The Migration Experience in Africa

The Migration Experience in Africa

Edited by
Jonathan Baker & Tade Akin Aina

Nordiska Afrikainstitutet, 1995

Indexing terms:

Migration
Rural–urban relations
Gender
Africa

Cover: Detail from painting by Ismail Diabaté, Mali

Language checking: Elaine Almén

ISBN 91-7106-366-8

© the authors and Nordiska Afrikainstitutet, 1995

Printed in Sweden by GOTAB, 1995

Contents

List of tables

List of maps

List of figures

Preface

In September 1991, a third conference under the auspices of the *Urban Development in Rural Context in Africa* research Programme at the Scandinavian Institute of African Studies (SIAS) was held in Kristiansand, Norway. The conference was entitled *The dynamics of internal non-metropolitan migration and linkage in Africa.*

The conference was an attempt to address a range of issues relating to *non-metropolitan* migration flows and other types of linkages in Africa. All too often, the focus has been on migration to the primate and other very large cities in Africa. It was hoped that the conference would help redress this situation. Approaches which explored the myriad of links (urban–rural, rural–urban and rural–rural) and which would increase our understanding of underlying processes were sought. However, with such an important and exciting topic as migration, it was decided that a range of broader conceptual and theoretical themes was required, as well as chapters on regional migration dynamics, refugees, pastoralists and gender issues. Moreover, some chapters do have the small town as a main focus, reflecting one intention of the original conference.

Unlike previous conferences where a selection of papers presented were published as proceedings by SIAS, the majority of the chapters in this present volume represent invited contributions from experts in the field of migration.

The preparation and publication of this book involved the contributions of many people. We would like to especially acknowledge the efforts of the invited contributors who responded so willingly and promptly to our requests for chapters. We would also like to thank those conference participants whose papers are included in this volume for their patience in a preparatory and publication process which took longer than anticipated.

We would like to acknowledge the assistance of the many individuals who helped bring this book to fruition. Karl Eric Ericson, Sonja Johansson and Åsa Berglund of the Publishing Department provided invaluable advice on editorial matters. Håkan Gidlöf, documentalist at the Institute's library, was of great help in re-checking many references as well as tracking down some obscure ones. Kjerstin Andersson drew most of the maps. Christer Krokfors made a number of useful suggestions regarding the literature. Kent Eriksson and Inga-Lill Belin provided important logistical support. Annabelle Despard translated Samir Amin's chapter from French, and Caroline Malcolm translated Jean-Bernard Ouedraogo's chapter from French. Elaine Almén did a superb job in reading the chapters and making many insightful comments and suggestions which improved the volume stylistically. Ingrid Andersson, Assistant to the *Urban Development in Rural Context in Africa* programme, deserves special mention for her patience and efforts in correcting, typing and formatting the chapters. We would also like to acknowledge the assistance provided by Per H. Iversen, ably assisted by Inger Kristiansen and Gunn Egeland, of Agder College, Kristiansand, who had responsibility for making local arrangements for the original conference in September 1991.

The editors would like to make two personal acknowledgements. Jonathan Baker and Tade Akin Aina would like to express their deep gratitude to Pernille and Florence, respectively, for their great support and encouragement stretching over many years. This book is dedicated to them.

Uppsala, January, 1995

Jonathan Baker and Tade Akin Aina

Introduction

Tade Akin Aina and Jonathan Baker

As in all human societies, the phenomenon of migration is not new in Africa. It has, however, not remained static and unchanging both in its form and dynamics over time. It has responded to and has affected changing social, economic, political and ecological conditions and processes. Africa's recent history has been in fact that of a series of rapid changes in all these aspects. And of course along with these changes in structures and processes, the forms and dynamics of modern migrations have changed and been adapted to wider transformations.

In this book, we attempt to bring together the wide variety of recent work and thinking on the changes that have occurred in the phenomenon of migration in Africa.

Because of the variety, complexity and extent of these changes and how they have been understood and explained, we have deliberately not structured this volume to express a uniformity of theoretical approach, methodology and analytical trends. Emerging initially out of a conference intended to provide a platform for an exchange of ideas and experiences on the phenomenon of modern non-metropolitan migration in Africa and the documentation and understanding of its changing forms and dynamics, this book is structured to present and confront the wide range of work and interest in the field and to identify gaps and worthwhile directions for a research agenda. This book is also meant to carry forward previous efforts on the study of modern migrations in Africa, fill in gaps in areas such as gender and migration and other forms of migratory experiences, and identify the lacunae in research. In spite of this diversity of approaches and views, certain elements emerge to structure and unite the contributions. The first is the recognition of the validity of the variety of migration experiences and strategies as means by which peoples engage in or are compelled to pursue their livelihoods within the limitations of the contexts and resources available to them. The modes and patterns of these pursuits and the rationalizations and the visions that the actors, both collectively and individually, hold and value are considered to be of equal validity.

The second element is that the migration phenomenon like all human experiences throws up winners and losers and that these outcomes are determined by a combination of complex factors that are expressed in and through structures and agents.

These define the collective and individual capacities to command and deploy resources and to exploit circumstances and conditions either positively or negatively. An important element of this combination of factors is the actual existence of patterns of inequality and domination that have characterized most human societies.

Broadly speaking, the contributions in this book are organized around four main concerns. These are: (a) the preoccupation with conceptual and methodological questions; (b) the presentation of broad overviews of current work and findings on the subject both at the regional and subregional levels; (c) the discussions of the wide range of migration experiences; and (d) a focus on gender issues both as a methodological and substantive concern.

METHODOLOGICAL / CONCEPTUAL QUESTIONS

Although a number of the chapters in this volume discuss methodological and conceptual questions, the contributions principally concerned with these are those by Amin, Adepoju, Aina and Krokfors and, to some extent, those of Gould, Salih and Gugler and Ludwar-Ene.

The methodological questions that are posed here went beyond the conventional concern with the dichotomy between Marxist and Non-Marxist approaches that characterized earlier discourses (see Gerold-Scheepers and van Binsbergen, 1978).

The two major concerns that emerge with the methodological and conceptual questions can be broadly stated as attempts by authors to answer the questions: how do we understand migrations and how do we study migrations? Although closely interrelated because one question leads to the other, it is possible to confine the methodological and conceptual issues through trying to deal with them independently.

Perhaps more than that of any other contributor to this volume, Samir Amin's chapter is concerned with the question of how we understand modern migrations. In his characteristically provocative manner, Amin returns to the larger questions of modes of analysis and paradigms which he had posed in the early 1970s (Amin, 1972, 1974) and which remain relevant and not totally resolved, although there have been some major related advances at the broader level of the social sciences in dealing with such questions. Amin attempts to specify in his chapter the distinctive elements of modern migrations and their connections with the globalization of the capitalist economy. His chapter, although concerned with methodological questions rather than an emphasis on methods, commences with the clarification of various concepts central to this approach. It offers a profound critique of what he calls the conventional approach to the study of migratory phenomena particularly the theoretical framework on which it is founded, mainly that of marginalist economics whose assumptions he finds to be fundamentally erroneous. He also challenges the pillar of methodological individualism on which the approach rests. Demanding a more structural, historical and holistic methodology, Amin concludes that we learn nothing from the conventional approach which we do not already know and that its explanations are circular and tautological and therefore of little help. For him the methodological controversy with regards to the study of modern migrations is not between the empirical and the abstract analytical approach but rather "... concerns the very nature of the significant facts: the motivations alone (which are merely the rationalization of behaviour within the system), or the laws of the system (which cannot be revealed from the motivations)". It is this methodological direction that defines the analysis of the specificity of modern migration in Africa which Amin offers. The distinction between the process and its impact on the political economy is made in relation to Europe and America: "In Africa the migration model operates in utterly different circumstances. Emigration from the countryside is not followed by an improvement in productivity, but by its stagnation, not to say its degradation. It is thus not a 'surplus' of labour, but a headlong flight of the entire population, leaving in its wake a countryside devoid of people and of production." For Amin therefore African migrations have not demonstrated the same effect for industrialization and economic development as migration has done elsewhere.

Thus Amin points us at a way of understanding migrations in Africa that emphasizes structures, systems, conditions of existence and their historical development, although unanswered questions and issues remain. The point is that in this framework there are silences about actors as beings with the capacity for decision–making, and about the importance of cultural factors and ecology. All of these must have implications for migrations even if they do not completely explain or determine them.

It is these kinds of questions that Krokfors attempts to deal with in his chapter on poverty, environmental stress and cultural factors. The chapter is provocative even though the ideas still have to be fully developed. What Krokfors has done is to point at directions that tend to be overlooked by too strong an emphasis on structural factors. Without succumbing to the weakness of the modernization perspective as it concerns cultural factors, he invites us to recognize the links between cultural factors, ecology and the structure of the political economy. He also deals with all of this within a framework that acknowledges the importance of poverty and treats cultural resources as entitlements and elements of the actual strategies social actors use. In short, Krokfors opens up the possibilities for an innovative approach which may enhance our understanding of the phenomenon of migration.

This concern with broadening the analytical approach is also reflected in Aina's chapter. Again, the perspective recognizes and attempts to link the issues of migration with the changing nature of African political economies and social structures, particularly with what he calls the 'development process'. With regards to approaches, Aina emphasizes the methodological divisions based on the mode of apprehending reality through structuralist, systemic action, voluntaristic or behaviourist approaches, rather than those based on political/ideological divisions of Marxist/Non-Marxist analyses. Although the latter division is relevant and important, the modes of analysis based on the divisions he emphasizes themselves tend to cut across both Marxist and Non-Marxist analyses. The chapter criticizes, in the mould of Amin, the emphasis on 'economic rationality' as the basis of migration decision-making and draws attention to related contributions from the fields of organizational theory and the sociology of industry, where sustained criticism of Taylorist conceptions of the economically-motivated person has existed for a long time. The lesson here being that the study of migration can benefit from interaction with other disciplines in the social sciences that have attempted to confront the questions of human motivation and decision-making.

This call for the need to pay attention to the contributions of allied disciplines in the analysis of the motivation to migrate and the decision-making process is particularly applicable to the very serious contribution of Evans and Pirzada whose focus is on the examination of the role of rural households as producers allocating resources of land, labour and capital among alternative farm and non-farm activities as a means of diversifying sources of income. This is an interesting example of what is perhaps the closest link in this volume to the conventional economic model of explaining migration. As interesting and detailed as the contribution by Evans and Pirzada is, immediate problems emerge with the failure to problematize the notion and constitution of the household and the whole process of decision-making beyond that which is economically determined. Thus the discussion of the strategies of rural households along the lines of the three main options of merely surviving, minimizing risks and maximizing profits can be viewed as requiring further broadening. However, the chapter contains very useful insights as to what kinds of rural 'households' possess the capacity to migrate, given the right conditions. The authors recognize that the choice of a strategy depends partly on the household's resources, and partly on local environmental and economic conditions.

Aina also reiterates the need for an opening of the approach to the study of migrations by noting that '... with migration as with other social processes we are dealing with a complex, multi-faceted interaction and interconnection of structure, agency and consciousness. We are dealing with the interaction between the definitions of options and alternatives, the perceptions of these, and the willingness and capacity to make choices and implement them. In relation to migration, distance (physical and cultural), gender, age, kinship and lineage ties, information, contacts, education and skills, finance and the willingness and desire to move are all important. A sufficiently open–ended and flexible model that considers all of these simultaneously is needed'. The point is that although such a model might produce a way of understanding that might be complex and not very elegant, it will at least contribute to deepening our knowledge of the phenomenon and bringing it closer to reality.

From these discussions on ways of understanding, some approaches to studying migrations emerge, particularly those that point at a multidisciplinary approach that uses different tools and methods of study. Issues such as these are explored by Adepoju, Gould and Gugler and Ludwar-Ene. However, apart from Adepoju, their discussions are not focused on methods but rather on examining the weaknesses of data sources and the factors responsible for these. Adepoju in his chapter begins with an examination of the contributions of various disciplines to the development of improved methods and sources of data for understanding modern migrations. Of significance to his discussion is the fact that the 'engendering' of demographic data has opened up new areas of analysis in terms of gender issues which hitherto male-dominated and gender-blind methods have neglected. Gugler and Ludwar-Ene also deal with the same question, a point to which we shall return in greater detail when we look at gender issues.

Still on data sources, Gould devotes some of his chapter to pointing out the various difficulties that exist with censuses as sources of migration data and what alternatives there are. The discussion which is predominantly technical and procedural possesses a great deal of relevance and utility in terms of drawing attention to the need to develop and strengthen public and private data sources and methods of collection. Also as a re-examination and critique of a major determinant of migration analysis in contemporary Africa, Gould's discussions deserve some attention.

OVERVIEWS

Three chapters in this book can be considered as being concerned with providing broad overviews of migration issues. These are those of Adepoju which concentrates on providing an Africa-wide sweep, and those of Rogerson and Gould with more specific regional foci.

Adepoju paints a picture of migration in Africa situated within a historical context of changing determinants, as well as with changes in the phenomenon itself. Using the colonial experience, like Amin, as a major watershed, Adepoju sketches out the changing patterns of Africa's social and economic structures and the migration processes within them. Recognizing the existence of the immense variety within Africa, Adepoju attempts to capture the different patterns, directions and motivations of migration between and within countries and sub-regions. These differences, along with the current economic crisis and political instability, have given rise to various forms of migration.

This particular overview attempts to confront some recent migration issues such as autonomous female migration, the brain drain, the refugee question and the effects of the current economic crisis. However, central to Adepoju's discussions are two main elements: (a) that so-called international migrations in Africa are often extensions of internal movements across 'artificial boundaries' by large numbers of undocumented migrants; and (b) that the strong link to the family which ensures mutual support for both migrants and non-migrants, particularly through remittances from the migrant to the home place, is a common element of modern African migrations.

Rogerson and Gould focus more on regional dynamics and their determinants, thus reflecting the richness and diversity of the African migration problematic at the regional level.

Rogerson provides a very interesting overview of migration research and issues in South Africa pointing out that non-metropolitan migrations are literally 'forgotten places' on the research agenda in Southern Africa. He notes that the major questions for research have concerned the historical development and maintenance of an oscillatory system of labour migrancy, the struggle to overcome influx controls, apartheid, mass population removals and flows of international migrants. Only in writings concerning the persistence of circular migration do non-metropolitan places emerge as significant foci of research. In his review, the importance of apartheid is underscored and Rogerson points out how it "... gave birth to new geographies and an accompanying rise of new urban forms outside of South Africa's major metropolitan areas". This analysis needs also to be recognized for the potential it has for expanding the research agenda on migration in Africa. Rogerson's depiction of the impact of apartheid on urbanization and regional planning and its implications for migration and population movements provides a direction for a more explicit political analysis of forms of state, social movements, governance and migration issues. This is a relatively underdeveloped area in migration research. Beyond this, Rogerson's contribution deserves attention as it takes us into the relatively unexplored 'forgotten places' of South African migration studies drawing our attention to the existence of useful materials that are unpublished or only published within South Africa.

The chapter by Gould does for East Africa what Rogerson's work does for South Africa by examining migration and population movement in terms of some of the major current issues in the development process of the region.

The central elements in this regard are concerns with how the economic crisis and structural adjustment programmes have affected migration, the problem of AIDS, and the relationship between development policies and population movements. The approach utilized by Gould in dealing with these issues is an attempt at specific country reviews of some of these relationships as a way of exploring variety and common patterns between them.

For instance, in discussing Uganda, Gould analyses the implications of structural adjustment programmes for urban migration indicating that it has most probably provided an impetus to migration. On this he points out that: "Migration does not cease in a collapsed economy: it merely takes on different forms, and in particular reduces the relative importance of urban and long-distance migration". The same conclusions on urban-directed migration are drawn for the Tanzanian case. Gould points out that: "The 'liberalization' of the market with a floating currency, incentives to entrepreneurs and businesses and privatization of state enterprises, etc. has had the greatest effect where 'the market' is most effective: i.e. in urban areas and areas of commercial agriculture. These have been able to attract migrants from the poorer, generally peripheral areas of the country, those areas that had been most directly affected by *ujamaa* and villagization in the 1970s". The conclusion from this is that the impact of structural adjustment measures in Tanzania seems to have been to reorder migration propensities towards urban destinations.

Apart from structural adjustment programmes, this extensive regional overview also looks at the economic impact of labour migration in source regions, the relationship between migration and environmental factors, and the important question of AIDS and migration.

Recognizing with regard to the latter issue that evidence is as yet inconclusive, Gould notes that "the impact of AIDS on migration in Uganda cannot yet be separately identified from the impact of the more general economic disruption", an important connection indeed that requires further attention. On the same subject as it concerns Tanzania, he makes the observation that "... the relationships between AIDS and migration and AIDS and the rural economy are likely to be highly diverse, but the same general issues probably apply: that its incidence and impact on rural economies is highly variable, more likely to be high in areas of considerable in–and–out migration..."

THE RANGE OF MIGRATION EXPERIENCE

Six chapters constitute this section of the book. They express some of the variety and diversity that make up the range of migration experience in Africa. These include the retirement migration of the elderly as depicted by Margaret Peil, the migration of young school leavers as described by Anders Närman, that of the pastoralists migrating to small towns in Africa as documented by Mohamed Salih, and involuntary population movements portrayed by Johnathan Bascom. Vesa-Matti Loiske and Jonathan Baker deal with different dimensions of the migratory experience such as the effect of inequality, conflicts and rural–urban connections in Tanzania, and the impact of the role of the state in Ethiopia.

Margaret Peil's contribution is especially important as it deals with a little-studied phenomenon in the African context—that of the small town as a retirement centre. The empirical focus of her chapter is five towns: two in Nigeria, two in Sierra Leone and one drawn from Zimbabwe. Consequently, the choice of the material enables cross-cultural comparisons to be made. The reasons why the elderly retire to small towns are varied and complex. Small towns offer a range of welfare services and easy access to water, not found in village communities. Such towns also offer a range of investment possibilities (for example, in housing or small-scale trade) to meet daily cash needs, which enables the drudgery of agricultural work to be left behind. Finally, small towns often have supportive kinship networks. As small towns increasingly become more attractive as places for retirement, planners should give more consideration to the social, economic and political effects of an ageing population in such areas, including the provision of health facilities and shelter.

Peil demonstrates that whether one retires to town or to one's rural birthplace is differentiated on the basis of sex. For example, the movement of elderly women, often widows, to live with adult children in town and thus care for grandchildren, is on the increase. By contrast, elderly men with resources at the rural birthplace, such as land and traditional social and political authority, are less likely to settle in town where they would lack these resources.

Margaret Peil makes a very significant point which is that as small towns develop and become more economically diversified (better infrastructures and a wider range of employment opportunities), the need to move to the large city for either work or retirement decreases. As a corollary, policy makers should stress to a much greater extent than at present the benefits of supporting and investing in small towns.

Anders Närman addresses the serious issue of unemployed school leavers in Kenya—a problem shared by many other African countries. And yet in Kenya, paradoxically, there is a lack of skilled personnel, particularly in the technical sectors. Närman states that the number of news jobs created annually in Kenya between 1984 and 1990 was about 100,000, although the number of school leavers was two and a half to three times greater.

Using tracer studies of secondary school leavers with a technical training as a methodology, he shows how many in his sample have tried unsuccessfully to find work in urban centres, particularly in Nairobi and Mombasa. One major finding was that the unemployed preferred to remain at home, and of a total of 452 without work, 370 (82 per cent) were at home. Thus, at least in the Kenyan context, the conventional wisdom that unemployed school leavers move to the cities is challenged. However, Närman does draw attention to the fact that those who remain at home without being formally or permanently employed, do find some work (for example, repairing electrical equipment or making furniture) often on an irregular basis, particularly when they can use the technical skills acquired through their education. One other surprising finding was that the employment rate of school leavers was higher in smaller towns and rural areas.

His overall discussion is contextualised within a framework which suggests that until the year 2000, the great majority of new employment (75 per cent in urban areas and 50 per cent in the rural non-farm sector) will be in the informal sector. From this, he concludes that the Kenyan educational system should be re-oriented to stress self-reliance and production and that "the necessary processes of change have to be initiated in the rural areas and small towns".

Mohamed Salih investigates a neglected theme in migration studies, which is the migration of pastoralists to small towns in Sub-Saharan Africa. This neglect can be explained in, at least, two ways. First, pastoralists tend to be subsumed as a category under the broad rubric of rural populations and thus are assumed to have experienced similar processes of change and transformation as peasant societies. Second, there are few purely pastoral societies which do not practise some form of agricultural production or agro-pastoralism.

Salih makes the important point that pastoralists represent a marginalised sub-sector within the wider rural populations of Sub-Saharan Africa. In recent years, pastoralist societies have suffered the worst of political coercion, economic pressure and ecological stress. These pressures have contributed to the gradual transformation of pastoral movements from migratory patterns dependent on seasonal variation of pasture and rainfall to economically-induced rural–rural and rural–urban migration. This particular change has significant implications for pastoralists, not only in spatial terms (from herd-based to land-based systems or both, to town-based life support systems) but also as a means of structural transformation within the pastoral economy and society, as well as its relationship with other external forces such as the state and the dynamics of the market economy. These factors have tended to create a pool of migrant pastoralists living in small, medium and large urban centres in Sub-Saharan Africa. Pastoralist migration and patterns of pastoral–urban interaction can therefore be analysed in relation to transformations in the rural economy and society and their subsequent impact on pastoral production.

Salih presents three hypotheses. First, rural–urban migration and the political economy of resource management among pastoral societies have some similarities with peasant societies which have undergone identical processes. Second, pastoralists have suffered not only from an urban bias syndrome, but also from a cash crop production bias. Third, unlike migrant peasants, pastoralists are able to adapt to a multitude of career patterns, including town-based pastoralism, which has shielded them from absolute poverty.

Johnathan Bascom provides an insightful and comprehensive overview of involuntary and refugee migrations in Africa. In Sub-Saharan Africa where such movements are most prevalent, one person in every twenty-four is an involuntary migrant. At the beginning of 1994, Africa's 5.8 million refugees (people living in asylum outside their country of origin) exceeded the population of twenty-eight African states. In addition, nearly 17 million Africans are internally displaced within their own countries, and thus are beyond the mandate and protection of the United Nations High Commissioner for Refugees (UNHCR). Moreover, by 1990, the majority of African countries (42) were hosting refugee populations.

Bascom identifies a more recent category of involuntary migrants—"environmental" refugees—who are forced to flee their homes because of dramatic changes in physical conditions, such as a marked decline in precipitation. However, he adds that state policies such as disastrous agricultural strategies (as in Mengistu's Ethiopia) are not independent factors in creating environmental instability and refugees.

Bascom proceeds to analyse the causes and patterns of flight. The most common movement is a short *en masse* flight across the nearest international border. The number of refugees settling in formal reception centres and camps is approximately the same as those who self-settle, without assistance, in rural areas in border regions close to their home country. He indicates that many refugees avoid sponsored arrangements, such as camps, and use them only as "safety nets" as a last resort. The fear of losing autonomy over their lives is apparently a major reason for this.

Bascom discusses the environmental impacts of refugee concentrations in host countries and indicates that current knowledge is limited, although it is becoming a growing concern. Another theme which researchers are becoming more aware of are the social dynamics which operate inside refugee camps.

Finally, solutions to the refugee issue are discussed. Of the three solutions, long-term integration in the country of asylum, resettlement in a third country, or repatriation to their home country, the latter is the preferred solution. Repatriation which is totally voluntary is, as Bascom points out, rarely achieved. As this chapter reveals, the study of refugees is a complex and fascinating issue and one that, given current conflict situations, is likely to warrant an even greater focus than hitherto.

Vesa-Matti Loiske portrays a fascinating picture of processes leading to social and economic differentiation in the village of Giting in the Northern Highlands of Tanzania. He suggests that contrary to the commonly held view that the land reform in Tanzania in 1974 removed social differentiation and produced a rural egalitarian society, the reverse has, in fact, been the case. Loiske categorises villagers into three groups: the wealthy, the ordinary and the poor, with the latter constituting the majority.

The wealthy have no limitations whatsoever in creating wealth and acquiring assets and have access to large amounts of land and other resources. They invest their surpluses (in property and trading ventures) in nearby small towns and also further afield. The poor, by contrast, live on the margins of survival, are often indebted, and work most commonly as day labourers. While they have access to some land, they often lack the resources necessary to cultivate, and frequently their fields are cultivated by others.

Loiske makes the very valid and central point that the use and exploitation of resources beyond the confines of the village in towns and cities have brought great benefits to the wealthy, while this form of rural–urban interaction has brought no benefits to the poor because they are assetless, and thereby unable to exploit these external resources. Indeed, the wealthy manipulate local labour markets by hiring labour from outside the village to "avoid the social obligations that locally are attached to an employment contract", thereby exacerbating the condition of village impoverishment.

The drama in the village and increasing differentiation should be viewed against a backdrop of corruption and misappropriation of resources by the wealthy who influence and co-opt the local ruling party, the courts and district leaders. Moreover, Structural Adjustment Programmes imposed in the 1980s have strongly supported this process of differentiation, as communal assets have been taken over by wealthy entrepreneurs.

While the chapter by Loiske presents a case study at the micro-scale, Jonathan Baker attempts to provide a review of the Ethiopian state as the central agent in promoting and orchestrating the mass movement of people following the 1984–85 famine in Ethiopia. Baker begins by tracing the origins of the modern Ethiopian state and the role played by internal imperialism and colonialism in this process of conquest and state formation. The central component of this process of conquest, followed by consolidation, was the migration of impoverished northern peasants to alienated lands in the newly-acquired territories in the south. This pattern of migration was to be maintained until the revolution of 1974.

Baker then discusses some of the policies pertaining to rural and urban land of the Marxist-Leninist regime of Mengistu Haile Mariam. A plethora of administrative and other controls were put in place which considerably reduced the rate and intensity of rural–urban migration.

The focus then turns to the reasons why the regime initiated a programme for the mass evacuation and resettlement of 600,000 people from the northern highlands to less densely populated regions in the south and west, over a period of eighteen months during 1984 and 1985. There is no doubt that the northern regions had suffered environmental deterioration, in some cases very severely, over a very long period, although the dramatic and sudden decline in precipitation triggered off a phase of environmental non-sustainability. The necessity for people (Bascom's discussion on "environmental refugees" is apt in this context) to out-migrate became an imperative. However, the policies of the regime including the neglect of the peasantry, authoritarian and top-down approaches to rural conservation schemes, retrogressive pricing and quota policies for agricultural produce, government restrictions on spontaneous migration, and so on, must also be considered as additional factors of why pressures built up and which finally led to a situation bordering on rural collapse.

The selection of settlement areas is discussed and the impact on these often environmentally-fragile areas of many thousands of settlers is analysed. Many of the schemes failed to live up to expectations, largely because of the government's haste in planning which resulted in areas being selected which were totally ill-suited for settlements with dense populations. With the collapse of the Mengistu regime in 1991, resettlement programmes were abandoned and the majority of settlers have apparently left. In conclusion, Baker argues that the present Transitional Government of Ethiopia will have to confront the problem of continuing environmental degradation in the northern highlands which will necessitate the out-migration annually of many thousands of peasants to better resource-endowed regions in the south. However, he ends on the sombre note that the Transitional Government's ethnic regionalisation policies may lead to conflict as northerners migrate southwards in search of a better life.

GENDER ISSUES

An important element of migration hitherto neglected but clearly recounted in this volume is that of gender issues in modern migrations in Africa. Five chapters deal with different aspects of the relationship between gender and migration. This is a particularly important element of the problem as it embodies both methodological and substantive questions. These questions concern the approach and the methodology in terms of gendering the issue by making central the relations and conditions of inequality, domination and exploitation embedded in traditional gender relations in economy and society. Methodologically, there is also the need to engender the sources of data and modes of data collection and to grant the deserved visibility and relevance to gender elements in social and economic relations.

These issues constitute some of the main points raised by Josef Gugler and Gudrun Ludwar-Ene in their seminal and thought-provoking chapter on gender and migration. Their discussion should also be seen as providing the backdrop for the following chapters which address the gender dimension of migration. Their discussion begins by focusing on two central issues. First, that most of the literature on migration deals only with the migration of men. Second, even where women are considered as migrants, it is only in their capacity as dependents of male migrants, and "the independent rural–urban migration of women has been grossly neglected in African studies to date".

Gugler and Ludwar-Ene adopt a historical perspective to explain why African cities have traditionally had many more men than women. Colonial policies did much to shape the sexual imbalance in towns. In settler colonies regulations were designed which discouraged the permanent urban residence of Africans. Men rather than women entered urban employment and they commonly came alone. Moreover, cheap-labour policies also induced Africans to pursue circular migration strategies which resulted in many migrant males leaving their families in their rural areas of origin. The term "one family—two households" appositely describes this situation of household splitting which still pertains to this day.

While many women visit their husbands in town or stay with them for the long term, many women are increasingly moving to urban areas as independent migrants. As Gugler and Ludwar-Ene indicate women outnumber men in the urban populations of a number of countries. Three categories of women moving to urban areas independently may be distinguished: young, unmarried women with little formal education who typically work at first as domestics; educated young, unmarried women in search of commensurate employment; and separated, divorced, and widowed women whose position is precarious in patrilocal societies.

The rural areas of origin continue to provide the ultimate security for many urban dwellers. Even families settled in town for a working life frequently anticipate retiring eventually to the village. However, the security patrilocal villages offer is problematic for single, separated, divorced and widowed women. Consequently, and "to put it in a nutshell: women are more urban than men".

Gugler and Ludwar-Ene's discussion and analysis raise a multitude of central issues which provide abundant scope for further investigation. For example, given the saturation of the formal labour market in many African towns and cities, what income-generating strategies and options can independent migrant women with education pursue? Further, if the informal sector is also facing a similar situation of reaching its absorptive capacity, as some commentators suggest, what kinds of comparative advantages can poor and uneducated migrant women exploit, in a sector characterised by ease of entry, intense competition associated with declining market shares, meagre returns and so on? Will migrant women be obliged to return, if this is at all possible, to the patrilocal confines of their rural areas of origin? Or will migrant women adopt new forms of urban associational economic solidarity?

Lillian Trager's chapter provides an excellent account of the role of Nigerian hometown associations in tying women migrants to their areas of origin, often long after they have left them. While much of the literature has tended traditionally to view membership in such organisations as primarily an activity for men, Trager's analysis demonstrates that such attachments are very important for women as well.

The chapter argues that the majority of women migrants, of all statuses and occupations, maintain some connection with family and kin in their home communities. She uses recent empirical data from five communities in south-western Nigeria to illustrate the extent and kind of involvement that women migrants have in maintaining hometown links. Her analysis reveals that women migrants in general maintain ties with relatives and kin elsewhere through the exchange of visits and goods. However, it is primarily women of higher status who have the economic wherewithal who are most actively involved in hometown affairs. These activities include membership in organisations, contributions and participation in local development efforts. And, of course, such active participation by these women does enhance their status and highlight the important contributions which they make to hometown development.

In her chapter, Lillian Trager raises a central issue which has implications which go beyond a discussion of the hometown, but which has major relevance for the study of migration in Africa, namely the impact of the current economic crisis and Structural Adjustment Programmes on the flow of migrant remittances to households in home communities. The conundrum is as follows: on the one hand, as migrants face greater economic constraints it is more difficult for them to maintain their erstwhile level of remittances, and yet, on the other hand, there is a great imperative to maintain or increase them because of increasing economic hardship in receiving areas.

Finally, what Trager's analysis does is to dispel the notion of a rural–urban dichotomy and she views "rural and urban places as part of a single social field"; the hometown "provides a source of social identity and a web of social connections, which influence actions regardless of where a person is residing". This is what makes the study of migrants and their fields of opportunities and constraints so vital and exciting.

Lai Olurode presents a profile of migrant women who moved independently to the town of Iwo, located north-east of Ibadan in western Nigeria. As a background to his discussion he states that migration studies in Nigeria have been strongly influenced by male bias. For example, until recently, much academic writing on migration assumed that only men migrated. Women, if they moved, did so only to accompany their husbands. Moreover, social and cultural norms are such that independent migrant women are often discriminated against.

In his case study, Olurode presents data for 55 independent migrant women to the town of Iwo which has a population of over 700,000. The town is predominantly Muslim and consequently religious proscription tends to disapprove of independent women. Having said this, Olurode goes on to state that: "it is a sign of a significant change in social values that Iwo as a community tolerates these women who live on their own and also lets houses to them". He also suggests that townspeople view migrants as a positive force for the community in that they help the development of the town through their demands for goods and services.

In contrast to Lillian Trager's findings, migrant women in Iwo do not generally belong to hometown associations and are thus excluded from "significant social contacts and resources" during times of crisis. However, they participate more in new religious movements, which provide an alternative focus for interaction and identity than male-dominated hometown associations. Olurode concludes by identifying five major constraints—socio-cultural, political, religious, legal and academic—which hinder the activities of independent migrant women.

The out-migration of males from Burkina Faso to find work primarily in the Côte d'Ivoire is a well-established labour movement and one which is fairly well documented. However, little is known regarding female migration within Burkina Faso. Jean-Bernard Ouedraogo's chapter is an attempt to redress this lacuna. He provides a compelling analysis which cleverly weaves together the histories of young Dagara women who migrate from rural communities in the Dissin region in the south-eastern part of the country to Bobo-Dioulasso, Burkina Faso's second largest city.

He describes the traditional Dagara social formation which stresses the role played by male domination and authority, although within this framework women are allocated and enjoy some degree of freedom. As everywhere in Africa, change and transformation have occurred and are occurring: nothing remains immutable. He identifies three "turbulences"—colonisation, evangelisation and transformation (or modernization) of the Burkinabè rural sector. Colonisation, for example, initiated a process of individualism, the emergence of differentiation and the weakening of collective identity. Modernization introduced processes which excluded or by-passed women. Thus, migration provides young women with the possibility to escape from the confines of traditional male authority, on the one hand, and the exclusive processes of modernization, on the other.

Ouedraogo details the various stages in the decision to migrate. The "escape" from the village is viewed as a "collective enterprise" and female friends, mothers and grandmothers act as accomplices. The transition to urban life is facilitated by the ability to utilise established networks of acquaintances and kin (so common in other African contexts) and these "urban solidarity networks" are vital at the initial stage of finding a job. The girls find employment in informal sector activities primarily the bar and domestic service sectors and, less commonly, in small businesses.

Ambiguity surrounds the fact as to whether some of the girls "draw the curtain", i.e. engage in prostitution, although the established Dagara community in Bobo-Dioulasso sees this as the case. Consequently, "the migrant Dagara women experience a double marginalisation: confined to highly despised occupations, they are also cut off from the Dagara community established in Bobo, which views them as the expression of collective disgrace". As a result of this exclusion, the girls create new alliances, often with Togolese or Ghanaian girls sharing the same economic and social status.

Ouedraogo has provided some illuminating insights into the constraints facing Dagara migrant women in their struggle to establish their own identities and escape the kind of lifestyles others want to define for them.

Elvyn Jones-Dube also points out that the study of migrant women in southern Africa has been neglected, where it was long assumed that females did not migrate, and if they did it was as associational migrants, accompanying husbands.

Jones-Dube discusses the migration of women in Botswana and shows that, contrary to this assumption, women have migrated independently on a seasonal and permanent basis, both within the country and to neighbouring states such as South Africa and Zimbabwe. The major reason women migrate from rural areas is because of rural poverty and underdevelopment. Until rural conditions improve rural women will be obliged to engage in circular or permanent migration to both small and large urban centres in Botswana.

Jones-Dube suggests that much more needs to be done to make rural areas and smaller urban centres more attractive to a population with rising expectations, and which is becoming younger and increasingly educated and skilled. She views the role of government as a central agent in this process of rural and urban change.

CONCLUSIONS: RESEARCH ISSUES

The chapters collected in this volume address the migration issue from a variety of perspectives and in a number of contexts, and hopefully they have identified some new research arenas.

At the conceptual-methodological level, they raise questions about models utilized in our understanding. They question the usefulness of unilineal, closed single-variable models that reduce all the explanations to one set of variables be it economic, social, or political or to one mode of analysis be it structural, voluntarist, behaviourist or actor-oriented. The discussions call for more flexible and open-ended models that recognize the complexity of factors that permit the insertion of cultural, environmental/ecological and gender elements into the analysis.

Procedurally, research issues concern the validity and reliability of our data sources, research instruments and approaches. Data sources and data collection methods require greater sophistication and relevance in terms of the extent of disaggregation of data, their longitudinal nature, the number of variables taken into consideration and their gender quality.

However, there are still many unanswered questions and issues which require clarification and investigation. The following themes are some which could benefit from further analysis.

- The *political analysis* of the migration phenomenon in terms of issues of governance and politics. How do political structures such as the now-discarded apartheid system affect migration? What is the importance of good governance for migration? What are the political consequences of extensive migrations, and the effects of the refugee question?
- The study of *refugees* is an essential field within migration studies, and one that, given the current levels of refugees within the continent, warrants increasing focus. While the subject of environmental refugees is addressed in this volume, it is an area which is still under-researched and little understood.
- *Migration and gender* is an expanding, although still under-researched, field of enquiry, both in methodological and substantive terms. Consequently, the range of work that needs to be done is extensive.
- The relationship between *migration and health status* is another theme which requires more analysis, particularly regarding migration and AIDS.
- More attention needs to be directed at the theme *migration and the current African economic crisis*. For example, how have the African crisis and structural adjustment programmes impacted and, at the same time, been affected by migration? What kinds of coping and survival mechanisms are employed and are households becoming more multiactive and multispatial in order to survive and/or maintain living standards? An important part of the research agenda in this connection is the impact of economic crisis and declining incomes on the level of remittances made by migrants.

References

Amin, Samir, 1972, "Underdevelopment and Dependence in Black Africa—Origins and Contemporary Forms", *Journal of Modern African Studies*, 10:503–524.

Amin, Samir, (ed.), 1974, *Modern Migrations in Western Africa*. London: Oxford University Press for the International African Institute.

Gerold-Scheepers, Thérèse and Wim van Binsbergen, 1978, "Marxist and Non-Marxist Approaches to Migration in Tropical Africa", in Wim van Binsbergen and Henk Meilink (eds.), *Migration and the Transformation of Modern African Society*. Special issue of *African Perspectives*, 1. Leiden: Afrika-Studiecentrum.

Part I

Conceptual and Methological Frameworks

Migrations in Contemporary Africa
A Retrospective View

Samir Amin

THE NATURE OF THE MODERN MIGRATORY PHENOMENON

The displacement of peoples and of individuals is by no means a peculiarly modern phenomenon, nor one that pertains to Africa alone. History teaches us that all peoples have come from regions that are sometimes very far away from those they occupy today. What makes the modern migratory phenomenon unique is its connection to the globalisation of the capitalist economy. I will in this chapter endeavour to examine the dynamics of this relation in the case of contemporary Sub-Saharan Africa.

It is thus necessary, from the very onset, to distinguish the movements of peoples from labour migrations.

Migrations of people lead to the setting up of organised societies, structured and complete, within the newly colonised areas. These societies are often similar to those originally inhabited by the "migrants". Yet this is not always the case. Sometimes people indigenous to a conquered area are integrated, either as an alien submissive minority, or as an associate group symbiotically organised. In this case the new society will acquire distinctive features. However, it is likely that generally speaking the very absence of an original population (it having been dispersed or assimilated), will leave the new society free to escape from hereditary constraints that were more difficult to overcome in the area the migrants originally came from. This has been the case for example in the Senegalese new territories of the central eastern crescent colonised by the Mourides who came from former groundnut territory, or in some sparsely populated regions of the Nigerian Middle Belt; equally in certain originally virtually uninhabited regions on the Ivory Coast west of Bandama. This is not unique to West Africa. We know that in North America the new capitalist society created by the immigrants developed more rapidly and more radically than in its place of origin in Europe, because it was not blocked by the obstacle of a feudal heritage.

Modern migrations are migrations of labour, not of peoples. That is to say that the migrants take their place in an organised and structured host society. There they generally acquire an inferior status, such as wage-earners or share-croppers.

This distinction also roughly corresponds to a break in time. Before European colonization, Africa was the scene of great movements of peoples. After colonization the continent has provided the stage for vast movements of labour, although some movements of peoples are taking place before our very eyes.

Movements of labour can be classified in various ways

The first possible classification will be one of place of origin and of destination: rural–rural, rural–urban, urban–rural, internal and international migrations. In those parts of the world that are already heavily urbanised the urban–urban flow will form the main part of the migratory phenomenon (as in present-day Europe). In Africa the migratory phenomenon is still essentially a flow from one rural region to another, towards cities, or out of the country.

The duration of the migrations constitutes another classification criterion. When it comes to migrations that are mainly rural, it is essential to know whether or not the migrants take part in the seasonal cultivation in the areas they are leaving. This criterion will allow us to take into consideration the fact that today a significant group of migrants in Africa are merely temporary migrants.

The criterion of distance, measured geographically, has no importance whatsoever. Today distance is only of importance when it involves crossing a state border, since then the question of legal status as national or alien has become an important factor. "Ethnic distance" is no doubt an element to be taken into consideration, and is not to be confused with the legal status of citizenship. It is doubtless useful to know whether the immigrants belong to the same ethnic groups as the host population, or to neighbouring groups or to ethnic groups far away. However, this knowledge can only be of value if the ethnic factor is seen in relation to the political strategies both of the migrants and of the host community, these strategies being so different that in some cases the ethnic factor will be decisive, in others of no importance at all.

The fourth classification criterion is based on the qualifications of the migrant labourer. Here we can distinguish between migrations of unskilled workers, constituting the main bulk of migrants, and the specific movements of tradespeople, clerks and salesmen, skilled workers, and professional people (the brain drain). These migrations are totally different from those of the unskilled farm labourers and come under particular categories requiring their own methods of analysis and an evaluation of their global significance.

In the history of modern Africa (the colonial century from 1880 up to today), the extent of the migratory phenomenon has been and remains gigantic, probably more important in relative terms than anywhere else. It is therefore useful to single out those large regions whose shaping by capitalist modernisation has been subject to particular strategies where specific rationality has determined different migrations from one region to another.

However, before setting out our own view of the African migratory phenomenon, based on the organic relationship this has to the capitalist globalization and peripheralization which the continent has undergone, it is pertinent to put forward a criticism of the methods conventionally proposed for migration analysis.

CRITICISM OF THE CONVENTIONAL METHODOLOGY FOR MIGRATION ANALYSIS

Is it possible on the one hand to analyse the "causes" of migrations, and on the other hand to evaluate their "consequences"? Can one pin down the "causes" of the phenomenon relying on an observation of supposedly significant objective facts (such as the differences in income from one region to another or from one activity to another), facts laid down as such by a classic investigation of the individual motivations of migrants? Does an analysis in terms of economic "costs" and "benefits" as much for the migrant himself as for the economy in the regions (host region and region of departure) which attempts to measure and compare the effects of the migration on production, employment and revenue, allow us to evaluate the "consequences" of the migration, to conclude whether the movement is generally positive (and if so, for whom), or if it has become excessive, whether it becomes negative (and again, if so, for whom)? And does this analysis and the conclusions to which it leads give us a base to form a rational policy on migration and to advocate a coherent set of desirable measures for the regions in question, including migration limitation, incomes policies, development policies, social policies?

The conventional approach to migratory phenomena derives from a theoretical framework founded on the hypothesis that the "factors" of production (labour, capital, natural resources and not least land) are given *a priori* and geographically dispersed in unequal measure, again *a priori*. This is moreover the very basis for the conventional economic marginalist theory. Yet I would contend that this approach derives from an idea that is fundamentally erroneous, that the distribution of "factors" is *a priori* given and not the result of development strategy. The economic choice, termed "rational", by which the migrant leaves his native region is thus entirely predetermined by the overall strategy that decides the "allocation of factors". The problem is thus to become aware that the reasons underlying the choice are those of the overall strategy; and that this is where the ultimate cause of the migrations can be found. The rational choice of the migrant is nothing but the immediate and visible cause, a commonplace that leads us nowhere.

The second pillar on which the edifice of the conventional approach rests is of no more value than the first. In a number of works on migration there is a curiously "individualist" approach. Migrants are individuals who emigrate because they are attracted by the lure of better pay elsewhere. There is little study of the country they leave; it is presented as a conglomerate of individuals who have before them the choice between staying and leaving, and consequently no one asks the question as to which individuals of the country are the ones to leave.

On this basis the traditional theory of migration cannot teach us anything at all, as it is pure tautology. It "explains" migrations by referring to the existence of individuals who are likely to emigrate. One might as well talk about the soporific virtue of opium to explain why opium is soporific. This model sets out to explain the migratory phenomenon by using as its point of departure the motivation as perceived by the migrant himself. Supposing that the individuals are situated in a defined temporal horizon that constitutes the framework of their calculations, and that they have the means of appraisal that allows them to compare costs and benefits in the near or distant future, then it is possible to detect a pattern in the behaviour of potential migrants. As it is, the model does not teach us anything that we do not already know. For it is obvious that migrants are rational beings who move towards those regions where there is a chance of earning better money.

Nor can it simply be assumed that migrants come from all the "poor" rural areas, or that they are recruited at random from among all the "individuals" making up the population of these regions. The Bassari of East Senegal are among the most destitute of the region, and they do not emigrate; whereas the Serere, whose income is considerably higher, do emigrate. Equally, it is notable that in Tanzania the ("poor") Masai do not emigrate, whereas the farmers of the "rich" Kilimanjaro region supply a considerable percentage of migrants. These are but a few examples. Taking these facts into consideration it becomes clear that there is a push factor which 1) cannot be reduced to the single factor that the income in rural emigration areas is lower than that of the towns, 2) does not have the same force from one rural area to the next (a force independent of the "average income"). This push factor is closely linked to the kind of social transformations that the rural areas of the world are undergoing as a result of their integration into the global capitalist system.

Individual motivations are well-known; their "revelation" by a sociological investigation is mere empty talk. More seriously, these motivations may disguise the true reason. For the migrant, like any other individual, will rationalize the objective needs of his situation. The Zarma may leave for Kumasi as they used to go to war. Yet they do not emigrate because they have an "adventurous streak". They emigrate because the colonial system requires money of them. Just as the same colonial system forbids them to make war, the necessary migration takes the place of military adventure in their ideology. The necessity becomes the ideal.

The controversy is therefore not between those who claim to be "empirical", that is those who wish to deal only with facts, and those who would not hesitate to hurl themselves into "abstract" theories, ignoring the facts. The controversy concerns the very nature of the significant facts: the motivations alone (which are merely the rationalization of behaviour within the system), or the laws of the system (which cannot be revealed from the motivations).

It is therefore not possible to separate the "causes" of the migrations from their consequences. The migrations are not only the consequence of an unequal development, which could in itself be the result of "natural" causes, such as the different natural potential of different regions. Migration is also in itself a part of the unequal development, as it serves to reproduce the conditions and aggravates these.

MIGRATION, PART OF THE PROCESS OF PERIPHERALIZATION
OF AFRICA IN THE GLOBAL CAPITALIST SYSTEM

The carving up of the continent, carried out at the end of the nineteenth century, gave the colonisers the means of achieving the main objective of capitalism for the region. This objective is the same everywhere: to obtain cheap export goods. In order to achieve this the metropole takes charge of the production on site and there exploits not only the natural resources (wasting them, plundering them, that is to say paying for them at a price that does not allow for the setting up of alternative activities to fall back on when they are exhausted), but also the cheap labour. On the other hand the direct and brutal domination allows the metropole to do away with the additional expenses of upkeep to local social classes, with attendant channels of transmission, and to make use of direct political methods of coercion.

This said, even if the objective is the same throughout, one can note the development of different varieties within the system of colonial exploitation.

In the region that we have called "The Africa of reserves" the main need of the dominant capital of the metropole is to put to immediate use the numerous proletariat. This is where we will find significant mining wealth to exploit (gold and diamonds in South Africa, copper in Northern Rhodesia and Katanga) or an agrarian colonization, rare in tropical Africa (the original Boer colonization in South Africa, the new English settlement in Southern Rhodesia and Kenya). In order to gain rapid power over this proletariat the coloniser violently ousts the rural African communities, forcing them into regions purposely scanty in resources. Furthermore they keep them in these impoverished regions without means of modernization, allowing them to intensify their production. Thus traditional society is forced into being a purveyor of temporary or permanent migrants on a vast scale, supplying a low cost proletariat to the mines, to the European farms, and later to the manufacturing industries of South Africa, Rhodesia and Kenya. It therefore follows that one can no longer call this part of the continent a traditional society, as a society of reserves has a function that has nothing to do with "tradition": that of supplying a migrant labour force. Deformed, impoverished, the African social units even lose their appearance of autonomy: and the miserable Africa of Bantustans and apartheid is born.

In West Africa there was never significant enough known mineral wealth to attract foreign capital or bring about settlement. On the other hand, the slave trade that was so active on this coast had engendered and developed complex social structures that allowed the coloniser to set up a structure for the large scale production of tropical agricultural products for export on terms that would attract central capital to these products, that is to say, provided that the pay were so low that the products would bring more profit than any substitutes produced in the centre itself.

It is the sum total of these methods and the structures they engender that constitutes mercantile economy. The French have introduced a specific expression—l'économie de traite. The methods are furthermore as much political as economic, which is always the case. The principal methods are:

1. The organisation of a dominant commercial monopoly, that of the colonial import–export companies, and the pyramidal structuring of the commercial

network that they command, in which the old African merchants are reduced to occupying subordinate functions;

2. Demanding taxation in money from the agricultural workers which forces them to produce whatever one offers to buy off them;

3. Political support to social layers and classes that authorises them to take their share of the clan territories and the organisation of internal migrations from regions that are voluntarily abandoned because of their poverty in order to serve as labour reserves for plantations;

4. Political alliances with social groups who, within the theocratic framework of muslim fraternities, are interested in realizing the tribute they levy from the peasantry; and

5. Finally, last but not least, when the preceding methods do not prevail, recourse purely and simply to administrative coercion: forced labour.

Under these conditions traditional society is deformed beyond recognition; it has lost its autonomy, it has as its principal function production for an international market in impoverishing conditions that take away all perspective of radical modernisation. Thus this "traditional" society is not in transition (towards "modernity"); it is fully formed as a society, dependent and peripheral. This society will retain certain traditional appearances that constitute its sole means of survival. Mercantile economy defines the process of the subordination/domination relationship between this pseudo-traditional society integrated into the global system and the central capitalist society that shapes and dominates it. All too often unfortunately made a commonplace, the concept of mercantile economy has been reduced to its surface description: the exchange of agricultural products for imported manufactured goods. The concept of mercantile economy is infinitely wider: it provides an analytical description of the exchange of agricultural produce supplied by a peripheral society formed in this way with the products of centralized capitalist industry (imported or produced locally by European concerns).

The results of the mercantile economy have varied according to the regions of mercantile Africa. We have already analysed the conditions for its success, which are as follows:

1. An "optimal" degree of hierarchization of the "traditional" society which corresponds accurately to that of the zones delineated by the slave trade;

2. "Optimal" density of the rural population—from 10–30 inhabitants per square kilometre;

3. The opportunity to initiate the proletarianization process by calling in immigrants of different ethnic origins to that of the plantation zone;

4. The choice of "rich" crops that will yield a surplus per hectare and per worker from the very onset of its cultivation; and

5. Propping up the political power and putting within reach of the favourite minority the means (political and economic, not least agricultural credits) that will enable them to take over and cultivate the plantations.

The fully formed model of mercantile economy was to be effectuated on the Gold Coast from the end of the nineteenth century, and reproduced considerably later in British West Africa, then in French, Portuguese and Belgian tropical Africa, as well as in some parts of East Africa.

The mercantile economy assumes two principal forms. Kulakization—that is to say the forming of a class of native rural planters, pseudo-private ownership of the land by these planters, and the employment of a wage-earning labour force—is the dominant form in the Gulf of Guinea, where the conditions have allowed for a trade economy. Conversely in the savannah, from Senegal to Sudan, through North Nigeria, the Muslim fraternities would allow another form of mercantilism; the organisation of the production of exports (groundnuts and cotton) within the framework of vast zones subject to a theocratic-political power, that of the fraternities, the Mourides of Senegal, the "Sultanates" of Nigeria, Ansar and Ashiqqa of the Sudan—who remain socially dependent, but integrated into the international system because the surplus accumulated through the tribute levied from the village communities is itself commercially realised.

The organisation of the mercantile economy brought about the destruction of the pre-colonial commerce and the reshaping of the trade routes in directions dictated by the opening up of the economy. Before colonization the regions had complemented each other in their essential natural base (forest, savannah), reinforced by the history of the relations between the different societies in Africa. The kola nut and salt trade of the interior, the exchange between stock-breeders and farmers, the sending out of export goods and the distribution of imported goods formed a tight and integrated network, dominated by African merchants. The colonial trading companies found it necessary to staunch any such currents, diverting them to the coast, and for this reason colonization was to destroy trade in the interior of Africa.

On the regional level, the mercantile economy will thus necessarily bring about a polarization of the marginal and dependent development. The "wealth" of the coast will have as its inevitable corollary the impoverishment of the interior. Africa whose geography and history both called for a continental development organised around the great river axes of the interior (providing transport, irrigation, energy etc.) was reduced to being "valued" only for its narrow coastal strip. The exclusive allocation of resources in this latter zone, a policy planned in accordance with the mercantile economy, accentuates the regional imbalance. The massive emigration from the interior towards the coast forms part of the logic of the system: it puts (cheap) labour to the use of the capital where the capital requires it; and only an "ideology of universal harmony" could possibly consider this kind of migration as anything other than an impoverishment of the regions of origin. Balkanization is the ultimate term for mercantilism, the "beneficiary" micro-regions having no interest whatsoever in "sharing" any crumbs from the colonial cake with their interior labour reserves.

THE SCOPE OF AFRICAN MIGRATIONS: THEIR DRAMATIC CONSEQUENCES

Two examples will illustrate the extraordinary scope of the migratory phenomenon in Africa.

The first example concerns the whole of West Africa, west of Nigeria. Here between 1920 and 1970 the proportion of the population in the interior savannah region (formerly more populated and more advanced) to that of the coastal regions went from 50–50 to 33–66. There is no other known region of this size in the world that has in one half century undergone such a considerable transfer of population. This flow started with colonization at the end of the last century, but up to 1920 it remained limited and relatively slow, except for the cocoa belt of the Gold Coast. In the course of the 1920s and 1930s it accelerated at a gentle pace, before it speeded up from 1945–50 at a pace that has since not diminished. The migratory phenomenon is thus still in its expansive phase; in other respects it tends to manifest itself by splitting regions more and more distinctly into zones of immigration and zones of emigration, while "neutral" zones, off route, tend to wither rapidly. This is a flow still almost exclusively from certain rural areas, while urban–urban migration is up to now essentially a stop on the rural–urban link. This flow was up to 1970 mainly situated in the heart of those regions where this export-bound agricultural development was carried out. In the last 20 years the rural economic crisis has hastened the migration that is now almost exclusively to the cities. It is a question of migrations that are already well on their way out of the first phase which was largely one of short term migrations (under a year) to the fully-fledged phase, characterized by the permanence of the migration. In addition, although the movement of migrants who leave each year from a zone of departure consists, for the main part, of young men from 18–30, this proportion is decreasing because after a certain time lag it tends to follow that the women of the same age emigrate, accompanied by their children. The swelling of the migratory flow can be seen in the growing contrast between the age pyramid in the emigration zones where the population is growing older, and the host regions where the population never ceases to get younger. Despite the balkanization of the region, we are still talking about migrations that are not overly hindered by state borders and which essentially retain an international stamp. Lastly this is a question of the migrations of an unqualified, unskilled labour force. In relation to this dominant flow, the migrations of tradesmen, employees and skilled labourers, even professional people, is one of secondary importance, much as those who subsist here and there, but no longer have, relatively speaking, the importance they had before colonization.

In Nigeria we can witness an internal migration on the same scale although the flow is not directed exclusively from the Middle Belt towards the two "souths" (East and West), but equally towards the North, which remains attractive due to the fact that before colonization this was the most densely populated region of West Africa. Thus contrary to the marginalist theory of the geographical distribution of "factors", this heavy density has constituted a positive pull factor provoking colonial development accelerated by the mercantile economy.

Is it possible to compare this movement to that which in Europe with its double agrarian and industrial revolutions led to the massive migrations of the nineteenth century? The rise and development of agrarian capitalism in Europe drove from the countryside a swelling number of agricultural workers who lost access to the land and became proletarianized. In Latin America, in Asia and in the Arab world we see the same in our time. But in tropical Africa this is not always the case, far from it. On the contrary, the development of agrarian capitalism in tropical Africa generally either attracts a supplementary migrant labour force, or retains in the countryside a growing density of population. It is clear that this feature of the development of agrarian capitalism in Africa has numerous explanations:

1. The vitality of the rural community and the common rights of its members to the soil;
2. The relatively sparse density of the population;
3. The poverty of the particular type of agrarian capitalism which only makes modest use of "modern" equipment, at best animal traction, never machinery.

Under these conditions it became necessary to set the process of proletarianization going elsewhere than in the regions. This has become the role of the reserve regions.

An ideological apology that takes the place of sound knowledge will at all costs attempt to justify the migratory phenomenon by claiming that it is in the interest of everyone in the regions of departure as well as in the host regions. To arrive at this conclusion "cost-benefit" calculations are carried out firstly on an individual level (comparing the income earned by the migrant in the region where he settles to that which he could earn in his home region), then in pseudo-collective terms where the transfer of remittances from emigrants to their families is treated as flow of capital from rich areas to poor. I have set out another method of cost-benefit analysis, directly macro-economic, taking into account the net loss carried by the regions of departure when a labour force is formed whose work will benefit the host region. For West Africa the transfer deriving from the migrations from the interior to the coast represents an annual loss that can be valued at about 7 per cent of the GDP of the countries of the interior (20 per cent for Burkina Faso), and a gain to the amount of 5 per cent of the GDP for all the coastal areas (and more than 7 per cent for the Ivory Coast and Ghana).

The second example concerns South Africa and Southern Africa. The entire population has been redistributed by the systematic policy of organising migration to the mines either from the reserve regions, themselves having been submitted to a rigorous project of misery, in itself enough to provoke emigration (with the Bantustans of apartheid this kind of planning assumes the form of Hitlerian "rationality"), or from neighbouring countries, notably Mozambique and Malawi.

In retrospect, the migrations that have shaped the population patterns of contemporary Africa, brought about in close relation to the peripheralization linked to the system of global capitalism have their responsibility for the present "marginalization" of the continent, its "fourth worldization".

For the specific reasons outlined above, these migrations are different in nature from those which followed the central capitalist development in Europe and North America. In these latter cases the emigration from the countryside, either to cities or to America, went hand in hand with progress in agricultural productivity measured per hectare and per family-labour year. The results had a distinct effect on national industrialization. Above all the migration to America favoured the national working class in its struggle for better pay, in reducing the pressure on the labour supply. In this manner it prepared the ground for the social compromise between capital and labour and the regulation of the system by increasing earnings parallel to a rise in productivity. In Africa the migration model operates in utterly different circumstances. Emigration from the countryside is not followed by an improvement in productivity, but by its stagnation, not to say its degradation. It is thus not a question of a "surplus" of labour, but a headlong flight of the entire population, leaving in its wake a countryside devoid of people and of production. Attributed to climatic or ecological factors (the Sahel drought) this disaster has severely affected the way the local rural economy is integrated into world capitalism and in the political expression of this—the exclusion of peasants from post-colonial political power. In these circumstances the acceleration of the exodus from the countryside became progressively widespread in the 1970s and 1980s, even in regions not suffering from exhaustion of the soil and drought. By perpetuating the inclusion of Sub-Saharan Africa in the old international division of labour—as a supplier of specific tropical products—the association of ACP states (African, Caribbean and Pacific) with the European Community have paved the way for the present catastrophe.

In these circumstances, African migration does not form part of a process of accelerated industrialization. The stagnating rural areas are depopulated for the benefit of towns with no industry, without the ability to finance this development by tapping an agriculture that is itself undergoing a rapid progress. Migration to the local towns is therefore but a miserable substitute for an international migration (to Europe) that is necessarily limited.

I will here return to the thesis that I would propose concerning the polarization immanent in the global expansion of "really existing capitalism". Globalization by the integration of markets would not be likely to reduce this polarization unless the markets in question were opened parallel in their three dimensions: exchange of products, transfer of capital and an integrated world labour market (which would imply total freedom of emigration on a global scale). Yet obviously this kind of integration is not on the agenda of the politically possible. Also the globalization by the truncated market reduced to the two first dimensions must necessarily continue to reinforce the polarization and in this connection the fourth worldization of Africa.

The political consequences of the African migration connected to these forms of peripheralization are no less dramatic when one takes into account their impact on the state and national level. These migrations are largely international migrations as defined by present day public jurisdiction, as they are still largely inter-ethnic according to the idea of ethnicity in Africa as laid down by the sociologists. Yet the relations that the ethnic groups have to one another within the framework of present day migration, cover the whole range: assimilation, peaceful co-existence, and conflict. It is important to note that the nature of these relations does not issue mainly from historical tradition, or from cultural distance or proximity. These relations are distinctly dependent on the collective strategies of the groups, manipulated or spontaneous. These strategies are defined according to the problems of the modern society into which the groups are integrated. The elements of tradition or culture are brought out in one way or another according to the circumstances and the demands of the strategy in question, which clearly proves that it is not a question of cause but of means. Finally it should be unnecessary to point out that the strategy of the host society counts as much, if not more, than the will of the migrants. For generally the groups of unskilled, unqualified migrant labourers, condemned to subordinate status and position, though a crushing majority, will be neither assimilated, nor accepted on equal footing, due to the opposition of the host country. Therein lies the loss of the "advantage" of the exploitation of the inferior condition of the migrants. It would thus be an outrageous simplification to talk of societies that are inter-ethnic, multi-ethnic, pan-African, or regional. Nevertheless the framework of inter-ethnic or multi-ethnic societies is already in place.

The serious political question which then arises is whether, under conditions such as these, it is possible to work towards a democratic and progressive state structure. The very number of incidents, not to say inter-ethnic wars, that have broken out in the last few years by no means augurs well. The progress that has been achieved in the field of inter-ethnic relations that the national liberation movements have often had to put into effect, seems all of a sudden to be called in doubt. Yet can the cause of this regression be "ethnic atavism", as it is so frequently and so readily labelled? I have put forward another answer to this question. Once stabilized, neo-colonial power was based on a ruling class more or less unified on a governmental level. This class was largely trans-ethnic and threw in its lot with the government that gave it the means of exercising power locally. Doubtless the individuals who made up this class looked to supporters in their region of origin, and lacking the power and will to make use of normal political methods (defending social interests, challenging programmes etc., forbidden by the widespread system of the single party subordinated to the targets of so-called development), they appealed to ethnic solidarity. Therefore this kind of ethnic manipulation remained limited in its results and only gained momentum with the onset of global recession. The revival of ethnicity has thus taken the shape of a centrifugal movement produced by the crisis and the breakdown of the surplus, a choice base for those segments of the newly emerged ruling class who wish to provide legitimacy for their power. Thus instead of unanimously rallying around a single party of so-called development we see the proliferation of groups emerging from the same circles, attempting to start afresh in a multi-party guise that is often ethnic (though not always). If this evolution continues, it will lead to disaster. For the map of the population of Africa formed by its pre-colonial, colonial and post-colonial history is made up of an entanglement of ethnic groups and communities that no border could possibly unravel. If in the name of the rights of the "peoples" (in itself a hard task to define) to succeed, one were to call for the formation of new states (as is the case in Ethiopia), it would prepare the ground for endless wars with "ethnic cleaning" as their main object. We have already seen what this policy leads to in Yugoslavia.

It is not the object of this chapter to define the possible and necessary alternative and the migratory policies that would be needed to sustain it. I will be content to call to mind that this alternative presupposes truly popular power within a democratic setting as well as strategies of regional development benefiting from a large degree of autonomy (which does not preclude their opening out to the exterior, as long as it is a controlled opening).

In a truly African perspective of integrated development, it is clear that the large hinterland river valleys and the great lakes provided grounds for a different type of agricultural and industrial development which would have led to a different distribution of the regional population. Geographers have long realized the importance of waterways in the territorial organization of the economy. But one look at the map of Africa and it is clear that this potential has not been used, and that the water reservoirs have not formed the axes of an integrated regional and continental agro-industrial development.

There are cases where the grotesque effects of the development of periphery capitalism on settlement call for a strategy of redistribution of the population here and now. South Africa is a case in point. Apartheid has organised a spatial distribution of the population between the reserves of overpopulated Bantustans and the half-empty lands of agricultural colonisation and the belts of industrial cities populated half by long-term, and half by short-term migrants, a distribution where no political democracy could manage to wipe out the consequences of racially determined, intolerable economic inequality without a systematic new policy based on massive redistribution of population.

References

This study refers implicitly to previous work that is to be found in:

"Sous développement et dépendence en Afrique noire, les origines historiques et les formes contemporaines", *Tiers Monde*, No. 52, Paris 1972. (In English: "Underdevelopment and Dependence in Black Africa—Origins and Contemporary Forms", *Journal of Modern African Studies*, Cambridge University Press, Vol. 10, No. 4).

"Le développement du capitalisme en Afrique noire", *L'Homme et la Société*, Paris, No. 12, 1969.

Modern Migrations in Western Africa, ed. S. Amin, London: Oxford University Press for the International African Institute, 1974.

L'Empire du Chaos, Harmattan, Paris, 1991. (In English: *Empire of Chaos*, Monthly Review Press, New York, 1992.)

L'Ethnicité à l'Assaut des Nations, Harmattan, (forthcoming).

Internal Non-Metropolitan Migration and the Development Process in Africa

Tade Akin Aina

Migration is not a new phenomenon in the history of Africa. According to the literature (O'Connor, 1983; Hance, 1970), it has occurred on a substantial scale in many instances in the history of the peoples that inhabit the continent. Several reasons have been given for these periodic population movements ranging from wars of conquest, responses to ecological and other disasters, to the peaceful and gradual occupation of vacant lands by some groups.

As a specific form of population movement the phenomenon had its own functions and utility for different groups and societies which included the pursuit of sheer survival, the search for better opportunities and improved conditions, and of course, the consolidation of advantages and benefits. These broad elements have to a great extent governed the expression of this phenomenon of permanent (or in many cases in Africa extended) spatial relocation.

However, the patterns and the dynamics of the process have changed over time, as what constitutes the conditions and situation of contemporary African social formations has itself changed. These changes have included very important features such as European colonization of the continent which led to the construction of 'modern nations' which in itself has introduced different political dimensions to the definition and understanding of migratory processes to the extent that the distinction is now made between 'international' and 'internal' migration—a distinction that pre-colonial African structures and social organizations did not emphasize. Other aspects of these changes that accompanied the colonization of Africa include modernization, the monetization of the economy, and the setting into motion of what has been called the 'development process' which includes the introduction and expansion of capitalist exchange relations, the development of capitalist and related productive forces, and the creation and expansion of related institutions of law, business and public administration and supportive social and physical infrastructures.

The demands that these new institutions, structures and processes produced and reproduced on the social organizations, consciousness, beliefs and behaviours of African societies and peoples were different from those that obtained in pre-colonial and erstwhile 'traditional' societies.

African responses and in some cases initiatives, particularly with regards to migratory processes, therefore included the adaptation and modification of old practices and patterns, and in other cases, the introduction of new features and objectives. Migration, which is a process and phenomenon not unfamiliar to Africans, therefore had to take different forms and orientation as a result of changing circumstances.

It is these different forms and the changes that have occurred in them that concern us in this chapter. This is particularly with regards to what has been called internal non-metropolitan migration and the development process. What this theme embodies is in itself an expression and reflection of the changes which we are concerned with. In this case, the emergence of national boundaries, the metropolitanization of some areas within those boundaries, the emergent socio-economic and spatial relations and organization that are the result of the changes, and the relationship which these have with and their implications for the development process at both the national and global levels.

Because of the extensive nature of the theoretical, empirical and policy issues which this subject matter encompasses, we shall not attempt to cover all of them in any great detail. Rather, we intend to focus on some of the most controversial aspects that have been expressed in the literature and to raise questions about directions both for research and policy.

In order to carry out this task, the rest of this chapter is organized as follows: first, we begin with the necessary preliminary task of specifying and clarifying some of the key notions in this chapter namely: internal migration, the non-metropolis, and the development process. In doing this we not only clarify the concepts and notions but also confront the methodological questions related to some of them. For instance, a major question in this connection, is how do we understand the migratory process? Should it be from a structuralist, action, or behaviourist perspective? The next section attempts to relate the non-metropolis to the development process in contemporary Africa, while the concluding section examines the process of non-metropolitan internal migration in Africa and its implications for, and relationship with the development process.

CLARIFYING THE KEY NOTIONS: MIGRATION / INTERNAL MIGRATION

Migration which refers to spatial residential relocation over a relatively long period of time is an aspect of population movement. It includes international migration which is movement across national boundaries, and internal migration which refers to intranational more or less permanent (or long-term) changes of residence.

As was pointed out in the earlier part of this chapter, the distinction between international and national movements faces certain problems in the African context where until recently 'non-permanent moves of nomadic and circulatory nature play such an important role' (Clarke and Kosinski, 1982:7). Also, the issue of 'artificial boundaries' amongst African nations in which single ethnic groups are divided into different nations such as the

Somali, the Yoruba, and the Fulani create situations where cross-boundary movements take no cognisance of the political definitions. Migration has received extensive attention in the literature particularly because of its effects and implications for urbanization (Hance, 1970; O'Connor, 1983; Adepoju, 1976; Amin, 1974). The emphasis in this regard has been on rural–urban migrations and the problems created for the urban areas through these.

But as students of population distribution have noted, the phenomenon in Africa is complex and highly varied. Internal migration is therefore seen to consist of rural–urban mobility, rural–rural mobility, urban–rural mobility, and urban–urban mobility. All of these contain intricate and complex processes such as step-wise urban migration, circular-migration and return-migration (Mortimore, 1982:50; Adepoju, 1976:1–2; Peil with Sada, 1984:120). Since these notions have been extensively discussed in the literature, and are mentioned here only to underline the complexity of the migratory process, we need not delay ourselves with them.

However it needs to be said that even though a consensus exists on the use and definition of technical terms, more fundamental disagreements arise over analytical frameworks. This is particularly so with regards to the understanding and explanation of the migratory process. Shrestha (1988) attempts a broad dualistic classification of the formulations of migration into a conventional perspective and a neo-marxist/dependency perspective. While the classification delineates the location of the explanation of the migratory process either at the level of the socio-economic structure or system and that of individual behaviour, motive and action, it is not too useful in terms of the clarification of ideological and theoretical location. The reason for this is that there is a conflation of methodological orientation with ideological/theoretical positions. In practice, this may not be strictly so.

A helpful example in this light is the difference between the works of E. P. Thompson and Leon Althusser both of whom are Marxists. But while the latter is a structuralist, the former emphasizes agency, history and some form of voluntarism.

In examining closely the phenomenon and process of modern migrations in Africa, one cannot but be impressed by the fact of the weight of socio-economic structures, particularly the nature and role of the capitalist mode of production and social relations and how the colonial and post-colonial states serviced and nurtured its penetration and reproduction. Migration and migrant labour is an aspect of the way labour is organized within the context. But we can fall into the trap of reification if we fail to consider actors and concrete human agents, in terms of their actions, the situation of action and the meaning which they give to action.

The divisions in the literature as to the explanation of migrations are too stark and too unreal. The fall-back to the concept of the 'economic man' or 'economic behaviourism' as found in Todaro's work disregards the recognition that Alfred Marshall made long ago about the complex nature of the supply of labour. It returns us to a scientific management perspective. So also are the other positions that Shrestha (1988:183) identified such as the ecodemographic, spatial and the anthroposociological interpretations of migration. The point to note is that with migration as with other social processes we are dealing with a complex, multi-faceted interaction and inter-connection of structure, agency and consciousness. We are dealing with the interaction between the definitions of options and alternatives, the perceptions of these, and the willingness and capacity to make choices and implement them. In relation to migration, distance (physical and cultural), gender, age, kinship and lineage ties, information, contacts, education and skills, finance and the willingness and desire to move are all important. A sufficiently open-ended and flexible model that considers all of these simultaneously is needed.

Non-metropolis/metropolis

The Dictionary of Human Geography describes the word 'metropolitan area' as "an American term describing a very large urban settlement." (Johnston, Gregory and Smith, 1986:296). However, the term in the development and other social science literature connotes not only the large cities, but also the core or centre of administrative, economic, political and cultural functions and advantages.

In fact, this notion is a central element of Andre Gunder Frank's underdevelopment theory in which he elaborates on the nature of systemic inequality and exploitation that characterizes the world economic system. Gunder Frank utilizes interchangeably what he called centre/periphery and metropolitan-satellite relations. For the purposes of this chapter, non-metropolitan areas refer to spatial entities outside the large or primate cities of Africa. Leaving aside the national differences in the use of population size to classify urban areas, it refers to the small and intermediate towns and the rural areas that are part of the national spatial hierarchy and structure.

Of course within that structure, particularly in Africa, the primate cities are the most favoured in terms of the concentration of economic, political and cultural activities and advantages, basic services and infrastructures. More often than not, they are the creation of, or grew as a result of colonial selection. Given the position of Fred Cooper (1983:27) on the fact that colonial spatial planning served not to integrate but to emphasize distinctiveness, a position confirmed by R. K. Home's (1976, 1983) work on indirect rule and town planning in Nigeria, the primate cities represented a point of local domination in a global hierarchy which encompassed metropolitan areas at the centre of the world system, and the metropolises of the peripheral formations themselves.

Non-metropolitan areas in Africa are therefore spatial entities located at lower points of advantages, benefits, services and opportunities within the structure of the local socio-economic and spatial hierarchy. Within these, intermediate towns fared better than small towns, while the rural settlements were at the bottom. The 1917 Township Ordinance in Nigeria which made the distinction between First Class, Second Class, Third Class and Native Towns on the basis of administration and allocation of services, is a perfect illustration of the embodiment of the inequality of this spatial hierarchy in law.

The development process

It is best to begin by saying that it is almost impossible to have a non-controversial, non-provocative discussion of the development process. This is because of the different meanings across ideological and theoretical frontiers. The solution to making clear what one's position is, in terms of development is the use of adjectives such as participatory, sustainable or human to prefix development. For some, the development process is about economic growth and increase in per capita income. From these, other social and welfare benefits accrue such as access to increased and improved basic services. This group will gladly prefix its own conception of the development process with the term 'economic'. Those who include 'participatory', 'sustainable' and 'human' in their conception of development are thinking of issues such as political and human rights, social and economic equity, popular participation and ecological integrity. For these, the development process should go beyond the mere generation of wealth for a small minority located in the different metropolises of the world system.

In terms of the actual process as it relates to the development and expansion of the productive forces and the transformation of the lives of the majority of African peoples in terms of access to sustainable incomes, livelihoods and other basic needs, the benefits of the development process in Africa have been most uneven and inequitable.

Most current assessments of the 'African condition' have passed a judgement on the past two development decades as being failures. They have pointed out that rather than being a context in which there has emerged concrete improvements, what has happened in the 1980s has been a deterioration which has taken the living standards of the majority back to the level they were at in the late 1960s (O'Connor, 1991:109; The World Bank, 1989:2). In fact, such has been the extent of deterioration that the decade of the 1980s has been seen as a decade of stagnation and crisis rather than that of development. Things have become so bad that Anthony O'Connor (1991:1) could open the discussion of his latest book with a debate on the statement: "To think of Africa is to think of poverty". Sadly that statement is not a mere reflection of the manipulation by the Western media, or the consensus located within international aid agencies and their officials. Rather it is being confirmed by recent studies such as those of Jamal and Weeks (1988). The economic programmes of most African governments in response to the crisis of the late 1970s and 1980s, particularly the World Bank/International Monetary Fund-inspired Structural Adjustment Programmes, have contributed to this systematic impoverishment of the majority of their urban and rural low-income peoples. To the policy makers and planners, those programmes are necessary aspects of the development process.

The development process, as it operates in most of Sub-Saharan Africa today, is based on the emphasis on market forces as a means of encouraging sustained economic growth and the repayment of international debts. Emphasis therefore is on externally-oriented productive activities in the areas of export cash crops, and the exploitation of minerals and other natural resources both to pay back their external debts and ensure internal economic growth. The innate contradictions lodged in this approach have been discussed by several scholars such as Bangura (1989) and Ake (1989).

The non-metropolis and the development process in Africa

As was pointed out earlier in this chapter, it is important that the non-metropolis be considered in relation to the metropolis both in terms of its origins and its current dynamics and linkages. In order to do this meaningfully, certain important questions arise as to the nature and structure of these entities. They include looking at the ways in which the non-metropolis can be said to be driven by forces different from those of the metropolises. Also there is the extent to which the non-metropolis is oriented towards positive alternative development paths. Other questions include how effective and positive are the different components of the areas. Of importance also is the extent to which the non-metropolises can provide for and fulfil the basic needs of their inhabitants expressing less inequitable distributive and productive mechanisms and processes? All these questions are central to a correct understanding of the real situation of these areas. They ensure that we do not reify or romanticize the subject of our discussion. They also direct us at history and politics, particularly the role of the state in ensuring decentralization, participation and relatively autonomous accumulation and reproduction.

This is because 'metropolitanization' as a spatial-social structure and process is a more recent phenomenon, dating back mainly to the nineteenth century in Africa. Although certain parts of Sub-Saharan Africa contained pre-colonial towns and cities, the emergence of modern urbanization and the structures and relations that attended it are mainly the product of colonial and post-colonial arrangements. The example of the Yoruba which observers have considered as the most urbanized group in Africa (Mabogunje, 1968) is most illustrative here.

The urbanization that characterized pre-colonial Yoruba society was quite distinct from that introduced by colonization. Yoruba towns in essence could be called agrarian towns. The Yoruba lived mainly in these towns which served as the administrative and political centres of their kingdoms with their farmlands on the outskirts. Their rural populations consisted of small village-size settlements surrounding the urban centres and dependent on them for political control, economic activity, and even ritual and religious leadership. Although, Yoruba pre-colonial urban society contained clear-cut internal stratification, and a complex social and economic division of labour, it operated to a remarkable extent as an integrated pre-capitalist political economy within which there were organic linkages between its different spatial, social and economic components.

The metropolitanization of African settlements and the creation of a spatial hierarchy which gave rise to one or two primate cities and a predominant population of dwellers in rural areas and small and intermediate towns occurred with colonial development. The colonial development process should however be seen as part of the whole process of the reproduction of a world economic system in which the colonial rulers and their countries were the dominant players. Their concern was with the economic benefits mainly through the search for and exploitation of markets for raw materials, labour and finished products. Colonial administrative and legal order facilitated and ensured the economic processes.

With these emerged a spatial order manifested in the growth of certain coastal ports and strategically-located settlements such as Lagos, Nairobi and

Dakar rising in political and economic significance. In relation to the most important primate cities, other towns developed in relative order of declining importance depending on both their functions and location in the colonial development process. While these operated as minor administrative, commercial, agricultural (plantation), mining or other extractive industrial towns, the rural areas on the other hand served as sources of labour to be imported into the towns or as productive units manned by predominantly independent small-scale farmers producing cash crops for the export and home markets.

Despite the fact that many of the African colonies depended on agriculture for their export earnings and for financing their development process, the rural areas that represented the main source of production received little or no attention in terms of benefits such as the provision of basic services and infrastructures. Olatunbosun (1975:22–26) has documented the experience for Nigeria noting that the rural areas were characterized by limited or non-existent supplies of basic services and utilities such as water, rural electricity, health and educational services, and roads. The situation remained the same until 1986, when the Federal Government of Nigeria embarked on a more aggressive programme of providing rural areas with basic services and infrastructures through the agency known as the Directorate of Food, Roads and Rural Infrastructure (DFRRI). For the other towns that constitute the non-metropolitan constituency, the 1917 Township Ordinance ensured only a slightly better provision of amenities to the classified towns, while the towns described as 'native towns' suffered the same type of neglect as the rural areas.

For most of Africa, the post-colonial era did not fundamentally change the pattern of development and the spatial hierarchy. Rather, in some cases, increasing populations complicated matters through greater pressure on resources. Also post-colonial maladministration and increased dependence on an externally-oriented economic development process only further worsened the conditions of the majority of the peoples of Africa living in the non-metropolitan settlements. Poverty in the post-colonial era worsened (Jamal and Weeks, 1988). The development potential of most of these settlements also received little or no direct planning and administrative attention as the contributions in Baker (1990) have pointed out.

In short what emerges from the broad discussion of the place and role of the non-metropolis in the development process in Africa to date, is the important point of the nature and history of metropolitan—non-metropolitan relations. These, it must be pointed out, clearly are not merely spatial relations. They are social, political, economic and cultural relations embodied in a structure of inequality that is part of the overall process of the global structuring of the world economy and its attendant relations of domination and exploitation. The crux of our argument here is that the relative socio-economic, political and spatial underdevelopment of the non-metropolitan areas of African social formations was intensified and consolidated by the process of colonial accumulation and domination which was 'centre-based', i.e. with its locus in a hierarchy of centres, with the metropolitan centres at the apex, and the various urban, regional and national centres forming its other parts. The underdevelopment of the non-metropolis with its economic, political and cultural marginalization of the ordinary producers and workers took its familiar form from this process. However, the post-colonial administrations and political élites did not change this situation in any major way, in spite of their endless pronouncements of concern with the welfare of their poor and downtrodden populations. Rather, they reinforced and consolidated the domination and alienation of these ordinary people, denying them any real participation in the political process. What we have therefore is a development process that has alienated and exploited the majority of the poor living in both metropolitan and non-metropolitan settlements in Africa. A process which has emphasized marginalization and immiseration and in relation to which the ordinary people have developed a wide range of responses and coping mechanisms, one of which is the option of internal migration.

Non-metropolitan internal migration in Africa

In this section of the chapter, we examine the subject of concern from the following perspectives: causes, process, problems and policies.

Causes

The literature is replete with discussions of the causes of internal migration (See: Hance, 1970; Udo, 1975; Adepoju, 1976; Amin, 1974: Clarke and Kosinski, 1982; Peil with Sada, 1984).

The reasons offered as causes are multiple and contain tremendous variety. They include the following:

a. catastrophes such as wars, droughts and floods,
b. what Amin has called unequal development, that is regional inequality of economic development and incomes,
c. high population pressures,
d. low agricultural productivity,
e. poverty and hunger in certain specific regions,
f. 'the attraction of towns as centres of education, higher incomes and social amenities; and the importance of ethnic flows, assisted by voluntary associations in towns and cities' (Clarke and Kosinski, 1982:7).

A different, though related, kind of classification has been used by Hance (1970:1–187) who identified: (i) environmentally-related conditions, (ii) socio-cultural factors, (iii) modernization, (iv) political factors and economically related factors.

The relative weight of any of these factors or their combination cannot be effectively theorized in advance. More often than not, they depend on specific situations and combination of circumstances. However, there is some consensus in the literature that the primary motive for migration tends to be economic, while the main actors in Africa are predominantly young males. This last point needs some qualification though, as available studies that account for the predominance of men could themselves contain some gender bias.

Process

The process of internal migration can be classified according to the origin and destination of migrants and the duration of their stay (Peil with Sada,

1984:118). Movements, as has been pointed out earlier, can be rural–urban, urban–rural, rural–rural, and urban–urban. They can also be daily, periodic, seasonal, short-term, long-term and irregular. All of these depend on the reason and object of migration.

The migratory process involves a multiplicity of patterns. Some migrants go directly to their destination, others utilize step-migration moving from smaller settlements to larger ones up the urban hierarchy, while some operate what has been called multiple-migration which involves the search for opportunities in towns either large or small (Peil with Sada, 1984:121).

In the case of non-metropolitan internal migration, these different steps are more or less taken in search of opportunities in rural areas and small and intermediate settlements. Rural–rural migration operates to a great extent and has been studied by some scholars. In the Nigerian case, the situation is characterized by farmers and other agriculturally-based peoples moving from areas of land-hunger, or different ecological zones such as the savannah or Sahel region, into the forest belt. The arrangements of production that these enter are quite complex. They include that of pure wage-labour, farm-tenancy, sharecropping, etc.

Although rural–rural migrants at times operate as traders, craftsmen and artisans, there is a consensus that most moves of this kind are based on the attraction of fertile land for farming (Adepoju, 1976:18; Olusanya, 1976; and Udo, 1975).

In some cases, the migrants do not operate as independent producers but rather as labourers (see: Stichter, 1985). In these cases they are employed as agricultural labour on farms (either corporate or individually owned), and plantations. The sizes and scale of the farms vary in different regions. Some are large-scale, formally organized farms, while others are the farms of medium-sized or medium-income farmers. Again, duration and employment relations vary. In some medium-sized farms, labour is engaged only seasonally during the harvesting or planting period, while the migrants are involved in a complex combination of relations that include sharecropping and farm tenancy. These occur in the cocoa-belt of south western Nigeria. In the cases of some of the large-scale farms and plantations, while there might be a core of long-term waged labour, there are also seasonal hands during planting and harvesting periods. While the emphasis is on wage-labour, it is not uncommon to find migrants utilising or leasing the company or landlord's land for their own crops.

Other types of migrants who are not labourers can be found in the context of rural–rural migration. These include traders, fishermen, transporters and prostitutes. All of these particularly the traders, transporters and prostitutes provide their own brand of services, although these tend to be found more in small and medium-sized towns. Also migrant bands of beggars, destitutes, itinerant minstrels, beauticians and entertainers are often found in different African settlements.

The rural–urban, or urban–urban non-metropolitan migration that occurs is often to small and medium-sized towns. In the small towns, the range of opportunities and activities depends on the size, location and functions of the settlements. The presence of migrants is often a question of scale and needs in relation to these either in rural areas or in medium-sized towns. These vary extensively depending on their sizes, locations and functions. Generally, the medium-sized towns are more heterogeneous than the rural settlements and small towns. They are also often better serviced with utilities and infrastructures. Opportunities for employment in them range from the public and private formal sectors to, in some cases, agro-based or mineral-extracting industries, commerce and an extensive informal sector. There is a greater division of labour in these settlements and as Okafor (1988) has pointed out in Nigeria, further political and administrative decentralization in the form of state creation in Nigeria in 1963, 1967, 1975, 1985 and 1991 have resulted in 30 state capitals, all of which are some form of regional administrative headquarters. These are being developed through construction of offices, provision of services and infrastructures so that they can play their official roles effectively. They also become sites of employment creation in a wide range of social and economic sectors.

Migrants as traders, transporters and prostitutes from near and far often proliferate in these sites. There have been reports of sectoral specialization by different ethnic groups with the provision of bicycle and motor-bicycle taxis being the strength of some, while others are well-known for their control of the motor spare-parts and second-hand clothing trades. In some cases, prostitutes are recruited and incorporated into the sex trade via a sophisticated network based on ethnicity. Thus a great deal of labour, goods and services are provided in the non-metropolitan settlements by migrants who are either labourers, petty producers, traders, artisans and craftsmen or simply amongst the group of people, Marxists will call 'lumpens', i.e. pimps, prostitutes, beggars and petty criminals.

Problems

A wide range of problems have been identified with non-metropolitan internal migration. These are both concrete and analytical. The concrete problems include:

a. The pressure on, and lack of availability of basic services such as shelter, schools and health services for the migrants.

b. Their competition for employment and other resources with the host communities. They have been said to depress wages and prices, contribute to increases in rent and compete with host populations for jobs and the provision of goods and services. This has in some cases generated hostility from the host community.

c. Their vulnerability to intense exploitation and denial of basic human and employment rights by employers who at times, particularly in plantations and isolated mineral-extracting stations, run what seem like forced-labour camps.

d. The negative role of the state in relation to them through the existence of legislations and policies that define the activities, residences and at times the very existence of the migrants as illegal. We need to remind ourselves that the migrants are often preponderant in the 'informal sector' and often as casual labour.

The main problem related to analysis is that we do not have sufficient reliable data on the phenomenon. Several African countries have not produced recent comprehensive census data that can provide us with information on the dynamics and structures of small and intermediate towns, the nature of migratory flows into them, and the structure of productive activities, employment and occupations.

There is the need for various sources of information, ranging from censuses, through surveys to detailed ethnographic studies. These should do what Peil (1972) did with Ghanaian factory workers and Cohen (1969) with the Hausa cattle and kola nut traders in Ibadan.

Policies

Policies often emerge from the realm of interaction and struggles of the people, different groups and the State. For policies to be effective they must be adopted and pushed by interested and strategic parties. In Nigeria, the combination of ethnic and statist politics has forced a systematic process of further downward administrative decentralization. This is an imperative particularly in the context of non-metropolitan settlements. Here, political, administrative, and fiscal decentralization is important so that these settlements can be freed to grow their own way.

Along with decentralization, there must be both meaningful financial support and the strengthening of institutional capacity through human and other resource development. Also creative and autonomous forms of funding and revenue-generation are required at these levels.

Above all, the politics of the development process must shift to an effective participatory process in which the broad range of dwellers in these settlements must participate in decisions, planning and implementation of issues and problems that affect them. This requires an effective process of democratization and electoral politics not restricted to elite control and manipulation. In this way, the true interests of those most affected by the development process at the grassroots can be expressed in politics and policies, at least at the level of their own settlements resulting in their empowerment.

References

Adepoju, A., (ed.), 1976, *Internal Migration in Nigeria*. Institute of Population and Manpower Studies, University of Ife, Nigeria.

Adepoju, A., 1982a, *Rural Migration and Development in Nigeria*. Dept. of Demography and Statistics, University of Ife, Nigeria.

Adepoju, A., 1982b, *Patterns of Migration, Living Conditions and Community Development in Rural Areas of South West Nigeria*. Lagos: Federal Ministry of Social Development.

Adepoju, A., 1982c, "Population Redistribution: A Review of Governmental Policies", in J.I. Clarke and L.A. Kosinski (eds.), *Redistribution of Population in Africa*. London: Heinemann.

Aina, Tade Akin, 1989, "Urban–Rural Relations in the Context of the Democratic Transition in Nigeria", *Nagarlok*, XXI, 1, January–March.

Ake, Claude, 1989, *The Political Economy of Crisis and Underdevelopment in Africa: Selected Works of Claude Ake,* edited by J. Ihvonbere. Lagos: JAD Publishers Ltd.

Althusser, L., and E. Balibar, 1975, *Reading Capital*, London: New Left Books.

Amin, Samir, 1972, "Underdevelopment and Dependence In Black Africa—Origins and Contemporary Forms", *Journal of Modern African Studies*, 10, 4.

Amin, Samir, (ed.), 1974, *Modern Migrations in Western Africa*. International African Institute/Oxford University Press.

Baker, Jonathan, (ed.), 1990, *Small Town Africa: Studies in Rural–Urban Interaction*. Uppsala: The Scandinavian Institute of African Studies.

Bangura, Yusuf, 1989, *Crisis, Adjustment and Politics in Nigeria*. Uppsala: AKUT, University of Uppsala.

Caldwell, J.C., 1969, *African Rural–Urban Migration: the Movement to Ghana's Towns*. Canberra: Australian National University Press.

Clarke, J.I. and L.A. Kosinski, (eds.), 1982, *Redistribution of Population in Africa*. London: Heinemann.

Cohen, Abner, 1969, *Custom and Politics in Urban Africa: A Study of Hausa Migrants in Yoruba Towns*. London: Routledge & Kegan Paul.

Cooper, Fred, 1983, "Urban Space, Industrial Time and Wage Labour in Africa" in Cooper, F., (ed.), *Struggle for the City: Migrant Labour, Capital and the State in Urban Africa*. London: Sage Publications.

Gunder Frank, A., 1978, *Dependent Accumulation and Underdevelopment*. London: Macmillan.

Haggblade, Steven, Peter Hazell and James Brown, 1989, "Farm–Non-farm Linkages in Rural Sub-Saharan Africa", *World Development*, 17,8.

Hance, William A., 1970, *Population, Migration and Urbanization in Africa*. New York: Columbia University Press.

Hardoy, Jorge and David Satterthwaite, (eds.), 1986, *Small and Intermediate Urban Centres: Their Role in National and Regional Development in the Third World*. London: Hodder and Stoughton in association with the International Institute for Environment and Development.

Home, R.K., 1976, "Urban Growth and Urban Government, Contradictions in the Colonial Political Economy" in G. Williams (ed.), *Nigeria: Economy and Society*. London: Rex Collings.

Home, R.K., 1983, "Town Planning, Segregation and Indirect Rule in Colonial Nigeria", *Third World Planning Review*, 5,2.

Jamal, Vali and John Weeks, 1988: "The vanishing rural–urban gap in Sub-Saharan Africa", *International Labour Review*, 127,3.

Johnston, R.J., Derek Gregory and David M. Smith, (eds.), 1986, *The Dictionary of Human Geography*. London: Basil Blackwell.

Mabogunje, A.L., 1968, *Urbanization in Nigeria*. New York: Africana Publishing Corporation.

Mabogunje, A.L., 1980, *The Development Process: A Spatial Perspective*. London: Hutchinson.

Mazumdar, Dipak, 1987, "Rural–Urban Migration in Developing Countries", *World Bank Reprint Series*, 422.

Mortimore, M., 1982, "Framework of Population Mobility: The Perception of Opportunities in Nigeria", in J.I. Clarke and L.A. Kosinski, (eds.), *Redistribution of Population in Africa*. London: Heinemann.

O'Connor, Anthony, 1983, *The African City*. London: Hutchinson.

O'Connor, Anthony, 1991, *Poverty In Africa: A Geographical Approach*. London: Belhaven Press.

Okafor, F.O., 1988, "The Role of Medium-Sized Towns in the Spatial Integration of Nigeria", *African Urban Quarterly*, 3, 3–4.

Olatunbosum, D., 1975, *Nigeria's Neglected Rural Majority*. Ibadan: Ibadan University Press.

Olusanya, P.O, 1976, "Residential Patterns and Population Movement into The Farmlands of Yorubaland", in A. Rapoport (ed.), *The Mutual Interaction of People and Their Built Environment*. The Hague: Mouton Publishers.

Peil, Margaret, 1972, *The Ghanaian Factory Worker*. Cambridge: Cambridge University Press.

Peil, Margaret with P.O. Sada, 1984, *African Urban Society*. Chichester: John Wiley & Sons.

Shrestha, N.R. 1988, "A Structural Perspective on Labour Migration in Underdeveloped Countries", *Progress In Human Geography*, 12,2.

Stichter, Sharon, 1985, *Migrant Laborers*. Cambridge: Cambridge University Press.
Todaro, M.P., 1969, *Internal Migration in Developing Countries*. Geneva: International Labour Office.
Udo, R.K., 1975, *Migrant Tenant Farmers of Nigeria*. Lagos: African Universities Press.
The World Bank, 1989, *Sub-Saharan Africa: From Crisis to Sustainable Growth—A Long-Term Perspective Study*. Washington, D.C.

Poverty, Environmental Stress and Culture as Factors in African Migrations

Christer Krokfors

Migration represents one important demographic response to conditions of poverty and environmental stress in Africa. These migrations might be of very different kinds both in time and space and in relation to the societal context in which they occur. The large migratory flows of people from poverty-stricken and environmentally degraded lands to more favourable conditions in other areas, for example from the Sahel to areas further south, are rather well documented and understood. It is also believed that migratory or circulatory movements of labour from rural areas to primate cities or regional centres can easily be explained by overall macro-economic factors (cf. Todaro, 1976, 1989).

However, recent investigations have shown that cultural factors have to be taken much more into consideration than has been done earlier. This is even more important when looking for explanations and understandings of migrations/circulations within households as a response to local environmental, political and economic conditions. These movements are often spatially restricted and take place within a specific cultural realm. The emergence of multi-active and multi-localized households through migration/circulation as processes of adjustment to prevailing societal structures and ecological conditions is one theme of this chapter.

However, there are also cases where members of groups of households refuse to adjust to the prevailing conditions and start to seek new opportunities, often through migration to remote or virgin areas. Such migratory movements which often have a strong ideological or religious commitment or are led by a charismatic leader, have characterized much of Africa since pre-colonial times. These movements of secluded groups are the second theme of this chapter.

The intra-household migrations/circulations and the migrations of secluded groups will be analysed against a background of resource entitlements and the effects of differing entitlements and poverty on environmental conditions. The political economy of households will be elucidated against this background and the cultural options for improvements discussed.

ENTITLEMENT AND POVERTY

Entitlements to resources and means of subsistence are one of the central concepts in the writings of Sen (1981, 1984) and Drèze and Sen (1989). The mere presence of resources or means of subsistence does not entitle a person or a household to use them. In each social structure, given the prevailing legal, political, and economic arrangements, a person or household can establish command over some alternative bundles of resources or commodities. These bundles can be either very extensive or very limited and the set of alternative bundles over which a person or household can establish command represents their entitlements.

Entitlements must be enforced and an individual's or a household's capacity to do so will determine their control of resources or means of subsistence and/or capital accumulation. Such enforcements may depend on heritage, ritual, political or economic status. Poverty can thus be defined as the failure of certain capacities that are important for the well-being of an individual or a household. These failures can depend on the socio-political or environmental conditions in certain localities, but might also be due to the cultural realm not present in other localities and thus leave options for improved living conditions through spatial mobility.

LAND AS A PHYSICAL AND SOCIETAL RESOURCE

Survival for the majority of Africans is still mainly based on entitlements to land. Land as a resource is a complex phenomenon with specific physical and social capabilities,[*] with intrinsic qualities satisfying a particular use at particular places and times (Blaikie and Brookfield, 1987).

Physical resources are normally described as stock resources and flow resources (Rees, 1985; Saetra, 1975). Stock resources are either abiotic or biotic. Their common characteristic is that once depleted they are not renewable within a foreseeable timespan. Flow resources are, if their production base remains intact, renewed within a sufficiently short timespan to be of relevance to human beings.

Physically land is a flow resource continuously produced by abiotic and biotic processes. As long as the physical capabilities are reproduced at the same pace as they are used there is no land degradation. However, in specific socio-economic situations land *has to be* over-used. In this case, land has changed from being a flow resource to a stock resource, the physical capabilities of which are soon extracted and what is left is degraded land.

However, the productive value of land depends not only on its physical capabilities, but also on societal capabilities. These result from the politicization processes and the relational nature of the population-environment totality. The societal capabilities are manifested as differing access qualifications of land within this totality (Figure 1). The access qualifications are determined by the income opportunities that land as a resource can offer. The higher the access qualifications, the higher and more varying, the income opportunities. Land with poor physical capabilities (marginal areas, waste

---

[*] Land capability is defined indirectly by Blaikie and Brookfield as "degradation is defined as a reduction in the capability of land to satisfy a particular use" (1987:6).

land, slopes, peri-urban land and so on) has low access qualifications. At the same time, this land is in high demand quantitatively, but has a low return and is therefore easily over-used and degraded. Such differential access to land is characteristic of most of Africa.

Figure 1. *The politicization of population and land resources within the population environment totality*

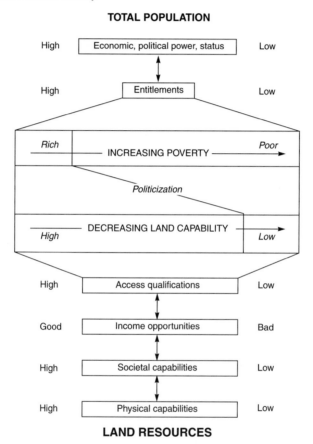

Source: Krokfors, 1989b

Households have varying entitlements to land depending on the access qualifications. These entitlements must be enforceable. Individuals must be able to exercise their rights *vis-à-vis* other people in respect of their entitlement (Curtis, Hubbard and Shepherd, 1988). This is done according to certain rules of legitimacy inherent in the overall ideological superstructure of the society, which locally is often based on political or economic power or status. Both degradation of land and human resources often occur as a result of shifts in entitlements (Sen, 1981, 1984).

Thus the politicized structure of the population is expressed in terms of entitlements, land-based income opportunities and their access qualifications. Each of these factors has implied relations of production, forms of surplus extraction, investment and accumulation possibilities (Blaikie, 1985). The part of the population that is entitled to high quality land has often benefited from various types of development projects like the introduction of high-yielding varieties, irrigation, well construction, cash cropping etc. This has often also meant that other people are forced to accept low quality lands and landholdings insufficient in size to permit a subsistence. In such a situation the risk for land degradation increases rapidly and new strategies for survival have to be developed. These include the household or part of the household searching for new entitlement options in new localities or a total rejection of existing societal conditions and attempts to construct a "new society" elsewhere.

THE CULTURAL REALM[*]

African spaces are above all social spaces. The continent is often described as the continent of peasants. Several studies on peasant relations to environmental resources have shown a great variety of adaptive strategies and coping mechanisms for environmental stress (cf. Richards, 1983, 1985, 1986; and for pastoralists, Dahl and Hjort, 1976; Dyson and Hudson, 1980). Behind these strategies are certain cultural and economic traits that explain the resilience of the peasant household in new circumstances and the capacity to find new survival possibilities.

In the 1960s in Western social sciences it became widely accepted that national patterns of social behaviour had displaced, at least in the West, those that could be thought of as local or regional. This thinking was exported, for example to Africa, in the form of nation-building and national economic growth. Interpretations of African development and performance, to a large extent, are still based on this view, emphasizing the national level and disregarding the locality and place identity.

In the African context the truth of the situation is the opposite. It is time-place specific actions and the myriads of day-to-day decisions at the micro-levels, not the performance of the state, that should be the concern when attempting an understanding of African and peasant realities, including spatial movements.

Contrary to the predictions of modernization theorists, social relationships grounded in assumed ties of blood, ethnicity, language, religion, place of origin, etc., remain powerful forces in Africa. Contemporary theories of political, economic and spatial development (cf. Mabogunje, 1989) are inadequate for understanding the role of these "primordial ties" (Hydén, 1980, Hoben and Hefner, 1991). The institutions in which primordial ties are grounded flourish in Africa today, as in the past, because people need them to cope with risk and pursue their interests. Thus, for instance, kinship, clan, ethnicity and religion can be interpreted as entitlements that buffer vulnerable people from the full force of natural as well as social calamity. Primordial ties provide access to natural and state resources. They provide a framework of social organization and moral sentiments of trust that facilitate the functioning of parallel markets and formal and informal enterprises. They enable groups

---

[*] See also Krokfors 1989a, 1991.

and individuals to internalize externalities and regulate competition for scarce natural, social and symbolic resources.

Primordial ties are not static, they are renewed, modified and remade in each generation and require creative effort and investment (cf. Krokfors, 1988). In rural as well as in urban Africa, primordial ties must be tended with a stream of social transactions to be kept fully active and ready for use. The lavish expenditures of African urban élites on the "traditional" ceremonies of their rural and urban kin or communities, are investments in security rather than adherence to antiquated rituals. Participation in primordial institutions has helped African farmers to cope with the effects of world recession, deteriorating terms-of-trade, effects of droughts and wars. In a situation of non-subsistence wage levels in the government sector, such participation has helped urban workers to survive, thus reducing the income gap between towns and countryside (see below). Hoben and Hefner (1991) have pointed out that the primordial ties in Africa today are robust, not because Africans are more "traditional" than people elsewhere, but because they, for a variety of environmental, political, and economic reasons, are more needed. The efflorescence of primordial micro-level politics in Africa, is in large part, a response to the problems and opportunities created by a weak state trying to survive through excessive controls and subsidies.

In a situation when individuals and groups have diminishing capacities to enforce entitlements, primordial ties function as reference points that are, at the same time, retrospective and prospective. In this sense, they provide security when looking for new options, for example new localities for subsistence income. This is certainly the case for individuals and groups spanning the rural–urban continuum, or secluded groups investigating the physical and social environments for new opportunities.

THE POLITICAL ECONOMY REALM

According to Barker (1989), one can distinguish between three circuits of economic activities in peasant economies. One is the domestic circuit which produces for household consumption, another is the market circuit where household land and labour is sold in external markets. The third circuit is the wage-labour circuit which creates and exports labour for work outside the community, and where remittances of some portion of wages are sent back for spending in local or external markets.

The three circuits are closely related and the operations in each are determined by the overall political-economic context. These circuits compete with each other by drawing on the same pool of labour; the two farming circuits also compete for the use of the same land. However, the circuits are complementary and can be interpreted as a kind of security against changing ecological and political-economic conditions. The function of primordial ties in peasant communities, and between peasant communities and the urban economy, should also be related to these circuits, for example the possibilities for wage labour in new localities. In this way the three circuits also function as a base for intra-household mobility.

Although the three circuits give peasant households flexibility and rationality, they are still subject to pressure and stress. Bernstein (1979) has dealt with the situation of African peasants in their role as rural producers. However, he does not discuss peasants in isolation but clearly points out that peasants in contemporary Africa are exploited through relations of commodity production and exchange which lock them into the international capitalist economy. Bernstein identifies what he calls "the simple reproduction squeeze" among peasant households. The "squeeze" is the effect of commodity relations on the economy of peasant households "that can be summarised in terms of increasing costs of production/decreasing returns to labour" (Bernstein, 1979:427). Production of items for exchange has become an integral part of peasant survival (Blaikie, 1988b). Deterioration in the terms-of-trade between commodities produced for the market, and items necessary for domestic consumption acquired from the market is transmitted to the household economy in terms of a reduction in consumption or an intensification of commodity production (i.e. through intensification of land use), or both. Because land and labour are the main means of production, the "squeeze" implies exhaustion of both. "The low level of development of the productive forces in peasant agriculture means that the household is extremely vulnerable to failure in any of its material elements of production" (Bernstein, 1979:428). Changes in prices of the produce can then result in a kind of super-exploitation of land that destroys the capability of it to satisfy the needs of the peasant household. A situation of sub-subsistence develops and members of the household have additionally to find new, and often not land-based, activities for survival. This means new social relations of surplus extraction, with less attention being paid to the maintenance of land, and the continuous loss of land capability to satisfy household needs. This is probably the most important element in intra-household mobility, or seclusion from a poverty perspective.

THE GEOGRAPHICAL TRANSFER OF VALUE AND SPATIAL MOBILITY

Land degradation in relation to the socio-economic structure of the population is best studied in a local setting. But this setting has to be related to higher levels of geographical and socio-economic organization. Most countries show uneven economic development, which is due mainly to the increased use of inputs from stock resources by the dominant capitalist mode of production. At the regional level, extraction of stock resources tends towards concentration of economic activities, as the extracted products have to be brought together for processing. This results in uneven distribution of capital accumulation based on transfers of values appropriated between the regions of a country.

   This spatial differentiation in accumulation can be attributed to two factors: one is the survival of pre-capitalist modes of production due to the uneven spread of the capitalist mode of production. The other is the qualitative differences within the capitalist mode due to different development of the productive forces and thus the ability to compete (Forbes and Rimmer, 1984). Again there will be a contradiction between harvesting flow resources and extracting stock resources. The higher the development of a region's productive forces, the more important are the inputs from stock resources, and the greater the appropriation of value from other regions. The values transferred are rent, interest and profits derived from two basic sources: the extraction of surplus produce from the pre-capitalist mode of production and the extraction of surplus labour from the production processes. Thus, the geographical transfer of these values reinforces exploitation of land and labour at the local level; some areas are left with only the possibility of harvesting flow resources with constantly decreasing returns. In the long run, the only resource left for these areas is labour, which as the only means of survival for households, has to be exported to areas of capital accumulation.

SURVIVAL THROUGH MOBILITY

Inequality in entitlements to land and assets is the main reason for land degradation (Figure 1). Once the degradation process reaches a level where the land capability cannot meet the demands of the user, than he/she has to find other means of survival than land-based production. As has been shown, this is often the case when land use practices, mainly based on harvesting flow resources, confront those using inputs based on extraction of stock resources. The result is a sub-subsistence situation. To manage such a situation households have to find new strategies of survival. These can either be adaptation to the new socio-economic situation like the "multi-active household strategy", or exiting from the situation using a "secluded-group strategy".

Multi-active households

The multi-active household exists in rural and in urban areas, as well as between the two. In this chapter multi-activity and multi-location are treated as survival strategies, not as capital accumulation strategies. Members of households engage in different income-generating activities. Some might be land-based, others wage-based but very often the activities are of a spontaneous and informal nature. Commonly households are not only multi-active, but also multi-localized. This means that the members earn income in different localities, often of several days time-distance from each other. Very often, household members use different income opportunities which exist along the rural–urban continuum (Hjort, 1979; Hesselberg, 1985; Bjerén, 1985). The interlacing of activities within the household enables the household as an economic unit to survive. In such a situation a large household with several income-generating members is an advantage. It is therefore not surprising that those countries in sub-Saharan Africa that have the highest development of the productive forces in the capitalist sector also have the highest rates of population increase (Kenya, Zimbabwe, Côte d'Ivoire). In these countries, the demand for commodities from the market economy is greatest and the simple reproduction squeeze most pronounced. The more members of the household, the more production that can be exchanged for commodities.

By being multi-localized the household also has a multi-resource base. This explains significantly the performance of African countries. The involvement of the household in different activities at different places using different resources is the core of the survival strategy (Krokfors, 1988). Household members in different places will be entitled to resources with differing access qualifications, with their practical consciousness[*] determining their resource use (Elwert, 1983). This implies new relationships between people and the physical environment. Resources that once were described as clearly belonging to a non-monetarized economy (for example "green leaves" in the diet) might suddenly become commercialized. The *one* member of a household in relation to members of other households has to use his/her innovative abilities to obtain access to resources that, in the best way, contribute to the survival of his/her own household. Locally, this entails a totally new form of man-environment relations. It is not any more a question of multiple use of the environment by united households. Instead there is competition for entitlement to resources in the same place by individual members of multi-active, multi-localized households. The ecological, demographic, and political consequences of these man-environment relations still have to be assessed and analysed in detail.

The secluded group

The secluded-group strategy implies exiting from a dominant societal superstructure characterized by a dominant mode of production and the simple reproduction squeeze. Seclusion is based on a new societal ideology, a superstructural reconstruction aimed at initiating the local population into a radically new community and thus avoiding encapsulation in a wider capitalist system. This reconstruction is often based on religion: Christian, Islamic, traditional African, or mixtures of these (van Binsbergen, 1981; Davidson, 1983; Lewis, 1955, 1956). The superstructural reconstruction is combined with an infrastructural reconstruction that entails new relations of the group's members to each other and to the means of production, i. e. land. This infrastructural reconstruction derives its strength through revitalizing an economy based on reciprocal assistance, local control of the means of production and a concern with production of use value for the community, before involving in exchange relations and taking risks.

Secluded groups in Africa have a long history going back to the pre-colonial period and only a few aspects of political relevance for maintenance of land capability are dealt with in this chapter. Seclusion has attracted much attention in connection with the independence of African states and in relation to the type of economic policy practised during the post-independence period. Through the emphasis on the local community and its survival under a specific superstructure different from that characterizing the post-independent state, the secluded groups have often made considerable economic progress compared with groups under the simple reproduction squeeze. This also means that members of secluded groups pay much more attention to the maintenance of land sustainability than is usually the case in African states. Land has often been reclaimed in remote areas (Clarke, 1982; Davidson, 1983; Hisket, 1984, for cases in Islamic West Africa; Lewis, 1955, 1956; Seger, 1986 for Somalia) or illegally occupied (for example, van Binsbergen,

---

[*] Practical consciousness is "tactic knowledge that skilfully applied in the enactment of courses of conduct, but which the actor is not able to formulate discursively" (Giddens, 1979, quoted in Krokfors, 1988:7).

1981). Secluded groups are often looked upon as a threat by the state authorities to the country's unity and therefore opposed (see, for instance van Binsbergen (1981) concerning the Lumpa uprising in Zambia, and Coulson (1982) regarding the Ruvuma Development Association, Tanzania, that developed an *Ujamaa*-type ideology and production infrastructure, too radical to be accepted by the state authorities).

CONCLUSIONS

Are local responses to the simple reproduction squeeze to be interpreted as mere survival strategies or as signs of development? The wide range of activities within the multi-household sector can hardly as a totality be assessed as development if the latter is to mean welfare improvements. On the one hand, there are households that through their utilization of rural–urban activities just gain a base for their existence and reproduction. On the other hand, there are households that for instance through the skilful use of urban or other non land-based activities, can accumulate capital for investment. However, the nature of these investments can vary considerably. If investments are made to maintain or increase land capabilities or for education and so on, they can contribute to the welfare of the household. Through investments in prestige enhancement, the status of the household can increase locally and thus the household's access to entitlements. However, the question remains whether these are signs of development or signs of a societal polarization process?

The more extreme response in the form of seclusion is also hard to evaluate. The new ideologies existing in some of these households can be fruitful alternatives to the dominating ideology of the society concerned, but are often, as mentioned above, viewed as a threat to the existing order and are suppressed. But in some cases they have gained propagation and have formed a base for a new societal order. Thus, a general conclusion can be that at least some of the survival responses can be a base for innovation and societal change.

References

Barker, J., 1989, *Rural Communities Under Stress: Peasant Farmers and the State in Africa*. Cambridge: Cambridge University Press.

Bernstein, H., 1979, "African peasantries: a theoretical framework", *The Journal of Peasant Studies*, 6, 4:421–443.

van Binsbergen, W.M.J., 1981, *Religious change in Zambia: Exploratory studies*. London: Kegan Paul International.

Bjerén, G., 1985, *Migration to Shashemene: Ethnicity, gender and occupation in urban Ethiopia*. Uppsala: Scandinavian Institute of African Studies.

Blaikie, P., 1985, *The political economy of soil erosion in developing countries*. London: Longman.

Blaikie, P., 1988a, "Environmental crises in developing countries: how much, for whom and by whom? An introduction and overview", in P. Blaikie and T. Unwin (eds.), Environmental crises in developing countries. *Institute of British Geographers, Developing Areas Research Group, Monograph*, No. 5, pp 1–6.

Blaikie, P., 1988b, "Explaining soil degradation". *Institute of British Geographers, Developing Areas Research Group, Monograph*, No. 5, pp 55–81.

Blaikie, P. and H. Brookfield, 1987, *Land degradation and society*. London: Methuen.

Clarke, P.B., 1982, *West Africa and Islam*. London: Edward Arnold.

Coulson, A., 1982, *Tanzania: A political economy*. Oxford: Oxford University Press.

Curtis, D., M. Hubbard and A. Shepherd, 1988, *Preventing famine: Policies and prospects for Africa*. London: Routledge.

Dahl, G. and A. Hjort, 1976, Having herds: Pastoral growth and household economy. *Stockholm Studies in Social Anthropology*, 2.

Davidson, B., 1983, *Modern Africa*. London: Longman.

Drèze, J. and A. Sen, 1989, *Hunger and public action*. Oxford: Clarendon.

Dyson-Hudson, H., 1980, "Strategies of resource exploitation among East African savanna pastoralists", in D. Harris (ed.), *Human ecology in savanna environments*. London: Academic Press.

Elwert, G., 1983, *Bauern und Staat in Westafrika: Die Verflechtung sozio-ökonomischer Sektoren am Beispiel Benin*. Frankfurt: Campus Verlag.

Forbes, D.K. and P.J. Rimmer, (eds.), 1984, "Uneven development and the geographical transfer of value". *Human Geography Monograph* 16. Canberra: School of Pacific Studies, The Australian National University.

Giddens, A., 1979, *Central problems in social theory: Action, structure and contradiction in social analysis*. London: Macmillan.

Hesselberg, J., 1985, *The Third World in transition: The case of the peasantry in Botswana*. Uppsala: Scandinavian Institute of African Studies.

Hiskett, M., 1984, *The development of Islam in West Africa*. London: Longman.

Hjort, A., 1979, "Savanna town: Rural ties and urban opportunities in Northern Kenya", *Stockholm Studies in Social Anthropology*, 7.

Hoben, A. and R. Hefner, 1991, "The integrative revolution revisited", *World Development*, 19, 1:17-30.

Hydén, G., 1980, *Beyond Ujamaa in Tanzania: Underdevelopment and an uncaptured peasantry*. London: Heinemann.

Krokfors, C., 1988, "The unique versus the general—some lessons for development geography", *Occasional Papers of the Finnish Association for Development Geography*, 23, pp 1-9

Krokfors, C., 1989a, "Population and land degradation: A political ecology approach", in A. Hjort af Ornäs, and M.A. Mohamed Salih (eds.), *Ecology and Politics. Environmental stress and security in Africa*, Uppsala: Scandinavian Institute of African Studies, pp 179–209.

Krokfors, C., 1989b, "The Political Ecology of Survival in Africa. A Conceptual Framework". Paper presented at the seminar *The Third World—The Fourth World: Dimensions of Development in the Peripheries*, October 26–28, 1989, Helsinki. *Occasional Papers of the Finnish Association for Development Geography,* vol. 26.

Krokfors, C., 1991, "Demystifying the rural/urban interface: Rural/urban interaction in an African context". *Paper presented to the NADG biennial meeting, December 6–8, 1991,* Kungsbacka.

Lewis, I., 1955, "Sufism in Somaliland: A study in tribal Islam I", *Bulletin of School of Oriental and African Studies,* 17, 3, pp 581–602.

Lewis, I., 1956, "Sufism in Somaliland: A study in tribal Islam II", *Bulletin of School of Oriental and African Studies*, 18, 1, pp 145– 160

Mabogunje, A. L., 1989, *The development process*. London: Unwin, 2nd edition.

Rees, J., 1985, *Natural resources: Allocation, economics and policy*. London: Methuen.

Richards, P., 1983, "Ecological change and the politics of African land use", *African Studies Review*, 26:1–72.

Richards, P., 1985, *Indigenous agricultural revolution: ecology and food production in West Africa*. London: Hutchinson.

Richards, P., 1986, *Coping with hunger: hazard and experiment in an African rice-farming system*. London: Allen and Unwin.

Saetra, H., 1975, Den økopolitiska sosialismen. Oslo: Pax Forlag A/S.

Seger, N., 1986, "Organization of the irrigated agricultural economy amongst the small farmers of the Mubaaraak/Lower Shabelle region", in P. Conze, and T. Labahn (eds.), *Somalia: Agriculture in the Winds of Change*. EPI Dokumentation Nr. 2, pp 153–163.

Sen, A., 1981, *Poverty and famine: An essay on entitlement and deprivation.* Oxford: Clarendon Press.

Sen, A., 1984, *Resources, values and development.* Oxford: Blackwell.

Todaro, M., 1976, *Internal migration in developing countries: a review of theory, evidence, methodology and research priorities.* Geneva: International Labour Office.

Todaro, M., 1989, *Economic development in the Third World.* New York: Longman, 4th edition.

Rural Households as Producers
Income Diversification and the Allocation of Resources

Hugh Emrys Evans and Gazala Pirzada

In many developing countries, especially in Africa where incomes are low and the modern sector is nascent, the bulk of production is undertaken at the level of the household. This is the case both in agriculture as well as in commerce, manufacturing, and most other non-farm sectors. Planners and policy makers concerned about promoting sustainable development, particularly in rural areas, need first to understand the behaviour of the household as producer, and the factors that affect the way it allocates resources of land, labour, and capital among alternative income-generating activities. Under one set of circumstances, the household may invest its resources locally in rural areas and nearby small towns, thus promoting local prosperity. Under other circumstances, the household may eschew local alternatives in favour of migration to the city, leaving the rural areas weakened and undermining the chances of achieving sustained local development. This chapter, therefore, is an attempt to explore the characteristics of the household as a production unit, and to shed light on key factors which influence the household's allocation of its resources among activities on the farm and off it.

The principal argument of the chapter may be summarized as follows. The household as a production unit has resources of land, labour, and capital, which it allocates according to objectives. Depending on the income level of the household, the objective to be maximized may be: merely surviving, minimizing risks, or maximizing profits. All three goals can be enhanced through diversifying the household's sources of income. When households are able to diversify their income, they are better able to accept risk in any one of their ventures. A higher risk threshold enables households to take actions, such as investing greater resources or adopting innovations, that improve their productivity as farmers or entrepreneurs. This in turn raises output and incomes, spurs demand, and creates further business and employment opportunities.

The rest of the chapter is devoted to elaborating elements of this argument, drawing mainly on empirical studies reported in the literature. We begin with a discussion of the household's attitude to risk, and the way it changes as income levels rise. Next, we discuss the rationale for diversifying incomes as a means of reducing risk, and how this helps households to become more productive producers, whether as farmers or entrepreneurs. Then follows a section documenting the tendency for rural households around the world to diversify their incomes, which is seen to be part of the larger structural transition from an agricultural economy to one based on a broader range of activities.

The main part of the chapter explores alternative strategies for diversifying the household's sources of income, and the implications for the use of the household's assets of land, labour, and savings. The first choice for rural households is often assumed to be migration to larger cities in search of employment. But there are other choices, including switching from subsistence to commercial agriculture, seeking local employment, and starting a non-farm enterprise, either on the farm itself or in an accessible town nearby. Of particular interest here are the factors which determine the household's choice of strategy, and their decision to deploy their productive assets locally or further afield. The chapter concludes with a brief discussion of the implications for planning and policy.

THE HOUSEHOLD AS A PRODUCTION UNIT AND ATTITUDES TO RISK

The notion of treating the household as a production unit for the purpose of understanding development problems first gained popularity with the concept of new household economics (Michael and Becker, 1973), but it is not without its detractors. Moock and others (1986) have argued that while the notion first originated with studies in Europe and Asia, it is not well suited to Africa. The different social conditions and structure of the family there make it difficult to maintain the idea that the household is a cohesive decision-making unit. Hyden (1986), for one, argues that the individual not the family or household is the relevant unit for analysis in any study of the agriculture sector.

However, for the purposes of the present discussion the household, rather than the individual, serves as the relevant unit of analysis, since we are interested in examining how the household as an enterprise or production unit allocates its collective assets or resources of land, labour, and capital among alternative income generating activities. In this sense, the household is not so much a single physical unit as an economic entity linked to several places and activities. A similar argument is made by Stark (1980) and Guest (1989) in examining household decisions concerning labour and migration.

As a production unit, the household allocates its resources to achieve certain goals. We postulate that the choice of goals depends on the household's level of income, and changes as incomes rise (see Figure 1). Among the poorest households, living on the edge of imminent disaster, the goal may be merely to survive, which as Shahabuddin *et al.* (1986a and b) suggest, may mean rationally taking big risks out of sheer desperation.

Just above the lowest income levels, the goal may be to minimize risk, to ensure at least a subsistence level of income to feed and maintain the household. Being close to penury, the household has minimum tolerance for accepting increased risk, and therefore rationally curbs spending on production, and avoids experimenting with new farming methods (Feder, Just and Zilberman, 1985). In a different context, Turner (1968) has also observed how low

Figure 1. *Income level, objectives, and risks*

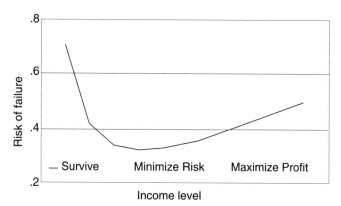

income squatter families also seek to minimize risk, in this case by avoiding potential confrontations with government authorities.

As incomes rise and the household becomes more secure, however, the objective may become the more conventional one of maximizing net income or profits in order to improve standards of living. With greater resources, the household can afford to accept higher levels of risk, and take actions that offer potentially greater returns.

RISK, INCOME DIVERSIFICATION, AND PRODUCTIVITY

As producers, rural households face risk and uncertainty from many directions, including environmental factors such as drought, flooding, pest and disease infestation, and economic conditions governing the supply of labour and other inputs, as well as the price of agricultural commodities on domestic and world markets. In addition, most actions to increase output or raise productivity involve risk of some kind. As Evans and Ngau (1991) point out, households expose themselves to further risk any time they invest larger resources in production, or adopt new methods of farming, since the outcomes can never be known for sure.

The household's choice of action depends largely on its assessment of the risks involved and its capacity to absorb losses in case things turn out badly. The household's assessment of the risks associated with a given action, and its capacity to undertake risk, largely determines its willingness to apply new production methods and technology, both in farming as well as small businesses.

In developing countries, where most families including those in the middle income bracket have low or modest incomes, they have a limited capacity to absorb downturns and losses, and can ill afford to take risks. Where the household depends largely or entirely on a single source of income, it is understandably going to be even more cautious in changing habitual practice and doing things differently.

Households can reduce risk, however, and improve their chances of achieving current goals—whether survival, risk minimization, or profit maximization—by diversifying their sources of income. Income diversification allows families to spread risk among a wider range of activities, and thus to insulate themselves better against calamity or loss of revenue in any one activity.

In so doing, income diversification allows households as producers to accept greater risk in individual activities, and thus to take actions that raise productivity in each of them, whether it be farming, a small business, or wage employment. As farmers, the household may hire more labour, spend more on inputs, or switch to higher value crops. As operators of a small business, the household may invest in equipment that raises productivity of labour. As wage earners, the household may finance one of its members to search further afield for a higher paying job, or even to train for one.

Income diversification also helps to raise the productivity of household assets in other ways. Income generated in one activity eases credit constraints, and provides cash to finance investment in another. The use of non-farm income to finance farming, for example, is well documented. Berry reports that non-farm earnings from trade or other cash employment as craftsmen or labourers were used by early planters in the expansion of Nigerian cocoa farming in the 1930s and 1940s (Berry, 1975:72). In East Africa during the 1960s and early 1970s, Kitching (1977:25) observed that increases in the area of land under cultivation were directly dependent on access to off-farm income for the purchase of land or the hire of labour.

EVIDENCE OF INCOME DIVERSIFICATION

Almost all studies report that rural households receive income from both farm and non-farm sources, but the shares of each in the total vary considerably. In Asia and Africa, for example, non-farm income ranges from 22 per cent to 70 per cent (Chuta and Liedholm, 1979), and in Latin America and the Caribbean from 30 per cent to 60 per cent (Deere and Wasserstrom, 1980). In the context of attitudes towards risk and potential for diversification, such percentages of non-farm income assume great importance.

Non-farm earnings may come from many sources, most commonly wage employment, farm-based non-farm activities, off-farm businesses, and remittances. As Chuta and Liedholm (1979) have shown, farm-based non-farm activities are likely to include a wide range of enterprises, such as brick-making, carpentry, handicrafts, and beer brewing, while off-farm business activities may include trading, retailing, petty manufacturing, and other services, often located in a nearby town.

Most authors seem to agree that for low income rural households, wage labour is the main source of non-farm earnings, but several report that it declines in importance among higher-income households. Kilby and Liedholm (1986) indicate that for the low income rural household, wage labour is the predominant source, while for the high income households salaries from administrative and manufacturing activities tend to predominate. From a review of ten studies carried out in Latin America, Deere and Wasserstrom (1980) report that wage labour has become the main source of income for the majority of smallholder households. In Puebla, Mexico, for example, it rises in importance from a low of 9 per cent of total income among business farm households with average landholding of 16 hectares, to 69 per cent and more among minifundio households with average landholding of 2 hectares or less (see Table 1). Rovira (cited in Deere and Wasserstrom, 1980:18) also indicates that wage income rises in importance as household income falls, although its contribution is smaller, from 1 per cent among large landowners to 16 per cent among small farmers.

Table 1. *Sources of non-farm income among rural households*

Sample	Sources	Per cent of Total Income	
Puebla (Mexico)			*1970*
Business farms	Wages		9.0%
Family farms			32.0%
Poor minifundios			43.0%
Very poor minifundios			57.0%
Prosperous minifundios			69.0%
Wage-earning minifundios			82.0%
Kutus (Kenya)			*1988*
All farms	Farm-based non-farm		5.8%
	Town business		26.3%
	Wage labour		33.5%
	Remittances		2.0%
Taiwan		*1960-62*	*1970-72*
All farms	Rental income	2.0%	3.0%
	Off-farm labour receipts	3.0%	10.0%
	Income from sideline	3.0%	12.0%
	Other non-farm receipts	3.0%	6.0%
	Total non-farm	11.0%	31.0%

Sources: Puebla-Deere and Wasserstrom (1980), Table 3:8; Kutus-Bendavid-Val *et al.* (1988), Table 6.3:77; Taiwan-Chinn (1979), Table 6:294

A study of farm households around Kutus in Kenya (Bendavid-Val *et al.* 1988:77, Table 6.3), however, shows wage labour contributing a fairly steady 30 per cent of farm household income across all income levels. Farm-based non-farm activities also contribute a steady 6 per cent, but town businesses rise sharply in importance from zero among the poorest group, to 4 per cent among middle income households, and almost 30 per cent among wealthier households. It was found that 40 per cent of farm household income originated from local rural activities, 28 per cent from non-farm activities in Kutus town, and 32 per cent from activities outside the study area, which covered a 10 kilometre radius of the town.

According to Bhalla (1978), income from non-farm sources in the Indian Punjab is high for medium- and large-scale farmers, many of whom have large earnings from hiring out tractors and tubewells. It also plays an important role in augmenting household income of marginal and small farmers, the main sources being wages from employment, followed closely by the sale of milk.

Another common source of non-farm income is remittances from household members working elsewhere. Case studies from Africa, India and Southeast Asia indicate that in comparison with earned income, the proportion of money and resources remitted is often substantial. As a proportion of the total income of recipients, Rempell and Lobdell (1978) concluded from their review of the literature that remittances accounted for up to 40 per cent in the

case of rural households, and up to 20 per cent in the case of urban households. A sample survey in Kenya found similar proportions among rural
households, but as much as 47 per cent for the poorest urban households,
which are usually newly arrived migrants or students (Knowles and Anker,
1981).

In general, remittances form a larger part of incomes among poorer households, and decline in importance as income levels rise. From their Kenya data,
Knowles and Anker (1981) report that net remittance receipts amount to 90
per cent of factor income among the poorest urban households, and over 35
per cent among the poorest rural households. Net remittances transferred by
urban households are highest in absolute and relative terms among middle-
income groups, amounting to as much as 10 per cent of factor income, but
fall in importance among higher-income groups. Net remittances transferred
by rural households amount to no more than 4 per cent of factor incomes,
and that occurs only among higher-income households. (Knowles and Anker,
1981). This trend is confirmed by Collier and Lal (1984:1016), who also find
that in Kenya the share of income sent by urban households declines as
income levels rise, and that the share of rural household income represented
by remittances received also declines as income levels rise.

RESOURCE ALLOCATION AND STRATEGIES FOR INCOME
DIVERSIFICATION

Conceptually, we hypothesize that households first establish an overall objective, then determine a strategy to achieve this objective, and based on the chosen strategy allocate their resources of land, labour, and capital accordingly.
In reality, few households probably do this in such a formal manner. But most
probably base their decisions implicitly or explicitly on some sort of similar
line of reasoning.

The strategy chosen is likely to depend on two sets of factors, one internal
having to do with the assets available to the household, the other external
having to do with physical and economic conditions. As Harris and Todaro
have suggested in the context of migration, the household as decision maker
has to take into account both potential returns from a given action, and the
probability of realizing those returns. While potential returns are a function
of such factors as soil fertility, levels of output, and prices, the probability of
realizing those returns has to do with less predictable variables such as rainfall, pest infestations, and market conditions.

Household resources or assets are an approximate indicator of relative levels of income and wealth. Households with less than average resources in all
three categories are likely to be among the poorest, those with more than
average in all three categories among the richest, and those with a mix of
more and less than the average somewhere in the middle. In terms of Figure
1, the poorest most destitute households with few or no resources apart from
labour correspond with the left end of the horizontal axis, and might rationally take highly risky actions out of desperation. Poor households with at
least some resources fall into the middle range of the horizontal axis, and are
more likely to be risk minimizers. Those with above average resources, partic-

ularly capital and other liquid assets, may be expected to be profit maximizers.

In the sections that follow, we examine in turn the rural household's use of land, labour, and capital. Ideally, to facilitate comparisons across countries, we need consistent sets of household data. However, in the absence of such data, we have to rely instead on a second best procedure of simply culling the literature for studies of household income and behaviour that shed light on the questions raised here.

The allocation of land

The amount of land available to a household largely determines the extent to which it engages in farming, and to a lesser extent the kind of farming it undertakes. Households with small landholding, but with little in the way of savings, are likely to be risk minimizers rather than profit maximizers. As such, we would expect them to use their land for subsistence farming, and perhaps low risk commercial agriculture, such as selling surpluses of staple foods.

Households with more land have other options. For those with more land but little savings, the probability increases that part of it will remain fallow or uncultivated due to the shortage of household labour, and the lack of funds to hire extra hands or needed inputs. Under these conditions, the household may be expected to lease it out to tenant farmers, assuming demand exists and local traditions permit. Larger households, and those with sufficient funds to purchase necessary inputs, can switch from subsistence farming to higher risk commercial production for the market, spending more on inputs, and switching to higher value crops, such as coffee or tea in place of maize. As the size of their landholding increases, households have greater opportunities to diversify their earnings within farming by cultivating a wider variety of crops. For households with larger landholding, therefore, we may expect to find that the relative importance of wage income and other non-farm income declines.

Such a trend is reported in a number of studies (see Table 2). In a comparison of data from five countries in Asia and Africa, Kilby and Liedholm (1986:9) show that among households with the least land, the proportion of total income from non-farm sources ranges from 50 per cent in Sierra Leone to 88 per cent in Thailand. Among households with the most land the non-farm share is substantially lower, ranging from 45 per cent in Thailand to as little as 16 per cent in Korea, indicating that these households are indeed relying on farming as their primary source of income.

Deere and Wasserstrom (1980:4) report a comparable situation in Bolivia. They cite the case of Chuquisaca department, where rural families derived a greater portion of their livelihoods from agriculture (64 per cent) than did their counterparts in either Potosi (40 per cent) or Tarija (30 per cent), where farms are smaller. On properties of less than one hectare, households derived only 27 per cent of their income from farming, a figure which increased to over 67 per cent on properties larger than five hectares.

Similar results are cited by Anderson and Leiserson (1980:233), from studies in Zambia, Pakistan, Korea, and Thailand, which all show that the non-

Table 2. *Farm and non-farm income related to size of landholding*

Country	Size of Holding (in acres)	Net farm income as share of total household income
Korea—1980	0.00–1.23	74%
	1.24–2.47	39%
	2.48–3.70	28%
	3.71–4.94	23%
	4.95–	16%
Taiwan—1975	0.00–1.23	70%
	1.24–2.47	52%
	2.48–3.70	44%
	3.72–4.94	39%
	4.95–	26%
Thailand—1980–81	0.00–4.10	88%
	4.20–10.20	72%
	10.30–41.00	56%
	41.00–	45%
Sierra Leone—1974	0.00–1.00	50%
	1.01–5.00	23%
	5.01–10.00	14%
	10.01–15.00	12%
	15.00–	15%
Northern Nigeria—1974	0.00–2.46	57%
	2.47–4.93	31%
	4.94–7.40	26%
	7.41–9.87	15%
	9.88–	24%
Source: Kilby and Liedholm (1986), Table 4: 9		
Southern Bolivia—1976–77	0.00–2.50	73%
	2.51–5.00	60%
	5.01–12.50	55%
	12.51–25.00	37%
	25.00–	33%
Source: Deere and Wasserstrom (1980), Table 4: 10		
Zambia—1966–68	4.9	22%
	22.8	6%
Pakistan	–6.25	39%
	6.25–12.49	22%
	12.50–18.74	22%
	18.75–24.99	8%
	–25.00	6%
Source: Anderson and Leiserson (1980), Table 3: 233		

farm share of household income tends to fall as farm size increases. In North Thailand, cropping intensity also emerges as a significant factor. The non-farm share drops from 42 per cent to 32 per cent as landholding increases on more intensely cropped farms, and from 76 per cent to 43 per cent on farms where cropping intensity is lower. Rietveld (1986), speaking of Java, mentions that in relative terms, income from non-agricultural activities is most important for the landless and small farm households, although in absolute terms, large farmers also derive sizeable incomes from this source.

We should be wary, however, of concluding that this is a universal phenomenon. There are undoubtedly cases where households with small landholding still derive most of their income from farming, and cases where households with large landholding earn most from non-farm sources. An example of the former is cited by Deere and Wasserstrom (1980) in the Peruvian highlands, which they attribute in part to the limited degree of development of the labour market.

Such instances point to the second set of factors mentioned earlier, which influence the household's allocation of its productive resources, namely prevailing environmental and economic conditions. These affect not only the scale of potential returns associated with alternative activities, but the probability of realizing those returns. In some cases, circumstances may encourage farm households to specialize more on farm production while in others conditions may induce farmers to diversify into non-farm activities. In agriculture, the scale of potential returns is largely a function of physical conditions, the scope for shifting to higher value crops, and expected future prices, which in turn depends on demand. The probability of realizing those returns is a function of many things, such as the predictability of rainfall and other climatic conditions, the likelihood of pest infestations, the stability of market prices, and the nature of government policies particularly those affecting farm prices.

Even where conditions in agriculture may be relatively secure, however, non-farm activities may offer even better opportunities for rural households to diversify their income. This may be especially true where households have easy access to nearby urban areas, and in countries where income levels are high enough to support demand for a wide range of non-farm goods and services. This situation is more likely in areas with a dense rural population, small individual holdings, and a decentralized urban system with lots of small towns. Such is the case, for example, in Taiwan, and in the Kutus area of Kenya, where higher-income rural households evidently prefer to diversify into non-farm enterprises (Chinn, 1979; Bendavid-Val *et al.* 1988).

The allocation of household labour

While land is fixed in a given location, labour is mobile and, from the point of view of the household as a producer, is free to be put to its most productive use. The decision to retain labour on the farm, to seek wage employment locally, or elsewhere, affects migration flows, and in part determines the rate of growth of population of rural areas, small towns and larger cities.

Conventional wisdom suggests that larger rural households with extra workers are the main source of migrants to the city. But this is not necessarily the case. The household may deploy its labour force in a number of ways, the choice depending as before on its objectives, the strategy selected to achieve that objective, and the availability of other productive resources.

Households with few workers, little or no land, and negligible savings, are almost certainly risk minimizers. Apart from subsistence farming, the only other viable option is wage employment in the local area, either part time, full time, or seasonal. With adequate funds, the household may switch from subsistence to commercial farming, particularly if it possesses a larger landholding. If not, the smaller household may opt instead to send one of its members to the city in search of work, often the male head or an older child.

Households with more workers may still be risk minimizers if they lack other resources. More workers may represent an asset in the sense of more hands to work, but they are also a liability in the sense of more mouths to feed. Having more workers and little land, the larger household is likely to seek employment locally rather than further afield. A strategy of local wage employment is likely to be preferred, since poorer households can ill afford to support job seekers in the city for an indefinite period. Wage levels may be lower in rural areas, but the costs of the job search are minimal, and the chances of landing a job are not necessarily any lower, may even be higher since the household is likely to have a wider range of contacts locally than in a distant city.

Risk minimizing households with additional labour might also engage in some kind of home-based non-farm production activity, as long as it requires minimal funds, though this is likely to be preferred less than wage employment. Sales are uncertain, some kinds of products—like baskets, weaving, or other craftwork—may entail costly marketing trips, others may be inferior goods for which demand declines as income rises.

As mentioned before, larger households with more land may opt for low risk commercial farming, or if they have the funds on higher risk forms of commercial farming. With adequate funds, larger households have other options if land is limited. They are better able to finance job searching in the larger city, and may even eschew wage employment in favour of operating their own business.

In most countries, the trend towards engaging in non-farm employment is strong, although estimates of the proportion of rural households that have members engaged in non-farm activities vary widely. Anderson and Leiserson (1980:229) present data for 15 countries showing that the percentage of the rural labour force primarily engaged in non-farm work falls between 20 per cent and 30 per cent. In some countries, where larger but essentially rural towns are included, the figure rises to 30 per cent to 40 per cent. (see Table 3).

From the 1980 Pakistan Census of Agriculture, Klennert (1986) calculates that 17 per cent of all economically active men belonging to marginal farm households were engaged in non-agricultural work. But the census counted only those men living permanently in the household, and excluded non-resident members living temporarily at their place of work. Taking these into account, Klennert estimates from his own survey that 40 per cent of all marginal farm households in rural areas included members either resident or non-resident that were engaged in non-farm work. He cites other similar studies in Pakistan which found proportions ranging from 58 per cent to 70 per cent, where off-farm income amounted to between 39 per cent and 43 per cent of the household's total earnings.

This variation in the proportion of households with members engaged in non-farm work may be explained by at least two factors. First, some part of the variation arises from seasonal fluctuations in demand for farm labour, which peaks at planting and harvest times. Second, the incidence of non-farm employment among rural households will depend on the availability of jobs

Table 3. *Rural household employment in farm and non-farm activities*

Country	Year	Employment (%) Farm	Non-farm
Kenya	1969	72	28
Iran	1972	67	33
Guatemala	1964	86	14
El Salvador	1975	68	32
Colombia	1970	77	23
Venezuela	1971	63	27
Chile	1970	70	30
Brazil	1970	88	12
Indonesia	1971	72	28
Thailand	1972	82	18
Philippines	1970	72	28
West Malaysia	1970	68	32
South Korea	1970	81	19
Taiwan	1966	51	49
India	1966–67	80	20

Source: Anderson and Leiserson (1980), Table 1: 229

Country	Year	Farm	Non-farm
Bangladesh	1981		
Village in Dhaka		41	59
Village in Chittagong		35	65
India	1982		
Villages in W. Bengal		59	41
Pakistan	1983		
Village A Faisalabad		49	51
Village B Faisalabad		55	45
Village in Jhelum		11	89
Sri Lanka	1983		
Village in Kandy		56	44
Village in Kurunegala		54	46
Thailand	1982		
Village in Suphanburi		60	40
Village in Kalasin		40	60
Village in Chiang mai		18	82

Source: Islam (1984), Table 1: 309

in agriculture and outside it, and relative wage levels. Manning (1988), for example, indicates that rapid agricultural growth in rural Java has been accompanied by increased employment in agriculture. He also argues that at least till the early 1980s, agricultural growth had weak linkages with non-agricultural employment creation.

Considerable differences have also been observed in the number of households with members engaged in non-farm activities as landholding or income levels increase. As was already seen in the case of income, households without land or with smaller landholding are more likely to have members working in non-farm activities. In a 1973 survey of rural households in Cajamarca department in Peru, Deere (cited in Deere and Wasserstrom 1980:14) found that 30 per cent engaged in artisan production, and 53 per cent in wage labour. Artisan production was a little more prevalent among households with larger landholding, 36 per cent versus 30 per cent among smaller farms, but the proportion of households with members engaged in wage labour fell off dramatically as the size of landholding increased, from 71 per cent among the smallest farms to 30 per cent among the larger ones.

Similarly, in a paper analysing non-farm activities in rural Asia using village level data from five countries (Bangladesh, India, Pakistan, Sri Lanka, Thailand), Islam (1984) concludes that employment in non-farm activities is substantial among rural households (Table 3) and varies inversely with the size of farm. He also claims, however, that wages from most activities are low, and that the growth of non-farm activities is more a symptom of distress, reflecting adaptation to increasing poverty rather than dynamic growth.

More often, however, studies report a trend towards the increasing participation of households in non-farm activities, and this is interpreted as a sign of a prospering local economy, and a reflection of rising rural incomes and the creation of new income-earning opportunities. It is also to be expected, given the long term structural transition from a predominantly agricultural economy to one based more broadly on non-agricultural activities. Using data from nine countries, Chuta and Liedholm (1979) show that the percentage of the rural labour force engaged in non-farm work had risen in all of them, much of it in small scale rural enterprises. Annual growth rates in rural non-farm employment ranged from 3.2 per cent in Korea between 1960 and 1974, to 9.4 per cent in Taiwan during the period 1955–66. In general, the growth rates varied with the type and size of enterprise, growth in employment being higher for larger size firms as measured by number of employees.

Chinn (1979) confirms the trend reported by Chuta and Liedholm in Taiwan, and Binswanger (1983) reports a similar situation in Thailand. There, between 20 per cent and 40 per cent of the rural labour force is engaged in off-farm pursuits, and the proportion also seems to be rising.

According to Carlsen (1980), however, there is often a marked difference in the returns obtained from rural non-farm production in part-time secondary occupations—particularly subsidiary household activities such as petty trade and home crafts—and those obtained in permanent full-time occupations of the informal variety. Furthermore, he suggests as rural incomes rise, the latter tend to displace the former. Carlsen reports that 43 per cent of the population were involved in non-farm production in a very poor area, while for three more prosperous areas the percentage ranged from 16.4 to 21.5.

In keeping with earlier conclusions, all this suggests that rural households with smaller landholding and having lower levels of income are more likely to allocate labour to non-farm activities than larger or high income households. This is understandable since the former have less access not only to land but also to other factors such as credit, infrastructure and other supporting services. Given the difficulties and risk involved for them to raise their productivity as farmers, they are more likely to deploy their labour in non-farm activities, both on and off the farm.

Household savings and investment

Perhaps, more than any other asset, the accumulation of savings enables the household to make the transition from a risk minimizing strategy to a profit maximizing one. The availability of liquid assets in the form of cash or live-stock provides the household with a cushion to ride through rough times in farming and downturns in other entrepreneurial activities. As such, the household can then entertain the notion of undertaking potentially more rewarding activities that may also be riskier.

The propensity to save

The propensity of rural populations to save is seen to be a function of income and investment opportunity. Until relatively recently, little effort was made to mobilize savings of the rural population, because it was assumed that most were too poor to save. However, the minimum income threshold at which savings can begin is likely to be lower in rural areas than cities, due to lower costs of living, the household's greater capacity to feed itself, and the more limited availability of consumption goods. From their study of rural savings in India, for example, Krishna and Raychaudhuri (1982) concluded that real per capita incomes need to rise only 10 per cent above the poverty line before a typical household starts to save.

Table 4. *Average and marginal propensities to save for rural households in selected countries*

Country	Year	APS	MPS
India	1970–71	6.9	22.0
Taiwan	1974	31.0	
Japan	1973	22.0	
Korea	1974	33.0	
Punjab (India)	1969–70	34.0	
Taiwan	1970		34.0
			56.0
			46.0

Sources: Adams (1978), Bhalla (1978), Krishna and Raychaudhuri (1982) and Ong *et al.* (1976)

Other empirical studies support the notion that rural households can and do save. Table 4 compares the findings of a number of surveys on rural savings in different countries spanning the period 1960 to 1980. From this it can be seen that the average propensity to save ranges from 7.0 per cent of house-hold income in India to 33 per cent in Korea, and the marginal propensity to save from 22 per cent in India to 56 per cent in Taiwan. The low rates reported by Krishna and Raychaudhuri for India reflect the fact that over 40 per cent of the rural population still remained below the poverty line at that time.

In countries for which time series are available, there is widespread evi-dence that average propensities to save tend to rise (see Table 5). Adams (1978) notes that in Japan it rose from 10 per cent in 1950 to 22 per cent by 1973, while in South Korea it rose dramatically from a low 4 per cent in 1965 to an unusually high 33 per cent in 1974, with smallholders recording 22 per cent, still a comparatively high figure.

In part, these increases may simply reflect the rise in income levels that took place during these periods. But more significantly, there is evidence to indicate that households save more when presented with increased incentives and profitable investment opportunities. In India, Krishna and Raychaudhuri (1982) report that there was a significant step-up in the savings ratio among rural households in the years beginning 1965–66, when agricultural price supports and new technology were introduced. Further, they find that while the savings rate for all rural households in the period 1966–74 was a low 3.5 per cent of net income, it was three to fifteen times higher in numerous irrigated regions where new technology had been introduced.

A second factor which affects the household's propensity to save is the relative attractiveness of alternative investment opportunities. The decision to invest in farming or non-farm ventures depends as before on the potential returns to be gained, and the probability of realizing those gains. The rates of return on investments in agriculture and non-farm activities depend in part on the domestic terms of trade, on advances in technology in each sector, especially in industry and agriculture, and the potential for adopting innovations. Normally technological advances favour non-farm activities, but advances in agricultural technology can also lead to substantial increases in investment in that sector, as witnessed by the Green Revolution in Pakistan, India and other countries.

Attractive opportunities for investment in rural areas may also arise from the growth of agriculture and rising rural incomes. In evaluating the impact of an irrigation project in the Muda region of Malaysia, Bell *et al.* (1982:187) report that savings were diverted from other uses to finance the balancing investments needed to increase the region's output of non-traded goods. They estimate that each dollar of downstream value added was probably supported by just over a dollar of additional investment in plant equipment in sectors that expanded in response to the project. In other words, local investment opportunities can attract savings that might otherwise be invested in urban activities.

The allocation of household investments

Numerous writers refer to the use of income from one activity as the means to finance investment in another. Typically, this means non-farm earnings being used to purchase agricultural inputs and sometimes more land or labour. But it may also mean earnings from agriculture being used to finance a non-farm enterprise.

In Pakistan, Klennert (1986) observed that off-farm employment improved the income of households with marginal farms directly and indirectly. Indirectly, the effects of off-farm employment were felt through the increase in agricultural yields of small farms, as 77 per cent of the households surveyed did not consume all the additional earnings, but used part of them to buy fertilizer and improved seeds, and to hire tractors and equipment (p 42).

In examining changes in farm household incomes in three provinces of Kenya, Collier and Lal (1984) found that "both non-crop income and liquid wealth significantly and powerfully contribute to crop income controlling for the direct inputs into production". They argue that the principal agricultural decisions which are potentially constrained by risk and cash flow are the use of purchased inputs and the mix of crops, which dictates need for inputs. They also point out that the shift from maize to coffee takes several years, implying high opportunity costs for food crop income foregone while coffee

Table 5.　*Changes in average propensities to save for rural households in selected countries, 1960–74*

Year	Taiwan Farm Size			Japan Farm Size			Korea Farm Size			India (Ludhiana District) Farm Size		
	Small	Medium	Large	Small	Medium	Large	Small	Medium	Large	Small	Medium	Large
1960	0.15	0.14	0.27	0.11	0.13	0.17						
1961	0.17	0.20	0.25									
1962	0.22	0.27	0.29				0.16	0.15	0.22			
1963	0.16	0.25	0.38									
1964	0.23	0.25	0.36									
1965	0.14	0.20	0.26	0.16	0.20	0.24	0.06	0.12	0.13			
1966	0.16	0.23	0.24				0.10	0.13	0.23			
1967	0.16	0.16	0.32							0.02		
1968	0.23	0.27	0.28				0.68	0.23	0.24	0.06		
1969	0.26	0.31	0.39							0.06		
1970				0.14	0.14	0.19	0.16	0.26	0.19	0.17		
1971				0.12	0.12	0.13	0.34	0.35	0.47		0.17	0.18
1972				0.19	0.16	0.24	0.34	0.30	0.30		0.23	0.22
1973				0.21	0.21	0.23	0.27	0.34	0.40		0.30	0.28
1974							0.35	0.43	0.40		0.26	0.25

Source: Adams (1978), Ong et al. (1976)

Note: For all the countries except India:

small farms　= 0.5–1.0 hectares,
medium　= 1.0–1.5 hectares, and
large　= 2.0 hectares and more

For India:

small units　< 3.5 hectares,
medium　= 3.5 to 6.0 hectares, and
large　> 6 hectares

tree plants reach maturity. They conclude that "the benefits of (agricultural) growth will accrue to those smallholders with characteristics which enable them to overcome cash flow and risk constraints", and that "a prime component of this group are those who participate in the urban economy" to generate non-crop income.

The use of income from farming to finance non-farm enterprises is less well documented, though examples exist. Household participation in non-farm enterprises is of course likely to be more prevalent in urban than in rural areas. A study by Vijverberg (1988:13) in Côte d'Ivoire, for example, indicates that participation rises from 27 per cent in rural areas, to 45 per cent in Abidjan, and a high of 51 per cent in urban areas outside the capital. The lower rate in Abidjan is mainly due to the wider availability of wage and salary employment there.

According to Vijverberg, 47 per cent of urban households operate a non-agricultural enterprise, and about half of these depend upon this enterprise for more than half their household income. While only 21 per cent of total urban household income originates from non-farm enterprises, households with such enterprises do not fall into the lowest welfare categories. In fact, in rural areas, they often rank in the highest income deciles.

In other urban areas, however, nearly half the males and half the females work on the family farm, only 43 per cent of male and 11 per cent of female workers being wage employees. The non-agricultural self-employed mainly comprise females, older workers, and foreign nationals. Thus, it seems that non-agricultural self-employment is an option for the household's secondary earners and for low income households, but not for primary earners in middle income households.

For Côte d'Ivoire as a whole, households with non-farm enterprises belong more often to the middle classes rather than to the poor, as has often been suggested in the literature. In Kutus, they are to be found among some middle income farm households, but mainly among the higher-income group within the sample, though these households are probably middle-income by most other standards (Bendavid-Val *et al.* 1988).

From the above examples, we conclude that even though lower-income rural households have a greater tendency to turn to non-farm employment, be it for reasons of survival or to raise cash for productive activities, it is the larger and middle income households who actually invest in non-farm enterprises. The former provide the labour, but the latter have access to the capital required for such businesses.

CONCLUSIONS

The bulk of production in less-developed countries takes place at the level of the household. As a production unit, the household has resources of land, labour and capital, which it allocates according to objectives. Depending on the income level of the household, the objective to be maximized may be: merely surviving, minimizing risks, or maximizing profits. All three goals can be enhanced through diversifying the household's sources of income.

Income diversification spreads risks across a range of activities, enabling households to take greater risks in any one activity, such as farming or a small enterprise. This allows the household to adopt new methods, hire additional labour, or switch to higher value crops, all of which helps households to become more productive as farmers and entrepreneurs. This raises output and incomes, spurs demand, and creates further business and employment opportunities.

Households can diversify their incomes either within agriculture through commercial production of a range of commodities for market, or outside agriculture through wage employment, either locally or further afield, or by establishing a business of some kind on the farm or off it. Some strategies imply investing resources in local small towns and rural areas, while others imply migrating to crowded cities in search of work. The first choice for rural households is often assumed to be migration to larger cities. But there are other choices. Households with sufficient land and savings can switch from subsistence to commercial agriculture, but only *if* markets are accessible. Households with little land and capital can seek employment locally, but only *if* there are expanding local job opportunities. And households with adequate capital and labour can establish a non-farm business, *if* there are vigorous small towns nearby to support such an enterprise and link producers to potential markets.

The choice of a strategy depends in part on the household's resources of land, labour, and capital, and in part on local environmental and economic conditions. Some of these factors are largely outside the control of planners, but many are not. To broaden choices and opportunities for households to diversify their incomes, planners and policy makers should seek ways of improving access to rural markets, providing necessary supporting infrastructure and services in small towns and rural areas, and creating an appropriate regulatory environment in support of farm and non-farm production and employment, themes taken up in greater detail elsewhere (Evans 1991). By assisting rural households to diversify their incomes in this way, planners can promote the larger goals of raising incomes, creating rural employment opportunities, and promoting sustainable development.

References

Adams, Dale, 1978, "Mobilizing Household Savings through Rural Financial Markets", *Economic Development and Cultural Change*, 26 (3), April.

Anderson, Dennis, and Mark W. Leiserson, 1980, "Rural Non-farm Employment in Developing Countries", *Economic Development and Cultural Exchange*, 28 (2).

Bell, Clive, Peter Hazell and Roger Slade, 1982, *Project Evaluation in Regional Perspective*. Baltimore: Johns Hopkins University Press.

Bendavid-Val, Avrom, *et al.*, 1988, *Rural–Urban Exchange in Kutus Town and its Hinterland*. Worcester, Mass: Clark University, Settlement and Resource Systems Analysis Cooperative Agreement.

Berry, Sara, 1975, *Cocoa, Custom, and Socio-Economic Change in Rural Western Nigeria*. Oxford: Clarendon Press.

Bhalla, Surjit S., 1978, "The Role of Sources of Income and Investment Opportunities in Rural Savings", *Journal of Development Economics*, Vol. 5, pp 259–81.

Binswanger, H. P., 1983, *Growth and Employment in Rural Thailand*. Washington, DC: World Bank, Report No. 3906-TH.

Carlsen, J., 1980, *Economic and Social Transformation in Kenya*. Uppsala: Scandinavian Institute of Social Studies.

Chinn, Dennis L., 1979, "Rural Poverty and the Structure of Farm Household Income in Developing Countries: Evidence from Taiwan", *Economic Development and Cultural Change*, Vol. 27, pp 283–301, January.

Chuta, Enyinna, and Carl Liedholm, 1979, "Rural non-farm employment: A review of the state of the art". *MSU Rural Development Paper* No. 4. East Lansing: Michigan State University.

Collier, Paul, and Deepak Lal, 1984, "Why Poor People Get Rich: Kenya 1960–79", *World Development*, 12 (10), pp 1007–1018.

Deere, Carmen Diana, and Robert Wasserstrom, (1980), "Household Income and Off-farm Employment among Smallholders in Latin America and the Caribbean". Paper for Costa Rica seminar sponsored by CATIE.

Evans, Hugh Emrys, and Peter Ngau, 1991, "Rural–Urban Relations, Household Income Diversification and Agricultural Productivity", *Development and Change*, July 1991.

Evans, Hugh Emrys, 1991, "Rural–Urban Linkages: A Key to Self-Sustaining Growth in a Developing Region". University of Southern California, School of Urban and Regional Planning. Unpublished manuscript.

Feder, G., R.E. Just, and David Zilberman, 1985, "Adoption of Agricultural Innovations in Developing Countries", *Economic Development and Cultural Change*, Vol. 33, pp 255–298, January.

Guest, Philip, 1989, *Labour Allocation and Rural Development: Migration in Four Javanese Villages*. Boulder: Westview.

Hyden, Goran, 1986, "The Invisible Economy of Smallholder Agriculture in Africa", in J.L. Moock (ed.) *Understanding Africa's Rural Households and Farming Systems*. Boulder: Westview Press.

Islam, Rizwanul, 1984, "Non-Farm Employment in Rural Asia: Dynamic Growth or Proletarianisation?," *Journal of Contemporary Asia*, 14 (3), pp 306–24.

Kilby, Peter, and Carl Liedholm, 1986, "The Role of Non-farm Activities in the Rural Economy". EEPA Discussion Paper No 7, November. Office of Rural and Institutional Development, USAID.

Kitching, G.N., 1977, "Social and Economic Inequality in Rural East Africa: The Present as a Clue to the Past". Swansea: University College, Centre for Development Studies.

Klennert, Klaus, 1986, "Off-Farm Employment in Marginal Farm Households: A Hidden Development of Parts of Pakistan's Poor", *Quarterly Journal of International Agriculture*, 25 (1).

Knowles, James C. and Richard Anker, 1981, "An Analysis of Income Transfers in a Developing Country", *Journal of Development Economics*, Vol. 8, pp 205–226.

Krishna, Raj and G.S. Raychaudhuri, 1982, "Trends in Rural Savings and Capital Formation in India, 1950–51 to 1973–74", *Economic Development and Cultural Change*.

Manning, Chris, 1988, "Rural Employment Creation in Java: Lessons from the Green Revolution and Oil Boom", *Population and Development Review*, 14 (1), pp 47–80.

Michael, Robert T., and Gary S. Becker, 1973, "On the New Theory of Consumer Behaviour", *Swedish Journal of Economics*.

Moock, Joyce Lewinger (ed.), 1986, *Understanding Africa's Rural Households and Farming Systems*. Boulder: Westview Press.

Ong, M.L., D.W. Adams, and I.J. Singh, 1976, "Voluntary Rural Savings Capacities in Taiwan, 1960–70", *American Journal of Agricultural Economics*, 58 (3), August.

Rempel, Henry and Richard A.Lobdell, 1978, "The Role of Urban-to-Rural Remittances in Rural Development", *Journal of Development Studies*, 14 (3), pp 324–41.

Rietveld, Piet, 1986, "Non-Agricultural Activities And Income Distribution in Rural Java", *Bulletin of Indonesian Economic Studies*, 22 (3), pp 106–117.

Shahabuddin, Quazi, and Stuart Mestelman, 1986a, "Uncertainty and Disaster-Avoidance Behaviour in Peasant Farming: Evidence from Bangladesh", *Journal of Development Studies*, Vol. 22, pp 740–51.

Shahabuddin, Q., S. Mestelman, and D. Feeny, 1986b, "Peasant Behaviour Towards Risk and Socio-Economic and Structural Characteristics of Farm Households in Bangladesh", *Oxford Economic Papers*, Vol. 38.

Stark, Oded, 1980, "On the Role of Urban-to-Rural Remittances", Discussion, *Journal of Development Studies*, 16 (3), pp 369–74.

Turner, John F.C., 1968, "Housing Priorities, Settlement Patterns, and Urban Development in Modernizing Countries", *American Institute of Planners Journal*, November.

Vijverberg, Wim, 1988, "Non-agricultural Family Enterprises in Côte d'Ivoire". Washington, DC: World Bank, *Living Standards Measurement Study*, WP No. 46.

Part II

National, Regional, and Sub-Regional Themes

Migration in Africa
An Overview

Aderanti Adepoju

In order to understand fully the current migration-development interrelations in Africa, migration in its historical perspective will be examined followed by a review of the contemporary situation. Some observers have amply described Africa as a "continent perpetually on the move" (Ricca, 1989). More appropriately, the people of Africa are perpetually on the move perhaps more so than other regions in the world. Significantly, the movements are both intra— and inter—continental migrations.

Africa is undoubtedly a continent of considerable migration. Various forms of population movement in response to political, economic, religious, and security situations, and demographic factors, have been recorded from early times (Hance, 1970). Spatial mobility has been a fundamental social and historical aspect of African life. However, the different patterns, directions, and motivations of migration have been severely affected by the colonial experience which, in turn, influenced economic, sociocultural, political, and demographic development (Prothero, 1968; ECA, 1981).

In spite of the apparently distinct phases of African history (the pre-colonial, colonial and post-colonial era) migration assumes a considerable measure both of diversity and continuity in its causes, magnitude and effects on African society and economy. Because the economic, social, cultural, demographic and colonial experiences have differed, so do the pattern and motivations of migration which have been largely influenced by these factors. The historical evolution of African countries, colonial experience, post-colonial development strategies and the current political and economic situation are linked to migration in the region.

DATA SOURCES

The problem of data on migration, in terms both of quality and availability is a perennial one in Africa. The sources of data for the study of migration which are quite varied have improved overtime. Originally, data on migration in Africa were found in localised studies conducted by anthropologists. Their interest usually focused on the determinants of migration among relatively small communities. Close on the heels of the anthropologists were sociologists who looked at migration from the perspective of the social structure. As urbanization spread on the continent and aspects of modernism, alien to African societies, started penetrating all corners of the continent, sociologists saw migration as a response to the disintegration of the social structure. Their focus was therefore more on the migrants themselves rather than on the communities.

Table 1. *Literature sources on migrations in Africa by theme*

Theme	Number of Studies Cited	Major Issues Addressed, Papers Presented
Data, methodology	128 (8.5%)	Data sources, scope, and limitations; Conceptual issues and problems.
Labour migration	202 (13.4%)	Internal: rural–rural to wage sector and rural–urban migration; International: direction, types (especially brain drain), and effects.
Resettlements/ spatial	153 (10.2%)	Post-independence resettlement process, types, results, and problems; Demographic and socioeconomic challenges of resettled areas.
Urban system/ urbanization	219 (14.5%)	Migrants' adjustment in urban milieu; Relationships between migration and urbanization.
Linkages to migration	100 (6.6%)	Networks and linkages of internal and international migrants with areas of origin; Indices of linkages: visits, remittances, sociocultural ties.
Female migration	37 (2.5%)	Lack of studies on female migration and gender roles.
Refugees	103 (6.8%)	Sources and destinations of refugees; Causes and consequences of refugeeism and displacements.
Nomadism	25 (1.7%)	Nomadism in Sahelian countries and Kenya; Process, determinants, and consequences of nomadism.
Migration and regional integration	34 (2.3%)	International migration in the context of regional integration/cooperation institutions in African national subregional economies.
Migration and basic needs	53 (3.5%)	Migration and provision of food, shelter, education, health, etc.
General interrelationships and policies	453 (30.1%)	General internal and international migration studies; Migration-influencing and migration-responsive policies.
All themes	1,507	

Source: Oucho and Gould (1993)

The pervasiveness and the different types of labour migration brought economists into the fray. Economists started documenting migration on a slightly larger scale, focusing on the dynamics of labour migration in response to wage differentials between rural and urban areas (Adepoju, 1984c).

It was however not until demographers came onto the scene that data sources for migration studies started improving and expanding dramatically. For demographers the issues of interest in the study of migration which they helped focus attention on were the differentials and selectivity of migration.

To fully understand these phenomena larger data sets were necessary. Thus the 1960s and 1970s saw the burgeoning of sample surveys with enough cases to study the different variables that interested demographers. These efforts were boosted by the round of censuses in the 1970s and 1980s which included place of birth and duration of residence in their schedules (see Adepoju, 1990 for a detailed discussion).

To date there is a much richer spectrum of data for migration studies as is shown in Table 1. While the quality of data has also improved considerably, there are however some special topics such as female migration and international migration, of which the latter is very scantily covered in censuses, for which there are still serious gaps.

Nonetheless it is evident that migration is now of central concern for planners and it is expected that data sources will not only expand but the existing ones will be refined. In response to United Nations inquiry, most African governments have cited migration as the most important population phenomenon, ahead of mortality and fertility, in the last five consecutive years. Good data however continue to be relatively elusive. Unlike fertility and mortality where comparable data sets have been generated through the World Fertility Survey, the Demographic and Health Surveys and Contraceptive Prevalence Surveys, such data sets are conspicuously lacking for the study of migration.

MIGRATION IN HISTORICAL AND CONTEMPORARY PERSPECTIVE

The phenomenon of migration in Africa can be better understood within the context of the political and historical evolution of African societies. The effects of colonization and decolonization on the economy and indirectly on migration are most visible when examined in the context of the pre-colonial, the colonial and post-colonial eras.

Pre-colonial Migration: Africa has a long history of population movement aimed at restoring ecological balance and, more important, of individuals in search of subsistence food, better shelter and greater security. In the pre-colonial era, movements now regarded as international migration occurred over a wide area, restricted only by warfare (Hance, 1970).

Migration in Africa is not a homogeneous phenomenon: various forms of movements across and within national boundaries have been promoted by commerce, pastoralism, natural disasters, warfare, and the search for employment (Addo, 1975). Such factors have influenced the composition, direction and characteristics of movements. Pre-colonial movements of Africans as explorers and labourers were unsystematized and entire villages, tribes and clans are known to have moved to escape the ravages of internecine warfare, or to avoid unfavourable agricultural and climatic conditions resulting in famine and drought (ECA, 1981). In West Africa, in particular, commercial migration (Sudarkasa, 1974–1975) and movements connected with trade and evangelization (Addo, 1975) also featured during this early period: indeed migrants have always considered most parts of the region as a free zone within which people moved freely.

Migration in Colonial Times: In west, east and southern Africa, especially, colonial rule paved the way for relative peace and political stability; movements hitherto associated with internecine warfare ceased or were reduced. Thereafter most of the population movements were linked to the economic strategies of the colonial governments. The development of the foreign export sector, emphasis on the urban sector and exploitation of the rural sector resulted in considerable inequality in both sectors. The stage was therefore set for a new framework for migration, deriving from the labour requirements for plantations and later the administrative apparatus (Amin, 1974). The colonial administrators imposed a series of economic measures to obtain labour in the required number and place in South Africa (Thahane, 1991). The forced-labour and compulsory cropping systems in former French and Portuguese colonies of western and eastern Africa were designed largely to obtain the labour-force needed for export crops—cotton in Mozambique and Angola—and to consolidate labour supply. This was also the case of construction of roads and railways in Uganda (Kaberuka, 1992), plantation agriculture in Côte d'Ivoire (Anan Yao, 1990) and former Rhodesia (Stahl, 1981). Initial forced migration through forced labour, taxes and compulsory cropping, later became institutionalized into regular migration in various African countries (Hinderink and Tempelman, 1978). The strategy of dispossessing Africans of their land in Rhodesia and South Africa (Thahane, 1991) in Namibia, Angola, Rwanda and Burundi (Zolberg *et al.*, 1989) created the strongest push thus far for labour migration.

In time, forced recruitment gave way to free migration of individuals and families in search of better living conditions. Thus the attractive alternatives on the cocoa farms of Gold Coast (now Ghana), the plantations and forest industries of Ivory Coast (Côte d'Ivoire), the groundnut fields of Senegal and The Gambia prompted streams of migration of unskilled labour from the landlocked countries—Upper Volta (now Burkina Faso), Mali, Niger, Chad—towards these coastal countries. Similar movements were observed from Mali, Senegal River Valley toward the Senegambian groundnut zone and the urban areas of Senegal and Côte d'Ivoire (ECA, 1981; Mabogunje, 1972; Findley and Ouedraogo, 1993).

Movement was north-south to areas of prosperous agricultural activity in the coastal region. Migration was short-term and male dominated. The major source of seasonal migrants was the savannah, peasant agricultural areas in the north, especially during the long dry season when economic activity was at its lowest (Amin, 1974). Indeed as Prothero (1968) observed, West Africa has been characterized by greater seasonal migration than elsewhere in tropical Africa. These migrations which still persist are largely spontaneous and uncontrolled (Adepoju, 1983a).

In West Africa, such north-south movements from the savannah to the forest zone, involved the Mossi migrants who moved to the coastal areas of Ghana and Ivory Coast; migrants from northern to south-west Nigeria and Ghana; from Mali to southern Ivory Coast and from the north-east to the cocoa areas in southern Ghana (Mabogunje, 1972). In some cases, such migrations took the form of primary group movement of people themselves of the same origin. The migrants later reconstituted into homogeneous groups at their destination. This was the case of Nigerian immigrants in Ghana. The transmission of information by relatives and kinsmen of available opportunities in the new locations facilitated such chain migration.

Here lie the roots of the temporary, target migration pattern, which involves "international" migration, in the African context: workers circulate between home and the plantations (East Africa) or mines (South Africa) or coastal forest zones (West Africa). The poor earnings and inadequate welfare services reinforced the cycling of the migration, leading to the temporary nature of migration observed in eastern and southern Africa (Mitchell, 1959, Elkan 1967).

Thus, while population movements in several parts of Africa dated back several centuries, and evidently predated colonial rule, their patterns, volume, intensity and direction have been substantially altered by colonial administrations. By accelerating some pre-existing migration patterns, colonial rule exerted a notable impact on the motivations for migration (Thahane, 1991; Oucho and Gould, 1993). However, the different African regions were not homogeneous in their colonial experience. In east, south and central Africa, unlike west Africa there were large concentrations of European settlers. Also West Africa escaped the use of large plantations as was the case in East Africa. These factors explain the differential impact of colonial rule on labour migrations in particular (Adepoju, 1988a).

Up to the mid 1970s Ghana, Côte d'Ivoire (and to a lesser extent Senegal) were the major destination of immigrants in West Africa. They were joined by Nigeria in the late 1970s. Burkina Faso, principally, Togo, Mali and Guinea were the sources of emigration. The introduction and/or expansion of mining and cocoa farming and the systematic orientation of the economy towards export products created a huge demand for labour which the indigenous people were unwilling or unable to satisfy. As a result labourers were recruited from Togo, Upper Volta (Burkina Faso) and Nigeria. In 1969 Ghana expelled a large number of foreigners under the Aliens Compliance Order but by the late 1970s, economic problems in the country had led many Ghanaians to emigrate to Nigeria and Côte d'Ivoire (Addo, 1975; United Nations, 1982; Adepoju, 1991c).

To summarise, the introduction of international currencies, the development of transport and communications systems, the end of internecine warfare, and labour conscription encouraged labour migration. Also the development of tracks, roads and railways to link the hinterland to the capital cities and ports further contributed to the process. By opening up large tracts of land, they reduced the physical efforts hitherto necessary for long-distance travel, accelerated the pace of existing migration, provided employment and quick transmission of messages and information about the range of opportunities in the different areas, and thus intensified migration.

Post-Colonial Migratory Movements: The post-independence period intensified the developmental pattern inherited from the colonial administrators. The urban based development strategies, the introduction of free primary education and high population growth rates reinforced the volume, intensity and determinants of migration, mainly towards the capital cities, and other urban centres (Adepoju, 1990).

The selective development of resource rich areas (mines, minerals, plantation agriculture) and urban areas: the line-of-rail region in Zambia, capital cities-Lagos, Nairobi, Kinshasa, Dar-es-Salaam, Addis-Ababa, Lusaka, etc.—

which serve as the administrative, political, commercial and educational centres, immensely attracted migrants.

Shortly after independence, national governments, building upon the foundations of the colonial development strategy, invested in industry, commerce,
administration, and especially post-primary schools and social amenities. The
export-oriented development path, and the concentration of investment in a
few cities was a major cause of regional inequality, rural to urban migration,
and in regions where plantation economies predominate, rural to rural migration, became a logical response by migrants to the prevailing regional inequalities in development, income, employment and living conditions (Adepoju, 1988c).

Cyclical migration, a feature of the African migratory scene, is mainly
rural–rural designed to meet labour demands in various parts of the continent
(Oucho and Gould, 1993). The rural–rural migration pattern is not confined
to domestic movements; most inter-country migration, particularly in West
Africa, is also of the rural–rural migration pattern: amongst frontier workers,
seasonal and short-term (temporary) migrant workers who regard the movement as an extension across national boundaries of internal movements and
of rural–rural migration (Adepoju, 1984b). Migrants are usually confined to
neighbouring countries and, in particular, to areas with similar cultural,
socio-economic and ethnic characteristics (Adepoju, 1991a).

The literature on migration indicates that the primary push factors in rural
areas of Africa include extremely low income, the unfavourable rural socio-
economic structure, low skills in peasant farming, displacement of small
farmers for large-scale farming, landlessness, and concentration of available
land in the hands of few landlords. In Lesotho for example, the majority of
labour migrants to the Republic of South Africa comes from rural areas, as
arable land continues to decline and a large proportion of rural households
are landless (Thahane, 1991). In most African countries, young men, both
single and married, tend to migrate *alone* to the cities, to more easily available urban jobs and accommodation and to save enough money to pay for the
transport and maintenance of wives, children, and relations who might subsequently join them (Oucho, 1990, 1991).

Most migrants both within and across national borders are adults, aged
15–39, unskilled and, if married, usually leave their wives and children at
home. The result is a division of labour among adult family members: men
migrate for wage employment while the women maintain the farm. This also
necessitates frequent home visits by migrants and, usually, high labour turnover (Adepoju, 1988c).

The picture during the colonial era, where educated persons tend to
migrate to urban areas while uneducated ones "gravitate towards agricultural
employment" (Oucho and Gould, 1993) has changed, as illiterate persons
have increasingly migrated to the urban informal sectors. In effect, skilled
persons, including those in pursuit of training are attracted to urban areas
while the unskilled and poorly educated tend to prefer rural–rural migration.

In general, therefore, migrants attracted to the cities, tend to be young,
educated persons. By contrast, rural–rural migrants are mostly unskilled persons in their middle adult years: the economic activities in the rural sector are
closely related to their work experiences and skill level. In this way, these

migrants avoid the uncertainties of migrating into urban unemployment, problems of housing, transportation, high costs of living and other uncertainties associated with an urban environment.

What should be noted is that Africa is predominantly a rural continent. And as living conditions in the rural areas deteriorated, unemployment, underemployment and poverty intensified. Rural dwellers believe strongly that with not much to lose, many are willing to, and do in fact, risk privation and uncertainty in the towns for a chance of giving their children the education they never had, and of participating in the bursting city life, exchanging misery without hope in the rural areas for misery with hope in the cities especially in the urban informal sector which largely absorbs migrants, albeit at subsistence wages.

The picture depicted above is far from static: indeed the results of Ghana's 1984 census show that the dominant migration was urban–urban (34 per cent) followed by urban–rural (22 per cent) and rural–urban (16 per cent) comes last. This is not surprising as 83 per cent of all industrial establishments are concentrated in the Greater Accra, Eastern and Western Regions with Greater Accra accounting for 31 per cent, and Ashanti Region 30 per cent. Also 83 per cent of all people working in industrial establishments live in these regions: 35 per cent in Greater Accra, 24 per cent in Ashanti, 14 per cent in Western and 10 per cent in Eastern Region (Boateng, 1994).

INTERNAL AND INTERNATIONAL MIGRATION

The poorly policed boundaries which lack (permanent) physical features, the complementarity of the economies of neighbouring countries and the cultural affinity between ethnic groups in different countries, especially where immigrants and host populations speak the same language and share the same customs blur distinctions between internal and international migration in Africa (Adepoju, 1991c). Besides, in general, both derive from the same set of fundamental causes. However, the limitations imposed on international migration are greater, or more easily enforced. The linkage between both internal and international migration and factors which influence both also imply—in the context of Africa—that in general, internal migration is an extension of external migration (Conde, 1984). Owing to the relatively small size of African states, some migration that would elsewhere fall into the category of internal movement in Africa occurs across national frontiers. The overall direction is the same: from the relatively remote and peripheral parts of a country to the coastal areas (Mabogunje, 1972; Adepoju, 1984b). Thus, what distinguishes international migration in Africa is the blurring of the distinction between internal and international migration and the ineffective policing of the long national frontiers, the absence of national geographical barriers and the arbitrary setting of borders which cut across homogeneous social and ethnic groups (Adepoju, 1991c).

A great deal of migration across borders has been largely undocumented. Long, unpoliced borders lacking physical landmarks facilitate the free flow of migrants. In the cases of Ghana/Togo and Nigeria/Benin, for instance, frontier workers commute daily between their homes and their places of employment (Adepoju, 1983a).

The vulnerability of some African countries especially the land-locked countries of the Sahel region to environmental degradation—drought, flood or other disasters—also results in a wave of migration of displaced persons who literally cross national borders and settle in the neighbouring countries, usually the coastal countries, to continue their familiar occupation near the borders (Adepoju 1983a). In fact undocumented migration and seasonal labour migration have taken place routinely in all regions of Africa, particularly West Africa (UNDP; 1992). Migrants, in desperation, often move from one poor country to another to escape unfavourable climatic conditions, ethnic conflicts and the like.

In West Africa, "commercial" migration of both males and females is significant; labour migration is essentially male dominated. In fact, intra-regional migration has been encouraged by sub-regional economic union: indeed, the complementary economies of neighbouring countries, close cultural ties between ethnic groups spilled over into adjoining countries and the historical record of free labour migration make economic integration in Africa imperative. All told such economic units as ECOWAS in fact stimulated the homogeneous society which once existed in the subregion (Adepoju, 1991b). Similar examples include the defunct East African Community and the Southern African Development Co-ordination Conference (now the Southern African Development Community). Thus, in spite of different political systems and ideology, national currencies and language, the porous "international" borders which divide homogeneous groups hardly hinder full flows of males and females, traders, peasants, fishermen, nomads, labour migrants and, in recent years, professionals (Adepoju, 1991b).

The Sahelian countries are inhabited mostly by nomads, semi-nomads and sedentary farmers. Among the nomads, the most numerous pastoralists are the Fulani (also known as the Peul) who live in Niger, Mali, Côte d'Ivoire, Nigeria, Senegal and the Somali ethnic stock in Somalia, Ethiopia, Djibouti and Kenya. Nomads normally criss-cross borders during the seasonal search for water, paying no regard to international borders (Findley and Ouedraogo, 1993).

The frontier, seasonal and short-term migrant workers in West Africa regard their movements as "simply an extension across national boundaries of internal movements and of rural–rural migration". Indeed, it is difficult to establish, in most cases, just when a traveller crosses international borders. The mixture of people, the so-called ethnic groups, can be very fascinating: the Mende-speaking people live in Liberia and Sierra Leone; so do the Vai and Kroo in both countries. Yoruba are found in Nigeria and Benin as are Ewe in Togo and Ghana. So are the Makonde in Mozambique and Tanzania, and the Kakwa in Uganda, Sudan and Zaire (Adepoju, 1991c).

FEMALE MIGRATION

Until recently, female migration received relatively little attention compared with male migration. Part of the reason is that researchers have tended to focus more on economically-motivated migration. Thus, women are usually stereotyped as associational migrants. However, the engendering of data permits a more incisive analysis of female migration (Pittin, 1984). Recent studies in Zimbabwe, Uganda, Nigeria and Mali have shown that autonomous female migration is directed towards attaining economic independence through self employment or wage income: education facilitates entry of females into the organised labour market and autonomous migration is the vehicle that gives them greater control over their productive resources (Vaa *et al.*, 1989; Oppong, 1980; Adepoju, 1984a).

Up to the late 1970s, women migrants have often been regarded not as free decision makers but rather as followers of men, being dependent on the decision and act of migration by their husbands. But a number of factors influencing female migration have promoted autonomous migration among them. Foremost among these are the changing structure of economic activities which influence female migration to a greater extent than male migration, because they are linked to socio-cultural factors defining sex roles; education acts as a major catalyst to the spatial and occupational mobility of women (Adepoju, 1983b). The relative opportunity structure and the nature of employment for women in Africa in general are conditioned in part by their relative skills, the prevailing sex segregation and discrimination in the organized labour market, the perceived role of women and the type of occupational structure. All these are however now changing dynamically.

In most parts of Africa, the structure of employment requires mostly men to work in plantation agriculture, industry, commerce and mechanized transportation. Thus, men tend to migrate alone, leaving their wives behind. Furthermore the cultural factors that initially favoured the education of males over females have had the effect of confining women to the lower cadres of formal employment, given that employment in the organised labour market is highly correlated with education. Hence, the disadvantaged and least educated groups are confined largely to commerce and distributive trade.

One significant aspect of male-dominated migration is the growing number of female-headed households not only in Botswana, Lesotho and Swaziland (BLS) but also in Zambia and Kenya. In Lesotho, a full three quarters of all rural households especially in the mountainous areas are female-headed. As men increasingly migrated from rural areas, smallholder agriculture became increasingly "feminized". In some districts of Luapula and Northern Province in Zambia, for instance, between 50 and 70 per cent of smallholder farms were managed by women; in eastern and central province of Kenya, the proportion rose to 90 per cent resulting in women making key agricultural decisions. Indeed between 40 and 50 per cent of rural households in several parts of Zambia are in fact female-headed (Safilios-Rothschild, 1994).

The circumstances discussed above have shaped the perception of sex roles, which tend to associate women almost exclusively with the tasks of housekeepers and mothers within the household economic structure (Oppong, 1980; Adepoju, 1984). But recent evidence depicts migration as a major women's strategic response to the situation. Indeed, research on female migration in Mali shows that women in fact engage in (viable) economic activities in support of their families concurrently at place of origin and destination (Vaa *et al.*, 1989).

Tienda and Booth (1988) note that "male absenteeism, cash-cropping and declining land quality are pushing many more women out of rural areas".

The poor quality, indeed lack of access to land, strongly push rural women out of traditional agriculture. In Kenya, for instance, the land reform legislation denies independent access to land to women who are single heads of households and married women without sons.

In BLS a significant number of the men who migrate to work in the mines and plantations in the Republic of South Africa (RSA) for a contract period of two years at a time, only to return home periodically between contracts, often spend up to between fifteen and twenty years in RSA during their active working life (ages 15–50 years). Consequently, female-headed rural households in Lesotho, offshoots of the out-migration by the males, are paradoxically among the poorest. In such cases, the men are not readily available for the arduous tasks of ploughing and planting; women with or without the assistance of their children find it increasingly difficult to adequately offset the labour contribution of their absentee husbands. This is especially the case in situations of seasonal labour demand at peak periods (Makinwa-Adebusoye, 1990; de Vletter, 1985; Adepoju, 1990).

In Lesotho where 51 per cent of the adult males work in the Republic of South Africa (RSA) the women left behind bear the key responsibility of farm production management, and increasingly, decision making of a short-term nature. As a result, family responsibilities, decision making processes and the status and role of women are undergoing considerable changes. This is particularly so with respect to the land tenure system: owners of land left uncultivated for up to two years normally lose title to such land. Increasingly, therefore, women have to cultivate the land in the absence of their husbands including some who visit home erratically. The day-to-day management of the farm is undertaken by migrants' wives as few male kin offer any form of assistance especially in arranging for and supervising (male) hired labour (Adepoju, 1988c; Ware and Lucas, 1988; de Vletter, 1985; Palmer, 1985).

Traditionally, the men migrate leaving behind wives and children who may subsequently join them. Cases of family migration initially are uncommon, and women either accompany or join husbands. Autonomous female migration was sanctioned by a variety of customs—in Swaziland's traditional set up the woman's labour is the property of the husband and his kin and made the more difficult by job segregation and discrimination in the urban labour market: the gender bias is all too pervasive (Makinwa-Adebusoye, 1988; Adepoju, 1991d).

An ever-increasing proportion of women is responding to this set of social and economic circumstances by migrating autonomously. Migration affects a woman's life in a variety of ways, but in general it gives her access to or strengthens her economic independence and exposes her to wider horizons and opportunities. In addition, it is associated with the change in the traditional roles of women. Most women migrate in search of better opportunities, in response to natural disasters or flight from war and internal strife. The depletion of male labour through migration also affects women left behind who have to devise survival strategies, of which migration is increasingly one, to cope with the children, the elderly, the family farm, etc., often with limited resources and without decision-making authority (Oppong, 1992).

The 1960, 1970 and 1980 rounds of censuses confirm that women in Africa are migrating to urban areas in greater numbers in search of wage employment. Two main reasons have been advanced for this phenomenon: the deteriorating living and working conditions of women in rural areas and the instability of marriage (Findley and Williams, 1990; Pittin, 1984). Thus, women in east Africa often migrate to urban areas in the expectation of greater autonomy. Single women in Uganda are able to improve their social position by increasing their autonomy through urban employment; the migration *per se* provides an alternative to their subordination in the villages (Tienda and Booth, 1988).

But female migration is not directed to urban areas alone: women sometimes accompany their husbands when they migrate to the rural areas (Adepoju, 1984a). Whatever the direction, recent empirical evidence tends to suggest that the very fact of migration tends to increase women's recorded participation in economic activities, and in particular the occupational mix among these migrants (Pittin, 1984).

Education is one of most important factors in female autonomous migration. Several studies document the fact that over a half of female migrants have at least some primary level schooling: 57 per cent in Juba City, Sudan; 54 per cent in Monrovia, Liberia (Findley and Williams, 1990). Widespread education among females means that educated women have, in recent years, greater opportunities for employment in the formal sector. This also enhances their ability to compete and participate increasingly in both non-domestic and formal sector activities. Another result of the increasing proportion of educated women is the accelerated movement of females (especially the young) into urban areas to seek further education and jobs. Thus fully 40 per cent of the female rural–urban migrants in Burkina Faso are aged 20–24 years. In Kenya, 38 per cent belong to that age group (Findley and Williams, 1990). In Bamako, capital of Mali, for example, in 1983 where migrants are disproportionately young with the peak between age 16 and 35, women migrants are almost as numerous as male migrants (Vaa *et al.*, 1989).

A significant proportion of educated women, single and married alike, have migrated alone in search of "greener pastures" to the developed countries. In June 1990, for example, about 5,000 female nurses/midwives and 264 doctors were recruited from Port Harcourt, Nigeria by agents who established recruitment centres for work in Saudi Arabia (Adegbola, 1990).

Female autonomous migration in West Africa is unique in one respect. Trading activities are the domain of women in West Africa a situation that has facilitated their visibility in both internal and international migration. Studies by Sudarkasa (1974–75) aptly document this phenomenon, especially among the Yoruba-speaking women in Nigeria and Benin. Women dominate short-distance rural to rural migrations, while men predominate in international and internal rural–urban migrations (Adepoju, 1983b, 1984).

Thus in a reversal of the traditional sex roles, female autonomous migration, especially of the educated and the more commercially enterprising, is leading to a situation where the men are left at home to look after the children in the absence of the womenfolk. Indeed, female migration has intensified child fostering: in Ghana during the period of economic downturn of the late 1970s to the early 1980s, children of female migrants were left in the care of grandparents, as is widely practised in Botswana also (Ingstad, 1994).

BRAIN DRAIN

The harsh economic conditions, sluggish economic growth, economic auster-
ity programmes combined with the rapid growth of the labour force have
resulted in sharp deterioration of the employment situation in Africa since
1980. Low salaries of professionals, salary cuts of up to a third and wage
freezes drastically reduced the real wages of those still in employment (ECA,
1988). Others were retrenched in both the public and private sectors in
response to economic adjustment measures (Adepoju, 1993a). Cumulatively,
these factors contributed to the sustained exodus of both skilled and
unskilled persons, males and females, and triggered an outflow of professionals to various African countries notably to Botswana, Zimbabwe, South
Africa's homelands, as well as to America, Europe and Canada (Adepoju,
1991b).

Uganda led the way in both the quantum and rapidity of exodus of highly
skilled persons in the early 1970s, closely followed by Ghana during 1970–
82, perhaps the bleakest in the history of Ghana's economy (UNDP, 1990).
Nigeria was a favoured destination, boosted by the oil-led expansion in the
industrial, educational and construction sectors. With the collapse of oil
prices of the early 1980s culminating in wage freeze, inflation, and as the
structural adjustment programme bit harder Nigeria also joined the league of
major labour exporters (Adegbola, 1990; Adepoju, 1990).

As Adepoju, (1991a) succinctly depicted the situation:

> A combination of political and economic mismanagement sparked off, and sustained the
> emigration of skilled professionals. The deteriorating working conditions of professionals
> and the poor working environment are rooted in large part to the foreign exchange short-
> ages in recent years which made it extremely difficult and expensive to purchase needed
> equipment, while research grants in the Universities have fizzled out. The lack of job satis-
> faction, and a system for recognising and rewarding efficiency have intensified the exodus
> of professionals in African countries, factors that have been compounded by the deteriorat-
> ing social, economic and political environment. In frustration, some professionals with the
> viable option of seeking employment in the developed economies of the West where their
> skills are in effective demand and whose skills and qualifications are of an international
> character have emigrated. For the unskilled migrants, the lure of higher pay, even in irregu-
> lar conditions, serves as a strong motivation for emigration. The devalued national currency
> enhances the comparable earnings of migrants, even at the lowest wage level in the coun-
> tries of the north.

Africa has gone through a devastating socio-economic crisis over the past
decade; consequently living conditions have worsened dramatically. Faced
with a chain of problems—poverty, unemployment, political repression—
Africans with the requisite skills, both men *and* women, have migrated in
search of more comfortable environments in the countries of the north (ECA,
1988).

To a very large extent, the direction of the migration has been from the
countries with historical and political links—francophone countries to
France, anglophone countries to United Kingdom; lusophone countries to
Portugal. Belgium continues to receive migrants from Rwanda and Zaïre,
while Italy hosts a large number of Ethiopians, and some Senegalese. USA
and Germany are favoured destinations for scientists, technical and professional staff in view of the well developed infrastructures for training and
post-qualification work opportunities for these kinds of skills (UNDP, 1990;
Adepoju, 1991b).

It is estimated that students constitute a substantial proportion of Africans in the United States—over 34,000 in 1985–86. Although current figures are not available thousands of African students were trained in and remained in universities and polytechnics in France, United Kingdom, Germany, Belgium and Italy (ECA, 1988).

Political instability, and civil strife in several countries—Ethiopia, Uganda, Sudan, Mozambique, Angola, Liberia—coupled with dictatorial regimes have stifled freedom of speech resulting in severe abuse of human rights. In several respects, the intellectuals, students, union leaders, etc., were targeted for harassment and intimidation (Adepoju, 1991b). Under such unstable political climates and deteriorating economic conditions, skilled professionals and technicians are often the first to leave or be forced out. More than half of Uganda's high level professional and technical personnel emigrated during the prolonged iron rule of Amin's regime, notorious for human rights abuses. Several Asian-Ugandans were also expelled: most eventually settled in the United Kingdom.

The lack of job satisfaction, and a system for recognising and rewarding efficiency have intensified the exodus of professionals in African countries, factors that have been compounded by the deteriorating social, economic and political environment

The structural adjustment programmes being pursued by several African countries have taken their toll through the brain drain especially in Nigeria, Zambia, Ghana that have devalued national currency, and where the living standards of the people had deteriorated drastically, the salaries of professionals have slumped and real purchasing power been rendered ridiculous in the face of hyper-inflation (Adepoju, 1993a). Although adequate statistics are scarce the outflow of especially medical personnel, pilots and technicians from Nigeria to the Gulf countries has reached an alarming proportion, as was the case of Ghanaian professionals in the late 1970s and early 1980s (Adepoju, 1989).

Precise figures on the stock of skilled emigrants from Africa in the countries of the north are not available. ECA (1988) estimates nevertheless that between 1960 and 1975, about 27,000 high-level Africans left the continent for the developed western countries. This number increased to 40,000 between 1975 and 1984. By 1987, nearly 70,000 such persons, or 30 per cent of the highly skilled manpower stock, had left Sub-Saharan Africa mainly for the countries of the European Community. In 1984, Nigerian highly skilled professionals numbered about 10,000 in the USA alone. In Egypt, about 2 million persons lived abroad in 1985 while 500,000 Sudanese worked abroad, up from an estimated 180,000 in 1978 and 334,000 in 1983 mainly in the Gulf Oil States. The trend depicted above bears close association with the levels of hardships of African economies. Ghana, for instance lost 60 per cent of her doctors trained in the early 1980s to the brain drain. For Africa as a whole, UNDP (1992) estimated that between 1985 and 1990, up to 60,000 middle and high level managers emigrated.

In Sudan, 90 per cent of the migrants to the Gulf were literate in a situation where 60 per cent of the population is illiterate; and 80 per cent of the migrants were skilled persons. The migrants are young (90 per cent were 20–39 year olds) and 10 per cent had had university education. Such a disproportionate number of skilled and educated persons obviously dented the man-power situation in the country; indeed, "17 per cent of all doctors and den-tists, 30 per cent of engineers, 45 per cent of surveyors and 20 per cent of university teaching staff left the country in 1978" (Ricca, 1989). Emigrants constituted 60 per cent of the total national stock of skilled workers at the peak of emigration to the Gulf States, a situation that created acute man-power shortages in critical skill areas. The result is that Sudan became both a labour exporting and labour importing country, like Jordan, welcoming Egyptians to fill the critical manpower gap (UNDP, 1992).

REMITTANCES

The sending of remittances by migrants is one of the strongest and most per-vasive phenomenon in Africa's migration systems. It is also one that demon-strates, perhaps in the most profound manner, the characteristic feature of African migration as fundamentally a family and not an individual activity. The practice of remittances pervades all forms of migration, with the excep-tion perhaps of refugee movements. Regardless of their age, gender, educa-tional attainment and place of destination, migrants are beholden to their families to remit some of their earnings (Adepoju, 1990; Oucho, 1990).

The literature of the 1980s views migration in Africa essentially as part of a family survival strategy. This is apparent in the deteriorating socioeconomic conditions in the region: drought in the Sahel, economic downturn in virtu-ally every African country, famine and internal conflicts. Thus in the expecta-tion that such remittances would be forthcoming and in the hope that the migrant would maintain close touch with the family through regular visits, families sponsor one or more of their members as an economic survival strat-egy to engage in the labour migration system. The family also expects to reap rewards from its investment in the education of one of its members—usually the first male child—who has been groomed for such migration in the urban formal sector (Oucho, 1990).

Sponsored, selective migrations, to ameliorate the dramatic impact of the structural adjustment programmes (SAP) on the family have become almost routine in Africa. As the SAP bites harder and deeper, the burden on the migrants to support other less privileged family members becomes very com-pelling. Indeed a new phenomenon of dual households has emerged among African migrant families trying to maximize the economic returns from both the home area as well as the destination.

The migrant member feels compelled to remit a substantial proportion of his earned income regularly to support the other members of the family left behind. For several families in the Sahel, but importantly in Lesotho, the remittance is the life-line, the dominant source of sustenance to pay house rent, meet medical expenses, school fees and a variety of communal commit-ments—(levies, contributions, rituals, etc.); to build a house or set up small enterprises in preparation for return home. Several surveys focusing on the remittance mechanism point to the fact that the migrants often remit up to 60 per cent of their earnings, regularly, to the homeplace through formal and informal channels. In some of the resource poor countries of Africa the importance of remittances—especially foreign currency remittances such as those received in some countries around the Horn of Africa from the Arab world and elsewhere—has been given full recognition by governments, which accordingly encourage such labour migration (Adepoju, 1991b; Oucho, 1991).

Possibly as a result of this strong relationship to the family as an economic unit, as well as a result of a few other non-economic factors common on the continent, the largest stream of migration in Africa is interregional: nomads, migrant labourers, undocumented migrants, seasonal and oscillatory migrants and refugees (Adepoju, 1988a).

REFUGEE MIGRATION

In the 1980s, and 1990s, refugees worldwide, have dominated international migratory movements. In Africa, special attention to refugees as migrants derives from several considerations: Africa is home to the world's largest refugee population; a large proportion of these "refugees" are internally displaced; refugees are confined to the continent, and result from a set of cumulative factors discussed below.

The refugee situation in Africa has been aptly described as a human tragedy. Africa has experienced the "most acute refugee problems in terms both of magnitude and complexity". The poorest of all regions, Africa is home to one of every two or three of the world's refugees. These refugees originate from and settle in countries designated as the least developed in the world, countries that are plagued with problems of famine, war, drought, and political instability (Zolberg *et al.*, 1989; Adepoju, 1982).

Historically, the struggle for independence, the rise of secessionist movements in independent nations and the struggle for autonomy are among the key causes of refugees in the region. The political situation in independent countries undergoing severe internal political and military strife, ecological disasters and breach of human rights has in recent years compounded the refugee situation. As the continent is torn by ravaging war and abuse of human rights by totalitarian regimes, the number of internally displaced persons escalates daily, while millions seek asylum in neighbouring countries (Adepoju, 1993b).

Varying estimates of the refugee population in the region reflect different definitions. The conventional definition has been modified by the OAU to fit the specificity of the African situation to include internally displaced persons. Indeed, the refugee situation in Africa is unique in several important respects. It is fluid and highly unpredictable: while old problems that gave rise to refugees are being solved as in Zimbabwe, Uganda, new ones surface and intensify the refugee crisis as in Liberia. The increasing desertification in the Sahelian region, drought in eastern, central and southern Africa, war in Chad, Uganda, Mozambique and Liberia and the war of liberation in southern Africa and Namibia, have generated and may continue to generate new or increased waves of refugees (Adepoju, 1982; 1993b).

Countries that generate large numbers of refugees also provide asylum for refugees from neighbouring countries. Thus, Sudan received refugees from neighbouring Ethiopia, Uganda, Chad and Zaire but also generated refugees (who sought asylum in Ethiopia) and displaced persons. Zaïre opened her

doors to refugees from Uganda, Angola and Zambia while refugees from
Zaire have sought asylum in Angola, Sudan, Uganda and Zambia.

Another significant characteristic of the refugee situation in Africa is that
refugees, drawn from one of the poorest regions of the world, also seek refuge
in equally poor countries within the region. Virtually all refugees are confined
to the continent, and are assisted by fellow Africans. Most of these relocate
spontaneously and their needs may be unnoticed by voluntary organizations
providing assistance to refugees in organised camps or settlements (Adepoju
1989; 1991a).

Perhaps more than elsewhere, the strains on refugees and the process of
adjustment to refugee life are considerably eased by the fact that nearly 60
per cent of rural refugees relocate spontaneously amongst the local population in the receiving countries. The ethnic and kinship ties between refugees
and host population, often near national frontiers, appear to relieve both the
host government and voluntary and international agencies concerned with
refugee issues of aid and assistance (Adepoju, 1989).

Observers believe that the Horn of Africa "remains perhaps the most complex region in the world for refugees and displaced people" and that about
4.5 million Sudanese have been dislocated by the war (USCR, 1991). More
dramatic is the estimate that a full 4 million (89 per cent) of these refugees are
southern Sudanese. These internally displaced persons are to be added to
those affected by the drought of 1990 and several thousands who died as a
result of war-induced famine. Yet, Sudan sheltered about three-quarters of a
million (726,500) refugees in late 1990, mostly from Ethiopia (700,000),
Chad (20,000) and a few Ugandans and Zaireans (USCR, 1991). The intensified civil strife in southern Sudan and the genocidal conflicts in Somalia
spurred additional waves of refugees fleeing to Ethiopia. Consequently, the
Horn of Africa was providing asylum for about 2 million refugees by early
1989. Most of these refugees also originate from the same countries of the
Horn: Somalia (350,000) Ethiopia (126,000) Sudan (348,000) (USCR,
1992).

Ethiopia, once reputed to be the largest refugee producing country in
Africa, currently hosts one of the region's largest refugee populations as the
escalating civil wars in Somalia and southern Sudan rendered thousands
homeless. These have sought asylum in an equally war-torn Ethiopia. In
1990, an estimated 500,000 Sudanese, mostly from the south fled to Ethiopia, Uganda, Zaïre and Central African Republic. Also Angola, in spite of its
internal problems, hosted nearly 100,000 refugees, mostly Namibians and a
few Zaireans and South Africans in 1988 (USCR, 1991; 1992).

By the end of 1992, there were about 6 million refugees in Africa up from
5.5 million in 1990, 4.5 million in 1989 and 4.1 million in 1988. These refugees sought asylum principally in Malawi, Sudan, Ethiopia, Somalia and
Zaire. The major sources of these refugees are Sudan, Ethiopia and Angola.
Indeed the magnitude and the rapidly changing map of refugees in Africa (by
source and asylum countries) over the years 1987–1991 is evident in Tables
2a and 2b. While these figures should be interpreted cautiously they nevertheless give an indication of the large mass of people displaced as a result of
human conflicts in these countries. Again, Sudan and Ethiopia top the list of
principal countries with internally displaced persons.

Table 2a. *Major African asylum countries: refugee stocks 1987, 1988, 1989,*
1990 and 1991

Asylum Country	1987	1988	1989	1990	1991
Malawi	420,000	630,000	812,000	909,000	950,000
Sudan	817,000	693,600	694,000	726,500	717,200
Guinea	–	–	13,000	325,000	566,000
Ethiopia	220,000	700,500	740,000	783,000	534,000
Zaire	338,000	325,700	338,000	370,900	482,300
Somalia	430,000	365,000	350,000	358,500	350,000
Tanzania	266,200	266,200	226,200	266,200	251,100
Côte d'Ivoire	600	800	55,800	270,500	240,400
Zimbabwe	150,500	171,500	185,500	186,000	198,500
Djibouti	13,500	2,000	46,500	67,400	120,000
Kenya	9,000	10,600	15,500	14,400	107,150
Burundi	76,000	76,000	90,200	90,700	107,000
Senegal	5,600	5,200	48,000	55,300	53,100
Swaziland	67,000	70,700	71,700	47,200	47,200
Mauritania	–	–	22,000	22,000	40,000
Rwanda	19,000	20,000	20,500	21,500	32,500
Namibia	–	–	25,000	25,000	30,200
Sierra Leone	200	100	100	125,000	17,200
Mali	–	–	na	10,600	13,500
Angola	92,000	95,700	26,500	11,900	10,400
Central African Rep.	5,100	3,000	2,800	6,300	9,000
Cameroon	7,300	4,700	4,200	6,900	6,900
Ghana	140	100	100	8,000	6,150
Total Africa	3,408,430[a]	4,088,260	4,524,800	5,443,450	5,340,800

[a] Sub-Saharan Africa only
Source: U.S. Committee for Refugees, 1989, 1991, 1992

Table 2b. *Refugee stocks by major refugee source countries, 1989, 1990 and 1991*

Source Country	1989	1990	1991
Mozambique	1,354,000	1,427,500	1,483,500
Ethiopia	1,035,900	1,064,400	752,400
Angola	438,000	435,000	717,600
Liberia	68,000	729,800	661,700
Sudan	435,100	499,100	443,200
Rwanda	233,000	203,900	208,500
Burundi	186,500	186,200	203,900
Somalia	388,600	448,600	202,500
Zaire	50,400	50,700	66,700
Mauritania	na	60,100	66,000

Source: U.S. Committee for Refugees, 1989, 1991, 1992

Angolan refugees in their thousands continue daily to flee from persecution or violence in their country—in a situation where the government is unable to adequately protect its citizens from genocidal attacks by rebel forces.

In all, the refugee situation in Africa has worsened dramatically over the past three years: new refugee-generating countries such as Liberia have been added to the list; the traditional sources of refugees—Sudan and Somalia—continue to generate additional refugees in their thousands.

Somalia, which in early 1978 became a major refugee hosting country in Africa, herself became a refugee producing country a decade later. Since then, and especially since late 1991, the situation has worsened as the persistent civil strife spread from the north to the south of the country, producing several thousand refugees and many more displaced persons within the country.

In April 1989 ethnic tensions flared up over a minor border dispute between Senegal and Mauritania leading to displacements of over 70,000 persons in both countries. As that year closed, the war in Liberia uprooted several thousand persons: about 125,000 Liberian refugees flocked to Sierra Leone and Côte d'Ivoire and 50,000 others fled to Guinea Conakry. That situation further deteriorated when in April 1991, troops from within Liberia invaded eastern Sierra Leone forcing refugees and the local population to flee for safety (USCR, 1991; Adepoju 1993b).

During 1990, about 1.2 million people were uprooted as refugees from Liberia at the peak of the civil war there and about 125,000 were trapped in Monrovia, the capital which for months was the battleground between several warring factions and later ECOMOG's forces. And by the end of that year, once more there were nearly half a million internally displaced persons in Somalia as fighting raged between "rebels" and government troops for the control of the capital, Mogadishu.

Among the countries of the world with the highest proportion of refugees to the local population in 1988, eight are in Africa: Swaziland, Malawi, Somalia, Sudan, Zambia, Zimbabwe, Burundi and Ethiopia. In 1981, eight out of twelve such countries were in Africa but both the composition of these ratios and the list of countries have changed: (Somalia, Djibouti, Burundi, Cameroon, Sudan, Swaziland, Zaire and Angola). Somalia stands out in the group, being the poorest of the twelve countries with an estimated ratio of refugee to the total population of 1:3 at that time (USCR, 1991).

Nearly 40 per cent of all refugees in Africa have in fact been displaced within their own countries by natural disaster, drought, ecological problems, internal conflict or wars of liberation. Hence these refugees include children, women, old persons, mostly of rural background. Countries of asylum face unpredictable problems of drought and food deficits. Famine and wars have become common. Until 1994, Malawi hosted nearly 1 million refugees from Mozambique, although most of these have now been repatriated. Sudan's refugees originate in Chad, Ethiopia and Uganda. Sudan and Somalia, have had to bear heavy refugee burdens, in spite of their frail economies. In the case of Somalia, for instance, the situation is accurately described as a crushing burden for the vacillating economy of a country classed among the ten poorest on the planet.

Refugees in Africa normally hope to return home when conditions permit: general amnesty in Zaire in 1980, change of regime in Uganda, Equatorial Guinea and Central African Republic; the attainment of independence in Mozambique (1975), Guinea Bissau (1974) and Angola (1975). The 1980s and early 1990s witnessed a series of repatriations in Africa: in Uganda (1989); repatriation of Ethiopians from Somalia which started in 1986; Zimbabwe (1980); Namibia (1990) (Adepoju, 1983 b), and Mozambicans from Malawi (1994).

CONCLUSION

This chapter has presented a general overview of migration in Africa, tracing the changes in both trends and types of migration over time. While in the distant past as in contemporary times, the population of Africa has always been on the move, recent times have seen migration increase in volume and new types of migratory forms emerge. The increase in volume of migrants was triggered off during the colonial period because of the labour and related policies of the colonial administrations, whilst post-independent African states fostered even greater rural–urban migration as a result of the unevenness of investments. Young men started flocking to the towns and cities in droves in search of better living standards through employment. Labour migration whether of a seasonal nature as in many parts of West Africa, or of a long term nature as in the mines of South Africa has always dominated the migration system in the continent.

The era of restrictions on so-called international migration coincided with the attainment of independence in the early 1960s when national governments enacted rules and regulations to control immigration into newly independent countries. In later years the formation of economic unions, the defunct East African Community and especially the Economic Community of West African States (ECOWAS), once again restored—at least in principle—free movement of labour between member states.

Economic survival strategies have expanded the types of migration found in Africa. As African economies deteriorated in the 1970s and 1980s through mismanagement or natural disasters such as famines, various migratory streams emerged. The brain drain of Africa's educated persons which started as a trickle, suddenly took on alarming proportions in such countries as Sudan, Zaire, Uganda, Ghana and recently Nigeria. Many of Africa's highly educated persons left the continent entirely for the developed world although some settled in other African countries. Similarly, autonomous female migration emerged in those decades as an important type of migration, derived from the women's need to supplement the household income in the absence of husbands' and other male labour. Education also gave women the confidence to challenge socio-cultural stereotypes that hitherto relegated them to the position of passive migrants, only moving at the behest of their menfolk.

But one common thread runs through all African migrants, and that is the strong link to the family; this link ensures mutual support of both migrant and non-migrant family members, the most evident of which are remittances from the migrant to the homeplace.

Refugee movements have increasingly taken a larger and larger share of migration in Africa, as a result of civil conflict. The peculiarity of refugee movements in Africa, home now to half of the world's refugees, is that the same countries which are a source of refugees, also host large proportions of refugees from neighbouring countries, creating an added strain on their fragile economies at the most crucial time.

For Africa, the future portends continued and even greater migratory movements as its populations, crushed by declining living standards, civil conflicts and environmental degradation, searches for a material and socio-psychological existence better than what is left behind.

References

Addo, N. O. 1975, "Immigration and Socio-Demographic Change" in J.C. Caldwell (ed.), *Population Growth and Socio Economic Change in West Africa*. New York: The Population Council.

Adegbola, O., 1990, "Demographic Effects of Economic Crisis in Nigeria: The Brain Drain Component", in *Conference on the Role of Migration in African Development: Issues and Policies for the 1990s*: Contributed Papers, Union for African Population Studies, Dakar.

Adepoju, A., 1982, "The Dimension of the Refugee Problem in Africa", *African Affairs*, 81, 322.

Adepoju, A., 1983a, "Undocumented Migration in Africa: Trends and Policies", *International Migration*, 21, 2

Adepoju, A., 1983b, "Patterns of Migration by Sex" in C. Oppong (ed.), *Female and Male in West Africa*. London: George Allen and Unwin.

Adepoju, A., 1984a, "Migration and Female Employment in South-western Nigeria", *African Urban Studies*, Vol. 18, Spring.

Adepoju, A., 1984b, "Linkages between Internal and International Migration: The African Situation", *International Social Science Journal*, 18, 1.

Adepoju, A., 1984c, Redistributing Population: Prospects and Challenges, Inaugural Lecture Series No. 66. Ile-Ife: University of Ife Press.

Adepoju, A., 1988a, "International Migration in Africa South of the Sahara" in R. Appleyard (ed.), *International Migration Today*: Vol. 1. *Trends and Prospects*. UNESCO and University of Western Australia.

Adepoju A., 1988b, "Overview of International Labour Migration in Africa" in *African Population Conference Dakar*, 1988, Vol. 2. Liege: IUSSP.

Adepoju, A., 1988c, "An Overview of Rural Migration and Agricultural Labour Force Structure in Africa", *African Population Studies*, No. 1:5-25.

Adepoju, A., 1989, "The Consequences of Influx of Refugees for Countries of Asylum in Africa" in R. Appleyard (ed.), *The Impact of International Migration on Developing Countries*. Paris: OECD.

Adepoju, A.,1990, "State of the Art Review on Migration in Africa", *Conference on The Role of Migration in African Development: Issues and Policies for the 1990s*. Commissioned Papers, UAPS, Dakar.

Adepoju, A., 1991a, "Africa: A Continent on the Move in Search of Solidarity with the Countries of the North" in Pontifical Council for the Pastoral Care of Migrants and Itinerant People: *Solidarity in Favour of New Migrants*. Vatican City, Rome.

Adepoju, A., 1991b, "South-North Migration: The African Experience", *International Migration*, 29, 2.

Adepoju, A., 1991c, "Binational Communities and Labour Circulation in Sub-Saharan Africa" in D.G. Papademetriou and P.L. Martin, (eds.), *The Unsettled Relationship: Labour Migration and Economic Development*. New York: Greenwood Press.

Adepoju, A., (ed.), 1991d, *Swaziland: Population, Society and Economy*. New York: United Nations Population Fund.

Adepoju, A., (ed.), 1993a, *The Impact of Structural Adjustment on the Population of Africa: The Implications for Education, Health and Employment*. London: UNFPA, Heinemann and James Currey.

Adepoju, A., 1993b, "The Politics of International Migration in the Post-Colonial Period in Africa", IDEP, DAKAR.

Amin, S., (ed.), 1974, *Modern Migrations in Western Africa*. London: Oxford University Press.

Anan-Yao, E., 1990, "National and International Labour Migrations in Côte d'Ivoire: Impact on Ivorian Institutions and on the Institutions of the Labour Exporting Countries", in *Conference on the Role of Migration in African Development: Issues and Policies for the 90s* (Spontaneous Papers). Dakar: Union for African Population Studies.

Arthur, J.A., 1991, "International Labor Migration Patterns in West Africa", *African Studies Review*, 34, 3, December 1991, pp 65–87.

Boateng, E.O., 1994, "Gender-Sensitive Statistics and the Planning Process" in A. Adepoju and C. Oppong (eds.), *Gender, Work and Population in sub-Saharan Africa*. London: ILO, James Currey and Heinemann.

Conde, J., 1984, "Socio-economic Survey of Malian, Mauritanian and Senegalese Immigrants Resident in France", *International Migration*, 22, 2, pp 144–151.

de Vletter, F., 1985, "Recent Trends and Prospects of Black Migration to South Africa", International Migration for Employment Working Paper No. 2. Geneva: International Labour Organization.

ECA, 1981, *International Migration: Population Trends and their Implications for Africa*, African Population Studies No. 4. Addis Ababa.

ECA, 1988, "An Enabling Environment to Retain Africa's High Level Manpower" background paper for *International Conference on the Human Dimension of Africa's Economic Recovery and Development*, Khartoum.

Elkan, W., 1967, "Cyclical Migration and the Growth of Towns in East Africa", *International Labour Review*, 96, 6, December.

Findley, S.E. and L. Williams, 1990, "Women who Go and Women who Stay: Reflections on Family Migration Processes in a Changing World", *Working Paper Series*. Geneva: International Labour Organization.

Findley, S.E. and D. Ouedraogo, 1993, "North or South? A Study of the Senegal River Valley Migration Patterns" contributed paper *IUSSP International Population Conference*, Montreal, August 24–September 2.

Gould, W.T.S., 1988, "Government Policies and International Migration of Skilled Workers in Sub-Saharan Africa", *Geoforum*, 19, 4, pp 433–445.

Hance, W.A., 1970, *Population, Migration and Urbanization in Africa*. New York: Columbia University Press.

Hinderink, J. and G. Tempelman, 1978, "Rural Changes and Types of Migration in Northern Ivory Coast" in W.M.J. van Binsbergen and H.A. Meilink (eds.), *Migration and the Transformation of Modern African Society*. Leiden: Afrika-Studiecentrum.

Ingstad, B., 1994, "The Grandmother and Household Viability in Botswana" in A. Adepoju and C. Oppong, (eds.), *Gender, Work and Population in Sub-Saharan Africa*. London: ILO, James Currey and Heinemann.

Kaberuka, W., 1992, "Migration and Development: Uganda's Experience, Paper No. 21, *Tenth IOM Seminar on Migration and Development*, Geneva.

Mabogunje, A.L., 1972, *Regional Mobility and Resource Development in West Africa*. Montréal: McGill-Queen's University Press.

Makinwa-Adebusoye, P., 1988, "Labour Migration and Female-Headed Households" in *IUSSP Conference on Women's Position and Demographic Change in the Course of Development*, Oslo, 1988, Solicited Papers, Liège.

Makinwa-Adebusoye, P., 1990, "Female Migration in Africa: An Overview", in Union for African Population Studies, *Migration and Development in Africa: Issues and Policies for the 90s*, Dakar.

Mitchell, J.C., 1959, "Labour Migration in Africa South of the Sahara: The Cause of Labour Migration", *Bulletin of the Inter-African Labour Studies*, 6, 1.

Ojo, K.O., 1991, "International Migration of Health Manpower in Sub-Saharan Africa", *Social Science and Medicine*, 31, 6, pp 631–7.

Oppong. C., 1980, *A Synopsis of Seven Roles and the Status of Women: An Outline of a Conceptual and Methodological Approach*. Geneva: ILO.

Oppong, C., 1992, "African Family Systems in the Context of Socio-Economic Change", background paper, for *Third African Population Conference*, Dakar.

Oucho, J.O., 1990, "Migrant Linkages in Africa", in *Conference on the Role of Migration in Rural Development: Issues and Policies for the 90s* Vol. 1. Commissioned Papers, Union for African Population Studies, Dakar.

Oucho, J.O., 1991, "Migration and Labour Utilization in Urban and Rural Areas of Africa", in A. Adepoju, (ed.), *Population, Human Resources and Development in Africa—Training Manual No. 1*. IDEP, Dakar.

Oucho, J.O. and W.T.S. Gould, 1993, "Internal Migration, Urbanization and Population Distribution" in National Research Council, *Demographic Change in Sub-Saharan Africa*. Washington: National Academy Press.

Palmer, I., 1985, *The Impact of Male Out-Migration on Women in Farming*. West Hartford: Kumarian Press.

Pittin, R., 1984, "Migration of Women in Nigeria: The Hausa Case", *International Migration Review* (Special Issue: Women in Migration), Vol. 18, 4, Winter.

Prothero, R.M., 1968, "Migration in Tropical Africa", in J.C. Caldwell and C. Okonjo, (eds.), *The Population of Tropical Africa*. London: Longmans.

Ricca, S., 1989, *International Migration in Africa: Legal and Administrative Aspects*. Geneva: International Labour Office.

Safilios-Rothschild C., 1994, "Agricultural Policies and Women Producers" in A. Adepoju and C. Oppong, (eds.), *Gender, Work, and Population in Sub-Saharan Africa*. London: ILO, James Currey and Heinemann.

Stahl, C.W., 1981, "Migrant Labour Supplies, Past, Present and Future; with Special Reference to the Gold Mining Industry" in W.R. Böhning, (ed.), *Black Migration to South Africa: A Selection of Policy-oriented Research*. Geneva: ILO.

Sudarkasa, N., 1974–1975, "Commercial Migration in West Africa with Special Reference to the Yoruba in Ghana", *African Urban Notes*, Series B, No. 1.

Thahane, T.T., 1991, "International Labour Migration in Southern Africa" in D.G. Papademetriou and P.L. Martin, (eds.), *The Unsettled Relationship: Labor Migration and Economic Development*. New York: Greenwood Press.

Tienda, M. and K. Booth, 1988, "Migration, Gender and Social Change: A Review and Reformulation", in *IUSSP Conference on Women's Position and Demographic Change in the Course of Development*, Oslo, Solicited Papers, Liege.

United Nations, 1982, *International Migration Policies and Programmes: A World Survey*. New York.

UNDP, 1990, *Human Development Report 1990*. New York: Oxford University Press.

UNDP, 1992, *Human Development Report 1992*. New York: Oxford University Press.

U.S Committee for Refugees, 1991, *World Refugee Survey: 1989 in Review*. Washington D.C.

U.S Committee for Refugees, 1992, *World Refugee Survey: 1992*. Washington D.C.

Vaa, M., S.E. Findley and A. Diallo, 1989, "The Gift Economy: A Study of Women Migrants' Survival Strategies in a Low-Income Bamako Neighbourhood", *Labour, Capital and Society*, 22, 2, November.

Ware, H. and D. Lucas, 1988, "Women Left Behind, the Changing Decision of Labour and its Effect on Agricultural Production", in *IUSSP African Population Conference Dakar, 1988*, Liège.

Zolberg, A.R., A. Suhrke and S. Aguayo, (eds.), 1989, *Escape from Violence: Conflict and the Refugee Crisis in the Developing World*. New York: Oxford University Press.

Forgotten Places, Abandoned Places
Migration Research Issues in South Africa

Christian M. Rogerson

With the objective of complementing other material in the volume, the task initially set for this particular chapter was to survey the 'state of the art' on research concerning aspects of the dynamics of internal non-metropolitan migration in South Africa. The production of such a review was, however, not practical as little substantive work so far has been undertaken on this theme in South Africa or the broader southern African context. Accordingly, in order to re-orient this chapter so that it might address interests relevant to the Scandinavian Institute of African Studies Research Programme on Urban Development in Rural Context in Africa two issues are isolated for investigation. First, the neglect of non-metropolitan migration in South Africa is contextualised within a broad canvas review on migratory patterns and migration research in the region, identifying key themes, strengths and omissions in existing literature. The argument in this section is that non-metropolitan centres, to a large extent, are 'forgotten places' on the migration agenda of South African analysts. With an eye to opening up this research agenda, the discussion in the second section narrows to examine certain issues concerning a group of these non-metropolitan places in South Africa. More specifically, attention centres on the question of the future prospects for migration from 'places created by apartheid' and now potentially set to become 'abandoned places' in the wake of changing policies and the transition in South Africa towards a new democratic, post-apartheid order. The conclusion highlights the importance of augmenting migration research for informing policy-making in a new South African political dispensation. Overall, this chapter should be read as a modest resource base for researchers interested in pursuing migration work especially in the non-metropolitan spaces of South Africa.

MIGRATORY PATTERNS AND MIGRATION STUDIES IN SOUTH AFRICA

In the broad picture of migration patterns and migration studies in South Africa, questions surrounding non-metropolitan areas in general and small towns in particular have not figured as a major research focus. Undoubtedly, the key themes have been the development and maintenance of an oscillatory labour migration system and the struggle of black migrants to overcome the 'influx control fence', which historically blocked their permanent movement into the urban areas defined as 'white space' in South Africa. Other important themes relate to forced population removals, flows of international migrants (including refugees), and the persistence of circular migration. Only in those writings examining circular migration do non-metropolitan places surface as significant foci on the migration research agenda.

Labour migrants and influx control

Historical research discloses that flows of black rural–urban migrants in southern Africa preceded efforts made by the colonial state in the late nineteenth century to organize a 'cheap labour' system for the region's mines and farms (see Delius, 1980; Crush, 1984). The mineral discoveries at Kimberley and on the Witwatersrand triggered the appearance of an important new actor in shaping migration flows, namely the aggressive activities of recruiters for workers to be channelled to the mines, construction or other urban activities (Jeeves, 1985). By the close of the century almost all parts of rural South Africa were incorporated into the region's expanding capitalist economy and with a progressive loss of control over their land "most (black) rural households henceforth found it difficult to avoid participation in the urban economy through selling the labour of one or more of their members in the towns or mines" (Mabin, 1992, p. 15). Accordingly, through a combination of powerlessness and processes of land dispossession, a system of oscillating labour migration was instituted, later to be reinforced and refined by state legislative fiat.

The shaping and contours of this migratory labour system for the mines, farms and industry of South Africa in the nineteenth and early twentieth centuries has been a well-researched theme (see Lacey, 1981; Yudelman, 1983; Jeeves, 1985; Crush *et al.*, 1991). As several works reveal, the voracious demands for cheap labour precipitated a spatial extension of South Africa's 'labour empire' with major flows of migrants from other regions of southern Africa (Jeeves, 1986; Crush, 1987a, 1991; Crush, *et al.*, 1991) and beyond (Richardson, 1983). In the making of labour migrancy in southern Africa the research emphasis shifted from the notion of a well-oiled labour machine to highlight the conflicts and contradictions which often threatened to tear the system apart especially in the formative years prior to 1920 (Crush and Rogerson, 1983). The complex patterns of uneven labour migration which emerged in southern Africa are explicable in relation only to the several themes of "the conflicts within the mining industry, and between it and other capitalist employers, over black labour; the ambiguous character of state action and response; the forces within African society promoting participation in and resistance to wage labour; the assertion of their powers of agency by individual migrants and commoner households and the struggles of disaffected groups to enlarge their influence within the system" (Crush, 1984, p. 116). Another more recent issue excavated by southern African scholars concerns the place and position of women in the migrant labour system. In particular, using the research technique of life-histories, the innovative works of Bozzoli (1991a, 1991b) and Miles (1991, 1993) recapture some of the neglected experiences and struggles of groups of migrant women in southern Africa.

During the 1920s and 1930s worsening landlessness and escalating rural evictions together with a tightening of state legislation combined to forge the basis for an exploitative system of 'cheap labour power' in South Africa which hinged on the oscillatory movements of (mainly male) black workers (Wolpe, 1972: Mabin, 1989, 1992). The most notable innovation was enactment of the notorious 'pass laws' which strengthened in force particularly after the 1948 elections bringing to power the National Party with its commitment to apartheid. The articulation, workings and effects of South Africa's 'closed city' programmes of influx control to contain permanent black urbanization in the country's so-termed 'white' metropolitan areas have been extensively interrogated (see e.g. Welsh, 1982; Giliomee and Schlemmer, 1985; Hindson, 1985; Posel, 1989). In particular, the works of Hindson (1985, 1987) are seminal in unpacking the implementation and shifting adjustments in the pass laws culminating in new strategies for controlled 'orderly urbanization' rather than closed city measures *per se*. Indeed, during the 1980s a sustained multi-disciplinary effort was launched by population researchers to demonstrate the scale and permanence of black urbanization in South Africa and to direct government authorities to the imperative need for the repeal of influx control legislation (which eventually occurred in 1986). This period saw the appearance of a number of policy-focused works addressing the shortcomings and misery generated by influx control measures (see e.g. Rogerson, 1984–85; Giliomee and Schlemmer, 1985; Bernstein, 1987; McCarthy and Rogerson, 1992, p. 40).

In the 1970s and 1980s new forms of labour migrancy began to evolve on the South African gold mines. The important works of Crush (1986, 1987b) and James (1992) track the restructuring of mine labour showing variously the extrusion of foreign labour, its replacement by domestic workers, and the new forms of recruitment which moulded major alterations in the spatial and temporal patterns of migrancy. "Inflexible migrancy" is the best description to stylize the more stabilized form of oscillating black migrancy between mines and rural labour reserves that crystallized in the 1980s (Crush, 1992). Towards the close of the 1980s, however, the question of a growing struggle against the migrant labour system as a whole loomed large on the policy horizon (Crush, 1987b; 1989; Crush *et al.*, 1991).

In the 1990s a number of policy-focused studies have appeared relating to labour migrancy, recent migration patterns and projected post-influx control black population movements in South Africa. Looking to the dismantling of the apartheid regime, de Vletter (1990) provides a thoughtful assessment of the several conflicting policy considerations surrounding foreign migrant workers in a future democratic South Africa. The writings of Simkins (1991) and of work produced by the Urban Foundation (1990, 1991) provide the most accurate contemporary picture and projections of migration in South Africa. Together this research reveals that contrary to popular opinion recently (the period 1980–85) blacks have not been moving in large numbers from rural homelands into the 'white' cities. Instead, they show that most movement has been occurring from white farming areas into burgeoning informal settlements, such as Inanda near to Durban and Winterveld close to

Pretoria; these are unplanned shack settlements situated within Homelands but adjoining the major metropolitan centres. Projections for the period 1990–2000 suggest that with the removal of influx control the dominant trend will be of outflows from homeland rural areas and major inflows into the metropolitan areas of South Africa (Urban Foundation, 1990, pp. 18–20).

Forced population movements, international flows and circular migration

Although migration research in southern Africa has been dominated over-whelmingly by the 'big' societal questions posed by oscillating labour migrants and influx control, a number of other studies are noteworthy (McCarthy and Rogerson, 1992). In particular, useful work has appeared concerning issues of forced population removals, international migration flows and, perhaps, most importantly studies on circular migrancy.

One of the most heinous aspects of apartheid social engineering was the uprooting and forced removal of established communities and their reloca-tion or, more correctly, dumping in remote and often barren rural slums (Map 1). This massive exercise in social engineering was one of the essential corner-stones of apartheid planning for 'separate' ethnic Bantustans (Freund, 1984; Platzky and Walker, 1985). The scale of mass population forced removals under apartheid planning has been calculated as touching, if not devastating, the lives of up to seven million people (Baldwin, 1975; Surplus People Project, 1983; Platzky and Walker, 1983, 1985). Despite coming under the spotlight of harsh international disapproval, forced population removals con-tinued apace into the 1980s phase of late apartheid (Newton, 1989; Roger-son, 1989; Grahamstown Rural Committee, 1991; Soni and Maharaj, 1991). These population removals have restructured the rural landscape of South Africa intruding new 'urban' forms such as the resettlement camp or closer settlements (Rogerson and Letsoalo, 1985). Moreover, beyond the group of ideologically-based removals, Mabin (1987, 1992) reminds us of the signifi-cance of another category of quieter, yet equally large-scale, population removals associated with private and state practices surrounding the eviction of (black) farm dwellers.

Key themes in writings on international population flows to South Africa have centred on the tempo, flows and assimilation of various white settler migrants, such as British, Greek or Franco-Mauritian communities (for review see McCarthy and Rogerson, 1992). The racial complexion and inter-national sources for migration flows to South Africa, have, however, under-gone changes especially in the last decade. One source of change has been the flow to South Africa of various refugee communities from surrounding coun-tries, most importantly from war-torn Mozambique (see Hart and Rogerson, 1982). Another movement has been that of returning black exiles to South Africa in the wake of the changing political environment of the 1990s. Equally significant has been a trend towards the voluntary migration of skilled migrants to South Africa from poor developing countries as well as increasingly from Eastern Europe. The work of Prah (1989, 1991) records the international 'brain drain' into South Africa's Bantustan areas from par-ticularly India, Ghana, Sri Lanka, Philippines and Uganda. These new migrants have been augmented by a more recent influx of illegal migrants

Map 1. *The Geography of Apartheid South Africa*

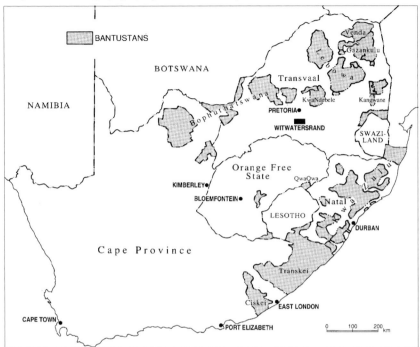

from India, Pakistan, and mainland China (Haffajee, 1993a). Finally, there is fragmentary evidence also of a new movement into South Africa of short-term economic migrants from several African countries, notably Zaire, Senegal and Ivory Coast; many of these migrants are involved in the burgeoning informal economy of South Africa's large urban centres (Ansell and Bond, 1992; Haffajee, 1993b).

Lastly, in terms of migration issues and patterns in South Africa, it is important to note the key findings of a recent stream of studies focused on the broad phenomenon of circular migration. South African migration writings have tended to focus on enforced migrant labour to the mines to the neglect of examining wider flows of temporary circulation. An important body of work by Mabin (1990) and of his students (Gaffane, 1990; Maluleka, 1990; Royston, 1991) provides evidence on the complex and circulatory patterns of short-term migrancy which exist in many parts of South Africa, often focused on small towns where wage-employment opportunities are available. From the empirical findings of these studies, it is clear that circular migration occurs both between and within urban and rural areas in South Africa (Royston, 1991, p. 79). Moreover, while the impact of apartheid legislation must be acknowledged, it remains that material economic factors are key factors in interpreting the micro-level patterns of circular migration (Mabin, 1990; Royston, 1991, p. 125).

ABANDONED PLACES

As argued above, the traditional focus of South African migration research
has been upon population movements into the country's metropolitan areas.
The relative neglect of non-metropolitan migration by population analysts
finds a distinct parallel in South African urban research which similarly
exhibits large-city bias. With a few notable exceptions (Bloch, 1987; Beavon
and Payne, 1988; Rule and Wills, 1988–89; Hart and Rogerson, 1989;
Drummond and Parnell, 1991; Dewar, 1993), the contemporary processes of
population change and economic development in South Africa's non-metropolitan urban places have generated few serious research contributions. In a
recent review of studies on local urban geography McCarthy (1992, p. 149)
stressed that small marginalised urban centres were overlooked, noting that
in comparison with major metropolitan areas "intermediate and small urban
centres remain relative lacuna in South African urban geographical knowledge". Nonetheless, it was argued that scholarly work on the role and functioning of these neglected urban centres should enjoy higher priority in the
era of post-apartheid reconstruction. Especially significant from a policy
viewpoint will be the future role of that set of places whose *raison d'etre* and
economic base were inseparable from the machinery of apartheid social engineering.

The making of apartheid places

Apartheid social engineering gave birth to new geographies and an accompanying rise of new urban forms outside of South Africa's major metropolitan
areas (Mabin, 1989; Soni and Maharaj, 1991). In particular, the Verwoerdian
project of forging separate 'independent' ethnic Homelands or Bantustans
resulted in a construction flurry of new grandiose 'capital cities in the veld'
(e.g. Ulundi, Lebowakgomo, Mmabatho) alongside the less-publicised, albeit
large-scale appearance of 'closer settlements' as miserable dumping grounds
for the victims of forced population removal (Rogerson and Letsoalo, 1985;
Murray, 1987; Drummond and Parnell, 1991; Pickles and Woods, 1992). In
addition, a vital aspect of attempts to legitimize the separate political status
of these artificially created 'states', was the government-sponsored attempt to
provide Bantustans with an industrial base through programmes of decentralization and growth centre planning (Rogerson, 1988, 1991; Pickles, 1991).

Since the late 1950s the South African government has pursued an active
regional development policy which targeted the decentralization of manufacturing into the country's peripheral areas (Rogerson, 1988). The goals of
regional development policy were conflated with those of apartheid social
engineering as the decentralization programme focused increasingly on a
selection of industrial 'growth points' bordering or within the Bantustans
(Map 2). During the early 1980s a more vigorous regional industrial development programme (RIDP) was introduced, designed to further siphon industry
away from South Africa's major metropolitan areas (most importantly the
Pretoria–Witwatersrand–Vereeniging (PWV) region) into a mass of peripheral
growth points with a special emphasis again accorded to Bantustan industrialization (Rogerson, 1991).

Map 2. *Some of the 'Abandoned Places' of Apartheid*

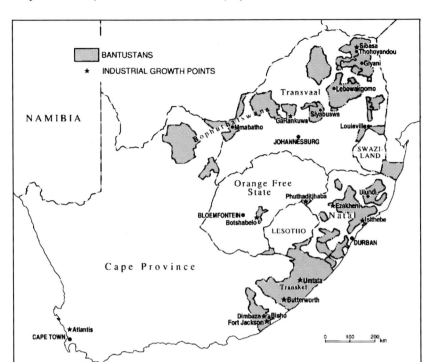

The effects of the state decentralization programme have been the source of much controversy and debate. In developmental terms, many critical observers draw attention to the programme's failure to achieve local linkages, the insecure and highly exploited work conditions of the predominantly female industrial workforce, and the footloose nature of much investment occurring in the Bantustans (see Hirsch, 1986, 1987; Cobbett, 1987; Rogerson, 1988, 1989; Soni, 1989). One impact of industrial decentralization undoubtedly was to restructure social relations in and around the growth points; on the one hand, the incorporation of rural women into wage labour allowed them a measure of autonomy and strength in the face of patriarchal controls in the family, on the other hand, it increased their vulnerability to exploitation as women workers in the factories (Pudifin and Ward, 1986; Mager, 1989; Jaffee, 1990; Msiza, 1992). Overall, it is clear that the generous incentives offered to manufacturers were responsible for the emergence of a new landscape of localized rural industrialization. Many of the growth points in the rural periphery recorded extraordinarily rapid rates of manufacturing expansion as new 'factories in the field' sprang up as features of the new apartheid-engineered geographies of several of the Bantustans (Pickles, 1991; Pickles and Woods, 1992). The impact of the industrial decentralization incentives was spatially uneven with the most rapid rates of growth taking place at growth points such as Isithebe, Fort Jackson, Dimbaza, Ezakheni, Butterworth, Botshabelo and Phuthaditjhaba (see Rogerson, 1988; Kabi, 1990;

Black *et al.*, 1991; Sarpong, 1991). The economic health of these 'new industrial spaces', artificially fostered by apartheid planning, began to be threatened as mounting criticism was directed at South Africa's decentralization
and growth centre programme.

Abandoned places

By the 1980s severe attacks began to be levied at the enormous financial costs
of the decentralization strategy. Critics drew attention to several shortcomings, *inter alia*, the absence of sustained industrial development at designated
growth points, the overly generous nature of incentives, mounting abuse of
the incentive scheme, the fact that too many growth points had been chosen,
few linkages established with local economies, and that the majority of
employment opportunities actually created at growth points were low-skill,
low-wage jobs leading to situations of widespread and abject 'poverty-in-
employment' (Rogerson, 1988, 1993). In short, it was argued that the RIDP
was politically motivated, highly costly, largely unsuccessful, and wasteful of
scarce development resources (Driver and Platzky, 1992). Accordingly, at the
end of the 1980s a re-thinking took place of regional policy led by a Panel of
Experts appointed by the Development Bank of Southern Africa (DBSA) and
by a parallel investigation pursued by the Urban Foundation (Rogerson,
1991).

Based on findings and recommendations made by the DBSA Panel of
Experts, South Africa's regional development policy was substantially revised
in 1991 and a new strategy phased into operation (South Africa, 1991).
Essentially the new RIDP shifts away from the past approach of selective
growth points and instead adopts a package of graded incentives that ostensi-
bly interfere less with the market, thereby encouraging greater economic and
financial efficiency rather than the support of inefficient firms. In financial
terms the new RIDP is far more modest than its predecessor. For the initial
two years of operation enterprises are given an establishment allowance and,
for the following three years, an allowance based only on the amount of profits made. A key aspect of the new programme is that it removes the spatial
discrimination which formerly favoured the official growth points (especially
those inside Bantustans) replacing it by a pattern of incentives which are
graded across different zones of the country (see Rogerson, 1991, 1993).

This new RIDP represents a major policy retreat from the old programme
which underpinned apartheid planning. No longer is industrial decentralization encouraged in the manner in which it was originally conceptualized (i.e.
firms relocating from white space to Bantustans and their borders) and func-
tioned for the past three decades (Driver and Platzky, 1992). Rather, the new
strategy de-emphasizes the former importance of industrialization in the
Bantustans, and, in the view of some observers, prepares the ground for policies geared to take 'people to the jobs' in the metropolitan areas rather than
taking 'jobs to the people' in peripheral regions (Platzky, 1989; Roux, 1991).
In particular, Roux (1989) presents the case for a radical reversal of past
regional policies arguing that the quickest and most efficient strategy for raising standards of living for the majority would be to encourage rural–urban
migration into the 'absorption zones' of South Africa's large metropolitan

regions and correspondingly, to drastically curtail expenditures on industrial decentralization. In future, it is argued migration "will play a much more prominent role in creating a more equal spatial distribution of per capita economic activity" (Roux, 1991, p. 47).

Although this radical option was not implemented in the 1991 RIDP, the consequences of the new programme are to dramatically reduce the competitiveness for new industrial investment of many of the formerly favoured industrial growth points (Wilsenach and Ligthelm, 1993). The impact of the new incentive programme on individual growth points, however, will vary enormously with some growth points having established a basis for viability, whilst the survival of others is in jeopardy due to the phasing out of incentives (Black *et al.*, 1991; Platzky, 1993). Already there is documented evidence of firms beginning to uproot and leave some of these growth points, often relocating to areas in and around the metropolitan regions (Driver and Platzky, 1992, p. 11). Other 'fly-by-night' enterprises, notably run by many Taiwanese or Israeli investors, have closed down their entire South African operations following the withdrawal of the lucrative investment concessions (Rogerson, 1991). Nonetheless, it must be acknowledged that not all the decentralized factories were marginal operations and that many factories will survive into the post-apartheid era of reduced incentives (Platzky, 1993). Driver and Platzky (1992, pp. 11–12) aver that:

> In spite of all the criticisms of industrial decentralisation policy, it may not be helpful to dismiss it altogether. It has made South Africa different from other developing countries in that it has helped to slow rapid migration to a poverty stricken prime city. It has provided some jobs—mostly for women, built some infrastructure, and given some people in the most remote rural areas independent incomes and exposure to industry. People in those areas are not merely passive recipients of apartheid policies or industrial restructuring; they respond to both in different ways, and their history of struggle will help to shape their development paths...

An important determinant of future patterns of migration into and out of these 'abandoned places' will be the varying local responses and development initiatives that are instituted in the new environment of reduced national incentives (Rogerson, 1993). Unless the post-apartheid government introduces new regional policy support for these places many of these artificially-induced small towns face the challenge to diversify their economic base and construct symbiotic linkages with the South African countryside (Dewar, 1993). Without local development initiatives to successfully meet this challenge, the prospect over the next decade is for deteriorating economic and social conditions in many of these 'abandoned places' thus precipitating new flows of out-migration to South Africa's metropolitan areas.

CONCLUDING REMARKS

The challenges of development, economic reconstruction and urban management that will be posed in the post-apartheid era underscore the policy relevance of migration studies (McCarthy and Rogerson, 1992). From a policy perspective it is evident that the shifting dynamics of international and internal migration flows require the attention of South African researchers. Emerging new patterns of international migratory movements, the impact of major legislative changes affecting internal migration or settlement in large urban areas, gender and migration, and the persistence of circulatory labour movements are just some of the issues that urgently demand scholarly analysis. Although it is likely that the local research agenda will continue to be large-city biased, there remains a strong case for addressing in greater detail certain issues relating to South Africa's hitherto largely forgotten non-metropolitan places. In particular, one important policy issue is the role of small and intermediate towns in diverting migrants away from the country's large and rapidly expanding metropolitan centres. A critical research issue will be to monitor the fate of those places that were artificial creations of apartheid and now face an uncertain post-apartheid future. The groups of Bantustan new towns and capital cities, the relocation settlements associated with compulsory population removals, and the 'abandoned places' of decentralization planning represent South African small towns where out-migration is possible in the short-term unless their economic base is restructured and revitalized in the next decade.

Acknowledgements

Thanks are due to the Centre for Science Development, Pretoria for funding my research. Opinions expressed are those of the author.

References

Ansell, G. and P. Bond, 1992, "The crazy pavement wars go on", *Africa South and East* (Johannesburg), November, p. 27.

Baldwin, A., 1975, "Mass removals and separate development", *Journal of Southern African Studies*, 1, 215–227.

Beavon, K.S.O. and R. Payne, 1988, "An analysis and typology of South Africa's non-metropolitan urban places", unpublished paper for the Urban Foundation, Johannesburg.

Bernstein, A., 1987, "The Urban Foundation, influx control and reform", in R. Tomlinson and M. Addleson (eds.), *Regional Restructuring Under Apartheid: Urban and Regional Policies in Contemporary South Africa*, 106–114. Johannesburg: Ravan.

Black, P.A., A.D. Roux and J.B. Standish, 1991, "Spatial patterns of industrial growth and its implications for regional policy in South Africa", unpublished report for the Development Bank of Southern Africa, Midrand.

Bloch, R., 1987, "Positive urbanisation strategy and non-metropolitan urbanisation in South Africa: the cases of Nelspruit-White River and Tzaneen sub-regions", unpublished paper for the Urban Foundation, Johannesburg.

Bozzoli, B., 1991a, *Women of Phokeng: Consciousness, Life Strategy, and Migrancy in South Africa, 1900–1983*. Johannesburg: Ravan.

Bozzoli, B., 1991b, "The meaning of informal work: some women's stories", in E. Preston-Whyte and C. Rogerson (eds.), *South Africa's Informal Economy*, 15–33. Cape Town: Oxford University Press.

Cobbett, W., 1987, "Industrial decentralisation and exploitation: the case of Botshabelo", *South African Labour Bulletin*, 12 (3), 95–109.

Crush, J., 1984, "Uneven labour migration in southern Africa: conceptions and misconceptions", *South African Geographical Journal*, 66, 115–132.

Crush, J., 1986, "The extrusion of foreign labour from the South African gold mining industry", *Geoforum*, 17, 161–172.

Crush, J., 1987a, *The Struggle for Swazi Labour, 1890–1920*. Montreal and Kingston: McGill-Queen's University Press.

Crush, J., 1987b, "Restructuring migrant labour on the gold mines", in G. Moss and I. Obery (eds.), *South African Review 4*, 283–291. Johannesburg: Ravan.

Crush, J., 1989, "Migrancy and militance: the case of the National Union of Mineworkers of South Africa", *African Affairs*, 88, 5–24.

Crush, J., 1991, "The chains of migrancy and the Southern African Labour Commission", in C. Dixon and M. Heffernan (eds.), *Colonialism and Development in the Contemporary World*, 46–71. London: Mansell.

Crush, J., 1992, "Inflexible migrancy: new forms of migrant labour on the South African gold mines", *Labour, Capital and Society*, 25, 46–71.

Crush, J. and C. M. Rogerson, 1983, "New wave African historiography and African historical geography", *Progress in Human Geography*, 7, 203–231.

Crush, J., A. Jeeves and D. Yudelman, 1991, *South Africa's Labor Empire: A History of Black Migrancy to the Gold Mines*. Cape Town: David Philip.

De Vletter, F., 1990, *Prospects for Foreign Migrant Workers in a Democratic South Africa*, Working Paper Mig WP. 48. Geneva: International Labour Office.

Delius, P., 1980, "Migrant labour and the Pedi", in S. Marks and A. Atmore (eds.), *Economy and Society in Preindustrial South Africa*, 293–312. London: Longman.

Dewar, D., 1993, "Reconstructing the South African countryside: the case of small towns", unpublished paper, University of Cape Town.

Driver, M. and L. Platzky, 1992: "Regional development: an overview of South African policy", unpublished paper, Development Action Group, Cape Town.

Drummond, J. and S. M. Parnell, 1991, "Mafikeng-Mmabatho", in A. Lemon (ed.), *Homes Apart: South Africa's Segregated Cities*, 162–173. Bloomington: Indiana University Press.

Freund, B., 1984, "Forced resettlement and the political economy of South Africa", *Review of African Political Economy*, 29, 49–63.

Gaffane, M., 1990, "Planning implications of persistent circulatory migration in a developing environment: focus on northern Transvaal migrants working in Johannesburg", unpublished MSc (Development Planning) discourse, University of Witwatersrand, Johannesburg.

Giliomee, H. and L. Schlemmer, (eds.), 1985, *Up Against the Fences: Poverty, Passes and Privilege in South Africa*. Cape Town: David Philip.

Grahamstown Rural Committee, 1991, "Between a rock and a hard place: forced removals and the Bantustans in the "Border Corridor" of South Africa", *Antipode*, 23, 137–141.

Haffajee, F., 1993a, "The invisible illegals", *Weekly Mail* (Johannesburg), 5–11 March, 16–17.

Haffajee, F., 1993b, "No fleas on these markets", *Africa South and East* (Johannesburg), June, p. 26.

Hart, D.M. and C. M. Rogerson, 1989, "Hawkers in South Africa's small urban centres: planning and policy", *Development Southern Africa*, 6, 295–310.

Hart, T. and C. M. Rogerson, 1982, "The geography of international refugee movements in southern Africa", *South African Geographical Journal*, 64, 125–137.

Hindson, D., 1985, *Pass Laws and the Urban African Proletariat*. Johannesburg: Ravan.

Hindson, D., 1987, "Orderly urbanisation and influx control: from territorial apartheid to regional spatial ordering in South Africa", in R. Tomlinson and M. Addleson (eds.), *Regional Restructuring Under Apartheid: Urban and Regional Policies in Contemporary South Africa*, 74–105. Johannesburg: Ravan

Hirsch, A., 1986, "Investment incentives and distorted development: industrial decentralization in the Ciskei", *Geoforum*, 17, 187–200.

Hirsch, A., 1987, "The industrialization of Dimbaza: population relocation and industrial decentralisation in a Bantustan", in R. Tomlinson and M. Addleson (eds), *Regional Restructuring Under Apartheid: Urban and Regional Policies in Contemporary South Africa*, 253–277. Johannesburg: Ravan.

Jaffee, G., 1990, "Industrial decentralisation and women's employment in South Africa: a case study", unpublished paper, University of the Witwatersrand, Johannesburg.

James, W.G., 1992, *Our Precious Metal: African Labour in South Africa's Gold Industry, 1970–1990*. Cape Town: David Philip.

Jeeves, A., 1985, *Migrant Labour in South Africa's Mining Economy: the Struggle for the Gold Mines Labour Supply 1890–1920*. Johannesburg: Witwatersrand University Press.

Jeeves, A., 1986, "Migrant labour and South African expansion, 1920–1950", *South African Historical Journal*, 18, 73–92.

Kabi, M.E., 1990, "Industrial decentralisation as an element of regional economic development: the case of Ezakheni", unpublished M. TRP dissertation, University of Natal, Durban.

Lacey, M., 1981, *Working for Boroko: The Origins of a Coercive Labour System*. Johannesburg: Ravan.

Mabin, A., 1987, "The land clearances at Pilgrim's Rest", *Journal of Southern African Studies*, 13, 400–416.

Mabin, A., 1989, "Struggle for the city: urbanisation and political strategies of the South African state", *Social Dynamics*, 15, 1–28.

Mabin, A., 1990, "Limits of urban transition models in understanding South African urbanization", *Development Southern Africa*, 7, 311–322.

Mabin, A., 1992, "Dispossession, exploitation and struggle: an historical overview of South African urbanization", in D.M. Smith (ed.), *The Apartheid City and Beyond: Urbanization and Social Change in South Africa*, 13–24. Johannesburg: Witwatersrand University Press.

Mager, A., 1989, "Moving the fence: gender in the Ciskei and Border textile industry, 1945–1986", *Social Dynamics*, 15, 46–62.

Maluleka, K.M., 1990, "Migration, urbanisation and development policy: a case study approach on implications for planning in South Africa", unpublished B.Sc TRP Dissertation, University of the Witwatersrand, Johannesburg.

McCarthy, J.J., 1992, "Urban geography and socio-political change: retrospect and prospect", in C. Rogerson and J. McCarthy (eds.), *Geography in a Changing South Africa: Progress and Prospects*, 138–55. Cape Town: Oxford University Press.

McCarthy, J.J. and C.M. Rogerson, 1992, "Unscrambling the demographic mosaic: population geography in South Africa", in C. Rogerson and J. McCarthy (eds.), *Geography in a Changing South Africa: Progress and Prospects*, 38–50. Cape Town: Oxford University Press.

Miles, M., 1991, "Missing women: a study of female Swazi migration to the Witwatersrand, 1920–1970", unpublished MA dissertation.Kingston: Queen's University.

Miles, M., 1993, "Missing women: reflections on the experiences of Swazi migrant women on the Rand, 1920–1970", *GeoJournal*, 30, 85–91.

Msiza, J., 1992, "Trapped and marginalised: a case study of the implications of decentralised industries at Babelegi on the women of the area", unpublished BA Hons Seminar Paper, University of the Witwatersrand, Johannesburg.

Murray, C., 1987, "Displaced urbanization: South Africa's rural slums", *African Affairs*, 86, 311–329.

Newton, D., 1989, "Forced removals in South Africa", in G. Moss and I. Obery (eds), *South African Review 5*, 403–414. Johannesburg: Ravan.

Pickles, J., 1991, "Industrial restructuring: peripheral industrialization and rural development in South Africa", *Antipode*, 23, 68–91.

Pickles, J. and J. Woods, 1992, "South Africa's homelands in the age of reform: the case of QwaQwa", *Annals of the Association of American Geographers*, 82, 629–652.

Platzky, L., 1989, "Capital and community in two industrial decentralisation points: some implications for a future regional development policy", unpublished Seminar Paper presented at the Centre for African Studies, University of Cape Town.

Platzky, L., 1993, "Comparative or cumulative advantage?: the impact of industrial location policies on Bantustan settlements", unpublished Seminar Paper presented at the Centre for African Studies, University of Cape Town.

Platzky, L. and C. Walker, 1983, "Review of relocation", in SARS (South African Research Service) (eds.), *South African Review 1*, 83–96. Johannesburg: Ravan.

Platzky, L. and C. Walker, 1985, *The Surplus People: Forced Removals in South Africa*. Johannesburg: Ravan.

Posel, D., 1989, "'Providing for the legitimate labour requirements of employers': secondary industry, commerce and the state in South Africa during the 1950s and 1960s", in A. Mabin (ed.), *Organization and Economic Change: Southern African Studies Volume 5*, 199–220. Johannesburg: Ravan.

Prah, K.K., 1989, *The Bantustan Brain Gain: A Study into and Causes of Brain Drain from Independent Africa to the South African Bantustans*, Southern African Series No. 5, Institute of Southern African Studies, National University of Lesotho.

Prah, K.K., 1991, "Is Africa losing its mind?", *Matlhasedi*, 10 (1), 77–78.

Pudifin, C. and S. Ward, 1986, "Working for nothing: gender and industrial decentralisation in Isithebe", unpublished M.TRP dissertation, University of Natal, Durban.

Richardson, P., 1983, *Chinese Mine Labour in the Transvaal*. London: Macmillan.

Rogerson, C.M., 1984–85, "Alternatives to influx control: policy response to urbanward migration in the Third World", *Journal of Contemporary African Studies*, 4, 37–70.

Rogerson, C.M., 1988, "Regional development policy in South Africa", *Regional Development Dialogue*, 9 (Special Issue), 228–255.

Rogerson, C.M., 1989, "The disaster of apartheid forced removals", in J.I. Clarke, P. Curson, S.L. Kayastha and P. Nag (eds.), *Population and Disaster*, 256–264. Oxford: Basil Blackwell.

Rogerson, C.M., 1991, "Beyond racial Fordism: restructuring industry in the 'new' South Africa", *Tijdschrift voor Economische en Sociale Geografie*, 82, 355–366.

Rogerson, C.M., 1993, "South Africa: from regional policy to local economic development initiatives", unpublished paper, University of the Witwatersrand, Johannesburg.

Rogerson, C.M. and E.M. Letsoalo, 1985: "Resettlement and underdevelopment in the black 'homelands' of South Africa", in J.I. Clarke, M. Khogali and L. A. Kosinski (eds.), *Population and Development Projects in Africa*, 176–193. Cambridge: Cambridge University Press.

Roux, A., 1989, "Regional policy options for a future South Africa", unpublished paper presented at the Lausanne Colloquim, Switzerland, 8–13 July.

Roux, A., 1991, "Migration and regional policy", *Urban Forum*, 2 (1), 41–58.

Royston, L. A., 1991, "Persistent circular migration: evidence, explanation and planning implications", unpublished MSc (Development Planning) discourse, University of Witwatersrand, Johannesburg.

Rule, S.P. and T.M. Wills, 1988–89, "Industrial decentralization: population migration to Newcastle", *South African Geographer*, 16 (1/2), 81–91.

Sarpong, E., 1991, "Butterworth—a growth pole", unpublished MA dissertation, University of Natal, Durban.

Simkins, C., 1991, "Population pressures", in M. Ramphele and C. McDowell (eds.), *Restoring the Land: Environment and Change in Post-Apartheid South Africa*, 21–26. London: Panos.

Soni, D.V. and B. Maharaj, 1991, "Emerging urban forms in rural South Africa", *Antipode*, 23, 47–67.

Soni, L., 1989, "Isithebe: hell for workers", *South African Labour Bulletin*, 14 (5), 72–79.

South Africa, Republic of, Office of Regional Development, 1991, *National Regional Development Programme: General Overview Volume 1*. Pretoria: Government Printer.

Surplus People Project, 1983, *Forced Removals in South Africa*, 5 vols. Durban: University of Natal.

Urban Foundation, 1990, *Policies for a New Urban Future: Urban Debate 2010: 1 Population Trends*. Johannesburg: The Urban Foundation.

Urban Foundation, 1991, *Policies for a New Urban Future: Urban Debate 2010—Population Trends: Demographic Projection Model*. Johannesburg: The Urban Foundation.

Welsh, D., 1982, "The policies of control: blacks in the common area", in R. Schrire (ed.), *South Africa: Public Policy Perspectives*, 87–111. Cape Town: Juta.

Wilsenach, A. and A.A. Ligthelm, 1993, "An evaluation of the RIDP and its preliminary impact on regional development in South Africa", unpublished paper, Development Bank of Southern Africa, Midrand.

Wolpe, H., 1972, "Capitalism and cheap labour power in South Africa: from segregation to apartheid", *Economy and Society*, 1, 425–456.

Yudelman, D., 1983, *The Emergence of Modern South Africa: State, Capital and the Incorporation of Organised Labour on the South African Gold Fields 1902–1939*. Cape Town: David Philip.

Migration and Recent Economic and Environmental Change in East Africa

W.T.S. Gould

The relationship between migration and development involves a two-way reflexive interaction: migration affects development and development affects migration (Gould, 1992). When people move from one location to another, as individuals or as groups, they affect the immediate and future development prospects both at the source of their move, the place of origin, and also at the destination of their move, the new place of residence. However, these moves are themselves conditioned by changing and economic and social circumstances at source and destination, as well as in other 'intervening' areas. In East Africa the continuously changing interrelationships between population movement and the development process are intricately bound into the changing geographies of the countries of the region: the changing balance between rural and urban production, between subsistence and commercial sectors in both rural and urban areas, the changing roles of the state and the market as prime engines of development, and, at an international level, the extent and type of interaction between the three states, with their neighbours in Africa and with the world economy at large.

Any overview of migration in East Africa, therefore, must focus on recent changes in patterns and processes of population movement as they affect, and are affected by, the patterns and processes of development, conceptualized as economic and social changes affecting the lived experiences of the population of the three countries, estimated in 1992 at 64 million (Kenya 23.5m, Tanzania 23.8m, Uganda 16.8m), some 14 per cent of the population of Sub-Saharan Africa. Within the last 30 years their broad national experiences have been widely different. Kenya has experienced relatively consistent and, by the standards of most African states, relatively successful economic progress in a 'liberal' (alternatively 'neo-colonial') economy. Tanzania has been transformed through the socialist experiment of the 1960s and 1970s followed by important changes in a series of structural adjustment measures in the 1980s and into the 1990s. The Ugandan economy was tragically undermined by devastating political collapse from 1971, and has exhibited only a very slow and halting recovery since the mid-1980s.

The diversity of their economic, political and social experiences has inevitably found its echo in the diversity of the migration experiences. In Kenya the emphasis on resettlement in the fertile Highlands, the area of European settler farms in the colonial period, in the 1960s and early 1970s (Odingo, 1971) gave way to the concern for urban growth, especially of Nairobi, in the 1970s (Obudho, 1984), and rural migration into the drier, more marginal districts in the north and east of the country (Dietz, 1986). In Tanzania, too, there was rapid growth of Dar es Salaam throughout most of the period, but much more attention of analysts and policy makers was directed to rural population redistribution through villagization policies (Thomas, 1982, 1985). In Uganda political instability disrupted the established migration patterns as the urban and coffee economies collapsed, but there was a substantial need for resettlement of refugees in rural areas, both of internal refugees from the 'ethnic cleansing' associated with civil disruption and of international returnees from Rwanda, Sudan, Zaire (Kabera, 1990).

Though there are many differences of style and substance in migration within the three countries, there are also important common features arising from the migration/development interaction round which an overview of migration in East Africa may be usefully structured. The first of these, the focus of Section 2 of this chapter, is a rather technical factor in that it is concerned with the range and type of migration data that are now available. In none of the three countries have there been large scale national migration surveys or major innovations in traditional migration data collection methods, to the extent that data collection and analysis seem not to have progressed to keep pace with the changing national developmental contexts in which the movement takes place. Furthermore, these contexts do have several important features in common, not least of which are the internal effects of macroeconomic changes, notably of structural adjustment policies and the changing regional and rural/urban balance of economic activity. The relationships between migration and structural adjustment and between migration and regional economic change in the source areas are the themes of Sections 3 and 4 respectively. Since the interrelationships between migration and the environment offer a theme of immense importance in all three countries, the role of migration as it positively and also negatively affects population/environment relationships is examined in Section 5.

PROBLEMS OF DATA AND METHOD

Traditionally the empirical analysis of migration in East Africa, as elsewhere in the Third World, has depended on both census and survey sources, and the availability of data has been an important factor affecting the sort of questions that could be addressed. Despite optimism in the 1960s and 1970s about the possibilities for improving both the quantity and quality of migration data that could be made available for migration analysis in Africa as a whole as elsewhere in the Third World, relatively little of fundamental methodological or analytical significance has been achieved since then in East Africa. The formulation of this overview of migration in East Africa, therefore, continues to be obliged in the 1990s, almost as much as it was in the

1950s at the time of Southall's classic overview (Southall, 1961), on partial, incomplete and often indirect sources.

Recent census sources in all three countries have asked place of birth information as the primary source of migration data, becoming more widely used than the ethnic data that had been the main source in colonial censuses (Table 1). These have allowed identification of basic patterns of inter-district movement as revealed by the matrix of place of birth by place of residence. They have also allowed identification of basic patterns of net-migration, rates of in- and out-migration to and from the specified units of account, and a generalized description of the major flows.

Table 1. *Census sources of migration data*

	Ethnic data	Birthplace data	No. of birth-places	Size of published source/ destination matrix	Time-specific question
Kenya					
1969	*	*	41	41x9	–
1979	–	*	41	41x9	one year
1989	–	*	41	?	one year
Tanzania					
1967	*	*	many	25x25	–
1978	–	*	many	25x25	previous census
1988	–	*	many	25x25	previous census
Uganda					
1969	–	*	18	18x21	–
1980	–	–	–	–	–

* = question included
– = question not included

Detailed analysis of the Uganda 1969 census showed the importance of a small number of large flows, largely for resettlement, between peripheral regions of the country (Kigezi to Ankole, West Nile to Bunyoro, Bukedi to Busoga), and a much larger number of rather smaller, but still substantial, flows into central Mengo, including the main urban area of Kampala but also areas of rural wage labour in the coffee *shambas* of Buganda (Masser and Gould, 1975). There were no migration questions at all in the 1980 census in Uganda. This was a very basic count taken at a time of very considerable civil upheaval (Uganda Government, 1982). Similar sorts of analyses were done in Tanzania using its 1967 census, with identification of the national catchment of Dar es Salaam, but also large flows over fairly short distances between rural areas (Claeson and Egerö, 1973). The Tanzanian place-of-birth material asked similar questions in the 1967, 1978 and 1988 enumerations, with an interprovincial 25 x 25 migration matrix being available, though, given that birthplace was defined by locality within districts, a much larger number of sources was specified in the raw data.

The main patterns of inter-district movement in Kenya had been established by Ominde using 1962 census ethnic data in combination with indirect estimates of patterns using population structures and sex ratios (Ominde, 1968). Subsequent censuses that provided place of birth data were able to refine and up-date these basic patterns slightly, but offered little by way of fundamental new insights (House and Rempel, 1980). The 1979 Kenya Census, for example, allowed identification of the pattern of net migration (Map 1a), rates of out- (Map 1b) and in-migration (Map 1c) for 41 districts, and inter-provincial flows for nine regions (Map 1d). These continue to reflect the importance of the densely populated former colonial 'labour reserves' as regions of out-migration, with major inflows to Nairobi, the primate capital city, and to Rift Valley province, the main area of planned resettlement schemes and also of wage labour in commercial farms in the Highlands.

Analyses based on these birth-place data suffer, however, from two sorts of problem that have become more apparent as development has proceeded. In the first place they provide a cumulative historical record that continues to reflect past movements rather than current trends. In Kenya, for example, most of the resettlement migration into the Highlands took place in the years immediately after independence in the 1960s and early 1970s, so that by the mid-1970s this organized resettlement had largely ceased. The flows into Rift Valley implied by the 1979 map (Maps 1b and d) therefore reflect a major geographical and economic restructuring that was at its height a decade before that enumeration, but the in-migrants of that earlier period remained to be enumerated in 1979. Since these birthplace data were not disaggregated by age in the published tables, it is not possible to even indirectly estimate the extent of 1970s movement from place of birth of children.

The problem of time can, in theory, be partly overcome by the inclusion of a time-specific question: "Where were you living at some previously specified time (normally one year or five years ago)?". This would allow only recent movements to be identified as a complement to the place of birth data as well as being useful in their own right. In particular, time-specific data would allow better identification of circulatory, non-permanent moves. The presumptions of the place of birth data are that there is a permanent move, a 'migration' in strict terms, from A to B, with no returns to A or any subsequent moves to C and perhaps to other locations. However, it is now widely recognised in migration studies generally, but in Sub-Saharan Africa in particular, that non-permanent moves are a characteristic feature of mobility phenomena, and need to be better identified (Gould and Prothero, 1975; Gould, 1992). There is a persistence of circulation (see below, Section 3) that is not adequately reflected in cross-sectional data collection methodologies.

Despite the attractiveness of time-specific questions in theory, in practice the results of their inclusion in censuses have been disappointing. The experience of Kenya, 1979, in including a time-specific question in the census was not successful. The data obtained were clearly not correctly conceptualized by the enumerators or the enumerated, and the Census Report concluded that:

> ...the data on place of residence in 1976 (i.e. one-year retrospective question) was bedevil-led by the biases that are liable to afflict all questions involving dating and reference periods in Africa. It is also possible that the question became garbled in the process of translation and was misunderstood; some people giving the name of their "home" district rather than the place they had actually been in 1978. It, therefore, cannot be recommended for inclusion in future censuses in Kenya (Kenya Government, 1982, p.64).

Although this was the conclusion in the Analytical Report of the 1979 Census, a time-specific question was indeed included in the Kenya 1989 Census.

Map 1a. *Net migration: Kenya 1979*

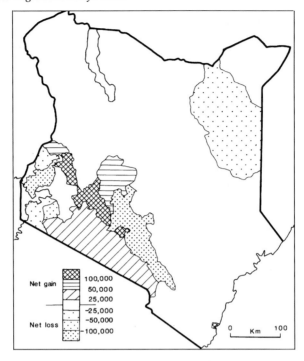

Map 1b. *Outmigrants per thousand born: Kenya 1979*

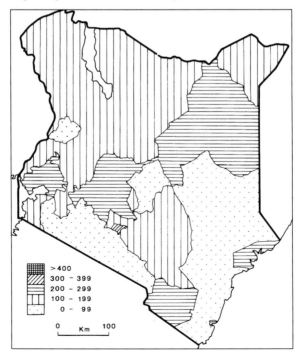

Map 1c. *In-migrants per thousand residents: Kenya 1979*

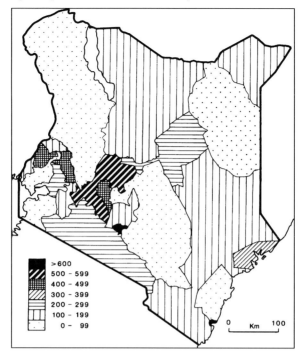

Map 1d. *Inter-provincial flows for nine regions: Kenya 1979*

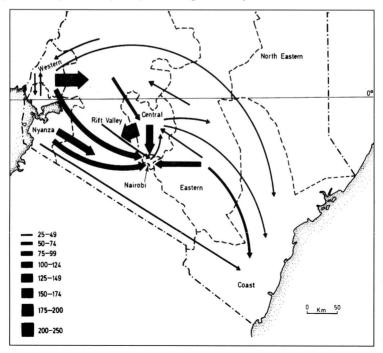

However, as with the whole of the data from that enumeration, no results have yet been published (to June, 1993), largely, it is assumed, for political reasons. A time-specific migration question was included in the Tanzania 1978 and 1988 enumerations: "Where were you living at the time of the last census?", but these 10-year retrospective questions have not been widely used for migration analysis.

The second type of major problem associated with census-based migration data concerns the spatial scale of the units of account. Since these are large districts (41 in Kenya with an average population of over 500,000) or provinces (25 in Tanzania with an average population of about 1 million), a lot of population movement—both permanent and temporary—occurs within them. The census scale over-emphasizes long distance moves—and particularly rural–urban moves, especially since the capital cities of Kenya and Tanzania are identified as separate destination regions. It under-records most intra-rural and rural to small town moves, yet these are clearly critical to understanding the whole process of population movement and its relationship with development.

The most obvious case of where the spatial scale of the census was inappropriate was in Tanzania in the 1970s. The villagization of rural settlement that came to a sudden climax with Operation *Vijijini* in 1973 was a major component of national development policy, gathering the traditionally dispersed rural population into permanent nucleated villages. Most resettlement migrations were over short distances. In Iringa District, the mean distance moved per person was 4.94 km, and the modal distance was 2.3 km, though 20 per cent of the moves exceeded 7.5 km (Thomas, 1985:148). This major and widespread national movement was almost entirely intra-district and therefore unrecorded by the census.

For these two critical reasons of problems of time and space, census-based migration analysis has become less important in East Africa, though it has not ceased altogether. Perhaps the most important example of its continuing value has been in the identification of very considerable in-migration into dry marginal districts in Kenya (Dietz, 1985). The analytical limitations have been compounded by the political and administrative difficulties associated with the publication of census results, and add to a general feeling of disenchantment with the efficacy of the census as a prime source of migration data.

The traditional alternative to census-based migration data has been in small scale surveys. These have continued, indeed have grown in numbers as more scholars, and particularly local scholars, have investigated migration. The institutional base in universities, to include the Population Studies and Research Institute (PSRI) in the University of Nairobi, the Demographic Unit in the University of Dar es Salaam and the UN Institute for Statistics in Makerere University, Uganda, has generated a number of analysts with interest in migration who have made contributions in unpublished research theses and papers as well as in published materials. These, however, are in a wide range of sources, many of restricted circulation (for example, in 'grey' material for donor agencies and NGOs, as well as in research libraries), and not yet fully integrated and synthesized even to definitive national overviews. Some of these studies are cited in the remainder of this chapter. In addition, however, some are given specific spatial reference in Map 2, where the main geographical focus of the study can be indicated. This is certainly not a complete or definitive map, but a summary of recent work known to this author. It can easily be extended with more detailed consideration of the range of sources.

Map 2. *Key to locations identified*

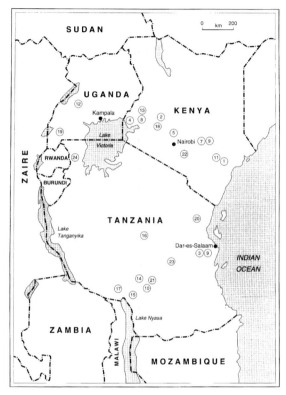

1 Alakoski-Johansson and Johansson, 1991
2 Ayiemba, 1990
3 Briggs, 1991
4 Cohen and Atieno-Odhiambo, 1989
5 Collier and Lal, 1984
6 Dietz, 1984
7 Elkan, 1985
8 Gould, in press
9 Hazlewood *et al.*, 1991
10 Holm, 1992
11 Hughes, 1984
12 Kabera, 1985
13 Lavrijsen, 1984
14 Lwoga, 1991
15 Mbonile, 1993
16 Nbara, 1992
17 Nkhoma-Wamunza, 1992
18 Odingo, 1971
19 Rutaremwa, 1990
20 Sender and Smith, 1990
21 Thomas, 1985
22 Tiffen, 1991
23 Van Donge, 1992
24 Weiss, 1993

Part of the problem is that the survey-based studies address a wide range of aspects—causes/effects, source/destination, individuals/groups, men/women —using a wide range of methodologies—from intensive questionnaires and rigorous statistical analysis to more qualitative insights—and are undertaken by analysts with a background in all the social sciences, as well as in medicine and natural sciences. The result is a disparate array of small-scale empirical conclusions with a disappointing reluctance to seek analytical or policy-relevant cohesion. Governments have been less concerned with migration than they have with fertility and mortality, and the apparent anarchy in migration studies remains, for there is no emerging or over-arching context into which these potentially insightful surveys can be set.

However, this need not be the case. Innovative data collection methods based on national migration surveys are available and have been proved successful and insightful elsewhere in Africa. There has been a long tradition of longitudinal and retrospective survey work in migration in West Africa, and most recently analysed in the case of the 1978–79 retrospective survey in

Burkina Faso (Piché, 1990). The only anglophone country which has had a National Migration Survey is Botswana, 1978–79, a country which, like Burkina Faso, has a long history of important external migration (to South Africa and Côte d'Ivoire respectively) and for which migration appears to government, as well as to external donors, as an issue that warrants considerable attention and allocation of resources for national survey to inform policy making.

The Botswana NMS reported in three volumes, was most concerned with internal migration (Botswana Government, 1982). Data were derived from four rounds of questionnaires to a nationally derived sample at six-monthly intervals, and it was able to overcome the basic shortcomings identified above as compromising the value of census-based work. It was able to identify the extensive amount of circulation and time-specific movement, including seasonal migration, both in the traditional sector between the large villages, the farming 'lands' areas, and the cattle posts, and also in the modern sector between town and country. It was able to identify the spatial patterns of short distance as well as long distance moves. It addressed questions and provided insights that the census could not provide, and was a valuable complement to the national censuses of 1971 and 1981. Furthermore, and probably more relevant to the East African context, it created a framework for policy analysis and overview into which several other independent and small-scale studies, at the time of the NMS and subsequently, could be contextualised. Such a survey is seriously lacking in East Africa. For any one of the countries a national migration survey would prove much more valuable to analysts and to decision makers than data from yet another round of census-based migration questions. The value would be direct, but the results would act as a focus for further analysis for existing work and for pointing the way forward to new directions. In the 1980s great attention was given, for perfectly valid reasons, to fertility surveys, including the Demographic and Health Surveys in Kenya, 1989 and Uganda, 1988, for these could be guaranteed international financial support. In the 1990s there is a strong case for similar efforts, using similar methodologies, being directed to migration analysis.

While Wilbur Zelinsky's 'Hypothesis of the mobility transition' made simplistic assumptions about the extent of mobility in poor societies, it did convincingly argue that development creates new forms of movement and restructures the mix of existing movements (Skeldon, 1990; Woods, 1993), and it offers a theoretical justification for moving the methods for the study of migration away from an aggregate, almost structuralist perspective, to one based on actual behaviour, as conceptualised for Africa by Akin Mabogunje (1971) in his systems model of migration. A new methodology will not by itself resolve the continuing theoretical and ideological disputes in African migration analysis, notably between the neo-marxists and structuralists on the one hand, and the behaviourists on the other (Gould, 1992), but it will shed new light on some old questions as well as on some new ones, and will be much more relevant to an examination of the interactions between migration and development in East Africa.

INTERNAL MIGRATION AND MACRO-ECONOMIC ADJUSTMENT

Since migration is responsive to economic circumstances at source and destination, the internal patterns and processes of movement will be affected by national economic circumstances and their spatially differentiated impacts. In general economic performance in East Africa, as elsewhere in Africa, in recent years has been weak and disappointing, with countries locked internally into a cycle of low urban and rural production, into underdevelopment in their relations with the world system, and into increasing indebtedness, often exacerbated by internal political conflict and policy failure. The three East African countries are sharply contrasted in their recent economic history and their macro-economic management, and between them offer a range of experiences that have differentially affected their internal migration.

Kenya, in many respects the epitome of a 'neo-colonial' economy, with strong links with the international economy through major exports of coffee and tea and through a thriving international tourist industry, has experienced least need for a formal macro-economic adjustment programme in recent years, yet there have been important changes driven by the IMF and World Bank (Mosley, 1991). The economy has remained relatively buoyant, continuing to earn foreign exchange and to afford foreign investment into the commercial sector in rural and urban areas. The spatial structures of core and periphery, of labour sending and labour receiving areas that had been established by the time of independence in 1964 have largely remained, with the growth of Nairobi and other major towns as a result of substantial rural–urban migration, much of which remains circulatory. Interaction between core and periphery continues to display an 'urban bias' (Gould, 1987). There have been changes in detail, such as the slowing of the growth of Nairobi relative to secondary centres (Obudho, 1990), slowing of rural–rural migration into commercial farming areas relative to migration, mostly spontaneous, to marginal drier land (Dietz, 1986), but essentially Kenya has seen a continuity in its migration system that reflects continuity in its macro-economic management.

In sharp contrast, Uganda and Tanzania, for quite different reasons, have experienced major macro-economic adjustments, in both cases associated with World Bank/IMF led structural adjustment programmes. Uganda's spectacular economic mismanagement and collapse under General Amin's regime in the 1970s, exacerbated by civil war and an effective collapse of government until 1986, with the winning of power by President Museveni's National Resistance Movement, had bankrupted the country, rendered its currency almost worthless, took most export earnings into the black-market and smuggling economies, and reduced the quality of life for most Ugandans (Hansen and Twaddle, 1991). However, food production did not fall significantly as most Ugandans learned to cope in a reversion to a subsistence and barter economy (Jamal, 1991). Urban populations that had grown substantially in the early 1970s, as migrants came to seek to take over Asian businesses after the expulsion of the Asians in 1972, probably fell as the wage economy collapsed and hyper-inflation seriously eroded the value of salaries in the public and private sectors. Many migrants returned to their shambas, and the once substantial rural–rural migration of wage labourers from peripheral districts and neighbouring countries to coffee and cotton areas in

Buganda evaporated. Internal migrations in that period were dominated by internal refugee movement and resettlement. A first priority after 1986 was for an emergency resettlement programme for returnees (Kabera, 1990).

Structural Adjustment measures with IMF support were first introduced by the Obote government in 1981, but proved ineffective in the face of continuing political instability up till 1986 (Banugire, 1989). After 1987 there was a more sustained effort in the Economic Recovery Programme (ERP) to stabilize the currency, reinvigorate exports and generally attempt to reintroduce a commercial economy, as in the more prosperous 1960s and earlier, based on agricultural exports (over 95 per cent coffee in recent years) and with a limited urban base. Success has been slow and limited and more obvious in urban areas, where 'the market' can operate, than in rural areas. In these circumstances urban migration has probably picked up. However, there are still major adverse impacts of the adjustment programme on the poor, as elsewhere in Africa, with the need, recognized by the IMF for a Programme for the Alleviation of Poverty and the Social Costs of Adjustment (PAPSCA) within the ERP. While much of the PAPSCA programme is targeted at seriously deprived regions and groups in rural areas, a significant proportion is targeted at the urban poor (Lateef, 1991). Banugire argues that substantial rural–urban exchange of food, goods and capital was critical to the economic survival of many poor and not so poor people:

> Within rural areas, several linkages between the rural and urban working populations must be recognized. First, many urban households obtain food remittances at subsidized prices from rural areas; these transfers have tended to increase with economic decline. Second, cash remittances from urban to rural areas have tended to decline as the urban standard of living deteriorated. Third, the urban rich are increasingly finding it socially useful, if not economically profitable, to invest in farm purchases and improvements, whether productive or unproductive.... (Banugire, 1991:96).

Migration does not cease in a collapsed economy: it merely takes on different forms, and in particular reduces the relative importance of urban and long-distance migration. However, as the economy recovers in a programme using IMF/World Bank guidelines and objectives, there will be an implicit presumption of the re-establishment of previous migrations systems rather than the creation of new patterns and processes.

In Tanzania too, there has been a programme of structural adjustment from the early 1980s, introduced at a time of severe economic difficulty, but not to the extent of beginning to approach the scale of the Ugandan experience, in particular that the state in Tanzania had not collapsed and there was little major civil disruption. The socialization of the economy that had been implemented in the 1960s and 1970s was faced with a serious crisis in the early 1980s as internally marketed production seemed to be falling, and externally the oil price shocks and declining world price for exports (coffee, cashew nuts, sisal, etc.) meant declining export revenues and a sharply increased import bill. To these must be added the cost of the war with Uganda which resulted in the ousting of General Amin in 1978 (Cheru, 1989). The strong presumption of rural bias in the policies of the 1970s has not prevented substantial and growing urban migration, and Dar es Salaam increased its population and attractiveness despite its losing its capital status and the relocation of some ministries to Dodoma (Hoyle, 1979), and systematic decentralization of government to regions and districts. Even though there was a policy presumption against urban places and urban migration, Obudho (1989) estimates that the urban proportion in the population of Tanzania grew from 6.9 per cent in 1970 (less than Kenya's and Uganda's 8.0 per cent) to 14.8 per cent by 1985 (still less than Kenya's 16.7 per cent in that year, but more than Uganda's 14.4 per cent), with an annual 6.0 per cent growth 1957–67, but 11.1 per cent for 1967–78. Dar es Salaam itself grew from 769,445 in 1978 to 1,217,590 in 1988, at a growth rate of 4.7 per cent p.a., a rate lower than the rate of growth of smaller towns in that period (Holm, 1992).

During the period of structural adjustment since 1981 the urban economy seems to have been strengthened relative to the rural economy. The 'liberalization' of the market with a floating currency, incentives to entrepreneurs and businesses and privatization of state enterprises, etc., has had greatest effect where 'the market' is most effective: i.e. in urban areas and areas of commercial agriculture. These have been able to attract migrants from the poorer, generally peripheral areas of the country, those areas that had been most directly affected by *ujamaa* and villagization in the 1970s. Mbonile (1993) has shown how migrants from Makete District, a poor isolated area of Iringa Region in Southern Tanzania, were in the 1980s much more likely to go to urban destinations than had been the case in the past, and that increasingly they were investing savings in land and business in these urban areas rather than in Makete itself. However, there is more migration to and opportunities from employment and informal sector business in the intermediate centres, such as Iringa and Mbeya. The attraction of Dar es Salaam and other long distance destinations has waned. These findings of Makete are similar to those found for Makambako, a less isolated town in Njombe district, also in Iringa Region (Holm, 1992).

In Tanzania the impact of structural adjustment measures seems to have been to reorder migration propensities towards urban destinations. The rural economy has not been given particular stimulus by the macro-economic changes, and in many regions there has been decline, but the majority of rural producers seem to remain attached to a rural economy that does not keep them out of the national migration system, but places greater emphasis on local coping mechanisms and survival strategies, especially for women and young people, that generate limited additional incomes locally in such informal sector activities as beer brewing, for example, in Mbeya Region (Nkhoma-Wamunza, 1992), or small scale agriculture, for example, in Dodoma District (Ndaro, 1992). These act to blur the wider policy issues, such as the conflict between 'state' and 'the market' and between 'town' and 'country' as locations for economic activity. There is little evidence of economic determinism in migration systems, though economic motivations for migration are strong. However, they are not sufficient in themselves to 'explain' the migration system, nor changes in it.

The broader basis of historical and cultural relationships acts in Tanzania, as elsewhere, to weaken the direct impact of national economic policies and circumstances on patterns of movement. Yet it is clear that these larger issues in the nature and structure of the national economic policy environment have their feedback to migration. In one important respect, however, there is conflicting evidence on the effect of structural adjustment on migration, and this

concerns the persistence of circulation. Circular labour migration, a form of
migration that characterized colonial East Africa, remains very prominent
into the 1990s, allowing migrants to become involved in the commercial,
modern sector, while at the same time permitting them to retain an economic
and social commitment to the rural source areas. The persistence of circular
mobility into independence has been widely documented for Kenya (Elkan,
1985), Uganda (Gould, 1992) and Tanzania (Lwoga, 1989), suggesting a persistence of the structural conditions that favoured circulation. In Kenya the
continuity of these conditions in a neo-colonial economy of sharp differentials between core and periphery has allowed substantial circulation to persist. These are most commonly associated with urban 'industrial' labour
(Tostensen, 1991), but wider conflicts in contemporary Kenyan society,
between 'town' and 'country', between 'modern' and 'traditional', remain.
These conflicts were strongly exemplified by the S. M. Otieno affair between
December, 1986, and May, 1987—the legal and political battle over whether
the remains of the dead man would be buried near Nairobi or at his rural
'home' area in Nyanza Province (Cohen and Atieno-Odhiambo, 1989: esp.
Afterword, pp. 133–39).

   In Tanzania, on the other hand, the incidence of permanent migration to
towns seems to have been higher, at least in a direct comparison between Dar
es Salaam and Nairobi (Hazlewood *et al.*, 1989: esp. p.277), and there is evidence, for example, in Holm (1992), Mbonile (1993) and Van Donge (1992),
to suggest that the importance of circulation has been further weakening
under the structural adjustment measures of the last decade. The major sisal
estates have been broken up and their labour force have either returned to
their original areas or have remained as peasant farmers on former estate
land. Former labour reserves now find migrants leave for nearby destinations,
predominantly urban, and they are less likely than they were in the past to
return to live or invest in productive farming or even in social facilities such
as schools in the rural area. Rather they develop a greater commitment to the
town in which they work or have business and visit immediate rural hinterlands (Baker and Mwaiselage, 1993:30).

   There seems to be an increasing divergence in experience between Kenya
and Tanzania with respect to the persistence of circulation, and the situation
in Uganda is clouded by the political uncertainties in that country, though the
uncertainty of urban life and the modern economy in Uganda would imply a
greater incentive to retain a rural commitment and continue involvement in
circular mobility. Much more needs to be known about the persistence of circulation under structural adjustment, and whether there is built into the
model for African economies that is being sought through macro-economic
policies the presumption, characteristic of the economic history of the Western development experience, of an urban transition at the end of which the
majority of the population will necessarily be living in towns in an advanced
and transformed economy.

ECONOMIC IMPACT OF LABOUR MIGRATION IN SOURCE REGIONS

While migrants in East Africa have clearly been attracted to towns and to
areas of commercial farming and the impact of their migration has been criti-

cal to the economic development of these destination regions, the impact of
the out-migration in the source areas of the migrants has seen widely differentiated effects. These sources are typically regions of African farming with varying and changing degrees of commercialization and integration with the
market economy. Within these regions, therefore, as within the destination
areas, there is a changing demand for labour, both in quantity and in type. In
particular, with increased commercialization there is normally a decline in the
relative importance (though not necessarily absolute importance) of family
labour relative to hired labour. The impact on labour supply and demand at
source and at destination of the migration flows clearly links with the issue of
the persistence of circulation that was raised above. If there were to be more
permanent out-migration, then there may be benefits if there is in that source
area considerable population pressure on scarce land resources, such that
more land and productive resources become available to those left behind.
On the other hand, if there is permanent migration of individuals from areas
of substantial potential for further rural development—and this is often the
case in the wetter highland regions in East Africa—the loss of labour and/or
the remittances, skills and knowledge of migrants will adversely effect the
household from which they leave as well as the economy of the area as a
whole.

However, it is still the case that throughout much of East Africa circular
mobility is important in the migration systems, and that there is a very substantial impact of rural–urban interaction on the rural source regions. The
general features and effects of the rural–urban interface at the local scale have
been well described, and in great detail, in the various case studies in Baker
and Pedersen (1992), so that there is no need to repeat them here. However,
the important point from the migration perspective is that the impact of
migration on the source regions is strongly differentiated within and between
each of the three countries of East Africa.

In Uganda the source regions for migration of internal migrants have traditionally been the peripheral and often densely populated regions of the country: in the south-west, in Kigezi on the border with Rwanda and Zaire, and in
West Nile in the north-west on the border with Zaire and Sudan. The reversion in the 1970s and 1980s to a coping subsistence economy with sharp ethnic conflicts has probably reduced the incidence of long distance migration
and long absences from source areas, especially from the north since 1986
with the establishment of a government dominated by and supported by people from the south and west. But in that coping situation the benefits from
more labour being available for food production have undoubtedly contributed to economic survival and community cohesion, particularly in the better
watered and fertile areas of the country, including Buganda along the northern shore of Lake Victoria. Here land is relatively abundant and fertile, and is
available for resettlement of internal migrants, especially in areas where
former immigrant labour on coffee farms, traditionally from Rwanda,
Burundi and south-west Uganda, have returned to their source regions and
countries with the collapse of the coffee economy. Some of these migrants
have come from towns and from the military, and with the end of the military
regimes, there have been structured resettlement packages targeted at demo-

bilized soldiers to return to their rural home areas and develop farming (Colletta and Ball, 1993).

The scourge of AIDS in Uganda has also had an economic effect on the migration system. Barnett and Blaikie (1992) identify a retreating frontier of cultivation in Rakai and other once economically vibrant districts severely affected by high HIV-sero prevalence and AIDS mortality. An area of in-migration has become an area of out-migration, with a downward cycle in the rural economy associated with that out-migration. In addition, the spread of the disease has been facilitated by migration—along the main lorry routes and by the migration of prostitutes into towns out of the affected rural areas and small settlements (Barnett and Blaikie, 1992, 27–8). However Barnett and Blaikie show that those agricultural systems most vulnerable to the impact of AIDS mortality (as a result of labour requirements per unit of output) are not those with highest levels of HIV-sero prevalence; nor are these the areas of highest out-migration in the past (Barnett and Blaikie, 1992, 144–8). The impact of AIDS on migration in Uganda cannot yet be separately identified from the impact of the more general economic disruption. However, it is certain to have affected patterns of land use and labour demand in affected areas, either to reduce outflows where labour is needed to replace the labour that is lost through the disease, or, and much more in evidence in the short-term, to accelerate permanent out-migration of the destitute population that remains, disproportionately comprising children and the elderly.

AIDS is also a serious problem in Tanzania, though its economic effects have been less intensively studied. Since it is a much larger country than Uganda, with a much wider range of economic and environmental conditions, the relationships between AIDS and migration and AIDS and the rural economy are likely to be highly diverse, but the same general issues probably apply: that its incidence and impact on rural economies are highly variable, more likely to be high in areas of considerable in- and out-migration, such as the Kagera Region in the extreme north-west of the country on the border with the most adversely affected district of Uganda (Weiss, 1993), and also more generally in towns (Baker and Mwaiselage, 1993:70–71).

For Tanzania a much more important issue for the nature of the migration system has been the regional differentiation of economic performance. There are a few regions of relatively buoyant economic productivity surrounded by large areas of limited environmental and economic potential and often very low population densities. Those areas of commercial peasant agriculture, such as Kilimanjaro (with coffee), Isamani in Iringa (wheat and tobacco), have traditionally used family rather than wage labour and so were not major regions of in-migration. However, various studies (for example, Collier et al., 1986; Van Donge, 1992) have indicated an increasing commercialization of the labour force in such areas, partly due to increasing inequalities within these regions creating a class of labourers, often casual day labourers, but also generating longer distance demands for labour.

Although it is clear from the high rates of urban growth in Tanzania that towns have become the preferred destinations, Collier et al. (1986) argued that urban migration in the mid-1980s was still having an impact on rural production through remittance of urban earnings. Their national sample (drawn from 18 districts in 8 regions with 600 households altogether) confirmed the importance of circulation:

> Migrants generally keep in touch with the village. Only a quarter of those who had migrated never returned to the village (p.37).

However they also argue that:

> Migration can be dichotomized into two distinct patterns, short-duration circular migration and permanent one-way migration. Those migrants who had returned to live in the village had mostly been absent from the village for only a short period. Indeed 70 per cent of them had returned either during the year of their departure or in the subsequent year. By contrast 80 per cent of those currently migrant had been absent from the village for longer than that (p.37).

More returned migrants than current migrants remitted money. They remitted a much higher proportion (over 30 per cent) of their total earnings and were an important source of income to those households (less than 20 per cent) with a migrant member. There is some further evidence in their data to support the case, discussed in the previous section of this chapter, for a shift from circular to permanent migration in Tanzania, but the sample cannot be disaggregated by region to investigate the extent to which there is a regional effect in that differentiation or in the ways in which the remittance income is spent.

There is very strong evidence from Kenya, however, that the impact of migration and return, and of remitted income in the source region is highly variable. In particular there is a great contrast between Central Province, on the one hand, and Western and Nyanza Provinces on the other. These are the three main regions of out-migration in Kenya, all 'labour reserves' in the colonial period with a persistence of circular migration of wage labourers, mostly men, with periodic return. In Central Province, however, near Nairobi, there is a vibrant rural economy with peasant production of vegetable products for the urban (and foreign) market as well as coffee and tea for export production. There is a strong rural off-farm employment sector in the formal and informal economy. In these circumstances there is still migration, mostly to Nairobi, but also some remittance of earnings to develop the rural economy. Collier and Lal (1984, 1986) have argued that in this area remittance income has been an important engine for rural development, with investment on the farm and in the off-farm sector.

In Western and Nyanza Provinces population densities, as in Central Province, are high and, again as in Central Province, rainfall is abundant and well distributed, and soils are relatively rich, such that environmental differences between these provinces are not great. However economic conditions are very different. Western and Nyanza Provinces are relatively remote from Nairobi and have not experienced such a development of a cash crop economy as Central Province. Farm incomes are much lower and the potential for productive investment on the land and in the much smaller off-farm sector is much more limited. Remittances in these much poorer conditions are a more significant proportion of household income, and more used for consumption and household survival rather than for investment to raise local income. Substantial sums in these circumstances are allocated to education and school fees so that the flow of migrants to urban jobs can be maintained or increased, for education and the subsequent mobility of the educated is perceived to be the key to urban income (Gould, 1988, in press). However, there are some areas of higher income and potential in Western Province, such as Bungoma District where rates of out migration are lower and there is potential for investment of migrants' remittances into the farm economy (Lavrijsen, 1984).

In the most densely populated and impoverished areas of western Kenya the continuing role of the migration system would appear to be to ensure household survival at the local level, and to maintain the major contribution of workers to the national migration system. In these regions circular migration seems to perpetuate, indeed exacerbate, the status quo of poverty and rural underdevelopment. In the more dynamic regions by contrast, circular migration appears to contribute to that dynamism through investment of remitted income. The local impact of migration is clearly sensitive to local economic conditions, and this is likely also to be valid for Tanzania and Uganda. However, we do not yet know how and why regional effects of migration on source regions are differentiated, and this is clearly a theme that further research needs to pursue. It is a theme that cannot be pursued using the small and spatially dispersed sample of 600 households from 18 districts that Collier *et al.* used in Tanzania. However, it is a theme that could be developed in a well structured national migration survey of the type described above for Botswana.

MIGRATION AND THE ENVIRONMENT

While the problems associated with and prospects for macro- and micro-*economic* change and their relationships with the national migration systems in East Africa have been the most prominent focus of the migration discourse in recent years, they have to be set against a larger set of problems and prospects associated with macro- and micro-*environmental* change. At the broad regional scale north-eastern Africa has been identified by FAO as being among the most critical regions, with a prognosis for medium-term environmental change towards progressive declines in precipitation and consequent expansion in the land area currently considered to be marginal for agriculture and, in the driest areas, marginal even for pastoralist economies (Parry, 1990:4–5). The migration implications of these predicted environmental changes would be to encourage permanent or even temporary (i.e. seasonal) settlement retreat to wetter areas out of north and north-east Kenya, Karamoja in north-east Uganda and from areas of central Tanzania to those areas where there are already higher densities of population and greater settlement concentration. This is in direct contrast to the general movement into drier areas in all three counties in the last few decades (Dietz, 1986; Kabera, 1985; Thomas, 1982). Furthermore, there are fairly high population densities along the East African coast, and in areas where livelihoods might be somewhat threatened by sea-level rise and loss of some land through salination or inundation, again with the implication of settlement retreat inland in the absence of elaborate and perhaps very expensive coastal management measures (Suliman, 1990). The area of the delta of the Rufiji, south of Dar es Salaam, might be particularly vulnerable in this respect. Although the impact of these predicted large-scale environmental changes is not yet directly apparent, this may need to be an issue for major policy and academic consideration in the medium and longer term.

A much more familiar consideration is the converse of this relationship: the impact of population movement on the environment, though operating at a more localized scale. Much mobility in traditional subsistence societies has been a response to population pressure to prevent over-cultivation or over-grazing. Traditional movement of cultivators in shifting cultivation systems and of pastoralists with their herds has been an integral feature of the mainte-nance of sustainable environmental systems, as in Samburu in Kenya (Ayiemba, 1990). However, movement into new areas also has an impact at destination. New problems are created in new areas. The high and continuing rates of population growth in recent decades in all three countries have cre-ated pressures for movement, either in spontaneous resettlement (for exam-ple, from Kigezi in south west Uganda into the traditional pastoralist lands of Ankole immediately to the east (Rutaremwa, 1990), or in organized resettle-ment schemes, the most celebrated of which was the 'million acre scheme' in the Kenya Highlands after independence as a political response to 'land hun-ger' in the overcrowded former African reserves (Odingo, 1971).

The nature of the relationships between population growth, migration and the environment in the most densely populated areas has been very much conditioned by their variable economic conditions. In relatively poor and impoverished high density areas, such as in south-west and north-west Uganda, in western Kenya (Gould, in press), in Kagera Region in north-west Tanzania, in the Ulugurus in Central Tanzania (Van Donge, 1992) and in south-west Tanzania (Mbonile, 1993), migration has remained an essential feature of household survival. There has been a continuity in the circular migration from the colonial period with out-migration of household mem-bers, usually men, to earn remittances that can ensure supplements to family income. In these areas family land is in short supply and there is little possi-bility of substantially increasing income from that land, for this would neces-sitate the adoption of a high risk strategy of a shift in land use from primarily subsistence production to primarily commercial production. Not only are these peripheral areas remote from the markets for commercial production, but there is usually insufficient land available to divert production from the first priority of basic subsistence. In the most accessible and more prosperous high density areas, such as in Central Province of Kenya and the Chagga homeland on Mt. Kilimanjaro in Tanzania, migration, as noted above, can become a source of funds for investment in the commercial farm economy. Furthermore, local off-farm employment is more readily available in these commercially vibrant rural economies, thus reducing the need for the migra-tion response to direct per capita land declines. In these circumstances the strength of the economic system is critical in mediating the migration/envi-ronment relationship and allowing the absorption of surplus labour (Living-stone, 1989).

Migration can assist the intensification process in situations of population growth by bringing stronger linkages between rural production systems and the broader commercial and economic structures of the nation. There is now increasing evidence of a positive relationship between population growth and per capita rural production under conditions of political stability and commercial development, as in Machakos District of Kenya (Tiffen, 1991) and in several communities in Tanzania (Eele *et al.*, 1992). However, it is clear that the potential for sustainable intensification under conditions of population growth is strengthened by the persistence of circular out-migration and the availability of remittance income, even though that persistence may itself be a factor in the continuing 'immiseration' of these rural regions (Tostensen, 1991).

Most government settlement schemes, however, have been premissed on a presumption of permanent migration to settle in the new lands, usually at densities well below the prevailing densities at the origin, for the environmental capacity of the new areas will usually be lower. Environmental problems can arise in the new settlements, with depletion of biotic resources of pasture and fuelwood, often in association with inadequate water management in low rainfall areas where irrigation may be essential for agriculture, and where, as in the schemes on the lower Tana River of Kenya, there has been serious and debilitating resurgence of malaria through anopheles infestation with the presence of additional water courses (Alakoski-Johansson and Johansson, 1991; Hughes, 1984). However, most resettlement onto marginal lands has been spontaneous and small-scale, but has brought small-scale pressures into local environments that may have disrupted their fragile stability. The most serious and most growing problems of environmental deterioration occur in East Africa in those marginal lands with relatively low but, as a result of in-migration, rapidly growing population densities, and not in the areas of higher densities from which the migrants tend to come.

A special case of such additional pressures on the environment as a result of population movement is associated with the villagization in Tanzania. The rationale for settlement concentration was that the social infrastructure could be better and more cheaply provided to larger settlements, and that the political objective of promoting more communal production would be more easily achieved. Both these objectives were met in part (the first being much less problematic than the second), but often at the expense of adverse environmental effects. Most of Tanzania, and particularly those poorer regions where villagization was most vigorously promoted, has low quality savanna environments that cannot, under normal circumstances, support high densities of population and permanent cultivation. In the new nucleated distribution of population, fields near the villages tended to be over-cultivated and pastures over-grazed (additional water supplies had often been made available in the village) so that severe environmental deterioration has often been the result (Kjekshus, 1977; McCall 1985). One response has been to encourage some settlement dispersal, at least seasonally, for some farmers, disproportionately women (McCall, 1987), to spend more time away from the village tending their traditional *shambas* at some distance. Intensification has not led to sustainable agriculture in the majority of environments, and environmental deterioration may be a more cogent explanation than communalization of agriculture for production shortfalls (Bryceson, 1990). In Kenya, by contrast, the essence of resettlement since the 1960s has been individualised holdings, consistent with the national individualist ideology, and thus farmers were immediately responsible for managing their own environmental resources and maintaining sustainable systems, though not without difficulty, as the Lower Tana experience, noted above, has shown.

The growing migration to towns also imposed additional burdens on urban and peri-urban environments. Rapid migration to large and to small towns has imposed substantial burdens on the urban infrastructure and on the sustainability of the whole urban system. Due to the predominance of commuting as a characteristic form of population mobility around small towns, this has not been a severe problem for small centres since housing and food continue to be provided from the family *shamba* (Ngau, 1991). For large towns, however, and particularly Nairobi and Dar es Salaam, the predominance of migration in their growth has serious environmental consequences. Housing and other infrastructure provision has failed to keep up with needs, resulting in familiar Third World problems of overcrowded and illegal housing with grossly inadequate water and waste management systems. Furthermore, the food provisioning of these towns has become a major issue. In Nairobi, situated near the fertile highlands of Central and Rift Valley Provinces, there is an abundant food supply, and the presence of a large and relatively prosperous urban market has indeed had a very favourable impact on rural production. In Dar es Salaam, by contrast, situated in a much less benign environment, the problems of food supply are more difficult, and solved by more cultivation within the urban area itself and with intensification and associated environmental pressures in the peri-urban rural areas (Briggs, 1991), as well as longer distance supplies, for example, from the Usambara mountains (Sender and Smith, 1990), from the Ulugurus (Van Donge, 1992) and from Dodoma (Ndaro, 1992).

CONCLUSION

In this highly selective overview of current issues in migration in East Africa, the emphasis has been placed on seeking to compare some of the local and national experiences of how development has affected migration and also how migration has affected the differential impact of development. Inevitably explicit consideration of many critical issues, such as the role of women in migration and the impact of basic needs and social provision on patterns of movement (Gould, 1990), has been omitted. Problems of synthesis are in part due to the principal issue raised in Section 2 of this chapter: the lack of systematic national migration surveys that can provide adequate reference points to which the range of empirical studies can be related. Since policy relevant and intellectually challenging migration research is seriously constrained by the absence of such a context, an overview of this kind is likely to raise more questions than it can provide answers. The developmental context for the study of migration is enormously variable and constantly changing, and the migration experience in Kenya, Tanzania and Uganda reflects that complexity.

References

Alakoski-Johansson, Gunilla and Stig Johansson, 1991, "From bushland to butcheries: concepts and adaptation in small town development in Bura, Kenya", Paper presented at a conference on *the dynamics of internal non-metropolitan migration and linkage in Africa*, Kristiansand, Norway, September.

Ayiemba, Elias H.O., 1990, "Environmental perception as a stimulant to rural migration in semi-arid ecosystems: a case study of Sambura District in Kenya", in Spontaneous Papers, Volume prepared from Union for African Population Studies *Conference on migration in the 1990s*, Nairobi, February.

Baker, Jonathan and Poul Ove Pedersen (eds.), 1992, *The rural–urban interface in Africa*. Uppsala: Scandinavian Institute of African Studies, Seminar Proceedings, no. 27.

Baker, Jonathan and Agnes A. Mwaiselage, 1993, *Three Town Study in Tanzania*. Report prepared for the Infrastructure Division, SIDA, March 1993. Uppsala: Scandinavian Institute of African Studies.

Banugire, Firimooni R., 1989, "Employment, incomes, basic needs and structural adjustment policy in Uganda", in Bade Onimode (ed.), *The IMF, the World Bank and the African debt*, Volume 2: the social and economic impact, 95–110. London: Zed Books.

Barnett, Tony and Piers Blaikie, 1992, *AIDS in Africa: its present and future impact*. London: Belhaven Press.

Botswana Government, 1982, *Migration in Botswana: patterns causes and consequences*. Final Report of the National Migration Survey. Gaborone: Central Statistical Office, 3 Volumes.

Briggs, John, 1991, "The peri-urban zone of Dar es Salaam, Tanzania: recent trends and changes in agricultural land use", *Transactions, Institute of British Geographers*, 16, 3: 319–31.

Bryceson, D.F., 1990, *Food insecurity and the social division of labour in Tanzania, 1919–1985*. Oxford: Macmillan.

Cheru, Fantu, 1989, "The role of the IMF and World Bank in the agrarian crisis of Sudan and Tanzania: sovereignty vs. control", in Bade Onimode (ed.), *The IMF, the World Bank and the African debt*, Volume 2: social and economic impact, 77–94. London: Zed Books.

Claeson, C.F. and B. Egerö, 1973, "Migration", in B. Egerö and R.A. Henin (eds.), *The population of Tanzania: an analysis of the 1967 population census*. University of Dar es Salaam, BRALUP, Vol. 6, 56–75.

Cohen, D.W. and E.S. Atieno-Odhiambo, 1989, *Siaya, The historical anthropology of an African landscape*. London: James Currey, Nairobi: Heinemann, Athens, Ohio: Ohio University Press.

Colletta, Nat and Nicole Ball, 1993, "War to peace transition in Uganda", *Finance and Development*, 20, 2:36–39.

Collier, P. and D. Lal, 1984, "Why poor people get rich: Kenya, 1960–79", *World Development*, 12, 10:1007–18.

Collier, P. and D. Lal, 1986, *Labour and poverty in Kenya: 1900–1980*. Oxford: Oxford University Press.

Collier, P., S. Radwan, S. Wangwe and A. Wagner, 1986, *Labour and poverty in rural Tanzania*. Oxford: Oxford University Press.

Dietz, T., 1986, "Migration to and from dry areas in Kenya", *Tijdschrift voor Economishe en Sociale Geografie*, 77, 1:18–26.

Eele, Graham, Alex Duncan and Andrew Lawson, 1992, "Environmental change and the response by small scale farmers: some evidence from Tanzania", Paper presented at a *conference on environment and population change*, Oxford, September.

Elkan, Walter, 1985, "Is a proletariat emerging in Nairobi?", in R.M. Prothero and M. Chapman (eds.), *Circulation in Third World countries*, 369–79. London: Routledge and Kegan Paul.

Gould, W.T.S., 1987, "Urban bias, regional differentiation and rural–urban interaction in Kenya", *African Urban Quarterly*, 2, 2:122–33.

Gould, W.T.S., 1988, "Urban–rural return migration in Western Province, Kenya", *Proceedings of the African Population Conference*, Dakar, International Union for the Scientific Study of Population, Liege, Vol. 2, 4.1:41–55.

Gould, W.T.S., 1990, "Migration and basic needs in Africa", in Aderanti Adepoju (ed.), *The role of migration in African development: issues and policies for the 1990s,* 142–55. Dakar: Union for African Population Studies.

Gould, W.T.S., 1992, "Population mobility", in M.B. Gleave (ed.), *Tropical African development,* 284–314. London: Longman.

Gould, W.T.S., in press, "Population growth, migration and environmental stability in Western Kenya: from Malthus to Boserup", in J.I. Clarke and B. Zaba (eds.), *Environment and population change.* Liege: Ordina Editions for IUSSP.

Gould, W.T.S. and R.M. Prothero, 1975, "Time and space in African population mobility", in L.A. Kosinski and R.M. Prothero (eds.), *People on the move,* 39–49. London: Methuen.

Hansen, Holger Bernt and Michael Twaddle, 1991, *Changing Uganda: The dilemmas of structural adjustment and revolutionary change.* London: James Currey, Kampala: Fountain Press, Athens, Ohio: Ohio University Press.

Hazlewood, Arthur with J. Armitage, H. Berry, J. Knight and R Sabot, 1991, *Education, work and pay in East Africa.* Oxford: Clarendon Press.

Holm, Mogens, 1992, "Survival strategies of migrants to Makambako", in Jonathan Baker and Poul Ove Pedersen (eds.), *The rural–urban interface in Africa,* Seminar Proceedings, no. 27, 238–57. Uppsala: Scandinavian Institute of African Studies.

House, William J. and Henry Rempel, 1980, "The determinants of interregional migration in Kenya", *World Development,* 8, 1:25–35.

Hoyle, B.S., 1979, "African socialism and urban development: the relocation of the Tanzanian capital", *Tijdschrift voor Economische en Sociale Geografie,* 70, 3:207–16.

Hughes, F.M.R.,1984, "A comment on the impact of development schemes on the floodplain forest of the Tana River of Kenya", *Geographical Journal,* 150, 2:230–44.

Jamal, Vali, 1991, "The agrarian context of the Ugandan crisis", in Holger Bernt Hansen and Michael Twaddle (eds.), *Changing Uganda: The dilemmas of structural adjustment and revolutionary change,* 78–97. London: James Currey, Kampala: Fountain Press, Athens, Ohio: Ohio University Press.

Kabera, John B., 1985, "Populating Uganda's dry lands", in J.I. Clarke, M. Khogali and L.A. Kosinski (eds.), *Population and development projects in Africa,* 112–22. Cambridge: Cambridge University Press.

Kabera, J.B., 1990, Implications of returned Ugandans for the rehabilitation of Uganda's economy, in Spontaneous Papers, Volume prepared from the Union for African Population Studies *Conference on Migration in the 1990s,* Nairobi, February, 603–12.

Kenya Government, 1982, *1979 Population Census, Volume II, Analytical Report.* Nairobi: Central Bureau of Statistics, Ministry of Finance and Planning.

Kjekshus, H., 1977, "The Tanzanian villagization policy: implementational lessons and policy dimensions", *Canadian Journal of African Studies,* 11, 2:269–82.

Lateef, K. Sarwar, 1991, "Structural Adjustment in Uganda: the initial experience", in Holger Bernt Hansen and Michael Twaddle (eds.), *Changing Uganda: The dilemmas of structural adjustment and revolutionary change,* 20–42. London: James Currey, Kampala: Fountain Press, Athens, Ohio: Ohio University Press.

Lavrijsen, J.S.G., 1984, *Rural poverty and impoverishment in Western Kenya,* Utrecht: Utrechtse Geografische Studies, 33.

Livingstone, I., 1989, "Population growth and rural labour absorption in Eastern and Southern Africa", in G. McNicholl and M. Cain (eds.), Rural development and population. Institutions and policy. Supplement to *Population and Development Review,* 15, 324–42.

Lwoga, C.F.M., 1989, "From long-term to seasonal labour migration in Iringa Region, Tanzania: a legacy of the colonial forced labour system", in A. Zegeye and I. Ishumo (eds.), *Forced labour and migration: patterns of movement within Africa,* 180–210. London: Hans Zell Publications.

Mabogunje, A.L., 1971, "Systems approach to the theory of rural–urban migration", *Geographical Analysis,* 2, 1:1–18.

Masser, I. and W.T.S. Gould, 1975, *Interregional migration in tropical Africa.* London: Institute of British Geographers, Special Publication, no. 8.

Mbonile, Milline, 1993, *Migration and structural change in Tanzania: The case of Makete District,* unpublished Ph.D. thesis, University of Liverpool, Department of Geography.

McCall, M., 1985, "Environmental and agricultural impacts of Tanzania's villagization programme", in J.I. Clarke, M. Khogali and L.A. Kosinski (eds.), *Population and development projects in Africa*, 123–40. Cambridge: Cambridge University Press.

McCall, M., 1987, "Carrying heavier burdens but carrying less weight: some implications of villagization for women in Tanzania", in J.H. Momsen and J. Townsend (eds.), *Geography of gender in the Third World*, 192–214. London: Hutchinson.

Mosley, Paul, 1991, "Kenya", in Paul Mosley, John Toye and Jane Harrigan (eds.), *Aid and power: The World Bank and policy-based learning*. London: Routledge.

Ndaro, Japheth M.N., 1992, "Local coping strategies in Dodoma District, Tanzania", in D.R.F. Taylor and Fiona MacKenzie (eds.), *Development from within: Survival in rural Africa*, 170–96. London: Routledge.

Ngau, Peter, 1991, "Commuting and migration to small urban centres in Kenya", Paper presented to the Conference on *the dynamics of internal non-metropolitan migration and linkage in Africa*, Kristiansand, Norway, September.

Nkhoma-Wamunza, Alice, 1992, "The informal sector: a strategy for survival in Tanzania", in D.R.F. Taylor and Fiona MacKenzie (eds.), *Development from within: Survival in rural Africa*, 197–213. London: Routledge.

Obudho, R.A., 1984, "National urban and regional planning in Kenya", *Third World Planning Review*, 6, 4:363–88.

Obudho, R.A., 1989, "Urbanization and urban policy in East Africa", in K. Swindell, J.M. Baba and M.J. Mortimore (eds.), *Inequality and development: case studies from the Third World.*, 292–315. London: Macmillan for the Commonwealth Foundation.

Obudho, R.A., 1990, "The changing nature of Kenya's urban demography", in Spontaneous Papers, Volume prepared from Union for African Population Studies *Conference on Migration in the 1990s*, Nairobi, February, 214–34.

Odingo, R.S., 1971, *The Kenya Highlands*. Nairobi: East African Publishing House.

Ominde, S.H., 1968, *Land and population movements in Kenya*. Nairobi: Heinemann.

Parry, Martin, 1990, *Climatic change and world agriculture.*. London: Earthscan.

Piché, Victor, 1990, "Potentialités et originalité d'une enquête rétrospective pour l'étude de la migration", in Aderanti Adepoju (ed.), *Conference on the role of migration in African development: issues and policies for the 1990s*. Commissioned Papers, Dakar: Union for African Population Studies, 283–313.

Rutaremwa, G., 1990, "Population resettlement in Uganda: past, present and future", in Spontaneous Papers, Volume prepared from the Union for African Population Studies *Conference on the role of migration in African development*, Nairobi, February, 576–86.

Sender, J. and S. Smith, 1990, *Poverty, class and gender in rural Africa: a Tanzanian case study*. London: Routledge.

Skeldon, Ronald, 1990, *Population mobility in developing countries*. London: Belhaven Press.

Southall, A.W., 1961, "Population movements in East Africa", in K.M. Barbour and R.M. Prothero (eds.), *Essays on African population*, 157–92. London: Routledge and Kegan Paul.

Suliman, Mohamed (ed.), 1990, *Greenhouse effect and its impact on Africa*. London: Institute for African Alternatives.

Thomas, I.D., 1982, "Villagization in Tanzania: planning potential and practical problems", in J.I. Clarke and L.A. Kosinski (eds.), *Redistribution of population in Africa*, 182–90. London: Heinemann.

Thomas, Ian, 1985, "Development and population redistribution: measuring recent population redistribution in Tanzania", in J.I. Clarke, M. Khogali and L.A. Kosinski (eds.), *Population and development projects in Africa*, 141–52. Cambridge: C.U.P.

Tiffen, Mary, 1992, *Environmental change and dryland management in Machakos District, Kenya. Population Profile*, Working Paper 54. London: Overseas Development Institute.

Tostensen, Arne, 1991, "Between shamba and factory: Industrial labour migration in Kenya", in P. Coughlin and G.K. Ikiara (eds.), *Kenya's industrialization dilemma*, 291–308. Nairobi: Heinemann.

Uganda Government, 1982, *Report on the 1980 population Census. Volume 1: the provisional results by administrative areas*. Kampala: Census Office, Ministry of Planning and Economic Development.

Van Donge, Jan Kees, 1992, "Agricultural decline in Tanzania: the case of the Uluguru mountains", *African Affairs*, 91, 1:73–94.

Weiss, Brad, 1993, "'Buying her grave': money, movement and AIDS in north-west Tanzania", *Africa*, 63, 1:19–35.

Woods, R.I., 1993, "Classics in Human Geography revisited. 'Zelinsky, W. 1971. The hypothesis of the mobility transition'". Commentary 1, *Progress in Human Geography*, 17, 2:213–19.

Part III

The Range of Migration Experience

The Small Town as a Retirement Centre

Margaret Peil

Small towns are sometimes seen as very similar to villages, though somewhat larger. This partly depends on the country's history and pattern of urbanization and the size of the town in relation to the size and level of urbanization of the country. It also depends on the level of economic development (what services the small town can provide, the state of the transportation system) and the nature of political life. (How centralized and democratic is governmental authority and are traditional forms of local leadership still functioning?)

People settle in small towns rather than in large cities or villages at various stages of the life cycle and for a variety of reasons. For many, it is accidental. They were born there, their family lives there, and the town is "home", regardless of whether they have spent all of their life there or merely return in old age. Others happen to get a job there and decide to stay. They buy land, build a house and raise their children there, establishing a new branch of their lineage. Still others make a purposive move, either because this is the nearest urban place to their village, because it seems to provide a good opportunity for their skill or business, or because they have relatives already settled there who can help them get established. Migrants today have more information on various alternatives than was the case thirty to forty years ago, but this information is still far from comprehensive and relies largely on word of mouth. The opening of a factory, new civil status (with more administrative posts) or the availability of secondary or university schooling may be the attractant, especially for people migrating for the first time in their teens or twenties.

Older migrants are probably better informed and make their decisions on a somewhat different basis, though the pull of economic opportunities and family ties continues to be important. This chapter focuses on the "senior citizens" (people over sixty) living in small African towns. Why are they living in these towns and what are the implications of this choice for them and for the town?

RETIREMENT MIGRATION

Africans have generally preferred to return to their place of origin, on retirement or before, rather than leaving for good and settling permanently in the host location. This preference has an economic base; in most cases they retain or can regain land rights and thus support themselves by farming at home. The continuing importance of this link has been demonstrated with the high inflation and food shortages of Ghana in the 1970s and the widespread redundancies in Nigeria in the 1980s. If the worker does not go home himself in times of trouble, he may send his wife and children home, where they can be self-supporting. Village primary schools may be less crowded than urban ones, and do not require parents' tax certificates as a condition of enrolment. In addition to economic reasons, social norms strongly support continued ties to the extended family, associated with the ancestral home. Many village leaders put considerable effort into maintaining migrants' interest, so that they will help with local development projects.

Finally, there is very little government welfare available in African countries and few people have pensions, so the dependent elderly rely on family assistance. Insofar as communal land cannot be sold, rights to it cannot be lost by migration and in theory can be revived whenever the migrant chooses. Contacts with the extended family at home are often maintained through remittances and visits. There are exceptions, based on choice or government policy. For example, Hausa migrants in northern Nigeria often sell their land when they leave and thus have no reason to return (Hill, 1972). Collectivisation of land in Tanzania means that those who are not members of the village cooperative have nothing to return to and thus generally plan a permanent stay, especially in Dar es Salaam. Severe overcrowding of the Communal Areas in Zimbabwe means that long-term absentees may have trouble finding land to farm at home.

For those who do go home (in the past at least, the majority of southern Ghanaians and Nigerians; see Caldwell, 1969), the timing often depends on the circumstances. Many people say that they will go home when they retire or when they are old, but causation and definition may well be in the other direction—they consider themselves old when they go home, or they retire from an urban job when conditions seem ripe for the return home. Middle-aged men may inherit the family farm or be elected to a chieftaincy, or may decide that they may as well carry on their trade or business in their home-town as in a major city. Many middle aged men returned to their provincial hometowns during the Nigerian oil boom to set up businesses—partly local chauvinism and partly because competition is less than in the capital.

Becoming a widow may precipitate a woman's return home in middle or old age, but they are more likely than men to prefer remaining in a town (large or small), because their children can support them there; they also continue their economic and social roles by trading and looking after the grandchildren. Women may not see moving to their husband's home or dependence on their own extended family as a worthwhile alternative.

A migration stream of increasing importance is the movement of elderly women, often widows, to towns and cities to live with a son or daughter. In the past, she would probably have remained at home, asking her children to send a grandchild to run errands and help around the house (Bledsoe and Isiugo-Abanihe, 1989). As parents increasingly prefer to educate their children in town, it seems more sensible for granny to join the family there. Another reason for moving to the city in old age is health care. While this is improving in villages, especially in Zimbabwe, health services are much better in towns and cities; old people can live with a son and his family while using these services, and may settle down permanently. Urban accommodation is often crowded, but if there is room having parents in the household or nearby may be seen as preferable to frequent long journeys to visit them at home. (Élites may well prefer and be able to afford separate accommodation for their parents, to retain authority in their own households and avoid criticism of their "modern" way of life.) From the old person's point of view, propinquity usually means more support than they would get at a distance.

Old men are less likely than women to agree to settle in an unfamiliar town, because they have larger economic, political and social resources at home. They usually control the land and help to run the village. They get more support from friends and relatives in the village than their wives do, since the latter are often outsiders who have married into the village. Thus, an elderly man would try to get his son to return to help with the farming rather than joining his son in town, whereas an elderly woman, whose life is centred on the household, is less uprooted when moving to join children and grandchildren in town (Masamba ma Mpolo, 1984).

SAMPLES

This chapter uses data from two studies of the elderly and an earlier sample census. While definitions of old age are necessarily imprecise in these countries, sixty has been used as the boundary for these studies because it is the official age for retirement from wage employment and because most people over this age consider themselves and are considered "old". Women may be classified as old much earlier, when they pass the menopause, but this partly depends on their continued energy and economic activities. Since a majority of the population are self-employed, continued participation in the labour force depends more on health, need and opportunity than on age, but focusing on the over-sixties is useful for comparative purposes.

The sample census was carried out as part of a study of housing, migration and support networks in Freetown, Bo and Kenema, Sierra Leone in 1981. Freetown was omitted from this chapter because it is the capital and largest city of Sierra Leone. Bo is 230 km from Freetown, and Kenema is 64 km from Bo, in south-western Sierra Leone. The southern Nigerians (studied in 1984) lived in two provincial towns in Ogun State, Abeokuta and Ijebu Ode, about 100 km from Lagos and from each other. The elderly Zimbabweans (studied in 1989) lived in Mutare, 263 km from Harare in the north-west of the country. All of these provincial towns have been clearly urban areas throughout this century. None has recently moved from village to urban status, though Mutare and Kenema have had a relatively small population for most of this period.

The Sierra Leone study was seen as preliminary to further work on the elderly. Both Freetown and Bo have populations which have been settled there over many generations and thus were likely to include reasonable numbers of elderly people. Bo was the second largest city until it was passed in the 1960s by Koidu, the main diamond mining town. Bo is now the country's third largest city and Kenema is the fourth, with populations of 39,000 and 31,000 respectively in 1974. Both are ethnically mixed marketing towns, with considerable government employment. Bo has long been an educational centre; the first school for sons of chiefs was established there. It is the urban centre for Sierra Leone's second university college, about 75 km down the road. It has fallen on hard times in recent years; since Bo voters supported the political opposition, government investment went elsewhere. Kenema has risen in importance as a centre of diamond mining and wealth from diamond dealing. According to our sample censuses of just under 100 houses in each town, 6 per cent of the population of Bo and 4 per cent of that of Kenema were over fifty five years of age—both relatively high for African towns. Since the numbers of elderly people in each and differences between the two towns are small, the data have been combined for this chapter. A majority of those questioned in both towns thought that urban life is preferable to rural life, which helps to explain why people chose to retire in town (Peil, 1990).

The two Nigerian towns were chosen because both are "traditional" Yoruba towns which produce large numbers of migrants (educated professionals and civil servants and less educated businessmen and women) who visit regularly while working away and often settle permanently at home on retirement. Both are ethnically homogeneous (over 95 per cent Egba Yoruba in Abeokuta and Ijebu Yoruba in Ijebu Ode). Abeokuta, the state capital, is about 160 years old and has at least 400,000 residents; Ijebu Ode is at least twice as old and has about half as many people. Large numbers of migrants from both towns have settled permanently in Lagos and Ibadan, the nearby metropolises; many of these still visit their hometowns at least occasionally.

Both of these towns have long been educational and commercial centres; Nigeria's first rail line linked Abeokuta to Lagos; it had a primary school before Lagos did and the first secondary school for girls in the country was opened there. However, during the half century 1920 to 1970 both towns became backwaters. Neither town took much advantage of opportunities for development, and educated indigenes had to find success elsewhere. Ijebu migrants are noted for their business acumen and many joined the civil service (Aronson, 1980). However, both towns managed to maintain the allegiance of many of these out-migrants, and the 1970s brought both of them a chance to use these educated, successful people for local development. Whereas in 1970 Abeokuta had no cinema and only a minimum of roads, it now has a small university and many new buildings and businesses. Progress was helped by its being designated a state capital in 1976 (ensuring a large increase in wage employment and business opportunities) and by the election of a businessman as Alake (traditional ruler). Indigenes of Ijebu Ode took development of their town very seriously, borrowing money abroad to build a large new market and investing in hotels and other businesses. While the state university was located in a much smaller town nearby most of its staff and students live in Ijebu Ode.

Mutare is the fifth largest town in Zimbabwe, with 70,000 people in 1982, the majority of whom live in suburban townships. It is ethnically mixed, mainly Shona, Manica or of European origin. Like most Zimbabwean towns, it was established by Europeans, on the line of rail to the Mozambique coast, and has grown very rapidly since independence. Africans were not encouraged to settle in urban areas during the colonial period, but a few have spent many years in Mutare; now they can buy their houses. A large majority of elderly people prefer rural to urban life, but given the overcrowding of the Communal Areas, at least some remain permanently in town. Their better-educated children are more likely to do so.

The differing size of these towns poses questions on the definition of 'small town', but they are at relatively similar positions in the hierarchies of their respective countries. There are at least seven Nigerian towns larger than Abeokuta, and from the point of view of Lagos and Ibadan (with populations of 6.5 and 4.5 million), they are indeed 'small'. They are certainly 'provincial' in the style of life they provide. In contrast, Mutare seems like a large town in the Zimbabwean context because its wide streets and decentralized, spacious housing spread out the population. The proportion of the population which is urban is about the same in Nigeria and Zimbabwe and higher in Sierra Leone, but Nigeria's total population is much larger and Sierra Leone's much smaller, so a third or fourth ranked town in Sierra Leone is necessarily small. Shopping facilities are best in Mutare, the commercial centre for its region; in the Nigerian towns alternatives are not far off and the Sierra Leonean towns have a relatively poorer hinterland. There are proposals for a mission-sponsored university on the outskirts of Mutare, the only one of these towns without university links.

MIGRATION STATUS

These towns illustrate the extremes of migration experience in African countries. The proportions of elderly men and women who were non-migrants, returnees or 'newcomers' to the town where they were living are quite different, as shown in Table 1. About two fifths of the residents of Ijebu Ode had not migrated at all, and about a quarter had returned to their hometown, sometimes after university studies or a relatively short period of employment. Thus, there was a large core of people who were permanently committed to their hometown. Others returned home during the oil boom, to set up a local business. There were relatively few elderly in-migrants; while some who had migrated to Ijebu Ode looking for economic opportunities (mainly trading, but also teaching) had remained after age sixty, opportunities for migrants are much better elsewhere in the area so its pull is not strong. There will also have been numerous migrants who stayed in the town for a while, then left to return home or try their luck elsewhere. Most of the female in-migrants had married an Ijebu man and came with him when he returned home.

Abeokuta's promotion to state capital status attracted many newcomers, some of them from Ijebu Ode. They were employed by the rapidly expanding bureaucracy or provided goods or services to the growing population. Two fifths of the in-migrants were still in the labour force and some will go home when they eventually retire. However, Abeokuta typifies a pattern of rural–urban links found in several areas of West Africa, where extended families maintain ties between villages and the nearby town; men and women from the surrounding villages may have family homes in Abeokuta and settle there in old age.

Table 1. *Migration status, by location and gender* (percentage)

Status	Ijebu Ode		Abeokuta		Sierra Leone		Mutare	
	M	F	M	F	M	F	M	F
Non-migrant	44	40	15	12	2	22	5	10
Returnee	26	23	17	21	10	0	0	3
In-migrant	30	37	68	77	88	78	95	87
Total	100	100	100	100	100	100	100	100
N	117	75	131	60	41	41	131	67

Women's migration status closely paralleled that of men in all five towns, though they were somewhat more likely than men to be in-migrants in Nigeria, non-migrants in Sierra Leone and indigenes in Mutare. Sierra Leonean men appear to be more likely than women to return to the town of their birth (unlike Mutare, where no men were returnees), but these towns do not appear to have a strong pull on indigenes who have migrated. Local women had married in-migrants in both Sierra Leonean towns and in Mutare; this pattern used to be common in most parts of Africa, a product of high urban sex ratios, whereas wives married elsewhere were brought back to the Nigerian out-migrant towns.

The pattern is probably shifting in Mutare, because independence in 1980 changed people's perspectives and opportunities. It became much easier to establish residence in town, and there is now more choice as to where to spend one's old age. It is interesting to note that several elderly people had moved to Mutare from larger cities (Harare, Bulawayo and Gweru) when they retired, whereas migrants from Freetown had moved to the Sierra Leonean provincial towns much earlier, for work, and decided to stay. A few "retirees" had taken up farming on the outskirts of Mutare rather than returning to their place of origin. We did not have the resources to investigate opportunities to acquire or rent land in this area, but obviously it is possible for strangers to do this, at moderate cost. Farms are very small in the hinterland villages we studied, and the location of the newest Mutare township (Dangamvura) in open country would allow a certain amount of unauthorized farming, in addition to the small "gardens" near their houses where many people raise food for the household. (Provincial towns have more space for "gardening" than large cities where many people live in multi-storey flats; 28 per cent of Mutare households grew at least half of the family food supply.) Living in town also facilitates trading, which is under less government supervision than before independence. Thus, although there were very few people who had been born in Mutare and only two women returnees, the next generation will have more people born here who may either remain or return to this pleasant town.

While a few elderly women in all of these towns have moved there in old age, this is far more common for both returnees and in-migrants in Abeokuta than in the other towns. Women were most likely to have settled in Ijebu Ode in middle age, as their older husbands returned home. They probably arrived or returned later in Abeokuta because husbands migrated there relatively late, when the town moved from lethargy to rapid growth, and or because like elderly women moving to the other towns they decided to join adult children who had settled there—whether this was "home" or merely a good opportunity. (Yoruba marriage often ends when no more child-bearing can be expected, and the wife is free to settle where she pleases.) Women arrived earlier in Sierra Leone and Mutare, probably because most of their husbands were in-migrants.

Table 2. *Age of migrants at arrival or return, by location and gender* (percentage)

Age	Ijebu Ode				Abeokuta				S.Leone		Mutare	
	Arrived		Returned		Arrived		Returned		Arrived		Arrived	
	M	F	M	F	M	F	M	F	M	F	M	F
>25	43	4	3	0	10	7	3	0	6	26	14	14
25–34	6	15	6	0	10	7	10	33	33	13	22	28
35–44	11	12	3	11	16	15	33	0	33	29	27	16
45–59	20	50	26	58	27	11	37	17	17	16	22	21
60+	20	19	62	31	37	60	17	50	11	16	15	21
Total	100	100	100	100	100	100	100	100	100	100	100	100
N	35	26	31	19	62	27	30	6	36	31	123	58

Half of the in-migrant men in Ijebu Ode had arrived early—for schooling or soon after it, at the beginning of their work careers, whereas men moved to Abeokuta later, when opportunities there greatly improved. Many of those born in Abeokuta returned home at the same time, whereas those born in Ijebu Ode delayed their return until they retired from wage employment. Most of the Sierra Leonean men had arrived between age twenty-five and forty-four, moving off the farm or being transferred from jobs in Freetown. The country has had no economic boom or limitation on migration, so their pattern is probably closer to what has been considered common for African male migration this century than the migration careers of the Nigerians or Zimbabweans. Rural–urban migration in Sierra Leone probably takes place at younger ages today than it did for these elderly people. The Zimbabwean pattern for both women and men shows a more even spread of arrivals; they were likely to have arrived at a somewhat younger age than the Nigerian in-migrants (except the Ijebu Ode men), but others had come in the last ten years as the war of independence ended and government control of migration ceased.

LABOUR FORCE PARTICIPATION AND HOUSING

The next stage is to investigate the economic basis for permanent settlement of migrants in provincial towns. The ability to continue earning money through trading or other economic activities or from rents gives elderly people more status and independence than being reliant on support from children, and many people continue some form of income-producing employment well into old age.

Status generally depends on the number of people and amount of resources one can control, so the house-owner with a large extended family at his beck and call is a "big man" by local criteria and maintains his position in the community well into old age, whereas the widow in ill-health who lives alone and has barely enough cash (mainly through gifts from her children) to feed herself may also have few friends and get little attention from the neighbours.

The official retirement age is not very important in countries where many people do not know precisely how old they are and a large majority are self-employed and with little or no savings. It seems to be quite possible to remain in wage employment after the official retirement age—both at the upper and lower levels of the labour force, but many people retire from wage employment much earlier in order to establish a business on their own. It was assumed that indigenous house owners (being more affluent than tenants) would be less likely to remain in the labour force in old age and that in-migrant tenants would be most likely, since cash income and continued employment are basic factors in their remaining in town. Men leaving wage employment might well relax because they are in ill health or have a pension. Women might remain in the labour force through small-scale trading or "retire" when their grandchildren need care so that daughters or daughters-in-law can work. Their status in the household is maintained by their continued contribution to its running.

Table 3. *Labour force participation by migration status, location and gender (Nigeria, Sierra Leone and Zimbabwe)* (percentage)

	Non-migrants					Returnees				In-migrants					
	Nig.		S.L.	Z.		Nig.		S.L.	Z.	Nig.		S.L.		Z.	
	M	F	F	M	F	M	F	Mª	F	M	F	M	F	M	F
Age at retirement[b]															
Under 60	1	5		0	(1)	5	4		(1)	1	3			7	31
60–64	3	6		(1)	0	5	0		0	8	5			12	10
65+	10	19		(2)	0	14	4		0	33	28			35	6
Not yet	86	75	(3)	(6)	(5)	76	92	(1)	(1)	58	64	64	55	46	53
Total	100	100				100	100			100	100	100	100	100	100
N	78	36	9	9	6	62	25	5	2	101	61	41	22	121	52
Per cent in labour force of															
Owners	77	0	(1)	(1)	NA	74	(3)	0	(0)	53	(5)	76	(3)	52	(4)
Kin of owners	93	76	0	NA	(1)	100	12	NA	NA	12	44	0	(4)	80	(1)
Tenants	96	67	(2)	(5)	(4)	72	0	(1)	(1)	84	79	55	(5)	52	47

[a] One of the five is a non-migrant.
[b] Those who have never been in the labour force, mainly Sierra Leonean and Zimbabwean women, are omitted in the first half of the table. Numbers are given in parentheses where the base is less than 10.

Table 3 suggests that when owners or tenants retire probably depends on individual circumstances. (For example, health is an important factor; blindness usually precipitates retirement and many Zimbabweans retire after industrial accidents.) Where the numbers are large enough for reliability, the majority of owners are still in the labour force, though half of the in-migrant Nigerian and Zimbabwean men who had acquired urban housing had retired. These are probably most characteristic of the strategy of investment in housing for retirement insurance. Indigenous kinsmen of owners were less likely to be retired than either owners or tenants; relatives living "at home" are expected to be self-supporting. In-migrants relatives, on the other hand, are likely to be being supported by their children and thus out of the labour force.

Official retirement does not necessarily mean a complete break from the labour force; many people continue to trade on a small scale and others use their savings and/or skills to start a new business. This is often a small shop, but some men who returned to Ijebu Ode in middle age set up substantial businesses in the interests of hometown development. Those who retire relatively early from wage employment are more likely to continue with some form of self-employment than those who continue in wage employment into their sixties (Peil *et al.*, 1985). Those retiring after age seventy are probably doing so because they no longer have the physical strength to continue; these often need physical as well as material assistance.

The national differences are largely due to the proportion of wage employment in their respective urban labour forces, the application of retirement legislation, and to the fact that many women in Sierra Leonean and Zimbabwean towns never enter the labour force or leave early, when they marry. Most southern Nigerian women combine work with managing the family, and seldom retire completely from the labour force until they are over 65. No man in Ijebu Ode had retired before age 60, but a tenth of the retirees in Abeokuta and a sixth of those in Mutare had done so; about a fifth of the Nigerian and Zimbabwean retirees left the labour force in their early sixties, but a majority left after age 65. (Most of those who have not retired are already over 65, whereas a substantial number of Sierra Leonean men in their early sixties had already retired.) Many in-migrant men (owners and relatives of owners more than tenants) retired after age 75, possibly too late to want to return home.

Table 4. *Present employment, by location and gender* (percentage)

	Ijebu Ode		Abeokuta		S. Leone		Mutare	
	M	F	M	F	M	F	M	F
None	16	29	40	42	42	64	38	40
Farm	8	1	6	0	0	2	4	6
Manual	26	3	11	0	27	2	34	10
Commerce	44	67	31	55	24	30	19	33
Non-manual	6	0	12	3	7	2	5	3
Total	100	100	100	100	100	100	100	100
N	117	75	121	59	41	41	131	67

Dependence on others often means lost status as well as a perilous existence. While most old people want to maintain some independent source of income for as long as possible, provincial towns tend to have a limited range of opportunities. Table 4 shows that trading is the major occupation of elderly men and women, plus manual work for men, these provide some income for the majority even though their resources of energy are diminishing. Land may be available for small-scale farming in or near provincial towns, but both farming and manual work require more energy and better health than small-scale trading. Few elderly people have enough education for non-manual work, and this is likely to lead to retirement at the prescribed age. Thus, non-manual jobs are usually held by relatively young in-migrants, who have fewer contacts which can be developed for trading or self-employed skilled work.

Manual work is least developed in Abeokuta and most available in Mutare, for both men and women. The Mutare pattern is an inheritance of the colonial era which is only gradually changing. Manual work is problematic for elderly people because it often requires strength; young men are usually preferred for unskilled labour, but old men may have to continue if they have no alternative. Many Nigerians have training for skilled jobs (carpenter, tailor, mechanic) which can be carried into old age. Skills training is less widespread in Sierra Leone, and many elderly Zimbabweans have a history of unskilled work as the only jobs available to them. Many of the women in Mutare had done domestic work, but none were still doing it; trading provides more time for the family.

One reason why retirement to a provincial town works well is that most of these towns are commercial centres, with many opportunities for trading on a small-scale, though this is less true in Zimbabwe than in West Africa. The only major market in Mutare is between the town and the largest township, and it is small by Nigerian standards. Petty trading is still mostly limited to officially designated places, whereas in Nigeria there is a great deal of street trading, providing opportunities for women who prefer not to leave the house or are physically unable to go far. Markets in Bo and Kenema are small given the size of these towns, but there are no limits on petty trading. Women have less education and training than men, and are therefore more reliant on trading for income. In a village, many women both farm and sell their produce; in a small town they may grow some household vegetables, but most retail goods they did not produce. Rural relatives can be useful for supplying these goods, but most buy from urban-based wholesalers.

The decision to retire in a town is more likely if the migrant owns a house, since control over property both facilitates and symbolizes commitment to a place. This is one reason why both towns and villages encourage their indigenes to build at home. Insofar as migrant residents of provincial towns are nearer to their homes than the majority of people living in capitals, being an urban landlord/lady may be a comfortable alternative to returning to the village on retirement; one can receive visits from rural relatives but have urban services at hand. Since it takes a considerable time to acquire land and accumulate enough capital to build a house in a town, most urban home owners are over forty (Barnes, 1986). Locally-born owners are often older than migrant owners, since the former can often inherit a house if they wait whereas the latter acquire urban housing as a safe and profitable investment. Traders and businessmen living in provincial towns are especially likely to spend their profits on housing, possibly because they have fewer alternatives than residents of cities and often find it hard to retain control over resources remitted home (Peil, 1981:133). Women are more likely to inherit a house from their husbands or a room in the family house than to build their own; the successful women traders who invest their savings in housing are more likely to be operating in a large city than in a provincial town.

Table 5 shows that ownership of housing or living in a house owned by one's spouse, child, sibling or the family collectively is much more common among both men and women in the West African towns than in Mutare.

Only a minority of the elderly Nigerians and about half of the Sierra Leonean immigrant men were in tenant households, compared to three quarters of the Zimbabweans. Over half of the Nigerian men owned their houses and two thirds of the women lived in houses owned by husbands, sons or other relatives; some Nigerian men also lived in family houses. Many of the other women are relatives of the rent-paying tenant rather than tenants in their own right.

Table 5. *Home ownership by migration status, location and gender (Nigeria, Sierra Leone and Zimbabwe)* (percentage[a])

	Non-migrants					Returnees					In-migrants					
	Nig.		S.L.	Z.		Nig.		S.L.	Z.		Nig.		S.L.		Z.	
	M	F	F	M	F	M	F	M[b]	M	F	M	F	M	F	M	F
Resident owner	52	3	(3)	(3)	0	62	15	(3)	NA	(1)	49	11	42	25	19	9
Kin of owner	17	66	(3)	(0)	(1)	9	66	0	NA	0	16	67	3	41	8	14
Tenant	31	31	(3)	(6)	(5)	29	19	(2)	NA	(1)	35	22	55	34	73	77
Total	100	100				100	100				100	100	100	100	100	100
N	81	38	9	9	6	63	26	5	0	2	106	63	36	32	123	58

[a] Numbers are given in parentheses where the base is too small for percentages.
[b] One of the five is a non-migrant.

Returnee men and women were somewhat more likely to own houses than non-migrants or returnees, but the differences by migration status were not statistically significant. Women were most likely to be owners in Sierra Leone, where none of them were returnees and a quarter of in-migrant women had acquired housing. This must have been largely through inheritance from husbands, since almost none of them would have earned enough to build a house. Inheritance practices often discriminate against women (e.g., in Zimbabwe, see Ncube, 1987), and changes in both custom and law need more study.

Aside from inheritance, house ownership is probably more closely related to income and aspirations than to migration experience: some men prefer to spend their savings at home in housing, land, cattle, etc. rather than invest in urban housing, while others see this as a secure and quick way to increase their income. Generally, the results suggest that in-migrants who acquire housing are likely to remain permanently in the town, and that out-migrants are especially likely to return if they have a house at home or can afford to build one. Sales of houses are rare in Nigeria because traditional attitudes toward property continue to be valued; undeveloped urban land is more readily available, though the Land Use Decree 1978, requiring registration of land transfers, has made it more difficult for the poor to acquire land (see Stren, 1985).

Government housing is much more common in Zimbabwe than in West Africa, where it is in very short supply and mainly allotted to upper-level government employees. In Zimbabwe, the colonial government's desire to control accommodation for blacks has left very little private accommodation except for the élites, and the independent government has only modified this to the extent of allowing people to buy council houses or build on site-and-service schemes. Thus very few Mutare residents, men or women, were owners, though several of the tenant men were buying their houses (through rent payments) under the new regulations and many younger migrants will take up this offer insofar as they can afford to do so. Although there are regulations against subtenancy, it is common on Zimbabwean housing estates; those fortunate enough to get council housing sublet rooms to help pay the rent. While only 11 per cent of men and 6 per cent of women in Mutare reported receiving rents, the proportion may well be higher because some tenant/landlords did not want to mention it.

Family housing is relatively common in West African towns (in Ghana and The Gambia as well as Nigeria and Sierra Leone) wherever families have been settled for several generations. Family housing for first generation migrants is less formally organized and usually individually owned, but extended family households are often found. The high proportion of women in Nigeria and Sierra Leone who were relatives of the owner demonstrates both ownership by spouses and by sons, and the ability of resident owners to accommodate their elderly mothers (see Table 6). There are numerous cases of people who moved to the towns studied when they retired from wage employment or became too old to farm. Living alone in rented accommodation is rare. For example, one man retired from farming and moved in with his son in Abeokuta at 90, when he felt too ill to continue on his own. A woman retired at 68 to her father's house in Abeokuta; she has her own room, but shares the house with elderly siblings. Another woman returned to Ijebu Ode from Lagos at 60, to live with her son. Several mothers and aunts had joined large extended family households in Bo and Kenema. A man who had spent some time in Mutare in his twenties returned there at 89 to live with his son, and several women in their sixties joined sons or daughters there. One man moved in his seventies from Harare, where his son lived, to Mutare, where he lived with a grandson.

Not all people who are tenant heads of household pay a commercial rent. A few poor women are provided with accommodation by successful men with whom a hometown connection can be established or fellow church members. Men may get free accommodation from employers or in return for services such as maintaining discipline in the house and collecting the rent. While those in the latter category are often kinsmen of the owner, this is not necessarily the case. Employees provided with subsidized housing may own a house of their own, which they rent out at a substantial profit. Several of the elderly tenants in Abeokuta were in this category. Retirement means loss of this subsidized housing, and often precipitates a return to their house at home.

SUPPORT

Housing reflects more than just accommodation; as people age, they often need physical and social as well as material support. Men tend to remain head of their households even after they cease contributing to household income; women often become head of a household or obtain greater power in it in old age. They often retain household duties (especially cooking) insofar as they are able, but the presence of younger people in the household is important for security and convenience (running errands) as well for various forms of support. Table 6 shows how households varied for men and women in these towns.

Table 6. *Household size and composition, by location and gender* (percentage)

| | Ijebu Ode | | Abeokuta | | Bo | | Kenema | | Mutare | |
	M	F	M	F	M	F	M	F	M	F
Household head	100	81	96	62	88	35	93	28	98	52
Lives alone	6	4	9	18	4	4	0	6	13	8
With spouse	62	15	65	20	65	17	93	22	64	33
With children	80	47	70	58	73	65	73	61	56	58
Grandchildren	36	62	31	58	31	52	27	50	28	48
Others	10	11	13	2	46	56	33	67	3	12
N	117	75	131	60	26	23	15	18	131	67
Mean size	4.3	3.8	6.6	6.2	10.1	12.2	11.9	11.3	3.6	4.2

Note: Totals are over 100% because many households contain several of these relationships.

Except in Sierra Leone, the majority of both men and women in these samples were heads of their households; very few men had given up their position, and many women had attained it because of their husband's death or separation. Very few men or women live alone. Urban housing is always in short supply, though densities are somewhat lower in provincial towns than in capitals. Men are more likely than women to be living in a nuclear family (with spouse and children), partly because custom allows couples to separate when the wife is no longer fertile and partly because many men marry younger wives when the first wife leaves if not before. Polygyny is common in Abeokuta and is rare in Mutare, but this makes no apparent difference in the proportion of men or women living with a spouse. Separation or divorce can be beneficial to both parties—an old woman may not be able to provide adequate service for an ailing husband, and relatives may not help if she is still in the household. On the other hand, she is more likely to get the help she needs from children or grandchildren than from her husband's family.

While the Nigerian men were more likely than the women to have at least one of their children in the household, the difference was smaller in Sierra Leone and negligible in Mutare. Women in all five towns were more likely than men to have grandchildren in the household. There were quite a few cases of women running a household for one or more young grandchildren whose parents lived elsewhere. This ensures that the children are fed and looked after while they attend school, and forms a close tie which may benefit the elderly person when this grandchild grows up. This is probably more important for isolated rural grannies than for those living in town (Bledsoe and Isiugo-Abanihe, 1989), but urban residence may be important where schooling (especially at secondary level) is not available in villages. The 'others' includes siblings, parents and other relatives. These were especially prominent in contributing to the large households in Bo and Kenema, where households often contained several siblings and their wives, nieces and nephews and other kin. Urban house-owners often put up new arrivals until they get on their feet, and siblings may resettle together in the family house.

Women living in family houses in Abeokuta tended to have their own room and an independent household, whereas men were more likely to have a wife or daughter with them to manage the household tasks.

Household size was fairly similar for men and women in each of these towns, though it differed considerably between them. Households were fairly small in Ijebu Ode and Mutare, somewhat larger in Abeokuta and much larger in Bo and Kenema, with up to thirty-nine people. This is partly a reflection of the relative ease of acquiring land for a family house (easiest in the smallest towns and most constrained in Mutare), but also a preference for living together under one roof. All of the largest households belonged to in-migrant owners; only one of the Sierra Leone indigenes lived in a household larger than nine people. It is clear that whole families are being established in these towns, which become 'home' in the same way that new lineages are established in Lagos through the development of property rights (Barnes, 1986).

In a country where post and telephone are unreliable or unavailable, visits are very important for maintaining family contacts. Thus in many African countries the roads fill up at weekends and national holidays with people visiting their parents at home. Links with home become less important after one's parents have died or joined the children in town. The data on visits are incomplete. Most in-migrants in the Nigerian towns claimed to visit their homes at least once a month, though a substantial minority in Abeokuta claimed that they never went home. Forty per cent of the Mutare men claimed to own land at home and 32 per cent owned cattle at home which they could pass on to their children (the figures for women are nine per cent and four per cent). This property serves to link urban residents to the rural areas, encouraging visits for economic as well as social reasons.

Table 7 provides data on the visits elderly people receive from and, less often, make to children and siblings. It is based on all of the children and siblings listed by the people interviewed who were not living in the same household or abroad, and hence means many visits to some people and none at all to others. Some elderly people have no living children and many have no living siblings. While people sharing the same household are most likely to support each other and may be indispensable for physical support, these data are more useful for examining migrant networks, since the people represented by the percentage section of the table are all living in other villages, towns and cities.

It is clear that sons are more frequent visitors than daughters, that brothers visit less often than children and sisters least often visit or are visited. This is partly a question of resources (males have more money for travelling than females) and distance (siblings may live further away than children; among in-migrants, they are less likely to live in the same town). But social norms strongly encourage children to visit their parents often, while sibling networks are more voluntary and hence selective. Nevertheless, there is obviously strong support for visiting siblings in Nigeria; many sisters were frequent visitors. There is an interesting difference between indigenous daughters, who are slightly more likely to visit their mothers than their fathers, and sisters, who visit their sisters less often than they visit their broth-

Table 7. *Frequency of visits by location, migration status, gender and relationship to contact* (percentage)[a]

| | Nigeria | | | | Zimbabwe | | | |
| | Indigenes | | Migrants | | Indigenes | | Migrants | |
	M	F	M	F	M	F	M	F
Male children								
>2/year	7	1	20	9	12	(1)	10	4
2–11/year	20	14	9	15	6	0	16	9
More often	73	85	71	76	82	(1)	74	87
Total	100	100	100	100	100		100	100
N	152	73	123	59	34	2	62	23
Female children								
>2/year	5	6	20	15	37	(1)	38	42
2–11/year	22	12	12	23	3	0	8	0
More often	73	82	68	62	60	(3)	54	58
Total	100	100	100	100	100		100	100
N	121	69	102	52	35	4	78	19
Male siblings								
>2/year	9	19	36	38	(4)	NA	53	82
2–11/year	23	35	11	14	0	NA	37	0
More often	68	46	53	48	(3)	NA	10	18
Total	100	100	100	100		100	100	
N	56	26	61	29	7	0	38	11
Female siblings								
>2/year	18	21	28	45	85	(1)	83	(6)
2–11/year	25	46	13	17	5	(1)	4	(2)
More often	57	33	59	38	10	0	13	0
Total	100	100	100	100	100		100	
N	60	33	46	29	20	2	24	8
Number in this town								
Children: M	52	14	52	19	3	2	19	8
F	34	15	37	16	2	0	6	3
Siblings: M	66	26	25	7	8	0	2	0
F	53	19	18	5	5	0	3	0

[a] Only children and siblings living outside the town but in the country are included in the percentages. Numbers in the last section do not include those in the household (see Table 6). 'Seldom' has been coded as under 2/year, 'sometimes' or 'occasionally' as 2–11/year and 'often' and 'always' as more often.

ers. This is probably related to the greater ability of brothers to provide financial help to their sisters, whereas elderly women would have little to give.

With the exception of sons visiting their fathers, Zimbabweans are consistently less frequent visitors than Nigerians even though the roads and buses are better in Zimbabwe. Given that Mutare residents are less likely to have any children, grandchildren or siblings living in the household or elsewhere in Mutare (who could visit more often), they appear to be considerably more socially isolated than old people living in the Nigerian towns. This has implications for their future as they age.

Family ties within the towns present a somewhat different pattern, telling us something about the nature of migration. Indigenous men and Nigerian indigenous women have more siblings than children (male and female) living in the same town, which is not true for in-migrant men or for other women. Part of the reason for returning home is to join the male leadership of the

family—shared with one's brothers. Women's migration on marriage sepa-
rates groups of sisters, and moving in with a son again gives women less
choice as to where to spend their old age. While Nigerian entrepreneurship
has been fostered by older brothers making room in their business or finding
a job for a younger brother, the strict regulation of migration and employment in colonial Rhodesia made it difficult for brothers to move to the same
place.

Having children or siblings living in the same town has many advantages;
on the whole, propinquity is used to make frequent visits, helping elderly people to feel at home. But we should not assume that all family members in the
same town visit frequently; even in a small town, some are seen less than once
a month. Urban areas provide more choice than villages, and excuses can be
made by those who want to avoid personal conflicts or bringing gifts. Nevertheless, these family members are resources which can be called on in emer-
gencies.

Most of the visits "under 2/year" are made at least once a year; if people
do not see each other at least that often, they tend to lose contact altogether—as many Malawians and Mozambicans living in Zimbabwe have
with their families at home. At the other extreme, many family members who
live in nearby towns and villages visit much more than once a month, sometimes more often than others who actually live in the same town. On the
whole, most Nigerian visitors, especially frequent visitors, came from the cities (especially Lagos and Ibadan) rather than from towns or villages. This
suggests that urban–urban links are stronger than urban–rural ones, and that
elderly people settled in provincial towns tend to lose links to their villages of
origin. Their children no longer live in the village and many other relatives
have moved out, so there is less reason to maintain what is essentially a tie to
a family rather than to a place.

However, it is also a question of resources in time and money. Migrants
working in Lagos and Ibadan are often in wage employment, with free time
for visiting over weekends and holidays; they also have money for cars or bus
fare. Relatives living in villages are often farming, which provides less income
for travel and gifts and less time defined as for leisure except after the harvest.
So if they visit at all it is less frequently than urban-based children and siblings. Also, children attending universities in these nearby cities can easily
visit their parents over the holidays or even more often since the distance is
short, whereas those in northern universities might only get home once a year.
Many children who were abroad (not included in the table) also came home
once a year.

DISCUSSION

What are the implications of these findings for small town development?
Small towns are often preferred as a place of retirement because they provide
services not available in villages (clinics and even hospitals, an easily accessible source of water) and facilitate visits from far-flung children. The heavy
labour of farming can be left behind, and savings can be safely invested in
housing or small-scale trade, which bring in enough cash for daily needs.

Small towns often provide a friendly, kinship-based environment, though this can be established in large cities as well.

Thus, planners should begin to think of the social, economic and political effects of an aging urban population, especially in small towns. The most obvious need will be in the field of health services, though the demand for improved education will continue, at least until fertility rates come down, because these households will frequently include grandchildren. Where health services are free or nearly so (as in Zimbabwe), many old people attend frequently, until one suspects that the clinic may become a social club. As tax-paying voters, increasingly with some education and with time to pay attention to what the authorities are up to, they expect service and may be able to complain effectively if they are dissatisfied. Health education, related to the ailments of old age, will be necessary to ration resources and improve their ability to care for themselves. Some sheltered housing may be needed for old people without families. This is increasing in Zimbabwe, but little is available in either Nigeria or Sierra Leone.

Elderly residents, especially indigenes, will also want a part in local politics and have the time to spend on it. When today's elderly were children, male elders played an important role in shaping and implementing policies. Retirees often want to continue this role even though political structures have greatly changed and the number of potential elderly participants has increased. They complain of loss of status when they are not consulted. In practice, many continue to settle family and neighbourhood disputes and thus play an important role in the maintenance of social control, a role for which the police are often grossly inadequate. Some accommodation needs to be made between traditional and governmental authority, maintaining if possible good relations between the local indigenous leadership and elected local councils, state and national authorities. There are advantages to be gained. Local councils will have plenty of advice from educated returnees on how to develop the town, and the enthusiasm and resources of indigenes can be used for development projects. But care must be taken that in-migrant's needs are not neglected, and local authorities will inevitably face factionalism and interference from men who aspire to rule. Some may have retired from very high positions and see in-migrant officials as interlopers.

Spending one's old age in a small town means that resources of the large cities are left to the young. Twenty years ago, it was thought right and proper for everyone to aspire to retirement in their home village. Today, there is less consensus as to whether one should go home or remain in town in old age, and much depends on the social support which various locations provide. As small towns develop a better infrastructure and greater variety of employment, it may be less necessary to leave town for the city and villagers may find work nearer to home, thus making the Ijebu Ode pattern far more common than it is today.

However, as more people decide to settle permanently in towns, villages will inevitably lose contact with many of their more successful migrants; some villages may cease to exist (as has happened in the USA) because there are not enough people for a school and not enough opportunities to keep young people at home. The few old people who remain will have to depend on the occasional visits or remittances from distant children. It is important for African development that farming include a smaller but more prosperous proportion of the population; the standard of living attainable from a quarter hectare of land will not keep people "down on the farm" or encourage retirees to return. The development of small towns may be a good solution to this dilemma.

References

Aronson, Dan R., 1980, *The City Is our Farm*. Cambridge, MA: Schenkman Publishing Co.

Barnes, Sandra T., 1986, *Patrons and Power: Creating a Political Community in Metropolitan Lagos*. Manchester University Press.

Bledsoe, Caroline and U.C. Isiugo-Abanihe, 1989, "Strategies of child-fosterage among Mende grannies in Sierra Leone", in R. Lesthanghe (ed.), *African Reproduction and Social Organization*. Berkeley: University of California Press.

Caldwell, John C., 1969, *African Rural–Urban Migration: The Movement to Ghana's Towns*. Canberra: Australian National University Press.

Hill, Polly, 1972, *Rural Hausa*. London: Cambridge University Press.

Masamba ma Mpolo, 1984, "Older persons and their families in a changing village society: A perspective from Zaire". Washington, D.C.: International Federation on Ageing.

Ncube, Welshman 1987, "Underprivilege and inequality: The matrimonial property rights of women in Zimbabwe", in A. Armstrong (ed.), *Women and Law in Southern Africa*. Harare: Zimbabwe Publishing House.

Peil, Margaret, 1981, *Cities and Suburbs: Urban Life in West Africa*. New York: Holmes and Meier.

Peil, Margaret, 1985, "Retirement in Nigeria", *Cultures et Developpement* , 17, 665–82.

Peil, Margaret,1990, "Sierra Leone's urban elderly: housing and support", in A. Jones, *et al.* (eds.), *Sierra Leone Studies at Birmingham 1988*. Birmingham: Centre of West African Studies, Birmingham University.

Peil, Margaret, *et al.* 1988, "Going home: migration careers of southern Nigerians", *International Migration Review,* 22, 563–85.

Stren, Richard, 1985, "Two Nigerian towns in the eighties: A socioeconomic survey of Idah and Makurdi, Benue State", Project Ecoville, Working Paper No. 21. Toronto: University of Toronto Institute for Environmental Studies.

The Dilemmas Facing Kenya School Leavers
Surviving in the City or a Force for Local Mobilization?

Anders Närman

> ...the educational level at which unemployment or inap-
> propriate employment begins has risen so that in many
> countries there are increasing numbers of unemployed
> among secondary-school leavers, and in countries like
> Kenya and Nigeria the economic situation has deterio-
> rated such that there are now college graduates who can-
> not find jobs (Tandon, 1987:12).

This quotation points to one of the major problems presently facing many
African countries, the possibility of acquiring gainful employment. This is
particularly related to the specific predicament of increased school leaver
unemployment. Since independence, Africa has experienced an unprecedented expansion of educational facilities. But there has been no way the
labour market could follow suit.

School leavers are trapped in a contradiction, in which "the education they
receive divorces them from the rural setting, without preparing them adequately for urban living" (Grey-Johnson, 1990:104). A search for "greener
pastures" in the cities is done both in anticipation of getting a job, and as a
response to family pressures.

During the colonial period, resources were directed towards primate cities
(Obudho and Taylor, 1979:102). This trend still prevails, as a consequence of
continuous external domination. African governments have not been able to
treat problems, such as urban unemployment "with imagination and the necessary initiative" (Mabogunje, 1989:199).

Mabogunje views the concentration of resources in metropolitan cities, as
counteracting an internal mobilization of the human resources available.
Political power and the control of resources must be more evenly spread over
the national space (Mabogunje, 1989:220).

With external policy directions on structural adjustment (including export
promotion) there is a serious risk that the negative labour market trends will
be aggravated further. Demands for greater efficiency in the administrative
sector will reduce the manpower requirement (Grey-Johnson, 1990). Industrial productivity is raised by an input of capital, rather than labour.

Modernization within the agricultural sector, to produce a surplus of
income from export, is resulting in competition for scarce fertile land. Cash
crop production will be concentrated on a number of indebted, but "successful" smallholder farmers. More traditional peasants are compelled to eke out
a living from marginal lands.

Integrated within this externally induced modernization strategy is the promotion of a basic mass education, primarily devoted to a set of "academic" subjects. "Scientific" economic calculations have "proved" this to be the most cost-efficient policy option. Attempts by African governments to initiate various programmes of vocationalisation or pre-vocational diversifications have been advised against by external funding agencies, led by the World Bank (World Bank, 1981:81–85).

Kenya can be used to exemplify the educational strategy in less-developed capitalist countries. The whole educational system has expanded at all levels, to pave the way for individual advancement in the society. Schooling could be regarded as the means to qualify for the urban labour market, mainly in the public service sector (Fägerlind and Saha, 1989:238).

This chapter will analyse some factors related to Kenyan educational development, as it is related to urbanization and the labour market. My intention is to give a broad overview of the present state of affairs. In addition to this some specific case studies will be discussed. A main question will be to find out if there are any alternative options open, which could mobilize the human resources for national development.

EDUCATION AND THE LABOUR MARKET

Since independence the Kenyan Government has emphasized the provision of education, both at the primary and secondary level. This has been in response to:

> the increasing demand for more educational opportunities for a fast growing population and the Government's commitment to make education accessible to all Kenyans and to train adequate manpower to meet the needs of a growing economy (Republic of Kenya, 1988:1).

Undoubtedly Kenya has been able to achieve a fast quantitative growth in education. Figures in Table 1 can be compared to the fact that at independence (1963) there were 314,000 school pupils in all, of whom less than 10,000 were in secondary education.

Table 1. *"School leavers" at different levels 1981–1990*

Year	Students enrolled (thousands) at		
	St 7/8	Form IV	Form VI
1981	369	106	11
1982	372	84	10
1983	385	101	12
1984	453	101	12
1985	360	116	18
1986	345	119	17
1987	368	151	22
1988	368	–	25
1989	415	139	32
1990	385	143	–

Source: Republic of Kenya: *Economic Survey*. Various issues.

It can be noted that during this period there was a change in the school system. Up to 1984 the final year in primary school was Standard 7, thereafter an additional year was added. At secondary level there was no Form IV in 1988, due to the same reform, which also abolished the upper secondary level from 1990.

Of course not all the students in Standards 7/8 or Form IV and VI leave school, but are enrolled at a higher stage, repeating or taking some kind of a vocational course. However, it can be expected that at least some 250,000 to 300,000 school leavers are annually joining the competition for available vacancies in the labour market.

The societal demand for educational facilities has been met to a large extent. However, this has hardly been in harmony with labour market development. It is a rather short-sighted populist approach to reform the school system by merely expanding the quantitative access, without realizing the need for a complete overhaul of the educational content.

It has not been possible to increase labour market opportunities to keep pace with educational progress. While decisions on the school structure are largely within the domain of the Government, manpower requirements are determined by a complex interaction of various forces, especially in a free market economy, such as the Kenyan one. Table 2 gives the number of salaried jobs (including the urban informal sector) 1984–90. Before that time the data are not comparable.

Table 2. *Total estimated salaried employment, 1984–90*

Year	Number employed (thousands)
1984	1385
1985	1462
1986	1537
1987	1636
1988	1731
1989	1807
1990	1899

During the period 1984 to 1990 there has been an average increase in the number of new jobs by some 85,000 annually. If we include vacancies created due to retirements, deaths, etc. the figure can be calculated to be close to 100,000 new jobs per year. This can be compared with the number of school leavers, which is 2.5 to 3 times as many.

While there are presently (1990) 1.9 million employees in the country, this can be compared to 6.2 million pupils in the formal school system (Standard 1 to Form IV). Within the next decade and a half most of them will compete on the labour market. This is a reminder of the serious predicament Kenya, like so many other African countries, finds itself in today.

Under such circumstances it is remarkable that the educational system is unable to produce the required skilled manpower.

Thus many industries cannot expand due to a shortage of skills at the professional, technical and artisan levels. In the Government itself, shortage of skills has hampered the implementation of projects which could generate substantial employment opportunities for both the skilled and the unskilled labour. One of the consequences of this imbalance is the importation of expensive expatriate personnel even in skills for which Kenya is well poised to produce (Republic of Kenya, 1983:12).

Not only is the school system unable to give the right skills for the labour market, but, as was noted above, there is a tendency to alienate school leavers from rural activities. A rather thought-provoking picture has been given by the Kenyan Government itself.

> Unless new workers can be attracted in large numbers to jobs in smaller urban centres and on prosperous farms, it will be necessary to build at least six cities the size of present-day Nairobi, or to watch Mombasa and Nairobi expand into cities of two to four million each (Republic of Kenya, 1986:1).

A major task for the Kenyan authorities, under such circumstances, must be to halt a flight of school leavers into metropolitan regions, where they will only join a growing cadre of unemployed. Otherwise one consequence will be that deteriorating socio-economic conditions will result in *"political instability and civil disturbances"* (Grey-Johnson, 1990:71).

Kenya has been mentioned in this context, as one of the few African countries in which *"economic, physical, and social planning has been adopted as a major part of government policy"* (Obudho, 1981:xi). The main question raised by this statement would be to what extent rhetoric is translated into actual implementation of policy. This will be discussed in the next section.

THE LABOUR MARKET AND SPATIAL STRUCTURES

In 1972 the ILO gave some views on the massive movement into the major urban centres in Kenya, primarily Nairobi and Mombasa. It was noted that most of the migrants are comparatively young men. Furthermore, it was stated that

> ...the likelihood of migration increases very rapidly with the level of educational attainment, and that Nairobi attracts a very large share of those with secondary and higher education (International Labour Office, 1972:45).

In addition to Nairobi and Mombasa, six other major towns are mentioned in the ILO report, namely Kisumu, Thika, Nyeri, Nakuru, Nanyuki and Eldoret. Further, it was claimed that even if unemployment was on the increase in towns and cities, the educated youth were not severely affected at that time. Research also indicated that migrants prefer *"to stay in their home areas if they could have had a job there with the same pay"* (International Labour Office, 1972:46–47). We have also come to a similar conclusion from the studies commented on below. Movements were most often directed towards a near-by town, because of the possibility to meet with relatives and friends. As will be seen below the role of the "extended family" is an important factor influencing the urge to move.

In the Development Plan 1974–1978 there seems to be a clear policy adopted to encourage a more even urban structure:

> To encourage the expansion of several large towns in addition to Nairobi and Mombasa, thereby providing more alternatives for the absorption of the migrant population and avoiding the problems arising from excessive concentration in these two towns (Republic of Kenya, 1974:119).

The main policy was to establish a hierarchy of urban centres, which would be provided with a set of service functions. It was then assumed, that this would give an impetus for commercial and industrial development and thereby *"provide improved employment opportunities"* (Republic of Kenya, 1974:120).

This planned structure would include eleven principal towns, namely Nairobi, Mombasa, Nakuru, Kisumu, Thika, Eldoret, Kitale, Nyeri, Kakamega, Embu and Meru. Some of these towns were fairly small in the population census conducted in 1969 (see below), but were supposed to adjust their boundaries to include a substantial rural population.

Next in the suggested hierarchy are 86 urban centres. Among these are some significant towns, like Nyahururu, Malindi, Machakos, Kisii, Kericho, Nanyuki and Naivasha. In addition, the emerging industrial towns of Athi River and Webuye could be found in this category.

Some specific service functions were also supposed to be allocated to rural (150), market (420) and local (1,015) centres.

However, in the Development Plan 1989–93 it was concluded that the continuous pattern included a heavy concentration of population in Nairobi, Mombasa and Kisumu (Republic of Kenya, 1989:74).

Still it can be observed, that during the last two decades some towns have grown substantially. In 1989 there were a total of 19 urban centres with populations above 25,000 (Table 3). A comparison is also made with corresponding figures from the two previous population censuses of 1969 and 1979.

Table 3. *Major urban centres in 1989, 1979 and 1969*

Urban centre	Population		
	1989	1979	1969
Nairobi	1,346,000	827,775	509,286
Mombasa	465,000	341,148	247,073
Kisumu	185,100	152,643	32,431
Nakuru	162,800	92,851	47,151
Machakos	116,100	84,320	6,312
Eldoret	104,900	50,503	18,196
Nyeri	88,600	35,753	10,004
Meru	78,100	70,439	4,475
Thika	57,100	41,324	18,387
Kitale	53,000	28,327	11,573
Kakamega	47,300	32,025	6,244
Kisii	44,000	29,661	6,080
Kericho	40,000	29,603	10,144
Malindi	35,200	23,275	10,757
Naivasha	34,500	11,491	6,920
Maragwa	30,600	6,980	1,230
Bungoma	29,100	25,161	4,401
Garissa	27,200	14,076	–
Webuye	25,700	17,693	–
Total	2,970,300	1,915,048	950,664

Note: The 1989 figures are still provisional.

Source: Republic of Kenya: *Economic Survey 1991* and *Population Census 1979*.

It can be pointed out that the growth of these urban areas has often been as a result of boundary extensions. Obvious examples of this, between 1969 and 1979, are Kisumu, Machakos and Meru.

Almost 14 per cent of the Kenyan population were living in urban centres with more than 25,000 inhabitants in 1989. Another 741,400 (3.5 per cent) found in towns with more than 2,000 inhabitants. In this category we find, for example, industrial towns, such as Nanyuki, Nyahururu and Athi River, the administrative centre of Embu (provincial capital of Eastern province), and major trading centres such as Wajir and Isiolo for huge pastoralist areas.

With more than one third of the total urban population, the primacy of Nairobi is obvious. Thereafter Mombasa, Kisumu and Nakuru are important centres from both an industrial and administrative (provincial capitals) point of view.

Of the total number of wage earners (excluding the informal sector) almost half (1989) are found in 20 towns (Table 4).

Table 4. *Wage earners in major towns, 1989, 1979 and 1969*

Town	Wage employees		
	1989	1979	1969
Nairobi	361,767	260,822	163,691
Mombasa	118,331	92,707	57,383
Kisumu	30,883	16,509	13,200
Nakuru	24,368	17,861	14,206
Eldoret	18,589	11,805	9,535
Thika	18,082	12,987	6,120
Machakos	11,652	3,326	1,836
Kericho	10,294	4,473	4,168
Nyeri	8,610	6,551	5,158
Kakamega	7,249	3,589	1,003
Kisii	6,530	3,695	1,798
Kilifi	6,428	2,783	600
Meru	5,962	5,043	4,007
Nanyuki	5,868	4,107	2,082
Embu	5,659	2,851	1,119
Kitale	5,495	5,527	2,032
Kiambu	5,434	3,512	839
Malindi	5,280	4,194	1,303
Nyahururu	5,185	2,391	2,035
Naivasha	5,008	3,203	1,759
Total	666,674	467,936	289,870

Source: Republic of Kenya: *Statistical Abstract*. Various Years.

In the national context, Nairobi is dominant in respect of the total number of employees. During the last two decades some 26–27 per cent of workers in the modern sector have worked in the capital. Together with Mombasa not less than 35 per cent of all wage earners work in these two main cities, although their share of the total population is only 8.5 per cent.

From this it seems obvious that Nairobi and Mombasa are attractive for youth seeking employment. Between 1969 and 1979 the growth in the number of jobs was in excess of the population increase for the same period. However, this trend was reversed in the 1980s.

For Kisumu, Nakuru, Eldoret and Thika the proportionate growth in job opportunities, was faster than the two metropolitan giants between 1979 and 1989. The remaining 14 towns in Table 4 have had a consistently rapid growth between 1969 and 1989. Especially during the 1980s vacancies increased far more rapidly than population growth.

It would seem rational, building on the experiences over the last decade, for a migrant in search of a job to give priority to some of the towns, below Nairobi and Mombasa in the urban hierarchy. A favourable trend can be noted for Kisumu, Eldoret, Machakos, Kericho, Kakamega, Kilifi, Embu and Nyahururu in the period 1979 to 1989.

To a large extent most of the new jobs are to be found in what can be broadly termed the "service" sector, such as the local administration or teaching profession.

Within manufacturing industries, Nairobi and Mombasa employ approximately half of all workers nationally, although there has been a slight proportionate decrease during the 1980s. Thika and Eldoret are also important industrial towns, with rapid growth experienced in the latter. Towns with a fair share of industrial employment are Athi River and Webuye. Traditional centres for manufacturing, such as Nanyuki and Naivasha, seem to have experienced a slight decline.

Both Nakuru and Kisumu are important industrial centres, but their labour market is primarily increasing within the "service" sector. For Machakos and Kericho, there is a positive trend both regarding industrial and administrative employment.

One important consideration in this context is the extent to which the Kenyan population can rely on this kind of job creation in the modern sector for their future survival.

> Historically, educated youth have sought urban, often white-collar employment. Although this tendency will certainly continue, it is clear that the modern sector will be unable to raise enough capital to employ more than a fraction of Kenya's workers from now to the end of the century (Republic of Kenya, 1986:54).

Under such circumstances, the adoption by Kenya of IMF/World Bank economic policies can hardly ameliorate the situation. Throughout Africa the "advice" given by these two agencies has always resulted in a deterioration of living conditions for the majority.

> Millions of jobs have been lost as a result of a reduction in the level of investment and cuts in social services. The resultant rise in unemployment has increased poverty and hardship in many African households (Grey-Johnson, 1990:42).

A natural reaction to such a trend could be a local mobilization to put human resources into some kind of productive use. Such an approach could be the labour-intensive informal, or *jua kali*, sector *"which is consistent with a relative abundance of labour"* (*Weekly Review*, August 30, 1991:29).

It has been estimated that 75 per cent of all new urban employment up to the year 2000 will be within the informal sector, while 50 per cent of the new non-farm rural activities will be in the same category. However, for such a development to take place new demands on the educational system will emerge. Priority must be given to skills training, both in the practical and entrepreneurial fields.

EXPERIENCES FROM SOME TRACER STUDIES

As an empirical illustration to what has been discussed above, some data from a couple of tracer studies will be presented. They were carried out from 1983 to 1986, as part of an evaluation of industrial/technical education in Kenya (Närman, 1985, 1988).

Within the study we tried to determine what happened to school leavers after completion of their Ordinary level examinations. Of course the data used cannot be taken as representative for the total secondary school system. First of all many of the students interviewed had a special technical diversification included in their school curricula.

The studies refer only to male students, as the examples are drawn from boys' schools. Furthermore, the schools selected are normally of a comparatively high calibre, in terms of examination results. These biases have to be taken into account in the analysis. The samples only include pupils who had left school, permanently or temporarily, at the time of the interviews.

From a follow-up tracer study, related to Industrial Education (IE), it is possible to draw some conclusions. Here we have a fairly high coverage rate for a larger sample. In addition to this, the tracing was done up to three years after the examinations. Initial interviews were conducted in twenty schools, both urban and rural, just prior to the examination in 1983. More than 1,500 students were included in the original sample. These were thereafter traced in 1984 and 1986.

One year after Form IV a high percentage was still in school. However, focus was on a group consisting of 63, that was working, and 452 not in school and out of work at the time of the interviews (Table 5). The location of this sample was categorised as follows:

(i)   "Still at home",
(ii)   Nairobi/Mombasa,
(iii) Major town, other than the above,
(iv)   Other towns or rural areas.

In this survey we included nearby Thika and Athi River in Nairobi, as they are characteristic of the same industrial structure. The major towns are Kisumu, Nakuru and Eldoret.

Of those working "at home", some were from Nairobi (10) or Mombasa (6). The rest were working in either western or central Kenya in the rural areas or small towns.

Table 5. *Location of sample at the time of interview*

Location	Working		Not working	
	N	(%)	N	(%)
"At home"	48	(76)	370	(82)
Nairobi/Mombasa	6	(9)	57	(13)
Major town	1	(2)	20	(4)
Other	8	(13)	5	(1)
Total	63		452	

It is obvious that most of the unemployed remained at home. Many of them admitted to a desire to be selected for higher education at a later stage. That was the most common reason for not actively looking for employment in urban areas. Furthermore, most of the interviewed did state that they actually preferred to remain at home, instead of moving to the cities. This is in accordance with the results obtained by the ILO, discussed above.

As was to be expected, Nairobi/Mombasa were most attractive for job seekers, even if few were actually employed. Some were also trying to find employment in one of the major towns of Kisumu, Nakuru or Eldoret. Mostly, this is done by students from the surrounding region, or with a relative working in the town. This result is similar to what was concluded by the ILO. It is noticeable that among this group only one (!) out of 21 was employed.

It is among the much smaller group moving to "other" towns or within the rural areas, that a higher share were employed (8), compared to unemployed (5).

During the first year after the O-level exams, 142 (28 per cent) of the students, either working or unemployed, had made an attempt to find work outside the home area. Only 22 (15 per cent) of them were engaged in some kind of income-earning activity at the time of the interviews. This is a clear indication as to the difficulty of entering the labour market in Kenya, even after eleven years of schooling. One startling observation is that:

> It is in fact the ex-students with the poorest examination results-Division IV or Failure, who most often have become employed or gained access to a job-related training program. Indeed, the trend is highly statistically significant. Superficially at least, this finding flies in the face of much writing, often based on impressions rather than empirical research, about the credentialist mentality of employers in developing countries (Lauglo and Lillis, 1988:252).

One noticeable factor from the study is that some kind of a practical component (such as IE) in the education is valuable to those who stay at home in the rural areas without being employed formally. This can be illustrated by a few representative quotations:

> I have kept myself busy and a little sort of self-employed by making simple furnitures which I could use at home or sell to neighbours to get my daily bread.

> I managed to employ myself by working and making carpentry work, first by borrowing tools from my friends and start my own business of carpentry and by now I have employed two people to help in my work.

> Due to IE I took at school, I do earn some little cash at home when I repair simple electrical devices.

Some kinds of practical skills must be useful to make a living, outside the formal labour market. It is even more obvious that three years after the O-level exams, many were compelled to utilize an advantage such as the one provided by a technical subject, as a survival skill.

Of those that were traced in 1986, more than one quarter were still at school/in training. Many of them had been at school continuously since the O-level exams. Some of those that were unemployed in 1984 had either joined some school/training or had obtained a job. However, many were still unemployed at this time. Among the Form VI leavers, some were still unemployed one year after their exams.

The labour market prospects can be illustrated by the fact that even three years after the O-level examinations more than half of those that were actually traced and were not in school/not training, were unemployed. Of course, many of them had been doing some temporary or casual jobs, for different durations. Some case studies may provide the best means to give a picture of the situation:

> The year 1984 ended without me doing a thing. In 1985 I decided to look for casual employment so that I could buy things that I badly needed but there was no one who could buy them for me. I succeeded to get some and I worked here and there for sometimes before there was nowhere to get casual employment again. In this year I've done totally nothing not even casual work.

> Since I left school that is the time from 1983 to this moment I have been doing casual jobs wherever found. Up till now I have not secured somewhere as a permanent employee. I could have joined a college, but I lacked school fees.

> After leaving Form IV in the year 1983, there is nothing specific I have been doing. All I usually do is any job that can earn me a meal for that day's survival.

Some had fallen into a situation of despair due to the few opportunities available:

> I am fed up with this kind of life—being idle and looking for what seems to be a non-existing job.

> Nobody wants to give a schooldrop out any worthwhile job.

The latter was said by a student who passed the O-level exams with the highest grade. In many cases, school results play an insignificant role for job seekers. Other "qualifications", such as good contacts, are of a higher value.

> I didn't know anybody in a big position to act as my protector, so I never came up with anything substantial. Months went by without getting any employment.

> I have in the whole of 1986 attended various interviews but due to malpractice like corruption I have never been able to secure any places at all.

In most cases, school leavers face fierce competition for *any* kind of a job.

> I've done various jobs: cement-mixing for 2 masons, waiter in a small cafe, working in a self-delivering van, a gas-cutter's help, etc.

Among the work mentioned by the school leavers employed at the time of interviews, were many examples in the categories, such as watchmen, cooks, telephone operators, office messengers, *jua kali* blacksmith, waiters, shop assistants, tailors, professional footballer, etc. However, the most common employment mentioned was that of teacher, in most cases unqualified. Many also gave their work as clerk.

Temporary work is often terminated due to the fact that the employer does not want to commit himself. The case below provides an example of the kind of negative impact of certain forms of external assistance:

> I was temporarily employed as an untrained teacher, a job that was terminated in July due to personnel aid from America.

In spite of the fact that the school leavers are faced with this kind of a harsh labour market reality, a surprisingly low number are actually trying to gain employment out of the home area. Of 493 students traced, as either working or unemployed, no less than 360 (73 per cent) were found "still at home". Moreover, 53 per cent did not have any source of income from either employment or self-employment.

Almost two thirds (142) of those classified as "still at home" were in either a small town or in the rural areas. Of the rest, most were in Nairobi (81), followed by Kisumu (18), Mombasa (14), Nakuru (9), Thika (7) and Eldoret (3). Among the Nairobi group the number at work is slightly in excess of the unemployed. The most difficult situation seems to be for school leavers originating in Kisumu, with 12 unemployed.

Attempts to leave home for urban employment have often been met with difficulties. Some have described the hardships encountered.

Looking for work in both urban and rural areas.

Moving from town to town where my relatives are, searching for small time jobs or where I can be assured of a job and hence money.

Nairobi is the single most attractive goal for school leavers in Kenya. This is obvious from the figures given in Table 6.

Apart from those actually being in urban areas at the time of our study, some 40 to 50 others indicated that they had been trying their luck to get a job, one or more times, in any of the cities and towns. Here, Nairobi is dominant, followed by Kisumu and Mombasa.

Table 6. *Location of school leavers outside home area, 1986*

Location	At work		Not working	
	N	(%)	N	(%)
Nairobi	30	(39)	37	(65)
Mombasa	10	(13)	9	(16)
Kisumu	4	(5)	3	(5)
Nakuru	1	(1)	4	(7)
Eldoret	3	(4)	1	(2)
Other	28	(37)	3	(5)
Total	76		57	

If we compare the situation here to the one two years previously, it seems that large towns, such as Kisumu, Nakuru and Eldoret, are fairly unattractive to school leavers. Some might have moved on to the two metropolitan areas, or returned home without any success.

One comment to the fact that a high proportion are working in other towns or rural areas is well worth making. In most instances, this does not show school leavers looking for a job, but is a result of transfers of the already employed. This can be within the teaching profession, the armed forces or local government.

Table 6 indicates that attempts to find employment in any of the cities are not easy. This is especially so in the case of Nairobi. Many case studies illustrate this:

I've been sometimes staying at home and sometimes here in Nairobi looking for a job. One day I got a temporary job, thus a friend of mine asked me to do that for him. It was one month only.

This year I left my rural home to come to stay here in Nairobi. During the month of August and September I held temporary employment with Caltex Oil Company (K) at their depot in Nairobi at industrial area and it terminated.

I went to Nairobi in early February (1984) to stay with my brother who was working there. After seeking for employment the whole year without getting, I went back home to join the other members of the family during Christmas holidays. In January 1985 I went back to Nairobi where I stayed for another full year without getting anything and in December I went back home. Again early this year (1986) I went to Nairobi but this time I didn't stay there for so long but about two months. The reason being my brother was sacked from job and I had no one to stay with.

It does not seem to be much easier for those trying in the other large cities:

Since I left IV Form I have been visiting places such as Nairobi (city), Nakuru town and Kisumu town, but employment has been a problem.

Since I left school in 1983 I went to our second big town, Mombasa, hoping that I would perhaps get employment, but my expectations were fruitless. So I wasted my two good years down at the coast doing nothing. I then travelled to Nakuru early this year, and I wasted my ten months here. And now I am at home doing a lot of nothing.

After one and a half years after my education I was taken by my cousin to Eldoret where I am staying up to the present moment. Here at Eldoret I have done work as casual labourer and then I stopped and then I am just staying without any job.

Some conclusions can be drawn from the data presented here. First, labour market conditions are not especially conducive to secondary school leavers. The situation has probably deteriorated seriously, simultaneously with the tremendous expansion of educational facilities.

One indication of the deteriorating labour market for school leavers can be given by comparing a pilot study, conducted prior to the main study. From this, some 300 ex-students from Kitui High School, with examinations from 1974-82, were followed up retrospectively. The response rate was 50 per cent.

From this study a low proportion was unemployed at the time of the interview. It is almost exclusively those with an O-level examination from 1980 or later that have been unable to find some kind of occupation. This cannot only be due to a shorter time out of school, but also to a continuous decline in labour market opportunities. An absolute majority are engaged in either teaching or office work, in most cases with the Government.

Most of the traced students were found in their respective rural home areas. In addition to this, many have tried their luck, sometimes successfully in the two major cities. Kitui is traditionally an area with a substantial out-migration to both Nairobi and Mombasa.

This is often made possible by the help of relatives in one of the two cities ("extended family"). Some of them seek work in vain and return to their home areas (Närman, 1985:45).

Presently an O-level examination seems to be an insignificant credential for wage employment. The prime advantage among job seekers in Kenya is a well-connected relative or other contact. However, some specific skills, such as IE, could contribute to acquiring a job.

However, the job tasks may have nothing to do with much of what has been learnt at school. In many cases, work done is of a casual or temporary nature.

A somewhat surprising result from this study is the low level of migration among school leavers. One should be aware of the bias in the material since it is easier to find those at home, than others. However, this main tendency is valid.

The majority of those at home stayed in their rural areas. Some were employed, mostly as teachers or in local government. Others seem to regard themselves as more or less idle, eking out a living from farming, or some kind of "survival skill".

Even if the decision to stay at home is not based on any calculated "cost-benefit" analysis, it seems to be the correct decision in view of the harsh urban labour market. There is nothing to suggest that the future will be any better.

The results from this tracer study are similar to those of one carried out in five technical secondary schools in 1985 and followed up in 1986. Among those traced who had left school, only 17 had a job or were self-employed.

Within the group at work almost all had acquired a job in their own home areas. The exceptions were a few, that had found employment in Nairobi or Mombasa. A majority of those working were engaged as untrained teachers.

Among the unemployed, nearly 30 per cent had left their home areas for a longer or shorter period to look for a job. Almost all of them indicated that they had tried in Nairobi, while a few had gone to the other major industrial towns, such as Kisumu, Nakuru, Mombasa, Eldoret or Thika. There were almost no exceptions to this.

CONCLUDING REMARKS

Obviously school leavers in Kenya, like in so many other African countries, are faced with a gloomy future. They are trapped in a situation of high expectations and few opportunities. This is so irrespective of whether they migrate to the cities and towns, or stay at home.

From the studies referred to above, it seems that fewer are now looking for jobs in the cities, compared to the situation reported in the 1970s. Still, however, the most attractive destinations for job seekers are the cities of Nairobi and Mombasa.

In a dependent development process there are few opportunities available. School leavers are forced to compete for a limited number of jobs in the modern sector which are often located in urban areas. Their existence is a struggle between the modern and the traditional. This is an extreme misuse of human resources.

Education cannot be offered exclusively to meet a social demand, with the primary goal to end up in the urban modern sector. It would rather serve a wider purpose if it could be adopted to provide a strategy for local mobilization. A reversal of the whole development perspective is badly needed. We have to regard the school leaver as a resource to be mobilized, and not somebody to provide employment *for*.

We have to revisit some of the original African concepts of education, such as the Tanzanian *Education for Self-Reliance*. What can it achieve in a situation not blocked by an external structure of dependency? Further, attention has to be given to the approach of *Education with Production*. It has to be realized that this is first of all a pedagogical tool, and not only an elaborate way of cost-sharing.

It is widely recognized that sustainable development cannot be achieved by measures imposed from above. The necessary processes of change have to be initiated in the rural areas and small towns. For school leavers to have an

integrated role in such a mobilization, their education has to be adjusted to
meet new demands for a self-reliant national development.

References

Fägerlind, I. and L. Saha, 1989, *Education & National Development—A Comparative Perspective.* London: Pergamon Press.
Grey-Johnson, C. (ed.), 1990, *The Employment Crisis in Africa—Issues in Human Resources Development Policy.* Southern Africa Political Economy Series. Harare.
International Labour Office, 1972, *Employment, incomes and equality—a strategy for increasing productive employment in Kenya.* Geneva.
Lauglo, J. and K. Lillis, 1988, *Vocationalizing Education—An International Perspective.* London: Pergamon Press.
Mabogunje, A., 1989, *The Development Process—a Spatial Perspective.* London: Unwin Hyman.
Närman, A., 1985, *Practical Subjects in Kenyan Academic Secondary Schools: Tracer Study.* SIDA, Education Division Documents No. 21. Stockholm.
Närman, A., 1988, *Practical Subjects in Kenyan Academic Secondary Schools: Tracer Study II Industrial Education, (three-year follow-up).* SIDA, Education Division Documents, No. 39, Stockholm.
Obudho, R. (ed.), 1981, *Urbanization and Development Planning in Kenya.* Nairobi: Kenya Literature Bureau.
Obudho, R. and D. Taylor, (eds.), 1979, *The Spatial Structure of Development: A Study of Kenya.* Boulder: Westview Press.
Republic of Kenya, *Economic Survey.* Government Printers, Nairobi. Various Issues.
Republic of Kenya, *Statistical Abstract.* Government Printers, Nairobi. Various Issues.
Republic of Kenya, 1974, *Development Plan 1974–1978.* Part I. Government Printers, Nairobi.
Republic of Kenya, 1981, *Population Census 1979.* Government Printers, Nairobi.
Republic of Kenya, 1983, *Report of the Presidential Committee on Unemployment 1982/83.* Government Printers, Nairobi.
Republic of Kenya, 1986, *Economic Management for Renewed Growth.* Government Printers, Nairobi.
Republic of Kenya, 1988, *Sessional Paper No 6 of 1988 on Education and Manpower Training for the Next Decade and Beyond.* Ministry of Education, Nairobi.
Republic of Kenya, 1989, *Development Plan 1989–1993.* Government Printers, Nairobi.
Tandon, Y., 1987, *Priority Needs and Regional Co-operation Concerning Youth in English-Speaking Africa.* Paris: UNESCO.
The Weekly Review, August 30, 1991.
World Bank, 1981, *Accelerated Development in Sub-Saharan Africa—An Agenda for Action.* Oxford University Press.

Pastoralist Migration to Small Towns in Africa

M.A. Mohamed Salih

Students of African pastoralism were until recently preoccupied with the analysis of pastoralists' response to seasonal and periodic climatic changes. Classics on the social anthropology of pastoralism have since been able to establish an association between migratory patterns and seasonal variations in rainfall and pasture. Pastoral movements were dealt with as regulatory processes mediated by seasonal predictability and pasture availability in dry and wet season rangelands (Evans-Pritchard, 1940; Gulliver, 1955; Hopen, 1958; Stenning, 1957 and 1959; Cunnison, 1966; Lewis, 1961). These studies have concluded that seasonal migration among pastoralists is an important mechanism for the interaction and hence the production and reproduction of people, herds and natural resources (pasture and soil). The relationships between people, herds and natural resources have further been analysed in terms of carrying capacities: household capacity to manage the herd, the herd capacity to satisfy the nutritional, economic and social needs of the household and natural resource capacity to sustain the herd and, when the climate allows, crop production. In this sense, pastoralists' migration is conceived as a direct response to the rhythm of the surrounding physical environment and its ability to satisfy, at a given time, the requirements of diverse resource users. Under such conditions, pastoralists' seasonal migratory routes regularly pass through towns and large population settlements where they exchange pastoral products (animals, milk, ghee and hides) for goods and services which they cannot produce themselves (cloth, sugar, tea, soap, flour-milling, modern medicine and so on).

During the 1970s and the beginning of the 1980s, the literature also provided examples of pastoralists inhabiting permanent settlements which were used as trade, and agricultural production centres to which the main herd trekked to distant pastures. Such settlements constitute small hamlets (Evans-Pritchard, 1940; Gulliver, 1955; Frantz, 1975) or large village settlements (Cunnison, 1966; Asad, 1964 and 1972; Ahmed, 1974; Lewis, 1961), which can hardly be denoted as urban centres. Iliffe (1987: 80) describes such settlements as:

population concentration rather than urban centres. They were built beautifully but imper-
mentantly of wood and reeds, moved quite frequently in response to political and environmental crises, and had neither markets nor economically specialized quarters.

Today, pastoral migratory patterns are under considerable ecological pressure
emanating from man-made interferences such as the expansion of crop production for food and cash, administrative control, game reserves and large-
scale irrigated schemes which restrict access to lands which were previously
part of what the pastoralists perceived as traditional grazing lands and farms
(Sørbø, 1985; Helland, 1980; Mohamed Salih, 1987; Ahmed, 1987; Rigby,
1992). Moreover, ecological stress has brought with it economic pressures
which have compelled primary commodity producers (such as pastoralists) to
sell more and buy less. The dynamics of the market economy negate any
notion that pastoralist migratory patterns are, like in the past, mainly determined by the natural sequence of the seasons. The increasing interaction
between pastoralists and urban centres also gives substance to the critique of
the conventional approaches which presented pastoral societies as if they
operate in isolation from sedentary populations. The thrust of this critique is
summarized by Barth's (1973:11) contention that:

1. nomadic societies can be depicted in relation to their total environment.
   Sedentary peoples and societies are part of this total environment, and the
   nomads' relations to them are revealed as part of an ecological, economic
   and political analysis.
2. to take a more symbiotic view, and seek to analyse the inter-connections of
   nomads and sedentary *populations* (italics added) as prerequisites for the
   persistence of each in their present form.

Other studies followed with remarkable contributions by Watts (1983 and
1987) and Galaty *et al.* (1980 and 1992) who developed the discussion further to point to the relevance of regional trade, economic interdependence
and political control to pastoralists. These and subsequent studies (Sørbø,
1985; Helland, 1980; Mohamed Salih, 1985; Ahmed, 1987; Hjort, 1990;
Rigby, 1992; Galaty *et al.*, 1992; Baxter, 1993) have revealed that contemporary changes in pastoral production have been augmented by proximity to
town, changes of consumption patterns and an increasing demand for goods
and services which were hardly known to the pastoralists a few decades ago.
Ecological and socio-economic processes have also encouraged adherence to
a complex and harmful system of resource management which at times forces
pastoralists to exceed the herd capacity as well as the pasture carrying capacity, in order to maintain the status-quo let alone improve the already deteriorating standards of living.

It is under such turbulent changes that the immigration of pastoralists
began to change and pastoralists' career patterns became diversified. While
some are still fortunate to have access to traditional animal routes and watering points, some have lost them to the expanding crop production sector.
Others have been displaced by drought and famine and migrated to towns,
thus developing linkages with small towns and other urban centres on which
they have become more dependent for their livelihood.

THE NEGLECT OF PASTORALISTS IN URBAN STUDIES

The relationship between rural populations and urban centres has been the subject of a few recent serious studies (Hardoy and Satterthwaite, 1986; Potter and Unwin, 1989; Baker, 1990 and Baker and Pedersen, 1992). However, in urban studies (except Baker, 1990) pastoralists do not even feature as a segment of the urban populations and most studies make no mention of pastoralist immigration or pastoral-urban interaction. Furthermore, few students of pastoral societies have ventured into devoting whole works to pastoral migrants (Hjort, 1990; Mohamed Salih, 1985 and 1992; Waters-Bayer, 1988; Bovin, 1990; Baxter, 1993; Markakis, 1993). Students of other social science disciplines such as Kameir (1988) have treated pastoral migrants as peasant migrants and applied all theories pertaining to the penetration of the capitalist mode of production and the impact of primitive accumulation. According to Kameir (1988) Nuer migrants in town are not different from any other migrants since they fall within the wider category of the working class. According to Kameir, the pastoral background of the Nuer migrants, therefore is of no relevance to their urban experience. The general opinion one gathers from the study is that the Nuer are peasants and not pastoralists or agro-pastoralists.

One explanation of this apparent neglect of pastoralists in urban studies could be that peasant studies tend to subsume pastoralists under the broader rubric of rural populations or the presumption that pastoralists have undergone processes of transformation similar to those experienced by peasant societies. Another explanation could be that, in Sub-Saharan Africa, there are few pastoral societies which do not practise some form of agricultural production (or agro-pastoralism). The view from Smith (1992:6), is that:

> those African countries south of the Sahara which have populations relying on domestic stock for their primary dietary, sociological and exchange needs constitute roughly a quarter of the continent's people. A further third are less dependent on their animals for food, but see them as a way of accumulating wealth and controlling the relations of production.

Therefore, it is unjustifiable to suggest that the wide prevalence of agro-pastoralism is used as a pretext to justify a crop production bias *vis-à-vis* pastoral production. Yet another untenable reason could be the low share of African livestock production in external trade and foreign exchange earning (less than 5 per cent of Africa's exports) relative to agriculture (60–80 per cent). It is obvious that the large share of agriculture in the export of cash crops determines development aid bias and orientations towards the cash crop sub-sector.

The evidence available suggests that most pastoralists are part of regional economies in which they barter or sell their products for grain and other commodities. Some used money or other medium of exchange even before the advent of colonialism (Bohannan and Dalton, 1962; Konczacki, 1978; Iliffe, 1987; Kerven, 1992). As in peasant societies, commercialization has induced significant economic transformations which include wealth concentration and surplus appropriation which is disproportionate with herd growth. Disproportionate surplus appropriation often results in impoverishment and hence sedentarization or rural–urban migration among the rural populations, peasants and pastoralists alike. In relation to these transformations, Watts (1987:194) observes that:

the possibility of herd decapitalization has been a major incentive for herders to take up cultivation of grain to circumvent the market altogether while other nomads are quite literally forced out of the pastoral economy by unequal exchange, having to liquidate all their animal assets. The cultural premium placed on pastoral *genre de vie* has naturally been a major incentive for herders to retain their classical cattle-based mode of operation.

Herd decapitalization (by market forces or natural disasters) has also fostered large-scale migration of impoverished pastoralists to urban centres where they have adopted a semblance of town-based pastoralism and other forms of adaptive and survival strategies.

The transformation of pastoral production from transhumance to sedentarization and other forms of settled pastoralism is not a simple change of means of production (from animal to farming), but one that involves structural transformation. At present, and unlike the past, a poor pastoralist cannot simply become a peasant, but is more likely to end up in the squatter settlements surrounding small or large urban centres and thus join the mass of the urban poor. Land appropriation by the state and the expanding interests of the wealthy and powerful agro-business classes indicate that the days when fertile lands were plentiful, and a poor pastoralist could easily settle and become a cultivator are drawing to a close. Hence, any attempt to encapsulate pastoralists under the broad category of the rural populations, would increase their marginalization and reinforce the injustices committed against them by administrators, planners and other functionaries of the African state. This however, is not to deny that both impoverished pastoralists and impoverished peasants do qualify for the category of rural poor or urban poor once they migrate to rural or urban areas. The difference however, is how they respond to these new livelihood situations.

The increasing numbers of pastoral migrants in African towns suggest that there are some specific forms of interaction and linkage with urban centres similar to those of peasant societies. As I have mentioned earlier, these linkages include the exchange of goods and services between rural and urban areas, the maintenance of family relations and primary group solidarity, support in the establishment of welfare organizations and institutions, and labour migration. The following section of this chapter discusses the factors which prompt pastoralist migration and its importance in pastoral–urban interaction, both between rural and urban areas as well as between settled pastoralists and the urban populations.

WHY DO PASTORALISTS MIGRATE?

Economic and social factors are considered prime determinants of migration among peasant societies and it is emphasized that rural–urban migration should be analysed within the wider politico-economic forces which have shaped the economies and societies of post-colonial Africa (Southall, 1979; Amin, 1974; Soja and Weaver, 1976; Simon, 1989 and 1992). Disparity between rural and urban areas, the concentration of employment opportunities and goods and services, have all contributed to the migration of rural populations, including pastoralists, from their homelands to towns. Since this chapter concerns rural–urban migration among pastoral societies, the aim is to examine whether some of the reasons given for migration among peasants are also relevant for pastoralists.

Nevertheless, it must be mentioned from the outset that some of the conventional reasons for peasant migration to town are of direct relevance to pastoralists. These can be summarized under four major factors or headings:

1. to gain access to education, health and other social services;
2. to seek employment, especially among school leavers whose skills cannot be absorbed by the pastoral economy, and their newly acquired needs and consumption patterns which cannot be satisfied within the pastoral economy;
3. to earn extra income in the slack period of crop and pastoral production in order to offset the deficit in the household budget;
4. displacement, and loss of stock and assets by natural disasters, or disproportionate surplus accumulation.

These factors have been the subject of many studies and I do not intend to dwell on them here. However, I intend to deal with migration among pastoralists as a direct response to social change, economic pressure and ecological stress. In this respect, some of the ideas developed by Barbara Harriss (1989) in her paper, *Commercialization, Distribution, and Consumption: Rural–Urban Grain and Resource Transfers in Peasant Society* will be used as a basis for a discussion aiming at comprehending the relevance of the processes which contributed to commercialization among peasants to pastoralists. Therefore, it is important to note that: 1) market exchange of grain is closely linked with market exchange of pastoral production hence direct exchange or exchange through conversion are important aspects of pastoral–peasant interaction and 2) the exchange relations between grain and livestock mediate certain socio-economic as well as political linkages which influence the processes of transformation in pastoral as well as peasant economies and societies.

Harriss (1989:205–6) argues that the commercialization of grain production is manifested in increased market exchange for three main purposes:

(i)   in order to purchase goods not produced by the household,
(ii)   in order to purchase goods produced but not owned by the household,
(iii) and in order to obtain cash.

All three categories of reasons as to why peasants have increased market exchange are also applicable to pastoral societies. Reasons (i) and (iii) are identical to those often given by pastoralists, and (i) in particular shows the importance of crop production for reinvestment in pastoral production and *vice versa*. As to (ii), it also indicates an increasing rate of differentiation in pastoral societies where herdless pastoralists begin to take up jobs as hired herders for wealthy pastoralists. Hired labourers or pastoralists who are entrusted by wealthy peasants to look after their animals are herd managers and not herd owners.

While Harriss's thesis is relevant to peasant societies, any substantive application of its implications for pastoral societies deserves some caution. For instance, market exchange according to Harriss (1989: 206) determines three conditions under which surplus from market sales is extracted:

(i)   where the agricultural marketing system is itself reasonably competitive and efficient, but where the power of non-agricultural classes is sufficient to manipulate price levels in such a way that the long term barter terms of trade are turned against the agricultural sector;

(ii)   where monopolistic merchants are able to depress their purchase prices (peasant producers' selling prices) below what they would be in a competitive market;

(iii)   where state pricing policies and other state interventions force prices below those of private markets, and compel peasants to sell to the state.

Contrary to Harriss's second argument which states that non-agricultural classes, turn the terms of trade against agricultural producers, it is evident that since the droughts of the 1970s and 1980s, pastoralists have not been sufficiently powerful to manipulate prices against the agricultural sector. This contradiction also applies to (iii) where I am not aware of any African country where pastoralists prefer to sell to the state through livestock marketing boards. This is mainly because as a principle livestock marketing board regulations usually set prices at levels far below the private sector. High administrative costs are paid for by the surplus extracted from pastoralists (and peasants). According to the urban bias thesis, low producer prices are often designed to supply cheap animal products (and food in general) to the politically vocal urban populations. Hence the marketing boards offer less encouraging prices to pastoralists than private wholesale traders. The market chain which involves several layers of middlemen and speculators also appropriates a considerable surplus from pastoralists. Nevertheless, the involvement of private merchant capital in the crop marketing sector adheres to market principles similar to those dealing with private wholesale livestock trade.

Despite differences in their response to the commercialization of primary commodities, pastoral societies share with peasant societies the same predicament. In Harriss's words (1989:211), "social relations of exchange will reveal themselves geographically in patterns of market places and a tracery of commodity flows, both between different rural areas and also between urban and rural areas". The impact of commercialization of pastoral production has not been accompanied by improvements in animal productivity to cope with increasing demands for manufactured goods, thus decreasing exchange ratios between livestock and agricultural production (Swift, 1982; Mohamed Salih, 1990 and 1992). Market forces have been aided by natural disasters (drought and large scale displacement) which also contributed to pastoralist migration to town. For instance, the economic and ecological crises and the subsequent decline of pastoral production, augmented by subsequent droughts during the early 1970s and late 1980s, aggravated the consequences of commercialization and accelerated the migration of displaced pastoralists to small towns throughout Sub-Saharan Africa (Hjort, 1990; Mohamed Salih, 1985 and 1992; Bovin, 1990; Baxter, 1993; Markakis, 1993). Harrison (1987: 224), sums up the responses of pastoralists to drought by stating that:

> the only sensible response was flight. Even then many families would lose most of their herds, or become involved in territorial disputes with other clans and tribes whose land they moved into.

Harrison then gives an indication of the magnitude of animal losses. He (1987: 224) points out that:

stock losses in recent droughts give some indication of the risk. In the Marsabit area of Kenya, 20–30 percent of all cattle died in the 1971 drought, and the same proportion died again a decade later. In the region north of Tahoua, in Niger, two thirds of the cattle and one third of the goats died in the 1973 drought. Eleven years later, when numbers had still not recovered to their previous level, the 1984 drought killed three fifths of the herds.

One implication of such magnitude of animal loss (or what Watts, 1987, calls decapitalization) is the displacement of large numbers of pastoral peoples and their relegation to the unenviable position of rural or urban poor living on international charity and food handouts.

As if natural disasters were not enough, most pastoral societies in the Sahel have been engaged in wars of liberation, self-determination or more autonomy from the grip of excessively centralized states or residual internal colonialism. I argue elsewhere (Mohamed Salih, 1990 and 1993) that by and large, the state of nations in Africa is one of defiance and resistance against the authority of the centralized government. Hence, the contradiction between state and civil society is compounded by another contradiction between societal interests and state policies which are insensitive to pastoralists. These wars have culminated in the displacement of 22.89 million people in eastern Africa alone of which 13.44 million have been affected by drought and food shortages and 2.8 million are war refugees most of whom are pastoralists, mainly Dinka, Nuer, Oromo, Beni-Amir, Somali, Afar and Baggara (SEPHA: 1991). For instance, following the intensification of the civil war in Somalia between 1988 and 1991, the formal economy had collapsed and exports of livestock, which make up Somalia's main source of foreign exchange, came to a total halt. The veterinary services were destroyed and because of unavailability of drugs and vaccines, epidemics spread and diseases increased. In October 1991, it is reported by SEPHA (1991: 67) that in central and southern Somalia livestock numbers have been reduced by 15 per cent, and one third of the animals surveyed showed signs of severe malnutrition. In the north it is reported that about 50 per cent of the goats and sheep have died in the past two years.

In Abyei District of Kordofan Region, bordering the war-torn Southern Sudan, it is reported (Mohamed Salih, 1993:26) that Ngok Dinka pastoralists attacked by tribal militias and the Sudanese Army migrated to northern and southern towns, or simply waited for death around a small town called Abyei, their administrative and market centre. With few skills and no one to help them during their stay in the towns, many Dinka and other Southerners died of starvation despite a mounting effort by relief organizations. Ryle (1988: 43) observes that, "there were about 20,000 Southerners who sought refuge in Abyei; four times the normal population of the town". Images of pastoral life being disrupted by war and famine are ghastly realities in most Sahelian towns where a large sector of the population is forced by all or some of the factors which I described above to migrate from their animal camps and villages to join an ever increasing pool of urban poor.

The factors which determine individual and households of pastoralists to migrate to town or to join relief centres in the outskirts of towns are not different from those of peasants. However, such reasons differ from individual to individual, group to group and from region to region. At the individual level, 100 heads of households which I surveyed in 1990–1991 among settled Somali pastoralists in Jigiga town (in Eastern Hararghe, Ethiopia) gave the following reasons for their migration: 35 percent lost their animals because of drought and epidemics, 15 percent fled the civil war in Somalia, 10 percent to educate their children, and the rest gave various reasons ranging from proximity to social services, and surplus milk selling to looking for employment opportunities. The rephrasing of the aggregate reasons given by individual heads of households falls within the general macro-pattern of rural–urban disparity, market exchange, drought, famine and wars. Pastoral–urban migration therefore is part of the general pattern of rural–urban migration.

Three points must be underlined before introducing the patterns of pastoralists' response to life in the urban centres. First, large sectors of pastoralists are gradually shifting emphasis from migration as a response to seasonal variation of the physical environment to economically induced migration, mainly influenced by the dynamics of the market economy. Second, disasters (drought, famine and wars) have taken prominence over conventional factors such as labour circulation and "the bright lights of town". Natural and man-made disasters have undermined most of what is left of pastoralist subsistence career patterns and forced large numbers of them to migrate to towns and large population centres. Third, pastoralists in town adopt a multitude of career patterns, and that the so-called urban-based pastoralism is only one among many other forms of adaptation.

PASTORALISTS IN TOWN OR URBAN-BASED PASTORALISM?

The meanings behind notions such as pastoralism in town and town-based pastoralism denote certain theoretical as well as practical implications for migrant pastoralists. In my paper on *Pastoralists in Town* (1985), an attempt was made to distinguish between patterns of pastoral responses to ecological and economic pressures resulting from the 1972–1973 and 1985–1988 droughts in the Sudan. These patterns suggest that urban-based pastoralism is only one form of pastoralists' adaptation. Some settled pastoralists do not even interact with town directly, but indirectly through middlemen, while others depend on peasant communities to purchase food for themselves and fodder for their animals. For example, I observed three distinct pastoral settlement patterns which have in the long-term reinforced their interaction with town (Mohamed Salih, 1985:3–4):

1. sedentary pastoralism along the banks of the Nile. Here pastoralists interact with the urban populations, peasants and fishermen. Their mode of adaptation is complex and involves livestock trade, milk selling, exchange of labour for fodder and animals for grain and vegetables.
2. rural sedentary settlements are also used as a dry season retreat from which pastoralists conduct long-distance trade and temporal visits to the large urban centres in order to sell their produce or purchase household requirements.
3. seasonal settlements around wells during the dry season, but constantly moving during the onset of the early rains and during spring. Most settlements are located alongside the main roads entering the town. Some pastoralists operate small shops and cafes, selling food and drinks to travellers.

Research results from the study of displaced pastoral groups living in the squatter settlements of small towns (Hjort, 1990; Baxter, 1993; Mohamed Salih, 1985 and 1993; Bovin, 1990) also demonstrate that such forms of pastoralism are prevalent throughout the African Sahel. My research experience among Somali migrants to Jigiga town, the capital of Eastern Hararghe Province, in Ethiopia, supports such a generalized pattern (see Fig. 1). As in the case of Omdurman (Kababish, Kawahla and Gwama pastoralists) the Somali settlements in the areas surrounding Jigiga have also emerged in response to the decline of the traditional forms of pastoralism due to drought, ecological stress and war (Map 1). The mode of pastoral adaptation associated with these two urban centres constitutes a unique system of livelihood where some new forms of pastoralism have been deployed. In these two cases, pastoralists were gradually moving away from complete dependence on the natural environment to an environment of their own making and a product of the urban centres on which they became dependent for the sale of their produce and the purchase of the necessities of life.

The three settlement patterns mentioned above are associated with socio-economic activities which do not include the urban pastoralist who has already been absorbed by an expanding 'urbanized' pastoralists have begun to adopt new consumption patterns, live in modern or European-type houses, use modern electric appliances (radios, TVs, refrigerators, air coolers), or became members of urban associations, trade unions and political parties. Neither can those who joined the urban labour market such as factory workers, porters and petty traders or those who took up various types of arduous jobs, be called pastoral based. This situation is not unique to Sudanese pastoralists. Bovin (1990:37–38) enumerated the following career patterns among the Fulani (also known as Fulbe or Fula):

> (1) beggars near roads and in urban centres, (2) jewelry sellers, (3) herbal medicine sellers, (4) petty traders, (5) night-watchmen, (6) car washing (7) hired farm labourers, (8) farmers depending on irrigation from water wells, (9) hair dressers, (10) calabash repairing (only by women), (11), domestic servants, (12) prostitution, (13) water carrying and selling, (14) workers in the construction sector and (15) carriers or porters, carrying heavy goods and luggage.

I add to these career patterns, milk sellers, casual labourers, skilled and semi-skilled labourers in small industries, government employees and self-employed businessmen. None of these career patterns are pastoral based and are certainly outside the domain of town-based pastoralism. Moreover, they reveal that pastoralists are highly responsive to new ideas and that they do look for opportunities outside pastoral production. To describe such pastoralists as persistent (Rigby: 1985) cannot be extended beyond the fact that pastoral production can be pursued in urban centres, not because pastoralists are traditionalists, but because they can adapt their mode or system of production to new situations.

Barth (1961) observes that the richest and the poorest pastoralists are often absorbed by new career patterns or find an exit from pastoral production, only the 'middle layer' remaining nomadic or pastoralist. In concurrence with this view, material collected from around Jigiga town in south-eastern Ethiopia (Brons *et al.*: 1993) suggests that highly educated and rich migrant pastoralists usually enter several town-based careers, and therefore cannot be

Map 1 . *Towns and ethnic groups mentioned in the text*

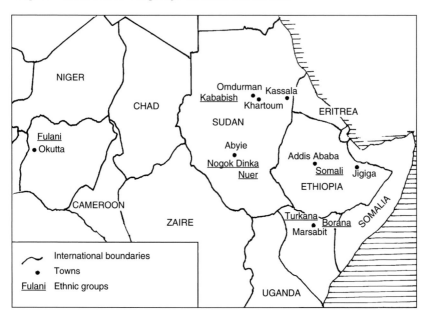

distinguished from educated urban dwellers with a peasant background. Another category of urban dwellers who cannot be distinguished by their pastoral or peasant background are the extremely poor who have lost all their stocks and assets before they decided to migrate to town.

Urban-based pastoralists (i.e. pastoralists who migrated to squatter settlements with some of their animals) fit into Barth's (1961) middle-layer pastoralists who can easily be distinguished from urban dwellers with peasant backgrounds, but who have no steady jobs or depend only on casual jobs. Such a peasant is part of the urban poor living under extreme poverty relative to the pastoralist who possesses some animals with which to practise urban-based pastoralism. Incomes from pastoral production in and around urban centres have become a shield which protects a large number of pastoralists from absolute poverty.

MIGRANT PASTORALISTS AND PROSPECTS OF SECURE LIVELIHOOD

The transformation and subsequent decline of traditional forms of pastoral production, coupled with the emergence of new forms of pastoralism around small urban centres, have created intersected social, political and economic problems for policy makers and town planners. Sociologically, pastoralists who migrate to town adopt a way of life largely influenced by the urban setting and the market economy which governs its dynamics. I have observed that pastoralists in town lose much of the institutional solidarity which they had enjoyed under the traditional system (Mohamed Salih, 1985). The commercialization of pastoral production signifies that the herd is no longer owned by groups of extended families or clan members, but by individual household members. As a result economic and social differentiation follows

which encourages the emergence of private property *versus* corporate ownership.

Furthermore, a problem of labour allocation may emerge as the household
size increases while the herd capacity to cater for household needs decreases.
A paradoxical situation may emerge when larger herds are needed to feed the
household and satisfy its newly acquired consumption patterns, while more
labour is needed for herd management. Any increase in the herd size beyond a
few cows, goats and sheep requires massive capital investment, expensive
feeding and higher labour capacity; all these are beyond the means of the so-
called middle layer of urban-based pastoralists.

Migrant pastoralists are generally among the least educated of the urban
populations, mainly because pastoral values and herding responsibilities allocated to children often draw them away from school and keep them within
the confines of their pastoral way of life. Child labour is an essential part of
pastoral production, including herding while adults attend farms or carry out
other social and political obligations. The lack of education undermines pastoralists access to job opportunities in the urban labour markets, especially in
situations where knowledge of some foreign language (English, French or
Arabic) is essential for communication and hence employment, even in jobs
that do not require any formal education or special skills. Therefore work
opportunities outside pastoral production are very few, a fact which compels
pastoralists to remain pastoralists in town. In other words, the persistence of
pastoralists in town is not a matter of resistance to change, but an adaptive
response to the predicament of traditional forms of pastoralism and the
opportunities which urban centres offer.

Nevertheless, migrant pastoralists are like peasant migrants in maintaining
linkages with relatives and kinsmen in town and in the rural areas. These
linkages include:

1. visiting relatives for maintenance of social relations or for medication in urban health services which are considered better than in rural areas;
2. living in relatives' houses during the initial period of migration;
3. exchanging gifts during religious celebrations, marriage and other life crises
   such as the mourning of relatives;
4. sending remittances to close relatives;
5. entrusting one's herd to relatives during migration;
6. attending and financing ethnic associations, regional political parties or
   representatives;
7. lobbying local government authorities on behalf of their communities;
8. contributing to the education of relatives' children, where there are no
   schools in their area.

Pastoralists in town are not without problems. For instance, one common
problem that confronts them is conflict with town authorities over access to
residential rights and the economic and social services that go with them.
Most of these conflicts emanate from deep rooted prejudices which administrators, planners and urban dwellers have held for decades about pastoralists.
For instance, town authorities in Omdurman in the Sudan have persistently
resorted to the use of the police and the army to evict pastoralists from squat-

ter settlements to distant camps which makes it difficult for them to commute to town for work (Mohamed Salih, 1985 and 1990).

The response of urban populations in Jigiga town in Ethiopia is identical to that in Omdurman in the Sudan, where the influx of displaced ethnic Somalis has created conflicts between pastoralists, urban populations and town authorities. Town authorities have prevented the immigrants from the right to food rations (flour, rice, cooking oil and sugar), forcing them to live under persistent fear of being removed to the very uncertain countryside from which they migrated. The excuses given by the town authorities to justify their prejudices against pastoralists include: 1) pastoralists are not registered town dwellers, 2) their food rations have already been sent to their areas of origin and 3) their animals create a health hazard and litter towns with dung and dirt.

Pastoralist milk sellers in Sahelian towns are regularly harassed by town health authorities who accuse them of mixing water with milk or selling reconstituted powdered milk (Mohamed Salih, 1985; Waters-Bayer, 1988). Such claims are often made by the owners of reconstituted milk factories and passed on to health authorities to discourage town dwellers from buying the relatively cheap and superior milk sold by urban-based pastoralists.

The urban populations in the above towns are often divided between those who sympathize and offer assistance to displaced pastoralists, and those who are antagonistic to the existence of large number of immigrants exerting pressure on health, education, transport and other social services.

In terms of livelihood strategies, the three patterns of settlement which I presented earlier, represent three spatially and occupationally interactive categories of populations: urban dwellers including urbanized pastoralists, urban based pastoralists, and rural or sedentary-based pastoralists (Fig. 1). It is within these complex exchange relationships that pastoralists adapt, and continuously change their strategies in order to maintain what Chambers (1988:1) defined as secure livelihood or the situation:

> whereby livelihood refers to stocks and flows of food and cash to meet basic needs, security denotes secure ownership of or access to resources, including services and assets to offset risk, ease shocks and meet contingencies. For a secure livelihood to be sustainable then, it has to lead to the maintenance or enhancement of resource productivity on a long-term basis.

The question is to what extent can pastoralists in town sustain a secure livelihood amidst increasing economic and political pressures and a dwindling resource base. Apparently, middle layer pastoralists can sustain a secure livelihood since they are increasingly dependent on more predictable feeding sources for their livestock under conditions of settled pastoralism. Their animals are close to water holes and only small quantities of fodder are needed which are obtainable from the market, as more farmers cultivate fodder and where feeding factories have been established (Mohamed Salih, 1992). Middle layer pastoralists are therefore outside the immediate impact of drought and other natural hazards. Proximity to town offers them better health services for themselves and their animals which also decreases the spread of epidemics and increases the possibility of steady herd growth.

Pastoralists who settled spontaneously also have the possibility of having indirect access to urban markets by commuting to town or through middle-

Figure 1. *Settlement patterns and pastoral–urban interaction*

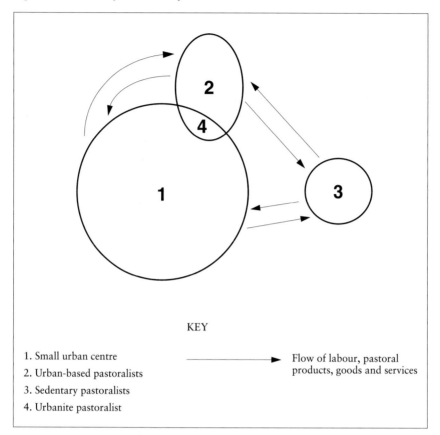

KEY

1. Small urban centre
2. Urban-based pastoralists
3. Sedentary pastoralists
4. Urbanite pastoralist

————————————▶ Flow of labour, pastoral products, goods and services

men who purchase their products and sell them in town. Pastoralists are disadvantaged in the sense that they continue to be dependent on middlemen who appropriate a considerable surplus of the market price (for example, 20–25 per cent of the sale of goat and sheep and 50 per cent of cattle sales), while transport adds another 10 per cent hence lowering pastoralists' earnings. The survival of rural sedentary pastoralists hinges on their ability to enhance resource productivity and maintenance on a long-term basis. These are largely associated with market behaviour and the primary commodity producers' position in the international division of labour. Other factors such as state agricultural policies, price regulations and other forms of urban bias are also detrimental to pastoralists, subsistence, urban-based and sedentary.

Poor or herdless pastoralists who are absorbed by town and settle there permanently are among the poorest in town (Mohamed Salih: 1992). They lack any stock, flows of food or cash to secure their basic needs. Their case as Baxter (1987:19) puts it is one in which:

> family and core social and economic relationships have taken a beat. Pastoral men have grown accustomed to having their skills devalued, and have adapted to migrant labour and shanty town life; as their womenfolk have adapted to getting by on relief handouts while trying to maintain, if they are lucky, a heifer or two and a few sheep and goats.

Poor pastoralists who live in urban centres can hardly maintain a secure live-lihood under such conditions, but middle layer pastoralists have some good chances to make ends meet. Poor pastoralists' standards of living can be improved through poverty alleviation and manpower development training schemes, if their existence as an impoverished sector of the urban population is recognized, and their need for specific skills derived from their pastoral background is acknowledged. What is unique about the middle layer of pas-toralists in town is that they continue with pastoral production as a modified career pattern, largely adapted to the urban setting. The knowledge acquired by this group of entrepreneurial pastoralists can be extended to poor pas-toralists who should be encouraged to be involved in income-generating activities, small-scale leather industries, small dairy farms, milk processing and marketing. Therefore, unlike peasants, migrant pastoralists can secure their livelihood provided that their skills are valued and their contribution to food and employment is taken seriously by administrators and town plan-ners.

CONCLUDING REMARKS

Although many studies continue to treat pastoralists as a remote and isolated sector of the rural population, recent evidence suggests that pastoral societies have undergone considerable transformations. The changing patterns of pas-toralists' migration (from dependence on seasonal variations to economically and ecologically induced migration) reveal an increasing tendency towards commercialization, sedentarization and rural–urban migration. All these are indicators of the distortions which plagued the so-called traditional forms of pastoralism and their increasing retreat in the face of mounting economic and ecological pressures.

Pastoralists in town pursue a variety of career patterns, including urban-based pastoralism. In this case, pastoral–urban interaction portrays a unique form of adaptation in which pastoralists are able to eke out their living from a small number of animals kept near their shacks and cardboard houses. Unlike dispossessed peasants, pastoralists in town are able to secure a limited advantage against absolute poverty. Even though it is apparent that the polit-ical economy and the factors which have contributed to the decline of pasto-ralism have some similarities with peasant societies, the two differ in their modes of adaptation to urban life. However, it is evident that rich and poor pastoralists, like peasants, can easily be absorbed by town life because they are in a position to divert their resources or labour from pastoralism to other urban-based activities.

References

Ahmed, Abdel Ghaffar, M., 1974, *Shayikhs and Followers*. Khartoum: Khartoum University Press.
Ahmed, Abdel Ghaffar, M., 1987, "National Ambivalence and External Hegemony: The Neglect of the Nomads in the Sudan", in M.A.Mohamed Salih (ed.) *Agrarian Change in the Central Rainlands of the Sudan*. Uppsala: Scandinavian Institute of African Studies.

Amin, S.,(ed.), 1974, *Modern Migrations in Western Africa*. Oxford: Oxford University Press for the International African Institute.

Asad, T., 1964, "Seasonal Movements among the Kababish Arabs", *Sudan Notes and Records, No. 45*

Asad, T. 1972, *The Kababish Arabs*. London, Hurst.

Baker, Jonathan, (ed) 1990, *Small Town Africa: Studies in Rural–Urban Interaction*. Uppsala: Scandinavian Institute of African Studies.

Baker, Jonathan and Poul Ove Pedersen, (eds), 1992, *The Rural–Urban Interface in Africa: Expansion and Adaptation*. Uppsala: Scandinavian Institute of African Studies.

Barth, F.,1961, *The Nomads of South Persia*. Boston: Little Brown and Co.

Barth, F., 1973, "A General Perspective on Nomad–Sedentary Relations in the Middle East", in C. Nelson (ed.), *The Desert and the Sown: Nomads in the Wider Society*. Berkeley, Institute of International Studies, University of California, Research Series No. 21.

Baxter, P.T.W., 1987, *From Telling People to Listening to Them*. Manchester Discussion Papers in Development, Faculty of Economic and Social Studies, University of Manchester.

Baxter, P.T.W., 1993, "The New East African Pastoralists" in J. Markakis (ed) *Conflict and the Decline of Pastoralism in the Horn of Africa*. London: Macmillan Press and The Hague, Institute of Social Studies.

Bohannan, P. and G. Dalton, (eds), 1962, *Markets in Africa*. Chicago: Northwestern University Press.

Bovin, M., 1990, "Nomads of the Drought", in M. Bovin and L. Manger (eds), *Adaptive Strategies in African Arid Lands*. Uppsala: Scandinavian Institute of African Studies.

Brons, M., M. Tegegn, E. Woldeysus, and M.A.Mohamed Salih, 1993, "War and the Somali Refugees in Eastern Hararghe, Ethiopia", in T. Tvedt (ed), *Conflicts in the Horn of Africa: Human and Ecological Consequences of War*. Uppsala: Environmental Policy and Society, University of Uppsala.

Chambers, R. 1988, "Sustainable Rural Livelihoods: A Key Strategy for People, Environment and Development", in C. Conroy and M. Litvinoff, (eds) *The Greening of Aid*. London: Earthscan.

Cunnison, I., 1966, *Baggara Arabs*. Oxford: Clarendon Press.

Evans-Pritchard, E.E.,1940, *The Nuer*. London: Oxford University Press.

Frantz, C. 1975, "Contractions and Expansions in Nigeria Bovine Pastoralism", in T. Monod, (ed), *Pastoralism in Tropical Africa*. London: Oxford University Press.

Galaty, J.G. and P. Bonte, 1992, *Herders, Warriors and Traders*. Boulder, San Francisco and Oxford: Westview Press.

Galaty, J.G., D. Aronson, P.C. Salzman, and A. Chouinard, (eds), 1980, *The Future of Pastoral Peoples*. Proceedings of a conference held in Nairobi, Kenya, 4–8 August, 1980. Ottawa: International Development Centre.

Gulliver, P.H., 1955, *Family Herd*. London, Routledge and Kegan Paul.

Hardoy, Jorge and David Satterthwaite, (eds), 1986, *Small and Intermediate Urban Centres*. London: Hodder and Stoughton in association with the International Institute for Environment and Development.

Harrison, P., 1987, *The Greening of Africa*. London, Glasgow, Toronto, Sydney and Auckland: Paladin Grafton Books.

Harriss, B., 1989, "Commercialization, Distribution, and Consumption: Rural–Urban Grain and Resource Transfers in Peasant Society" in R. Potter and T. Unwin, (eds), *The Geography of Urban–Rural Interaction in Developing Countries*. London and New York: Routledge.

Helland, J., 1980, *Five Essays on the Study of Pastoralists and the Development of Pastoralism*, Skriftserie, Occasional Paper No. 20, Bergen.

Hjort af Ornäs, A., 1990, "Town-Based Pastoralism in Eastern Africa", in J.Baker (ed), *Small Town Africa: Studies in Rural–Urban Interaction*. Uppsala: Scandinavian Institute of African Studies.

Hopen, C.E., 1958, *The Pastoral Fulbe Family in Gwandu*. London: Oxford University Press.

Iliffe, J. 1987, *The African Poor: A History*. Cambridge, New York, New Rochelle, Melbourne and Sydney: Cambridge University Press.

Kameir, E.M., 1988, *The Political Economy of Labour Migration in the Sudan*. Hamburg: Institute of African Studies.

Kerven, C., 1992, *Customary Commerce: A Historical Reassessment of Pastoral Livestock Marketing in Africa*. London: Overseas Development Institute.

Konczacki, Z.A., 1978, *The Economy of Pastoralism: A Case Study of Sub-Saharan Africa*. London: Frank Cass.

Lewis, I., 1961, *A Pastoral Democracy*. Oxford: Oxford University Press.

Markakis, J., (ed), 1993, "Introduction", in *Conflict and the Decline of Pastoralism in the Horn of Africa*. London: Macmillan Press and The Hague, Institute of Social Studies.

Mohamed Salih, M.A., 1985, "Pastoralists in Town", *Pastoral Development Network Paper*, No. 21 b. London: Overseas Development Institute.

Mohamed Salih, M. A., (ed), 1987, "Introduction" in *Agrarian Change in the Central Rainlands of the Sudan*. Uppsala: Scandinavian Institute of African Studies.

Mohamed Salih, M.A., 1990, "Pastoralism and the State in African Arid Lands: An Overview", in *Nomadic Peoples*, Nos. 25–27.

Mohamed Salih, M.A., 1992, *Pastoralists and Planners*, Drylands Networks Programme, Issue Paper No. 32. London: International Institute for Environment and Development.

Mohamed Salih, M. A., 1993, "The Decline of Pastoralism in the Sudan", in J. Markakis (ed) *Conflict and the Decline of Pastoralism in the Horn of Africa*. London: Macmillan Press and The Hague, Institute of Social Studies.

Potter, R. and T. Unwin, (eds), 1989, *The Geography of Urban–Rural Interaction in Developing Countries*. London and New York: Routledge.

Rigby, P., 1985, *Persistent Pastoralists: Nomadic Societies in Transition*. London: Zed Books.

Rigby, P.,1992, *Cattle, Capitalism and Class*. Philadelphia: Temple University Press.

Ryle, J., 1988, "The Road to Abyie", *Granta*, Vol. 10.

SEPHA, 1991, "Situation Report", *Special Emergency Programme for the Horn of Africa*. New York.

Simon, D., 1989, "Colonial Cities, Postcolonial Africa and the World Economy: A Reinterpretation", *International Journal of Urban and Regional Research*, Vol. 13, No. 1.

Simon, D., 1992, *Cities, Capital and Development: African Cities in the World Economy*. London: Belhaven Press.

Smith, A.B., 1992, *Pastoralism in Africa: Origins and Development Ecology*. London: Hurst and Company, Athens: Ohio University Press, and Witwatersrand University Press.

Soja E.W., and C.E. Weaver, 1976, "Urbanization and Underdevelopment in East Africa", in B.J.L. Berry, (ed), *Urbanization and Counterurbanization*. Beverly Hills: Sage.

Sørbø, G., 1985, *Tenants and Nomads*. Uppsala: Scandinavian Institute of African Studies.

Southall, A., 1979, *Small Urban Centres in Rural Development in Africa*. Madison: African Studies Program, University of Wisconsin-Madison.

Stenning, D.J., 1957, "Transhumance, Migratory Drift, Migration; Patterns of Pastoral Fulani Nomadism", in *Journal of the Royal Anthropological Society*, Vol. 87, Part 1.

Stenning, D. J., 1959, *Savannah Nomads*. London: Oxford University Press.

Swift, J., 1982, "Development of Livestock Trading in Nomad Pastoral Society: The Somali Case", in *Pastoral Production and Society*. Cambridge: Cambridge University Press.

Waters-Bayer, Ann, 1988, *Dairying by Settled Fulani Agro-pastoralists in Central Nigeria*. Farming Systems and Resource Economics in the Tropics, Vol. 4. Kiel: Wissenschaftsverlag Vauk.

Watts, M., 1983, *Silent Violence, Food and Famine in Northern Nigeria*. Berkeley: Berkeley University Press.

Watts, M., 1987, "Drought, Environment and Food Security", in H.G.Glantz *et al*. (eds), *Drought and Hunger in Africa*. Cambridge: Cambridge University Press.

The New Nomads
An Overview of Involuntary Migration in Africa

Johnathan Bascom

People are on the move all across Africa. Approximately twenty million Africans have chosen to leave home in search of better opportunities elsewhere, but even more must leave against their wishes. Nearly twenty-five million Africans are displaced persons, 5.8 million of whom live in asylum outside their own country (Hamilton, 1994). One hundred and one distinct populations of displaced persons exist throughout the continent. In the sub-Saharan region, where displacement is most endemic, one person in every twenty-four is an involuntary migrant. The chief objective of this chapter is to provide a well-informed survey of involuntary migration in Africa.

The structure of the chapter is as follows. Section one summarizes the magnitude of involuntary migration in Africa and categorizes different causal factors and flight patterns. The second section highlights patterns of flight and the prevailing forms of settlement for people who find asylum in neighbouring countries. Section three examines solutions to their plight and concentrates on the complexities associated with the return of refugees to their homeland. The final section reflects on the following issues: the new dimensions of involuntary migration in Africa; lessons learned for future refugee policy; directions for ongoing research; and the interplay between structure and agency in refugee settings.

MAGNITUDE: INVOLUNTARY MIGRATION IN AFRICA

In late 1960, the United Nations High Commissioner for Refugees (UNHCR) sanctioned its first relief operation in Africa. Political independence occurred in most African nations including Zaire, the site of UNHCR's first intervention, during the decade thereafter. Despite many spontaneous repatriations in the aftermath of victorious wars of independence, the total number of African refugees had exceeded one million by 1970 (Figure 1). Fifty per cent of the 1970 refugee total originated in liberation wars against the Portuguese in Angola, Guinea Bissau, and Mozambique (Hansen, 1993:149). While the number of refugees had grown significantly, the refugee crisis was largely confined to exiles of five different nationalities: 400,000 Angolans, 165,000 Sudanese, 150,000 Rwandans, 55,000 Guinea Bissauans and 35,000

Mozambicans. Nonetheless, nearly 45 per cent of the global refugee population under the mandate of the United Nations were Africans (UNHCR cited in Rogge, 1977:186).

Figure 1. *The annual refugee population in Africa, 1959–1993*

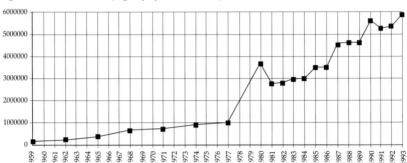

After independence, African states faced the challenge of establishing legitimate political systems, developing viable economies, and unravelling the legacy of colonial domination. These pressures, coupled with the added exigencies of superpower confrontation, created coups, counter-coups, ethnic conflicts, and more refugees. By 1980 the total number of African refugees reached 3.5 million. Observers could no longer hope that political transformation from colonies into states would rid the continent of refugees. Latent colonial activity in Zimbabwe, Namibia, and the Republic of South Africa accounted for only 10 per cent of the displaced persons on the continent (Hansen, 1993:149). The locus of Africa's refugee movements at this point was primarily central and eastern Africa. Ethiopia, Angola, and Uganda were the three largest source countries while Somalia, Sudan, Zaire and Kenya served the counterpart role as the principal host nations. In 1980, UNHCR (1981) reported that one in three people living in Somalia were refugees.

Refugee crisis became a Pan-African problem during the 1980s. While the total number of refugees reached 5.6 million by 1990, the number of nations hosting exiled refugee populations grew from eighteen to forty-two (Figure 2). Significantly, West Africa had began to play a growing role in refugee crises evidenced by hundreds of thousands of refugees in Guinea, Côte d'Ivoire and Liberia. By the beginning of 1994, the continent's population of 5.82 million refugees exceeded that of twenty-eight African states (Population Reference Bureau, 1993).

Not surprisingly, the amount of foreign assistance for African refugees has grown significantly during the last thirty years. The most significant portion—UNHCR's funds—grew from 2 million to 284 million dollars between 1970 and 1992 (Rogge, 1981:201; UNHCR, 1993a). This constitutes 27 per cent of UNHCR's total budget. UNHCR's role in refugee relief has shifted markedly during the last three decades as well. At one time the agency undertook "turnkey" operations entirely on its own. While UNHCR still provides the critical function of protection, the delivery of assistance is increasingly sub-contracted out to non-governmental organizations (NGOs) leaving UNHCR staff with mainly a supervisory and monitoring role. In the case of

Figure 2. *The distribution of African refugees in host countries, 1990*

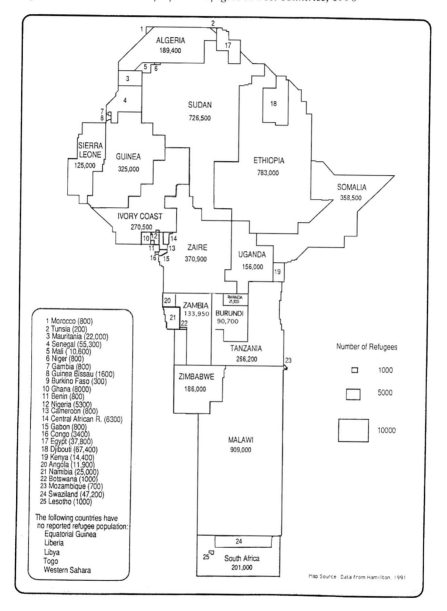

ALGERIA
189,400

SUDAN
726,500

SIERRA
LEONE
125,000

GUINEA
325,000

ETHIOPIA
783,000

SOMALIA
358,500

IVORY COAST
270,500

ZAIRE
370,900

UGANDA
156,000

RWANDA
2,500

ZAMBIA
133,950

BURUNDI
90,700

TANZANIA
266,200

ZIMBABWE
186,000

MALAWI
909,000

SOUTH AFRICA
201,000

1 Morocco (800)
2 Tunsia (200)
3 Mauritania (22,000)
4 Senegal (55,300)
5 Mali (10,600)
6 Niger (800)
7 Gambia (800)
8 Guinea Bissau (1600)
9 Burkino Faso (300)
10 Ghana (8000)
11 Benin (800)
12 Nigeria (5300)
13 Cameroon (800)
14 Central African R. (6300)
15 Gabon (800)
16 Congo (3400)
17 Egypt (37,800)
18 Djibouti (67,400)
19 Kenya (14,400)
20 Angola (11,900)
21 Namibia (25,000)
22 Botswana (1000)
23 Mozambique (700)
24 Swaziland (47,200)
25 Lesotho (1000)

The following countries have
no reported refugee population:
Equatorial Guinea
Liberia
Libya
Togo
Western Sahara

Number of Refugees

1000

5000

10000

Map Source: Data from Hamilton, 1991

sub-Saharan Africa, for example, UNHCR relies on as many as 125 NGOs as operational partners (UNHCR, 1993a:178).

Significantly, another category of displaced people exceeds the early 1994 total of 5.82 million official refugees. The United Nation's mandate limits its purview to those involuntary migrants who cross international boundaries due to a well-founded fear of persecution for reasons of race, religion, nationality, membership of a particular social group or political opinion. This distinction established by the Geneva Convention delimits the "classical" refugee from voluntary migrants, but it ignores two other categories of forced migrants in Africa—"internal" refugees and "environmental" refugees.

The vast majority of displaced people in Africa are refugees in every respect except that they do not, or, in many instances, cannot cross an international boundary. The number of involuntary migrants who remain inside their own country includes 16.8 million Africans (Table 1). This total is more than four times the number of refugees under the traditional terms prescribed by the first article of the 1951 Geneva Convention. Legally speaking, however, internal refugees remain under the sovereignty of the state in which they still live and thereby, beyond the purview of direct international intervention (Bascom, 1993b).

Table 1. *Significant populations of internally displaced civilians within African countries, 1993*

Sudan	4,000,000
South Africa	4,000,000
Mozambique	2,000,000
Angola	2,000,000
Liberia	1,000,000
Somalia	700,000
Zaire	500,000
Burundi	500,000
Ethiopia	500,000
Sierra Leone	400,000
Kenya	300,000
Rwanda	300,000
Eritrea	200,000
Togo	150,000
Djibouti	140,000
Guinea	80,000
Chad	50,000
Mali	40,000
Senegal	28,000
Total	16,888,000

Source: Hamilton 1994.

The United Nations is, however, beginning to break with its usual reluctance to violate national sovereignty. Based on humanitarian grounds, UN has recently intervened in Lebanon, Iraq, Bosnia and, significantly in the African context, in Somalia. The emergency division of the United Nations Development Program (UNDP) is inheriting the charge to respond to internal crises. In Africa, UNDP has begun to shift from monitoring to intervention by initiating the establishment of "peace villages", safe havens, or protected corridors. Demarcating such zones can serve three important functions. Internally displaced people can: a) flee without leaving their home region; b) return to a place closer to home before conflict completely subsides; and c) receive improved access to assistance from the international community.

A third category of refugees illustrates another set of significant structural forces at work in the lives of involuntary migrants. In 1985, the leading US public information agency regarding refugees added a new table to its annual world refugee survey. Nearly 600,000 people in Africa are displaced by "refugee-like conditions", the vast majority of whom are referred to as "environmental" refugees (Table 2).

Table 2. *Significant populations of Africans displaced by*
"refugee-like conditions", 1993

Burundi	170,000
Uganda	120,000
Egypt	103,000
Cameroon	40,000
Mauritania	22,000
Namibia	20,000
Algeria	4,000
Total	599,000

Source: Hamilton 1994.

The central issue beneath the semantic distinction between this category and other migrants is the origination or source of the pressures that causes people to move. "Ecocidal tactics"—burning crops, killing animals, mining fields, destroying irrigation systems—are a deliberate strategy of war (Wood, 1994). Undoubtedly, such forms of overt destruction have prompted large portions of the current population of "classic" refugees and "internal" refugees to leave their homes. However, Table 2 identifies displaced persons associated with two other kinds of environmental conditions—sudden natural disasters and longer-term manifestations of oppressive economic and political conditions. Put differently, there is a growing recognition that drought, degradation and famine which force people to move, are not independent of key forces that originate in economic or socio-political structures.

Prime examples of "environmental" refugees occurred during recent famines in Ethiopia and Sudan. A physical phenomenon—a marked drop in precipitation—was the proximate cause of a massive exodus out of rural areas in Ethiopia during the 1984–85 famine. Less immediate forces—disastrous agricultural policies dictated by the state and the deliberate obstruction of food aid into stricken areas—were no less important factors (Rahmato, 1987 and Baker, this volume). Sudan was relatively untouched by the intense Sahelian drought of the late 1960s. Twenty years later, however, more than one hundred thousand people left their homes to avoid starvation. Poor rainfall occurred on both occasions. The difference between the two events—and thereby the underlying reason for the recent migration—was an ongoing process of impoverishment linked to the disarticulated nature of the Sudanese economy, appropriation of labour and land by mechanized schemes, obstructionist tactics employed by merchant capital, and operative mechanisms of immiseration within the localized social relations of production (Bascom, 1989). Throughout Africa, political and economic contexts like these produce additional "environmental" refugees.

The three broad categories noted above reflect that definitions for refugees depend mainly upon what party is doing the defining. The United Nations administers the "classic" definition at one end of the spectrum:

Article 1 of the 1951 Geneva Convention defines a refugee as someone who is forced by a well-founded fear of persecution for reasons of race, religion, nationality, membership of a particular social group, or political opinion, to migrate involuntarily across an international boundary and remain outside his [her] country of nationality (Nobel, 1982:9).

All African countries but seven have ratified either the 1951 Geneva Convention or the 1967 supplementary protocol, designed for newly independent countries to ratify (Ricco, 1989). Many African governments—that actually effect refugee status—use a slightly broader definition. In 1969, leaders in the Organization of African Unity (OAU) determined that the Geneva Convention's definition did not match the realities of their region. Consequently, they expanded the basis for permitting refugee status by appending a second set of distinctions to those of the Geneva Convention:

> The term "refugee" shall also apply to every person who, owing to external aggression, occupation, foreign domination, or events seriously disturbing public order in either part or the whole of his country of origin or nationality, is *compelled to leave his place of habitual residence* in order to seek refuge in another place outside his *country of origin* or nationality (Nobel, 1982:10 *emphasis mine*).

Thirty-four African countries have ratified the 1969 Refugee Convention adopted by the OAU and several have taken specific action to expand their national legislation concerning the status of refugees (Ricco, 1989).

Relief agencies and the media expand the scope of meaning associated with refugees. They tend to base their actions and stories on refugees' condition rather than their motivation for leaving home. At least in some instances, however, refugees use a broader designation. In the early 1980s, for example, Ugandans who fled into southern Sudan did not consider themselves to be refugees until they entered a UN camp or settlement. As Harrell-Bond (1986:6) documents:

> After crossing the Ugandan/Sudan border, they believe they are still... not refugees. When they see you pack to come to the settlement, they say 'so you have accepted to be a refugees'. They use the 's' on the word 'refugee' even if you are a single person without knowing the connotation, even when they are actually refugees in the Sudan!

In sum, the United Nations, host governments, relief agencies, and refugees themselves deploy a long continuum of definitions. The most restrictive and explicit definitions are legal, political and administrative ones designed to establish dichotomous categories between those who make interstate movements and those who do not (Zolberg, Suhrke, and Aguayo cited in Hansen, 1993:145). However, the lines between these are becoming more and more blurred. This should not surprise us. The Geneva Convention's distinction was framed in the context of post-war Europe when refugees had crossed international borders as German forces advanced across the continent. In a monumental survey of refugee crises world-wide, Louise Holborn (1975:825) observed that "African refugee groups have proved to be very different from those in Europe in size, character and needs; and African refugee movements have occurred in an entirely different political, economic, social and cultural context". The rising numbers of "internal" refugees and "environmental" refugees since then attest to the truth of her observation. However, the remainder of this chapter focuses on the traditional categorization of refugees; those people who are forced by a well-founded fear of persecution to migrate involuntarily across an international boundary and remain outside his [her] country of nationality.

ASYLUM: PATTERNS OF FLIGHT AND FORMS OF RESETTLEMENT IN AFRICA

This section focuses on the prevailing patterns of flight and resettlement as refugees seek asylum in neighbouring countries throughout Africa. As a useful place to start, Kolenic (1974) offers a fruitful set of generalizations based on an intensive analysis of recurrent flight patterns in Africa. She links different characteristics of refugee flight to the country of origination:

1. *A direct relationship between the severity and immediacy of conflict and the size of refugee flows.* The fundamental dynamic that acts upon refugees is severity of the conditions that force them to leave their homes and migrate involuntarily out of the country. Open warfare produces "acute displacements" compared to smaller more sporadic flows due to less overt pressures (Kunz, 1973).

2. *A direct relationship between the refugees' perception of conflict and the size of flows.* A refugee's motivation to move is often dependent upon refugees' perception of the severity of conditions. It is for this reason that Kunz (1973) coins the expressions "anticipatory displacement" and "vintage" to denote different waves of refugees produced by refugees' changing perception of danger linked to the actual existence of such dangers.

3. *A direct relationship between the severity of conflict and the composition of flows.* Severe conditions within a source country produce a broad distribution of ages, more balance between different genders and a greater number of intact family groups. Smaller and slower movements are more selective in their composition (for example, young, intellectual, male adults who travel long distances to urban areas).

4. *A direct relationship between the severity of conflict and the length of flight.* During open warfare refugees want to get beyond the range of hostilities and tend to move shorter distances. Low intensity conflicts allow people more time to leave and they may chose to make a more distant urban centre the objective of their flight.

5. *A direct relationship between the length of flight and the permanence of involuntary migration.* Time produces inertia that reinforces the relationship between distance and permanence. The longer the period in exile, the less likely it is that refugees will ever return to their homeland.

For the vast majority of African refugees, flight ends in the country of first asylum. One in ten thousand African refugees moves on to resettle in a third country off the continent (UNHCR, 1993a). The United States, Canada and Australia are the only countries with planned levels for an annual intake of African refugees (3,000, 1,000, and 250 respectively). Those European countries that admit African refugees do so only on an individual basis. That avenue is now diminishing with the shift from a "welcome mode" into a "protection mode" (Rogge, 1991:9). Most African refugees cannot return home either. Eighty per cent of the current refugee population in Africa has been exiled for more than five years. Hence, this section turns to the only real option facing most African refugees—to settle in the country to which they fled.

The most fundamental difference among incoming refugees is that some settle without international assistance while others reside with the formal protection and help of the United Nations. The distribution of African refugees among these two categories has changed significantly since the mid 1970s; the ratio of unassisted refugees to assisted ones fell from a 4:1 ratio in 1976 to a 3:2 ratio in 1984, and then, to a 1:1 ratio in 1994 (Hansen, 1981; UN, 1984; Drumthra, 1994). Both categories can be subdivided into two forms of settlement—concentrations of self-settlers in rural areas or in urban enclaves and assisted refugees in either "temporary" camps or agricultural and wage earning settlements. The remainder of this section examines each of these four forms of settlement in a sequential manner.

Self-settled refugees in rural concentrations

The most typical pattern of flight is a short, *en masse* push across the closest territorial boundary away from the conflict source. Approximately 50 per cent enter formal refugee reception sites, camps or resettlement schemes. Just as many refugees, however, settle without assistance somewhere within the asylum country. The majority of these self-settling refugees generally congregate in rural areas along the border adjoining their homeland. The largest concentrations of unassisted rural refugees are in the boundary areas of eastern Sudan and Ethiopia, southern Zaire, south-western Uganda and Tanzania, eastern Malawi, north-western Zambia, western Ghana and Côte d'Ivoire, northern Liberia, and southern Sierra Leone.

Most refugees avoid camps and settlements as much as possible and tend to use them only as a "safety net" when all else fails as support for the most vulnerable family members, or where there are security problems (McGregor and Aikman, 1991:3). There are many related reasons why refugees dislike camps and settlements, but the basic one is that refugees lose more autonomy over their lives in such settings. The fear of forced repatriation, restricted social mobility, and governmental supervision threatens refugees' sense of control—already radically deteriorated after their flight—enough to persuade them to self-settle. Hansen (1993:17) encapsulates this "power calculus" in action:

> From the perspective of the refugee, self-settlement in the border villages is a sensible decision in terms of power. The village world is a familiar one, where the refugee may be able to transfer and maintain some status, rank, and prestige from the previous existence. Though material wealth was usually greatly reduced in flight, the refugee can continue to live in a world where his or her previous experience, skills, and acquired knowledge may be put to use to rebuild a new life....

An important body of opinion—suggesting that the social advantages of self-settlement far outweigh the material advantages of formal settlements (Betts, 1982; Harrell-Bond, 1986; Hansen, 1990)—relate at least in part, to an important connection between ethnicity and self-settlement. National boundaries run through as many as one hundred and eighty-six different ethnic territories within sub-Saharan Africa. The social integration of many transborder communities has played an important role in refugee crises. Zartman (1970:151) documents an early case from West Africa. The affinity between the inhabitants of Senegal and Guinea-Bissau was so strong that, in many cases, the local population shared everything with the refugees including lodging, tools, seeds, and food stocks. Harrell-Bond (1986) illustrates the deployment of ethnic affinities as a social resource by incoming Ugandan refugees in southern Sudan. However, the best documented case is that of Luvali-speaking people who are on both sides of the Zambian-Angolan border (Hansen, 1981, 1990, 1993).

> During and after the colonial era, a number of labour migration routes ran through this region to the rest of southern Africa. Migration eventually institutionalized political and social obligations into a network of dependable relatives and kin. Consequently, many Angolans did not flee indiscriminately across the border when fighting erupted as early as 1966. Instead, they relied on familiar routes and kinship relationships in Zambia to secure food and shelter at first, and for some to even secure land later. (Bascom, 1986 based on Hansen, 1981)

On the basis of his longitudinal observations among Luvali-speaking refugees in north-western Zambia, Hansen, (1993:17) draws this generalization:

> Self-settlement is even more attractive to refugees with host relatives. Being received by kin, and staying among them, means that the refugee maintains more of his or her previous social identity. Kinship relationships with the accompanying reciprocity-based rights and obligations mean that the refugee maintains more power over other people and more stability and power over his or her own life. These reasons provide powerful support for the popularity of self-settlement.

In sum, pre-existing forms of interdependence and migration have helped buffer many refugees from the break with "home". At the same time, however, researchers have begun to document the dissipating importance of cultural relations in refugee settings (Bulcha, 1988; el Shazali, 1987).

The last thirty years have witnessed significant changes in the nature of the settlement process in agrarian societies. In the late 1960s and early 1970s rural resettlement was frequently characterized as a process of "spontaneous" integration into a host society. The new reality is, however, one in which local integration is becoming much more arduous rather than spontaneous for unassisted rural refugees. The introduction of mechanization triggered widespread transformation of the African political economy in the late 1960s. The deepening commoditization of land, labour, agricultural inputs, and grazing rights spurred on the process of agrarian change in the 1970s and 1980s.

The historical process of agrarian transformation has serious implications for contemporary refugees. As recently as twenty years ago, most unassisted refugees could derive a livelihood from shifting cultivation or pastoralism on uninhabited land at the periphery of host countries. Now, however, refugees must establish a new livelihood in very different contexts; ones characterized by very competitive social relations of production rather than ones built on reciprocal exchanges of land, labour, and food (Bascom, 1993a). This factor helps to explain why the proportion of African refugees who self-settle has fallen 30 per cent during the last eighteen years.

Self-settlers in urban enclaves

The term "urban refugees" is the generic name given to the category of refugees who move directly or eventually from border areas into towns (Karadawi, 1987:115). Urban refugees go to great lengths to avoid camps and get into urban centres. One can generally identify two phases in their migration: a) movement to an initial point of safety in an asylum country—the refugee's involuntary migration to escape persecution; and b) movement to a town—often, a voluntary migration (Karadawi, 1987:119–20). A sevenfold categorization based on Karadawi's observations in Khartoum illustrates the wide range of motivations and backgrounds within one African city:

The Education Seekers
Although Ethiopian communities existed in Sudanese towns before the refugee phenomenon was officially recognized in 1967, the problem of urban refugees first began to be a subject of concern in Khartoum in 1971. By that time, approximately 100 students of Ethiopian origin had arrived from Addis Ababa as a result of government suppression of the militant student movement, which had begun to oppose the government in 1965. Although the Commissioner of Refugees (COR) admitted them as refugees, UNHCR suspected the genuineness of their motivation for leaving their homeland and labelled them "education seekers...".

Rural to Urban Migrants
These are refugees who first settled in rural areas or in refugee settlements. Their migration usually begins when they are hired to work on agricultural schemes such as the Gezira. Thereafter some of them move to nearby towns; other migrants move directly to Khartoum for employment or educational opportunities. After 1976, the centralization of administration assistance offered by the COR (especially the issuance of travel documents), as well as material assistance offered by the Refugee Counselling Service (RCS), has further encouraged refugees to move to Khartoum to seek help from these organizations for overseas migration or resettlement.

Army Deserters
This group includes military officers and soldiers who deserted from the Ethiopian army and escaped to Sudan. Although relatively smaller in number than the education seekers and the rural–urban migrants, the deserters pose considerable security and employment problems. For these reasons, the authorities in the provinces tend to send them to Khartoum.

Deserters from the Exiled Fronts
This group comprises individuals who were once fighters of Eritrean or Ethiopian political fronts opposed to the government of Ethiopia, most of whom deserted because of dissatisfaction with the internal factionalism within the Fronts. In 1978 a group of TPLF and Ethiopian Democratic Union (EDU) deserters arrived in Khartoum; the majority of deserters, however, are from the ELF and arrived in Khartoum immediately before and after it broke into two factions in April 1982.

Refugees-sur-place
This group includes Ethiopians who came to Sudan as migrant workers, but who subsequently became unable or unwilling to return home for fear or threat of persecution. They play a very important, informal role in the reception and orientation of newly arriving refugees. Because of their long residence in Sudan they tend to live in the planned residential areas rather than in the squatter areas. Newly arriving refugees locate with or near them, which explains why refugees in Khartoum seldom live in the poorer squatter settlements where Sudanese rural–urban migrants live. This informal assistance between the old-timers and the newcomers has a tendency to degenerate into an exploitative relationship, where the old-timers collect a great deal of money through counselling new arrivals.

The Activists
This group includes an array of exiled political organizations. The Eritrean groups, the ELF, PLF (People's Liberation Front), and EPLF, all have offices in Khartoum, Kassala, and Port Sudan. Each has organizations for their different membership, such as workers, women, or students. Although such organizations do not exercise total control over the refugee population, they perform an important role in providing alternative assistance to refugees, as well as being accepted as mediators between refugees and formal agencies such as COR, UNHCR, and RCS. Although young and poorly equipped, these refugee-based agencies have shown a good degree of efficiency in mobilizing refugees, gaining their trust, and helping them preserve their sense of identity. They should be encouraged and assisted by both UNHCR and the government of Sudan by extending to them legal recognition, by providing them with access to material resources, and by involving them as full partners in the whole refugee assistance structure, since to date neither RCS nor COR has proved effective in understanding and coping with the problems of refugees in the urban milieu.

The Opportunists
Clearly, many individuals migrate to Sudan to seek ways of emigrating overseas. They believe that in Sudan they can acquire the necessary travel documents, visas, and tickets, as

well as receive money from relatives and friends who are already abroad. This type of movement has been encouraged by the many opportunities offered in the oil-rich Arab countries and by resettlement programs to the United States and Europe. Many refugees who go abroad correspond with their relatives and friends in the home country, and encourage them to follow their example by coming to Sudan. Many of the refugees who express a desire to return home by volunteering for the repatriation program are persons who were unsuccessful in realizing their hopes of emigrating abroad (COR 1980).

(Karadawi, 1987:120–2)

One might expect that the number of city-settled refugees would mirror the rapid growth of urban populations, in general. Between 1950 and 1990 Africa experienced an average urban growth of 65 per cent per decade compared to 50 per cent for Asia and 43 per cent for Latin America (UN, 1980). In the 1993 report for the General Assembly, UNHCR identified a total number of 58,722 urban refugees within 13 African countries (UNHCR, 1993b). As such this would constitute only 1 per cent of the total refugee population as compared to Chamber's estimate of 4 per cent in the mid 1970s (Chambers, 1979). However, there are two basic reasons why most city-settled refugees remain "unidentified" and thereby subject to significant under-reporting. First, many refugees risk the prospect of urban deportation and therefore, work hard to maintain a low profile. Second, host governments may classify bona fide refugees as economic migrants. The Kenyan government has, for example, failed to acknowledge for political reasons that many Ugandans, Ethiopians, and Somalis living in Nairobi and Mombasa are "refugees".

Many cities in Africa clearly have sizeable refugee populations. The largest three concentrations identified in UNHCR's 1993 report included 26,775 in Burundi, 20,000 in Kenya, and 3,500 in Congo. In addition, Accra, Addis Ababa, Harare, Khartoum, and Kinshasa all have large enclaves of unassisted refugees. Refugees prefer primate cities like these, atop the urban hierarchy of a given country. They have a disproportionate amount of social and economic infrastructure. They also represent the usual "launch" point for resettlement opportunities to the industrialized countries of the West (Kebbede, 1991:100).

The integration of urban refugees is one of two main refugee issues that remain relatively unresearched and poorly understood (Rogge and Akol, 1989). (Problems associated with repatriation, including the process of reintegration and rehabilitation upon return, is the other main issue.) Previous studies of urban refugees in Africa, however, shed considerable light on the process of refugee integration within cities. The results of a study carried out in Kenyan cities revealed a surprisingly strong relationship between originating in urban places and subsequently settling in them. Ninety-five per cent of the sample resided in cities before flight (Billard, 1982:35). Urban refugees are generally younger, more educated, and more politically oriented than their rural counterparts. They are also predominantly single. Goitom (1987:138) notes, for example, that 80.9 per cent of the Eritrean refugees in his study sample from Khartoum were not married.

Urban refugees rely heavily on their predecessors to help them make cultural, psychological, and economic adjustments. Refugees who arrived first act as reference groups for those that follow. Goitom (1987:142) makes the apt point that:

It is a known fact that people exposed to external or internal dangers (socio-political and economic) tend to show a high degree of community solidarity on many levels. The refugees' level of survival is based on changing strategies, a mechanism demanding a continuous information flow. The more numerous a refugee's sources of information, the higher his chances of adjustment with the host system. This fact and the need for survival have always perpetuated a sense of mutual dependence within refugee communities.

Social norms, legal avenues, social contacts, and employment opportunities are all important aspects of the constant circulation of information among urban refugees.

Newcomers also depend on their predecessors to provide material assistance like housing and food. Goitom documented the density of refugees living in single-room dwellings throughout Khartoum. He derived the following proportions for refugees sharing the same space in one room: 36 per cent with 4 to 6 people; 28 per cent with 7 to 9 people; and 17 per cent with 10 to 12 people (1987:139). Refugee communities can become alienated from the indigenous residents, especially if refugees concentrate in a residential quarter. Severe tensions can erupt in cities because refugees cannot avoid exacerbating the chronic shortages of public services common to developing countries. In recent years, for example, violent outbursts between refugees and Sudanese have occurred in Kassala, Gedaref, and Kashmel Girba, the three largest towns in eastern Sudan.

Although housing is certainly a problem for urban refugees, employment is the strategic factor on which their successful integration depends most heavily. The present author's observations in Khartoum illustrate the kinds of formal employment commonly held by fortunate urban refugees. Some foreign companies hire Eritrean refugees as cheap, yet highly trained and English-speaking labour. The Sudanese government occasionally deregulates employment restrictions for refugees to compensate for an important gap national Sudanese cannot fill in the employment market, such as nursing, English competency, higher education, and specific skills are three critical ingredients that enable a refugee to land a job in the formal sector. Without these extra assets, urban refugees usually resort to the informal sector or illegal alternatives such as clandestine restaurants (which largely serve fellow refugees) or prostitution. Goitom's survey included the following occupational structure for refugees in Khartoum: unemployed (50 per cent); domestic service (8.5 per cent); day labourers (6.5 per cent); receptionists or bartenders (4 per cent) (1987:139). A later study, focused on refugee women, found that 76 per cent of those with jobs worked as domestics (Kebbede, 1991:102). Urban refugees who are unemployed, underemployed or poorly employed must turn to others to cover the shortfall in their earnings. Goitom's case study revealed, for example, that a majority of the sample were dependent on extra support. Twenty per cent were dependent on relatives or friends living in Khartoum and 30 per cent more totally depended on, or supplemented their low incomes from, remittances sent by relatives or friends working abroad (Goitom, 1987:139–40).

Relief for urban refugees has been slow for a number of reasons. Relief agencies can ignore urban refugees on the false assumption that if refugees reach a city, they are able to take care of themselves. Host governments can regard urban refugees as being a transient, temporary problem who will resettle in a third country or repatriate back home. This assumption can allow asylum states to remain in a passive mode regarding the problems of urban refugees. In 1979, however, the Pan-African Conference at Arusha called for special efforts to create opportunities for the employment and retraining of urban refugees and for the re-evaluation of their qualifications (Eriksson, Melander and Nobel, 1981:37). The OAU's Bureau for the Placement and Education of African Refugees (BPEAR) has worked to achieve these goals. Significantly, BPEAR deals with refugees on a case-by-case basis and thereby, places its emphasis on individuals rather than groups (Karadawi, 1987). In the face of growing numbers of urban refugees, however, African governments are beginning to explore collective responses. Some governments have begun relocating less trained and poorly educated refugees to wage-earning settlements. In 1993, for example, the Djibouti government agreed to transfer 30,000 non-assisted refugees and displaced persons in Djibouti-ville to the four existing refugee camps within the country (UNHCR, 1993b:9).

Assisted refugees in UN camps

UN-supervised camps and settlements are the other basic form of settlement for African refugees who integrate in the country to which they first flee. Approximately one half of the African refugee population lives under this "umbrella" of direct UN supervision and protection (Stein and Clark, 1990:3). Camps are distinguished from settlements by little or no prospect or attempt for refugees to achieve self-sufficiency.

Camps also vary from settlements in their geographic location. Two opposing pressures define and demarcate the zone for camps and settlements within the receiving country. On one hand, the greater the intensity and the closer the proximity of physical violence, the deeper refugees want to push into the country of refuge. UNHCR commonly requires that permanent settlements remain at least fifty kilometres from an international boundary to qualify for financial aid. The basic rationale for this requirement is to prevent border skirmishes from spilling over into refugee settings. On the other hand, the host governments are usually eager to keep reception camps as far away from urban centres as possible. Isolating camps and their blighted conditions is not only politically less embarrassing, but distance decreases the likelihood of urban migration and the added impact of refugee populations in cities.

Most refugee camps are conceived and created as a temporary holding site, but over time become permanent settlements perpetuated by a paradoxical state of semi-emergency. Reception camps lose their dramatic aura of emergency as the time between initial flight and eventual repatriation grows, but they still maintain an emergency identity because they depend on external sources of food. During the last decade researchers have examined the "dependency syndrome" so commonly associated with camps. Among others, Kibreab (1991:38) challenges the common stereotype of people languishing in camps:

> Whether or not African refugees in camps are in the grip of "dependency syndrome" is an empirical question. It cannot be assumed that because it happened in Europe and Asia it should happen in Africa. A considerable proportion of the literature deals with the origin of the problem, but no attempt is ever made to establish whether or not the problem exists. ... In my rather extensive survey of the literature on refugees in camps in Africa, I have yet to come across a single piece of evidence to suggest that African refugees in camps are in the

grip of "dependency syndrome". In fact all available studies on refugees in camps show that they leave no stone unturned to earn an income, either to supplement their diet, to make up for things not included in the aid package or to make material progress. On the contrary the refugees in the camps are described as hardworking, persevering and creative.

Physical resources are a key constraint on refugees' livelihoods and, at the same time, one of the chief impacts upon the regions in which refugees settle. This is particularly true in Africa where most camps (and settlements) are located in environmentally fragile rural areas. Camps in Somalia were some of the first in Africa to demonstrate the potential scale of environmental strain and degradation associated with holding concentrated refugee populations for long periods of time in relatively fragile ecosystems.

> The camp areas are totally cleared of trees and small vegetation, as is up to five to eight kilometres of the adjacent land. The refugees have cleared the areas in the process of getting fuel for cooking. This is still going on and the areas are slowly being transformed into a stony, arid desert. (Christensen, 1982:11).

More recently, the presence of Mozambican refugees has necessitated reforestation and rehabilitation of large tracts of land in ten districts throughout Malawi (UNHCR, 1993b:5). The current state of knowledge about environmental change in refugee-affected areas is still quite limited, but there is little doubt that it is quickly becoming a topic of growing concern (Black, 1993).

Researchers are also becoming aware of less obvious social dynamics inside camps. The central dynamic of food can mould social differentiation. Grain stockpiling created three social strata within camps in Somalia (Christensen, 1982). When food supplies became irregular the marginalised members (10 to 15 per cent) suffered severe malnutrition that required supplemental feeding centres. The middle majority in each camp managed to secure ample food and thereby, constituted a second stratum in the social hierarchy of the camp. Still others in each camp managed to accumulate food surpluses. This upper tier engaged in regular exchange of their extra rations—grain, milk, and oil—to obtain fresh foods or cash. Food rations can become, in this fashion, a strategic basis for cooperation and exchange with the host community as well as a key factor underpinning the process of social differentiation among camp populations.

Assisted refugees in UN settlements

Designated settlement schemes are envisioned as a more useful long-term solution for refugees. The design of such schemes is to replace dependency with productivity by giving refugees a place and resources to tap cultivation skills or wage-earning potential. Organized settlements are particularly advantageous for vulnerable refugees and they offer better prospects for fostering their own religion and culture (Wijbrandi, 1990:73). Governments favour schemes for different reasons. "Negative motivations" involve concerns about national security (the most often publicized reason) and fears that the absorption capacity of self-settlement areas is too limited: for example, overexploiting common property resources and overtaxing social services (Hansen, 1993; Kibreab, 1990). Positive rationales include a desire to: (a) foster as high a level of self-sufficiency as possible; (b) integrate the latent manpower resource of the refugees into the regional economic structure of the area into which they move; (c) maximize benefits for the government because the investment costs of the physical and social infrastructure are borne by international donors; (d) assert greater control of refugees' activities; and (e) prevent the flow of refugees from migrating into urban centres to compete for employment, scarce resources and social services (Rogge, 1987; Kibreab, 1990). At least in theory, settlement schemes can reduce the burden of refugees upon host countries and contribute to the local, regional, and national economy. Tanzania has made some of the best efforts to devise self-sufficient agricultural schemes for refugees, primarily from Rwanda, Mozambique, and Zaire. President Nyerere envisioned schemes as a significant component of the *Ujamaa* plan for agricultural development and therein integrated refugee settlement programs into national social and economic policies.

Holding camps provide little, or no, opportunity for refugees to move towards self-support, but that is the avowed goal for organized settlements. UNHCR established more than 170 organized refugee settlements in Africa between 1961 and 1987 (Kibreab, 1990:2). Stein and Clark (1990) concluded that only 13 per cent of the settlements organized in Africa before 1982 had clearly achieved the basic goal of economic self-sufficiency. (The standard of living enjoyed by the nationals in surrounding areas is often used as a proxy for self-sufficiency.)

Significantly, settlements in the Stein and Clark study experienced even more difficulty reaching a point of integration. (Integration is usually measured in social, political and legal terms.) Refugees in many settlements were not as concerned about the need for further assistance, but about questions of protection from abuse of authority by local officials, and about equity issues, such as having some input into how to use the money they pay in taxes or fees (Stein and Clark, 1990:47). This concurs with Wijbrandi's assessment that assistance plays a minor role in the process of integration (1990:75).

In sum, a negligible number of past settlements have become a "durable" solution for their inhabitants. Meanwhile, the future prospects for settlement success are diminishing. Donor interest in Africa is falling. Growing problems and populations beset reception countries. (Both factors will force new settlements onto marginal lands.) Although Uganda and Senegal have brought the issue under consideration, only three sub-Saharan countries have granted citizenship and permanent residency to refugees—Tanzania, Botswana, and Burundi (Rogge, 1991:9–10).

SOLUTIONS: THE SUCCESS OF THE PREFERRED SOLUTION
TO REFUGEE CRISES

In 1984, the Executive Committee of the United Nations High Commissioner for Refugees (UNHCR) identified three "durable" solutions for refugees. Long-term integration of refugees in the country of first asylum—albeit in cities, camps and settlements, or concentrations along the border—is the *de facto* solution in Africa. Resettlement to a third country of asylum is the *exceptional* solution, evidenced by the fact that only one in ten thousand African refugees resettles off the continent (UNHCR, 1993a). This section examines a third solution. Repatriation is the return migration of refugees from exile back to their homeland. This is generally considered the most *desirable* solution of the three.

Between 1970 and 1990 an estimated 3.5 million African refugees returned home (Rogge, 1991:3). Two significant repatriation initiatives have begun during the last two years. The consolidation of the peace process in Mozambique is opening the way for as many as 1.5 million refugees to repatriate, most of whom are expected to return home without assistance (UNHCR, 1993b). Meanwhile, an important repatriation operation has commenced in eastern Sudan. As many as 75,000 Eritreans have returned home of their own accord since the war with Ethiopia ended in May, 1991. UNHCR anticipates that an additional 150,000 Eritreans will repatriate in an organized repatriation operation which began in early 1994 (UNHCR, 1993b).

In spite of these welcome developments, the near universal position that repatriation is a "natural" outcome of refugee movements on the African continent is increasingly in need of re-evaluation (Rogge, 1991:7). Figure 3 illustrates the widening gap between the total number of African refugees that remain in exile and the total number that repatriate.

Figure 3. *The annual number of African refugees repatriating versus in exile, 1973–1993*

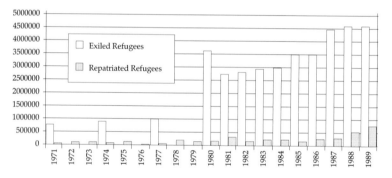

Until the mid-1970s most refugee movements in Africa were associated with a struggle against the imposition of colonial power. For that reason, host countries maintained a high degree of solidarity with incoming refugees with the shared expectation of ultimate victory and subsequent repatriation (Stein, 1992:3). (Repatriation of 43,000 Namibians before independence in 1990 was the last "colonial" case on the continent excepting the controversial case of South Africa.) However, internal conflicts—like those in Rwanda, Liberia, and Sudan—are not as decisive as the earlier independence movements. Hence, voluntary repatriation is becoming significantly more difficult to begin, and, even when it eventually does occur, it is more delayed and incomplete than in the past (Stein, 1986). Unsure of their status, refugees may choose to remain in exile. Meanwhile, governments are often slow to facilitate the return of refugees in order to garner more resources from donors and, in some instances, to rid themselves of certain segments of the exiled population (Bascom, 1994a).

Ideally, repatriation is a decision that is fully voluntary, fully informed, and only occurs when the conditions that prompted flight no longer exist. Realistically, however, repatriations rarely follow this "textbook" scenario. Ruiz (1993) identifies three common permutations that blur the classic model of voluntary repatriation. First, refugees may choose to repatriate outside the auspices of the United Nations even in the face of unsafe or uncertain conditions at home. In the mid-1980s, for example, 400,000 refugees returned to Ethiopia from Somalia and Djibouti without assistance, as did 75,000 Ugandans from southern Sudan and 29,000 Ugandans from Rwanda. The UNHCR did not assist a 1985 repatriation of 200,000 Ethiopians from eastern Sudan; in fact, both UNHCR and the United States actively opposed their return (Cuny and Stein, 1989:298). The difference in scale of as much as 100 to 1 between spontaneous and organized repatriations suggests that the refugees and UNHCR hold different standards of safety and perceptions of appropriate timing in regard to repatriation (Cole cited in Cuny and Stein, 1989:305). So-called "spontaneous" repatriations frequently occur on the part of unassisted refugees who were settled outside official camps. Refugees choose to remain outside refugee camps to counteract the diminished sense of power and control associated with displacement, but the same can be said of refugees who make the decision to return home on their own accord, at least in part, to try to ensure the success of their reintegration.

Second, host governments may choose to send refugees home. In 1982, for example, Djibouti claimed that it could no longer shoulder the burden of hosting Ethiopian refugees. The government began forced deportation, or refoulement, of refugees, the single worst possible violation of the 1951 UN Refugee Convention (Crisp, 1984).

A third, and more common, scenario is that relief agencies "help" refugees repatriate by withdrawing assistance when they determine that it is safe for refugees to return home. In such cases, UNHCR and/or donors believe that refugees should repatriate, but that they will not begin because they are more comfortable in exile than at home. In the past UNHCR has taken steps to encourage refugees to repatriate by lowering food rations, withdrawing services, cutting funds, and shifting refugees to new locations. Chadian refugees in western Sudan, for example, have received such treatment in recent years. Cases like these beg serious questions posed by Stein (1986:7). How voluntary is voluntary? Does it mean free will or are some inducements allowed? When does push become a shove (refoulement)?

The UN High Commissioner for Refugees proclaimed the 1990s as the "decade of repatriation". The first half of the 1990s has already witnessed two new initiatives associated with repatriation. Both involve the country of origination rather than destination because, as Kibreab (1990:33) so aptly stresses, "The central issue of the African refugee problem is to examine ways and means by which to bring about changes in the refugees' countries of origin...." The recent saga of intervention in Somalia has made the United Nations recognize the need to: (a) incite and expedite conflict resolution in the source country so refugees can return; (b) take vigorous action—including emergency response to crises and the provision of international protection on site—to eradicate the causes of flight before refugees flee; and (c) initiate more proactive intervention to prevent the development of conditions that might impel people to leave in the first place (UNHCR, 1993a). The United Nations is also working hard to create economic conditions that will induce people to repatriate home and, keep them there once they return. The central fact of the matter is that if repatriation is not linked to the rehabilitation of productive capacity, a vicious circle of renewed disintegration and displacement is likely to emerge (UNHCR, 1993a).

CONCLUSIONS: REFLECTIONS ON REFUGEE MIGRATION IN AFRICA

This chapter has attempted to provide a compact survey of involuntary migration in Africa. The summary discussion focuses on four main conclusions.

First, new dimensions in the African refugee crises: late April 1994 marked a new and unprecedented threshold in the modern history of refugee migration in Africa. More than 250,000 Rwandans fled the country in a period of twenty-four hours, thereby constituting the biggest and fastest exodus UN officials said they had seen (Associated Press, 1994). Other kinds of serious precedents are occurring elsewhere on the continent. The case of Liberia has prompted a new level of military involvement by Africans in an African refugee crisis. Ghana, Nigeria and Senegal sent peace-keeping troops to Liberia only to find themselves trapped in the conflict. The case of Somalia has created a new and ugly twist on the theme of refugee dependency. During the 1980s, the Somalis learned to depend on refugees as a vehicle to bring food, financial assistance, hard currency, employment opportunities, and used vehicles into the country. The price of this entrenched, "false economy" is now being paid. The mass media stereotypes the clan issue as the cause of the current conflict rather than the long-term "starvation" of the Somali economy and the struggle to control the "entry gate" for future assistance (Samatar, 1992). Raw food has become the prize for warring parties who pay themselves by looting (Jean, 1992:49). This tactic makes the country depend even more on relief agencies who must bring sufficient quantities of grain into the country to reduce tension, lower prices, "saturate the warriors" and then, at last, to help Ethiopian refugees (Jean, 1992:49).

Second, important policy implications: the basic poverty of many policies and programs is that many variables lie beyond the control of the international community. Limitations aside, the 1990s have already witnessed new and important policy initiatives. At least two bear mention. Beginning in 1992 UNHCR began to forge cross-mandate approaches to refugee crises in all three major regions of Africa, namely the Horn of Africa, Southern Africa, and West Africa:

> In Somalia and Mozambique, the United Nations has recognized the complex relationship between peace-making, peace-keeping and humanitarian action and is seeking to ensure that the needs of a range of populations, such as returnees, internally displaced persons and other impoverished nationals are adequately addressed...
>
> In this context, UNHCR will continue to work closely with Governments, the Department of Humanitarian Affairs (DHA), concerned United Nations agencies and NGOs to build on these efforts and establish a "modus vivendi" for protection and assistance to all affected populations.... (UNHCR, 1993b:6).

UNHCR has also begun to provide assistance to refugees outside formal camps and settlements. Researchers have long advocated that UNHCR provide the self-settling refugees with "creative, fine-pointed forms of assistance" so that they could receive aid without sacrificing their ability to control where they want to live (Chambers, 1979; Neldner, 1979; Hansen, 1982; Harrell-Bond, 1986). Some funding is now available for projects assisting "refugee-affected areas" through UNDP, and from the EEC under LOME IV, Article 255 (McGregor and Aikman, 1991:4). In 1993, twenty-five per cent of UNHCR's 284 million dollar budget for Africa was designated for non-camp settings (UNHCR, 1993b). The \$22.4 million spent on "local settlement" compares to \$166.4 million for refugees in camps and settlements, \$71.4 million for voluntary repatriation programs, \$14.5 million for administration, \$9.1 million for emergency assistance operations, and \$0.8 million for third country resettlement programs. It is an empirical question as to how much assistance actually reaches self-settled refugees. At least in theory, however, the need to put refugees in camps in order for them to be counted and qualify for assistance has been obviated (McGregor and Aikman, 1991:4).

Third, future research: partial understandings still shroud many key themes and relationships despite an acceleration in the growth of African refugee studies. I have chosen to highlight three important facets of the refugee experience that suffer from incomplete explanations. The first one involves the dynamic between refugees and the people that host them. Studies of African refugees still struggle to move beyond what Chambers (1986) termed as a "refugee-centric" perspective that overlooks the impact of refugees on their hosts. The literature contains examples of cases in which nationals have benefited from a large refugee presence and others in which an influx of refugees impoverishes a host population (Kibreab, 1991; Chambers, 1986). What are needed to understand why some members of the host population do well while others suffer are detailed longitudinal studies that are begun, if possible, before refugees arrive. Such work could be strengthened significantly by grappling more deeply with a sizeable body of literature on the African peasant economy (for example, Amin, 1972; Bernstein, 1979; Barker, 1989; Samatar, 1989; Watts, 1989).

Intra-household relationships are a second key facet that requires more investigation. Becoming refugees usually involves major cultural and social transformations that precipitate fundamental changes in the constitution of refugee households. Although donors are placing more emphasis on women and children (Martin, 1992; el Nagar, 1992), researchers generally treat the dynamics within refugee households in a loose, imprecise and static way. Empirical data on refugee women, children, men, elderly, youth, and vulnerable has not been adequately conceptualized in the wider social environment in which they operate (Daley, 1994). Researchers have made significant headway conceptualizing intra-household dynamics amid the more circumscribed social context of a settlement or camp environment (Harrell-Bond, 1986; Daley, 1991; Wilson, 1992). However, the prolific growth of the African refugee literature during the last decade has positioned researchers to move the level of explanations above isolated case examples. Many issues need more systematic explanations. Some of the more relevant questions related to the conceptualization of the refugee household include: the erosion and replacement of "traditional" authority structures (Harrell-Bond, 1985); the breakdown of the household as a unit of production and consumption (el Shazali,

1985); the production of new sets of decision making roles, particularly for women refugees who become "heads of households" (Rogge, 1991); and the restructuring of the rules, roles and responsibilities that govern interaction within the household during exile and reintegration (Bascom, 1994b).

Repatriation is a third key area for research. The literature on repatriation in Africa remains the least developed compared to other phases of the refugee experience. The theme of refugee flight predominated in the literature of the 1970s. The focus of attention shifted to resettlement during the 1980s as the magnitude of the refugee crisis grew throughout Africa. Repatriation has become the "lead" theme of the 1990s. Although much of the initial writing on repatriation focused upon legal or logistical matter, the focus of study is now shifting to the socio-economic and psychological dimensions of repatriations (Rogge, 1991:2). Researchers need to continue moving in this direction for two major reasons; socio-economic factors play a growing role in determining whether repatriation becomes a normative response among an exiled population as well as a key role in the process of reintegration after return home.

Fourth, the tension between choice and context: Simon and Preston (1993:48) note that refugee research "... is pulled in one direction by the need for links with established social theory... and, in another, by attempts to define its own parameters". Unassisted settlement in rural areas throughout Africa is one example of the ongoing tension between using social theory or establishing "indigenous" refugee theory to explicate the dynamics of refugee migration. One important body of opinion emphasizes that refugees make real and important choices in the process of resettlement and repatriation (Betts, 1982; Harrell-Bond, 1989; Hansen, 1993). Meanwhile, however, another body of opinion stresses the importance of placing refugee settlement and repatriation into the context of larger processes operative in agrarian societies (el Shazali, 1987; Black, 1991; Bascom, 1993a). After an in-depth analysis of the current literature, for example, Black (1991) underscores a continuing trend of assigning "exceptional status" to refugees that tends to abstract refugees from the larger context in which they exist. On the basis of an ongoing study in eastern Sudan, the present author concludes elsewhere that resettlement is a process whereby refugees negotiate their subsistence from the "opportunity structures" afforded by the host society and economy (Bascom, 1993a). All facets of the refugee experience—migration, resettlement, repatriation, and reintegration—represent an ongoing process of choice played out in a changing context. Thus, we should study and understand the interplay between choice and context—agency and structure—as the central dynamic at work in the African refugee experience.

References

Amin, S., 1972, "Underdevelopment and dependence in black Africa", *Journal of Modern African Studies*, 10:503–524.

Associated Press, 1994, "250,000 Rwandans flee into Tanzania", *The Raleigh News and Observer*, pp. 11a, (April 30).

Barker, J., 1989, *Rural communities under stress: Peasant farmers and the state in Africa*. Cambridge: Cambridge University Press.

Bascom, J., 1986, "Self-settling refugees in Africa", *The Rural Sociologist*, 6:290–5.

Bascom, J., 1989, "Conceptualizing food security and famine in Sudan", *Northeast African Studies*, 11, 2:1–19.

Bascom, J., 1993a, "The peasant economy of refugee resettlement in eastern Sudan", *Annals of the Association of American Geographers*, 83:320–46.

Bascom, J., 1993b, " 'Internal refugees': The case of the displaced in Khartoum", in R. Black and V. Robinson, (eds), *Geography and refugees: Patterns and processes of change*: 33–46. London: Belhaven Press.

Bascom, J., 1994a, "The dynamics of refugee repatriation: The case of Eritreans in eastern Sudan", in W. Gould and A. Findlay, (eds), *Population Migration and the Changing World Order*: 225–48. London: John Wiley & Sons.

Bascom, J., 1994b, "Reconstituting households and reconstructing home areas: The case of returning Eritreans", Submitted paper, *Symposium for the Horn of Africa on the social and economic aspects of mass voluntary return movements of refugees*, United Nations Research Institute for Social Development, Addis Ababa, September. (Forthcoming, James Currey Ltd.)

Bernstein, H., 1979, "Concepts for the analysis of contemporary peasantries", *Journal of Peasant Studies*, 6:421–43.

Betts, T., 1982, *Spontaneous settlement of rural refugees in Africa*. Research project commissioned by Euro Action/Acord, Great Britain.

Billard, A., 1982, *Refugees magazine*, Number 1, Geneva: UNHCR.

Black, R., 1991, "Refugees and displaced persons: Geographical perspectives and research directions", *Progress in Human Geography*, 15:281–98.

Black, R., 1993, "Refugees and environmental change: Global issues", Presentation, *Symposium on refugees and environmental change*. London: Kings College, (September).

Bulcha, M., 1988, *Flight and integration: Causes of mass exodus from Ethiopia and problems of integration in the Sudan*. Uppsala: Scandinavian Institute of African Studies.

Chambers, R., 1979, "Rural refugees in Africa: What the eye does not see", *Disasters*, 5:381–92.

Chambers, R., 1986, "Hidden losers? The impact of rural refugee programs on poorer hosts", *International Migration Review*, 20:245–63.

Christensen, H., 1982, *Survival strategies for and by camp refugees*. Geneva: UN Research Institute for Social Development.

Crisp, J., 1984, "The politics of repatriation: Ethiopian refugees in Djibouti", *Review of African Political Economy*, 30:73–82.

Cuny, F., and B. Stein, 1989, "Prospects for and promotion of spontaneous repatriation", in G. Loescher and L. Monahan, (eds), *Refugees and international relations*: 293–312. Oxford: Oxford University Press.

Daley, P., 1991, "Gender, displacement and social reproduction: Settling Burundi refugees in western Tanzania", *Journal of Refugee Studies*, 4:248–66.

Daley, P., 1994, "The situation of refugees in east Africa", paper presented to the 1994 annual meeting of the *International Research and Advisory Panel for Refugee Studies*, Refugee Studies Programme, Oxford University (January).

de Sherbinin, A., 1992, "Mauritanian refugees: Casualties of rural development?", paper presented at the *1992 Annual Meeting of the Association of American Geographers*, San Diego (April).

Drumthra, J., 1994, Personal communication. US Committee for Refugees (March).

el Nagar, S., 1992, "Children and war in the Horn of Africa", in M. Doornbos, *et. al.*, (eds), *Beyond conflict in the Horn: Prospects for peace, recovery and development in Ethiopia, Somalia and the Sudan*: 15–21. London: James Currey.

el Shazali, S., 1985, *Peripheral urbanism and the Sudan: Explorations in the political economy of the wage labor market in greater Khartoum, 1900–1984*. Ph.D. dissertation, University of Hull, Department of Political Science.

el Shazali, S., 1987, *Eritreans in Kassala*. Joint research project of the Development Studies and Research Centre, University of Khartoum and the Centre for Development Cooperation Services, Free University of Amsterdam.

Eriksson, L., G. Melander, and P. Nobel, 1981, *An analyzing account of the conference on African refugee problems, Arusha, May, 1979*. Uppsala: Scandinavian Institute of African Studies.

Goitom, E., 1987, "Systems of social interaction of refugee adjustment processes: The case of Eritrean refugees in Khartoum, Sudan", in J. Rogge, (ed), *Refugees: A third world dilemma*: 130–42. Totowa, NJ: Rowman and Littlefield.

Hamilton, V., (ed), 1994, *1994 world refugee survey*. Washington, DC: US Committee for Refugees.

Hansen, A., 1981, "Refugee dynamics: Angolans in Zambia 1966–72", *International Migration Review*, 1:175–94.

Hansen, A., 1982, "Self-settled rural refugees in Africa: The case of Angolans in Zambian villages", in A. Hansen and A. Oliver-Smith, (eds), *Involuntary migration and resettlement: The problems and responses of dislocated people*: 13–36. Boulder: Westview Press.

Hansen, A., 1990, *Refugee self-sufficiency versus settlement on government schemes: The long-term consequences for security, integration, and economic development of Angolan refugees (1966–1989) in Zambia*. United Nations Research Institute for Social Development Discussion Paper No. 17. Geneva: United Nations.

Hansen, A., 1993, "African refugees: Defining and defending their human rights", in R. Cohen, G. Hyden, and W. Nagen, (eds), *Human rights and governance in Africa*: 226–266. Gainesville: University of Florida Press.

Harrell-Bond, B., 1985, "Humanitarianism in a straitjacket", *African Affairs*, 86:3–14.

Harrell-Bond, B., 1986, *Imposing aid: Emergency assistance to refugees*. Oxford: Oxford University Press.

Harrell-Bond, B., 1989, "Repatriation: Under what conditions is it the most desirable solution for refugees? An agenda for research", *African Studies Review*, 32:41–69.

Holborn, L., 1975, *Refugees: A problem of our time*. Metuchen, NJ: The Scarecrow Press, Inc.

Jean, F., 1992, *Populations in danger*. London: John Libbey.

Karadawi, A., 1987, "The problem of urban refugees in Sudan", in J. Rogge, (ed), *Refugees: A third world dilemma*: 115–29. Totowa, NJ: Rowman and Littlefield.

Kebbede, G., 1991, "The agonies of displacement: Ethiopian women refugees in Khartoum, Sudan", *GeoJournal*, 23:99–106.

Kibreab, G., 1990, "Host governments and refugee perspectives on settlement and repatriation in Africa", paper for the *Conference on Development Strategies on Forced Migration in the Third World*. The Hague: Institute of Social Studies (August).

Kibreab, G., 1991, *The state of the art review of refugee studies in Africa*. Uppsala Papers in Economic History, Research Report No. 26.

Kolenic, P., 1974, *African refugees: Characteristics and patterns of movement*. Master's thesis, Ohio University, Department of Geography.

Kunz, E., 1973, "The refugee in flight: Kinetic models and forms of displacement", *International Migration Review*, 7:125–46.

Martin, S., 1992, *Refugee Women*. London: Zed Press.

McGregor, J., and S. Aikman, 1991, "Avoiding camps", *Refugee participation network*, 10: 3–4.

Neldner, B., 1979, "Settlement of rural refugees", *Disasters*, 3: 393–402.

Nobel, P., (ed), 1982, *Refugee law in the Sudan*. Research Report 64. Uppsala: Scandinavian Institute of African Studies.

Population Reference Bureau, 1993, *1993 World Population Data Sheet of the Population Reference Bureau, Inc*. Population Reference Bureau: Washington, DC.

Rahmato, D., 1987, "Famine and survival strategies: A case study from northeast Ethiopia", *Food and Famine Monograph Series*, No. 1. Institute of Development Research, Addis Ababa University.

Ricco, S., 1989, *International migration in Africa: Legal and administrative aspects*. Geneva: ILO.

Rogge, J., 1977, "A geography of refugees: Some illustrations from Africa", *Professional Geographer*, 29:186–89.

Rogge, J., 1981, "Africa's resettlement strategies", *International Migration Review*, 15:195–212.

Rogge, J., 1987, "When is self-sufficiency achieved: The case of rural settlements in Sudan", in J. Rogge, (ed), *Refugees: A third world dilemma*: 86–97. Totowa, NJ: Rowman and Little-field.

Rogge, J., 1991, "Repatriation of refugees: A not-so-simple "optimum" solution", *Symposium on social and economic aspects of mass voluntary return of refugees from one African country to another,* Harare, Zimbabwe, March 12–14, United Nations Research Unit for Social Development (March).

Rogge, J., and J. Akol, 1989, "Repatriation: Its role in resolving Africa's refugee dilemma", *International Migration Review*, 23:184–200.

Ruiz, H., 1993, "Repatriation: Tackling protection and assistance concerns", in V. Hamilton, (ed), *1993 World Refugee Survey*: 20–9. Washington: US Committee for Refugees.

Samatar, A., 1989, *The state and rural transformation in northern Somalia, 1884–1986*. Madison, WI: University of Wisconsin Press.

Samatar, A., 1992, "Social decay and public institutions: The road to reconstruction in Somalia", in M. Doornbos, *et al.* (eds), *Beyond conflict in the Horn: Prospects for peace, recovery and development in Ethiopia, Somalia and the Sudan*: 213–16. London: James Currey.

Simon, D., and R. Preston, 1993, "Return to the promised land: The repatriation and resettlement of Namibian refugees", in R. Black, and V. Robinson, (eds), *Geography and refugees: Patterns and processes of change*: 46–63. London: Belhaven Press.

Stein, B., 1986, "Durable solutions for developing country refugees", *International Migration Review*, 20:264–82.

Stein, B., 1992, "Policy challenges regarding repatriation in the 1990s: Is 1992 the year for voluntary repatriation?", paper commissioned by the *Program on International and U.S. Refugee Policy,* The Fletcher School of Law and Diplomacy, Tufts University.

Stein, B., and L. Clark, 1990, "Refugee integration and older refugee settlements in Africa", paper presented at the *1990 meeting of the American Anthropological Association,* New Orleans (November).

UNHCR, 1981, *International assistance to refugees in Africa*. Report of Secretary-General, 36th Session of UN General Assembly.

UNHCR, 1993a, *The state of the world's refugees 1993: The challenge of protection*. New York: Penguin.

UNHCR, 1993b, *UNHCR activities financed by voluntary funds: Report for 1992–1993 and proposed programmes and budget for 1994*. Part I. Africa, A.AC.96/808 (Part I).

UN, 1980, *Patterns of urban and rural population growth*. ST/ESA/Series A.68, Tables 4 and 48. New York: United Nations.

UN, 1984, *Declaration and program of action of the second international conference on assistance to refugees in Africa*. A/Con. 125/L.1, July 10, Geneva.

Watts, M., 1989, "The agrarian crisis in Africa: Debating the crisis", *Progress in Human Geography*, 13:1–41.

Wijbrandi, J., 1990, "Organized and spontaneous settlement", in T. Kuhlman, and H. Tieleman, (eds), *Enduring crisis: Refugee problems in eastern Sudan*: 55–83. African Studies Centre: Leiden, The Netherlands.

Wilson, K., 1992, *A state of the art review of research on internally displaced, refugees, and returnees from and in Mozambique*. Report prepared for the Swedish International Development Authority (SIDA/ASDI), Stockholm.

Wood, W., 1994, "Hazardous journeys: Ecomigrants in the 1990s". (Forthcoming).

Zartman, I., 1970, "Portuguese Guinean refugees in Senegal", in E. El Ayouty and H. Brooks, (eds), *Refugees south of the Sahara: An African dilemma*: 143–61. Westport, CT: Negro University Press.

Social Differentiation, Conflicts and Rural–Urban Interaction in the Babati Area, Tanzania

Vesa-Matti Loiske

The aim of this chapter is to examine who benefits from rural–urban interaction. Who appropriates the resources generated? In order to understand this, changes in social stratification and changes in power relations as well as economic strategies of different social strata in a village in Tanzania are analysed. How structural adjustment policies interact with this development are also discussed. The empirical material used here is derived from fieldwork conducted in Giting village located some 50 km south-west of Babati town in the Northern Highlands of Tanzania.

THE STUDY AREA

Giting village is located on the north eastern slope of Hanang mountain (Map 1). The mountain can be characterized as a green island in the midst of a vast expanse of semi-arid savanna. Mt. Hanang is an extinct volcano covered with evergreen mountain forest, continuously providing the surrounding area with precious water. The agricultural conditions are reasonably good.

The main town in Hanang District is Katesh with 12,887 inhabitants (1988). Katesh is growing rapidly like other small towns in the area. At a distance of approximately 18 kilometres many villagers regularly walk to town and back to visit the monthly market, the hospital, the district authorities, etc. Katesh is not as commercially developed as Babati, the second closest town, but is nevertheless an important junction along the Arusha to Singida road.

Babati, the capital of neighbouring Babati District, with 21,794 inhabitants (1988), is one of the main stops on the road between Arusha and Dodoma. From both Babati, located some 50 kilometres from Giting, and Katesh, agricultural products are exported to the densely populated Arusha and Moshi areas.

The Iraqw, an agro-pastoral ethnic group, have made up the majority of inhabitants in Giting village since the 1920s when they squeezed out the Barabaig, a pastoral group. Iraqw society is described as an egalitarian soci-

Map 1. *The study area and the location of Giting*

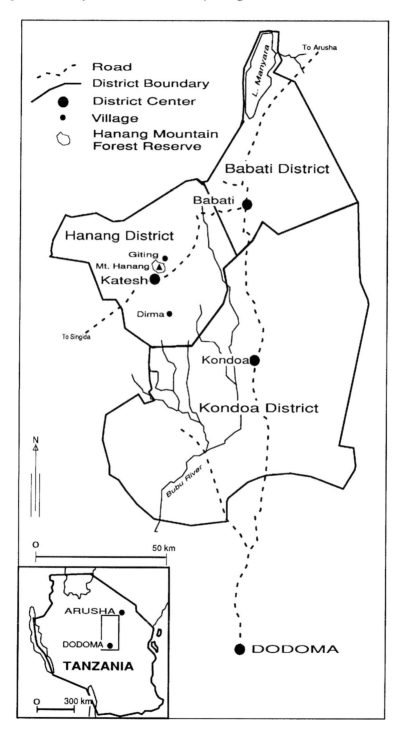

ety (Thornton, 1980:5), though several decades of rapid economic change have made inroads on Iraqw social organization. This is particularly connected to the colonial government's effort to build an "African prosperous yeoman farmers' class" among the Iraqw which according to Shivji, transformed Iraqw society into a socially differentiated, cash-crop producing appendix to the world colonial economy (1976:50–54).

In the 1950s the agriculturally favourable land of Giting was allocated to five African households who came to possess hundreds of acres each. In 1967 all land in Tanzania was taken over by the state. A major land reform was undertaken in Giting in 1974. Each resident household was allocated four acres of agricultural land and a one acre household plot. Five hundred acres were set aside as a communal village field. The land allocation was carried out in haste and under somewhat chaotic conditions. A few well off farmers managed to be allocated more than four acres.

The land reform was intended to create equality between households and change the whole agrarian structure. The colonial unequal structure did, however, survive. The patriarchal bonds created during the colonial period, were strong. The five families that dominated Giting during the colonial period are still, 19 years after the land reform, the most wealthy and most powerful families in the area. Social differentiation has increased contrary to expectations in 1974.

SOCIAL DIFFERENTIATION IN GITING

All households in Giting village have been ranked according to wealth. The method used in mapping the social differentiation is a variety of "wealth ranking" (cf. McCracken *et al.* 1988:30; Grandin 1987) frequently used in rapid rural appraisal to obtain an approximate view of social differentiation in local communities. Local people's own perceptions of "wealth" provide the categories used in the ranking. In Giting 18 villagers were asked to do the ranking. These key informants were carefully selected among people well informed about village affairs and who, for a variety of reasons, knew people in all income groups in the village. After they had completed the ranking, the informants were interviewed and the criteria they had used were noted. In this way seven wealth groups were identified.

More than 15 per cent of the households in each wealth group were randomly selected for interview. Households in different wealth groups were asked about strategies used to maintain their economic and social positions. It turned out that access to resources in nearby urban areas and neighbouring villages was vital to economic success. For the purpose of this chapter I have merged the wealth groups 1–3, 4–5 and 6–7 into three as the differences regarding access to outside-village resources between the households in each of these three groups are small. A more detailed classification than this did not increase the stringency of the analysis. The distribution of the households into three groups is summarized in Figure 1.

As shown in Figure 1, social stratification in Giting is substantial, contrary to the common view that the land reform of 1974 removed rural differentiation and that the social structure in rural Tanzania is fairly egalitarian. The three groups identified are described below based on the wealth ranking and subsequent interviews.

Figure 1. *Distribution of village households in three groups*

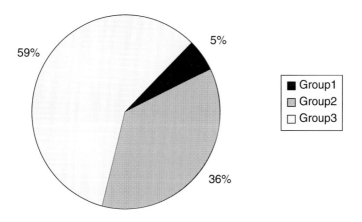

Source: authors field notes

Group 1: The wealthy

The uppermost stratum in this group (five households) has, in the local perspective, only one criterion: they face no limitations what so ever in terms of wealth creation. This group has free access to land and is not limited to making use only of village resources. In addition they have great influence on the local ruling party, the courts, among district leaders, and so on.

They live in modern, corrugated-iron roofed concrete houses. All five households have pick-ups for transporting day labourers and agricultural inputs. The pick-ups are also used for transporting cash crops to Katesh and Babati. An additional income from the pick-ups is public transport. They also own tractors. The main income from the tractors comes from contracted ploughing. The tractor owners cultivate big areas in both Giting and neighbouring villages. Oxen are, in this group, mainly used as an alternative if the tractors break down or in times of fuel shortage. Pesticides, improved seeds, fertilizers and semi-bred cattle are commonly used. Two people own lorries used for long distance trade, mainly to Arusha, Dar es Salaam, Singida and Mwanza. They employ day labourers from Giting but also from other villages and surrounding towns. Their resource base includes surrounding villages, nearby small towns and major towns in other regions. In the village their emphasis in production is on agriculture, while in the surrounding villages they are engaged in cattle rearing, and, finally, in town, they invest in trade, transport and real-estate.

The middle stratum of this group (15 households) is involved in agriculture and cattle rearing. Two of them have tractors and the others have more than two ox-teams. They do not own lorries or cars. They have access to agricultural land and grazing outside Giting. They use improved seeds, fertilizer and pesticides in cultivation. In Giting they increase their cultivated area through "sharecropping" and land renting arrangements. Two of them have dug fish ponds and grow fruit trees, bananas and coffee in an agroforestry system. They have modern houses. They also have second dwellings in other villages.

The less well off in this group (10 households) are mainly involved in petty trading, most of them having small shops in the village. They have modern houses. No one owns cars, tractors or lorries. They use fertilizers, improved seeds, pesticides and plough with oxen.

Group 2: The ordinary

The upper stratum in this group (110 households) manage to cultivate a few acres more than the four acres they have been allocated and they employ day labourers from the village during peak periods in agriculture. They have 1–2 teams of oxen, oxcarts and ploughs and tin-roofed traditional houses. They have sporadic contacts with towns and five have plots or real estate in Katesh or Babati. Seven of them have access to land in other villages. The majority of their cattle are grazed in other villages. A few milk cows are kept in Giting. They manage fairly well and their position is only threatened in times of severe drought or flooding. A specific feature of this group is the cooperation between households. They collectively own their means of production (oxen, oxcarts, ploughs, etc.), work together and give support to each other when needed.

The less well off in this group (121 households) manage to crop their four acre fields but they do not have possibilities to sharecrop or rent additional land. They are limited to the village resources. They cooperate with each other and own oxen and ploughs together. Five of the households own oxcarts and most of them have a plough of their own. The average number of oxen per household is 2.4. One ox-team comprises four oxen which means that most households have to cooperate to get access to a full ox-team. The houses are traditional, sometimes with corrugated-iron roof, but commonly grass thatched. The houses are big and well maintained.

Group 3: The poor

No one in this group manages to cultivate their 4 acres. The upper stratum (170 households) cultivates on average three acres out of four, while the lower stratum (201 households) cultivates one. About 50 households do not manage to cultivate at all every year. Everyone in group three lives mainly as day labourers. They live from hand to mouth and especially the months before harvest they are semi-starving. The households are often indebted to the well-off farmers. They live in grass thatched traditional mud houses, often of low quality. They do not have access to modern means of production. They retain formal control of their land, but frequently their fields are cropped by other farmers.

RESOURCE ACCESS AND SOCIAL DIFFERENTIATION

Group 1 has access to resources in nearby rural towns, surrounding villages and, of course, in Giting itself. On and off they do business in the major towns of Arusha, Singida, Mwanza and even Dar es Salaam. Group 2 has frequent contacts with surrounding villages, but only sporadic interactions with rural towns. The poor farmers in group 3 are limited to the resources in Giting. They cannot, however, utilize more than a small fraction of the village resources as they lack the basic means of production. The varying resource access has created a specific set of social relations in the village that is reflected in the various strategies that the people in the three groups use to maintain their social positions.

Strategy of Group 1: Multi-activity and multi-spatial entrepreneurship

In Tanzania, registered villages are identified either as agricultural or pastoral. In 1974, when Giting achieved its registration, it was noted as predominantly engaged in agriculture. This had the consequence that a limit on cattle keeping was imposed. Nine head of cattle was decided as the maximum number allowed for each household. Rich people are particularly active to make sure that this restriction is upheld. The reason is that they have access to grazing opportunities in other parts of the district. Hence their strategy in Giting is to concentrate on agriculture. One way to increase agricultural land is to open up the limited grazing areas for agriculture. Another is to complain, via the village government, and force cattle keeping households to migrate to other villages. By reducing grazing pressure in this way, farmers in group 1 hope to increase their cultivation area. And, indeed, a major reason for out migration from the village today is lack of grazing. This strategy has created conflicts between groups 1 and 2, as the latter try to combine crop production with livestock keeping, having limited access to grazing land outside the village. An additional reason for the well-off farmers in Giting to cultivate the grazing areas is that they get larger units of land that is cheaper and less labour demanding to cultivate with tractors than rented or sharecropped four acre plots.

Group 1 also have resources in neighbouring villages. The most common strategy to get access to resources in other villages is to establish a second dwelling there. There are some villages, e.g., Dirma, with uncultivated lands. The Giting household sends a son or relative with some cattle to the village claiming to be a pastoral household which is a precondition for becoming accepted as a member of that village. Once the second dwelling is well established the same strategy for expanding cultivation is used as in Giting. There are examples of farmers from Giting who have 200 acres of land in Dirma. The cropping conditions in semi-arid Dirma are poor. Droughts, as well as flooding, are frequent. The soils are vulnerable and increased cropping as well as intensive grazing will effect the ecology of the area negatively. Several thousand head of cattle are distributed by Giting farmers into the surrounding villages. They are kept either by relatives or by poor farmers who need to borrow cows to get milk.

Another relation between Giting and other villages is the labour market. Labourers from other villages and towns in the surrounding area come to

Giting during peak periods in agriculture. There is also a minor out-migration of labourers from Giting. Giting has one of the biggest labour markets in the area but also has many underemployed labourers as a result of the social stratification. One of the reasons why rich farmers go far beyond the local area to employ labourers is that they avoid the social obligations that locally are attached to an employment contract. Traditionally the employer has responsibility for the reproduction of the hired local labour the whole year, and has hence to feed the employed household the whole cropping season. If, however, the labour employed comes from far away these obligations do not apply. Labour recruited from outside the village has only occurred over the last few years.

In the nearby towns of Katesh and Babati, well-off Giting farmers have plots, houses, shops or guest houses. A relative or friend is employed to run the business. Farmers make frequent visits to these towns for social reasons but also to control their businesses.

The income from trade is important in the daily running of the household economy, while major investments are financed by selling cattle. Cattle are still the most reliable way of increasing and saving capital. During the last few years it has become more profitable than previously to own real estate in town and it, to some extent, competes with cattle keeping as a way of saving and investing capital today.

Katesh had 4,000 households on a waiting list to obtain residential plots in the town in 1991. The majority of them, according to the district office, are well-off households from nearby villages. If everyone was allotted a plot overnight, it would more than double the number of inhabitants in Katesh! Land prices and living costs have, of course, been affected accordingly. Investments in real estate have in recent years been very profitable.

The increase in urban population also increases the demand for food products. Food is sold to town dwellers by well-off farmers in the surrounding rural areas. Seven farmers in Giting who have access to transport facilities buy their neighbours' excess production and sell it in the rural towns. The two who have access to lorries transport crops to Arusha, Dar es Salaam, Singida and Mwanza, where the prices are more than double those in Katesh or Babati. Capital created in this way may be used to improve housing in Giting, but investments outside the village are far more important and include real estate in towns, transport and cattle.

Strategy of Group 2: Agro-pastoralism and cooperation

Villagers belonging to group 2 organize their lives in a rather different way, much closer to the traditions of Iraqw society. They consider agro-pastoralism, with cattle and agriculture spatially incorporated, to be the most viable mode of production.

Another traditional feature is cooperation between households. Households often own means of production together, rear cattle communally and work together in peak periods in agriculture. This group is also concerned about soil fertility and uses manure and soil conservation methods more frequently than other groups. They are not totally limited to the village resources but claim that they are forced to use other villages' grazing resources due to lack of grazing opportunities in Giting. They complain bitterly about the well-off farmers' strategy in cultivating the grazing areas of the village. Some of them have cattle and second dwellings in nearby villages but they prefer to have both agriculture and cattle integrated in the same area. The top stratum in this group has invested in small houses in Katesh or Babati. They are involved in petty trading in markets in Katesh or Babati and a few have small "kiosks" in Giting. Petty trading commonly supports grown-up sons or daughters who have not managed to get access to land. They also complain about the problems of getting land for their children. These households have the highest average size (10.9) of all households.

Strategy of Group 3: Few alternatives and semi-proletarianization

The third group are more or less cut off from all resources and even though they have formal access to four acres of land they rarely manage to cultivate it. They grab whatever opportunity comes along in times when day-labour is in demand, but are without income for long periods of time, especially since the employers started to recruit cheap labourers from other areas. Production on their land is less than half of the average per acre production in the village. Modern agricultural inputs are not used. Their fields are often ploughed by those who own tractors or ox ploughs. In return they are allowed to plant 2-3 acres and take the harvest.

The people belonging to group 3 eke out a meagre existence, which also has repercussions for their social lives. Family life often revolves around the wife who takes on the main responsibility for the well-being of the children. Consequently women prefer payment in kind for their day-labour. They are the ones responsible for food on the table, even if it often has to be without contributions from the husband. Many men in this group consume their cash drinking local brew (*pombe*).

Many families in this category struggle with problems of physical illness, mainly TB and malaria. If a family member falls ill it often has very severe long term repercussions. The costs of transport, medical assistance and medicines will indebt the family and increase its dependence on better-off neighbours.

Most households have access to, at least, one cow (the range being one to seven) borrowed from more well-off relatives or friends. No one owns modern agricultural equipment and they are totally dependent on the goodwill of the well-off farmers.

STRUCTURAL ADJUSTMENT IN TANZANIA

Structural adjustment in Tanzania has gone through three different phases. These are the National Economic Survival Programme (NESP), the Structural Adjustment Programme (SAP), and the Economic Recovery Programme (ERP). The NESP was a programme devised by the Tanzanian state itself in 1981–82 as an effort to revive agricultural and other non-traditional exports in the wake of the breakdown in negotiations with the IMF. It was also meant to increase industrial output for the same purpose while reducing public expenditure. The aim was to raise, by the end of the programme, a targeted amount equivalent to USD 903.5 million. The targets were, however, unrealistic and the result was that both crop production and industrial output fell (Mbelle, 1982:73).

Perhaps due to the frustrations born of the failure of NESP, the SAP (1982–1985) was much more comprehensive and encompassed a greater part of the national economy. Among the policies adopted were the partial devaluation of the shilling, the partial liberalization of internal and external trade, and partial liberalization of agriculture, especially through the formulation of the National Agricultural Policy in 1983 which for the first time since 1967 allowed private ownership of land. Emphasis was put on further reductions in government spending and rationalization of foreign exchange use (Campbell, 1988:5; Chachage, 1992:5).

The ERP (1986–) is a further extension of the SAP, leading to wholesale structural adjustment efforts on the economy and in the political life of the nation. Some of the policies involved have been the rehabilitation of infrastructure, the market adjustment of producer prices and the decontrolling of the cooperatives, the privatization of land ownership, and the restoration of internal and external balance of payments through prudent fiscal policies. All subsidies have been removed from agricultural inputs and urban food supplies and a reintroduction of direct taxation has been combined with cuts in social services expenditures (Mbelle, 1982:34; Chachage, 1992:7). At the political level, multi-partyism is suggested as the preferred form of democratic governance.

Reports from the planning departments of the Tanzanian government indicate that the economy has experienced real growth from 1986 and onwards. The annual report of the Bank of Tanzania for 1991 pegged this growth at 4 per cent. Other knowledgeable observers of the Tanzanian socio-political scene, however, believe that these programmes have only benefited local and international private capital at the expense of the less endowed social groups in the country (cf. Chachage, 1992).

STRUCTURAL ADJUSTMENT IN GITING

The liberal conditions for economic activities, as well as more relaxed political conditions resulting from structural adjustment programmes, have had a profound impact in Giting village. The last decade has been characterized by clashes between both the political leadership of the village and ordinary villagers and between affluent villagers and the less powerful people over access to resources. A major change that has occurred is that several previously communal assets have now been taken over by private entrepreneurs.

At the time of the land reform in 1974 a village field of 500 acres was set aside to cater for investments in communal development. Plots for a school, a dispensary and a commercial centre were also demarcated. Communal investments included a school, a dispensary, a cattle dip, a milling machine, piped water, a village tractor, a lorry, a village silo, a butchery and a village shop.

These investments threatened to, and were indeed intended to, take over business from privately owned shops, tractors, milling machines, transport, etc. There was, as a result, a continuous struggle between a small group of rich people, members of the upper stratum of group 1 identified above, and the rest of the village, over the control of these resources. The village made its communal investments from the late 1970s up to 1986 on the political initiative of the village government that was led by its secretary. During these years the secretary came to be the focus of attacks by the property owners in the village, making up at most a quarter of the population. By 1986 they had, however, managed to control the majority of votes in the village government. The secretary met with direct opposition and was eventually also accused of several crimes, the most serious being the murder of a villager in 1987. He was arrested by the police, but released from jail after two weeks, due to lack of evidence. The campaign to get rid of him continued, however. Finally, in 1989, he was transferred to another village, eleven kilometres away. The whole structure of communal investments, so laboriously erected, fell into a shambles. Private entrepreneurs took over. Below, details are provided as to how this occurred.

Misappropriation of communal resources

Giting has had a piped water system since 1985. The system serviced the school, the dispensary and a few livestock watering points. In 1989 two well-off farmers connected their households to the system without the consent of the village government. Both built two big water tanks on their household plots. Their additional consumption thus decreased the already insufficient water supply to other parts of the village. This annoyed many people in the village, some of who are reported to have sabotaged the water pipe. Today, the supply of piped water is erratic due to this conflict.

A village shop was established in the 1970s to provide the people of Giting with agricultural inputs and other necessary commodities. Before the shop was privately owned. The village shop sold at officially controlled prices until the shop was closed in the late 1980s for a variety of reasons. Meanwhile, several new shops have been established in Giting. The price level is considerably higher here than in shops in other nearby villages. Many people are growing increasingly indebted to the owners of the shops.

A silo was built by the village cooperative in 1984 and was used by the cooperative to store cash crops awaiting transport. The official buying agents started to refuse to buy poor peasants' crops on the pretext that their crop had too poor a quality. However, when the very same crops were sold to a rich peasant at less than half the price and taken to the silo they were accepted as prime quality. This is another example as to why poor people lost faith in local public institutions.

The village bought a lorry at the beginning of the 1980s to transport crops to far away markets where prices are higher. Two persons in the village government were responsible for the maintenance of the lorry and the buying, selling and transportation of the crops. Because of its comparatively low charges the village lorry managed to take much of the business from the two privately owned lorries in the village. A maintenance fund was established for the lorry from the profits. At the beginning of the 1990s, however, the lorry had a major breakdown that needed a substantial amount of money to repair. When the two-man committee decided to draw from the maintenance fund to repair the lorry the money was not there. No one in the village government could be held accountable for the disappearance of the money. The lorry has been idle ever since and the profitable transport business is back with the two private lorry owners.

A village tractor was bought to help the villagers cultivate their communal field and also to help the villagers with ploughing and transport services. Up to the late 1980s the communal field was cultivated by the village tractor, hence giving good income to the village. Many of the peasants in the village also had their fields ploughed with the village tractor which was cheaper to rent than the private ones. Just as in the case of the lorry, a separate maintenance fund had been set aside for the tractor. However, when this fund was needed in 1989 to repair the tractor the money was nowhere to be found. The tractor was out of use up to the 1992 cultivation season when it was repaired on orders from the Regional Commissioner in Arusha. While the tractor was broken down the communal field was not cropped and the village finances deteriorated. In the 1992 cultivation season a small part of the village field was cultivated, again on direct orders from the Regional Commissioner.

Land laws and corrupt courts

In 1989 the village government decided to redistribute land to open up opportunities for landless young people while at the same time also allowing space between the fields for roads in order to make the fields accessible for tractors and oxen. About forty of the land owning households lost land to the new roads. These households had been promised compensation in the new areas intended for young households. The compensation, however, never materialized and the households who had lost land decided to take their case to court.

The court decided that the village had no legal right to allocate land and as such the forty households should just accept the hard fact that they had lost their land. A few of them protested to the ward secretary who in many respects formed a sort of court of last appeal. They were not listened to. Instead the ward secretary, who was responsible for redistributing the land, and who has the right to confine "troublemakers", detained them for nine days. When they came out from detention they were asked if they were prepared to drop the case. Several of the protesters who maintained that they would pursue the case were repeatedly confined until they "saw" the wisdom of dropping the case.

The village government decided to distribute the new lands to those who were already registered as households in the village and who could pay a "registration fee". The landless youth who had initiated the redistribution process, hence failed to get plots while a number of well-off households in Giting received an additional half acre or acre of "coffee or pyrethrum plots" on the well-watered slopes close to the mountain.

In another case, ten of the rich households in the village were taken to court by the village government to answer charges of "invading" areas set aside for grazing. The court case dragged on for about one year. Finally, the village lost the case on the technical point that it had no legal mandate to allocate land for any use in the village.

This judgement actually staggered the whole land tenure system in the village. As a result the few farmers who controlled large tracts of land before the land reform, started proceedings in court to regain their pre-reform lands. The court has not made any judgement in these cases yet. However, it is possible to speculate on what will happen if these litigants win their cases. One of the big land owners, for example, had 500 acres before the land reform, which means that more than 100 families will be evicted from their land if only this farmer regains his previous land.

Leadership accountability

At the initiative of a party official a collection of money was undertaken in Giting ward in 1991. The money collected, Tsh. 4.5 m, was meant to purchase a bus. The problem of public transport is severe in the whole ward as the private bus companies charge high fares. The idea was well received by the inhabitants of the ward who hoped that the ward was more able to handle a transport business than the village government. The party official did not, however, purchase the bus but diverted the money into some other use. In early 1992 he had promised the villagers to return the money. Very few believed in that promise. The matter was reported to the district party headquarters. The party official, however, was not punished by the district party branch despite the fact that they investigated this matter.

Following complaints from the villagers, the Regional Commissioner for Arusha visited Giting in 1992. As a result of that meeting the Regional Commissioner ordered, among other things, that the village should rehabilitate its communal resources and cultivate the communal field. He also nullified the redistribution of land of 1989 and initiated an investigation on the irregularities of the village finances. The party branch at the district level was ordered by the Regional Commissioner to investigate the complaints. It resulted in the dismissal of the village chairman and the transfer of the village secretary to another village. The members of the land committee in the village government were also dismissed while the investigation was carried out.

CONCLUDING DISCUSSION

The Giting area is not poor, indeed Giting is considered as one of the richest villages in the region, but the social stratification blocks the possibility for a majority of the population to utilize the village resources because of a small group of rich farmers who appropriate the surplus production and invest the profits outside Giting. Whereas in the 1970s neighbours were mutually dependent on each other and "forced" by social as well as political pressure to cooperate, a system of private ownership and individualistic organization is now being established. Village resources are transferred from communal to private hands and local labour is being replaced by imported labourers.

Giting village is, as shown, highly socially stratified today. Five households dominate the economy. A majority of the households (58.6%) are poor and unable to utilize all the land they have been allocated and form a proletariat in the village. The poverty in Giting results in low wages and easy access to land for the elite. This provides the opportunity to produce cheap crops and to sell them dear in urban markets.

The interaction between the village and towns is now totally in private hands and the towns form only one additional resource that is utilized by the village elite. The village of Dirma constitutes another resource and the poverty of people a third. The local rural élites in the village live in and use the village as a base for their economic and social activities and this case study is not, therefore, an example of a village that is economically exploited by the surrounding towns because it is local Giting entrepreneurs who make the profits. It is not, on the other hand, an example where rural–urban interaction improves the living conditions for the majority of villagers. The resources of Giting are utilized without being reinvested or redistributed; hence the present strategy of the local entrepreneurs retards the development of the village. Part of the surplus is invested in small towns in the vicinity (investments in real estate and trade) but the lion part is invested in the national and international economy (tractors, cars, lorries, building material). The centre of the process is the local entrepreneur and his antipode—the day labourer.

Giting provides us also with an example of how difficult it is to influence development by political means. The local elite have successfully worked against the former very strong political ambitions of the country to distribute the means of production equally between the peasants. The strongest possible political efforts have been made here; a very radical land reform and the creation of communal economic resources that financed investments in infrastructure and development of the village, but these achievements did not survive even 15 years. The political struggle that has been carried out so successfully by the rural elite has resulted in a *laissez-faire* situation where individual economic self-interest commands village life. The structural adjustment programmes imposed since the early 1980s have strongly enhanced this process.

The physical resource base in Giting is now threatened. An incipient land degradation resulting in decreasing per acre production in agriculture is obvious today. If the profits created in the village continue to be exported to national and international markets without any reinvestment to maintain soil fertility and the infrastructure of the village, the result will be increased underdevelopment.

References

Campbell, H. 1988, "Tanzania and the World Bank's Urban Shelter Project: Ideology and International Finance", *Review of African Political Economy*, 42:5–18.

Chachage, C.S.L., 1992, "Agriculture and Structural Adjustment in Tanzania". Paper presented at a workshop on *The State, Structural Adjustment and Changing Social and Political Relations in Africa*, held at the Scandinavian Institute of African Studies, Uppsala, 19–21 May.

Grandin, B.E., 1987, *Wealth Ranking in Smallholder Communities: A Field Manual*. Nairobi: ILRAD.

Mbelle, A.V.Y., 1982, *Capacity Utilization under Foreign Exchange Constraint: The case of selected industrial linkages in Tanzania*. Unpublished MA Dissertation, University of Dar es Salaam.

McCracken, Jennifer, *et al.*, 1988, *An Introduction to Rapid Rural Appraisal for Agricultural Development*. London: IIED.

Shivji, Issa G., 1976, *Class Struggles In Tanzania*. Dar es Salaam: Tanzania Publishing House.
Thornton, Robert J., 1980, *Place, Time and Culture Among the Iraqw of Tanzania*. New York: Academic Press.

Migration in Ethiopia and the Role of the State

Jonathan Baker

The purpose of this chapter is to illustrate the central role of the state in facilitating and directing internal migration in Ethiopia. The main focus is on the post-1974 period when an attempt was made to transform Ethiopia into a Marxist-Leninist state, guided by the Workers' Party of Ethiopia (WPE). The mixing of tenses, particularly in the section on land reform and institution building, is deliberate because some uncertainties surround the precise responsibilities of institutions constructed by the Mengistu state but retained by the present Transitional Government.[1] This chapter does not consider the movement of millions of refugees into or out of Ethiopia.

IMPERIALISM AND THE FORMATION OF THE ETHIOPIAN STATE

Present-day Ethiopia is of recent creation. Unlike the situation in the rest of Africa where European colonialism created dependency and reshaped the continental map, Ethiopia developed as a result of an alliance between northern Amhara-Tigre colonisers. Through a series of military campaigns, Emperor Menelik II (ruled 1889–1913) greatly extended the boundaries of Abyssinia and in the process tripled the size of the country, doubled the population (McClellan, 1984:657) and "incorporated a myriad of religious, ethnic and linguistic groups into the Empire" (Baker, 1990:212).

Menelik's desire to create a modern, centralised state required the expansion of state revenues and extraction of southern resources such as spices, civet, ivory, gold, hides and, most important of all, coffee, provided him with the wherewithal to achieve this ambition.

The consequences of Menelik's imperial endeavours are increasingly being documented and the details need not detain us (see, for example, McClellan, 1978, 1980, 1984; Donham and James, 1986). However, it is appropriate to mention the mechanisms through which Menelik maintained and consolidated control of his newly-acquired empire.

In the newly-conquered territories, Menelik established a number of military garrisons (*ketema*) which were governed by military commanders. In addition, soldiers of the imperial army, who in turn were accompanied by their families, were rewarded for their services by grants of expropriated land (*rist-gult* and *gult*) and were assigned a number of tenants *(gabbar)* from among the conquered peoples. *Gabbar* were obliged to cultivate *gult* lands for their new patrons and to provide a range of other services (Baker, 1990:212). Thus, in the space of two decades, a feudal system had been firmly implanted in the southern regions of Ethiopia. For a discussion of the variety and complexity of land tenure systems which were established in the south of Ethiopia and which prevailed until the 1974 revolution, see Cohen and Weintraub (1975) and Pausewang (1983).

Menelik's efforts at creating a centralised state also involved the expansion and modernisation of the tax-collecting system, the extension of communications and transportation, and the establishment of a new and permanent capital, Addis Ababa, in the 1890s at the geographical centre of the Empire. The success of pacification campaigns in the south meant that *ketema* settlements acquired new non-military functions and many evolved into centres for the extraction of the rural surplus.

The southern conquests, however, required a steady flow of northern peasant farmers willing to cultivate alienated land, and thus maintain and consolidate the feudal structure and promote the process of Amharaisation in non-Amhara regions. Moreover, the increasing impoverishment of peasant households in the north through increasing land degradation and scarcity (McCann, 1986:369–411) meant that there were many peasants willing to migrate to take advantage of the new opportunities.

As McCann puts it:

> The north-south migration that took place in Ethiopia between 1890 and the post-war years was perhaps *the most significant single process* in the foundation of the modern Ethiopian social formation. Menelik's conquests meant little without a ready population of soldier/settlers willing to leave the cycle of subsistence production in the north and settle into the huge tracts of alienated land offered in the wake of the imperial conquests (McCann, 1986:399) emphasis added.

Haile Selassie continued the process of modernising and centralising the Empire inherited from Menelik. Poor peasants continued to migrate out of the north. Between the 1950s and the 1970s, an estimated one million people migrated because of insufficient or degraded land and drought (Kloos and Aynalem, 1989:115).

THE ROLE OF THE STATE IN POST-REVOLUTIONARY MIGRATION PROCESSES

While migration during the imperial era may be characterised largely as being spontaneous, although the state played an enabling role through pacification campaigns in southern regions, during the post-1974 period the great majority of population movements were state controlled and directed or, at least strongly influenced.

With the overthrow of the imperial regime in 1974, the revolutionary government committed itself to a programme which was "to liberate Ethiopia from the yokes of feudalism and imperialism, and to lay the foundations for the transition to socialism" (Halliday and Molyneux, 1981:100). Apart from nationalising large industries and the banks, the government enacted one of the most far-reaching rural and urban land reforms ever attempted by an African country.

Land reform and institution building: Consequences for rural–urban migration

In 1975 and 1976 the government introduced legislation pertaining to the organisation and ownership of rural and urban land. All rural land was nationalised and usufructuary rights were redistributed to tenants and the landless (Negarit Gazeta, Proc. 31 and Proc. 71, 1975). The upshot of this legislation was to dispossess the landowning class of all but the legal maximum amount of land permitted per farming household of one-quarter of a gasha, about 10 hectares[2] (Negarit Gazeta, Proc. 31 and Proc. 71, 1975).

Furthermore, the rural land reform meant that tenant farmers and the rural landless gained user rights to agricultural land, thus greatly improving their economic status. All feudal obligations were abolished including the onerous *gult* system in the south of the country, whereby tenants were often obliged to surrender more than 50 per cent of their harvests to the landowning class. In order to implement the redistribution of rural land, peasant associations (PAs) were established throughout the countryside. PAs had the responsibility for not merely distributing and redistributing land (as a result of population growth) but also for administering and controlling the lives of all rural Ethiopians. PAs vary in size although a legal minimum area of 20 *gasha* (about 800 hectares) was a requirement for the establishment of an individual PA.

In the urban sector, the government introduced policies which broke the power of the landowning elite. Proclamation 47 of 1975 pertains to the ownership of urban land. Under this law all urban land was nationalised (but not housing) and landlords were dispossessed of their rights to own more than one house. Extra houses became the property of the state and these in turn were rented to those in need of accommodation. In practice, private tenants became tenants of the state. Overnight the government eliminated landlordism as a phenomenon and landlords as a class. Land speculation came to an end. This had two immediate results. First, the elimination of a class which might have emerged as an enemy of the revolution and second, the redistribution of housing with secure tenancies to those in need. However, one very negative longer-term effect was to severely reduce the construction of new dwellings for rent which led to a chronic shortage of urban housing. The destruction of the rentier class meant that the main supplier of urban housing disappeared. Moreover, the housing supply shortage was exacerbated by the inability of the government to construct anything like the number of dwellings required or, indeed, to maintain the existing stock of housing (Clapham, 1988:141–142; Wendt *et al.*, 1990:227–248).

To implement the new urban policies, urban dwellers' associations or *kebele* were established in all urban centres with a population of more than 2,000. In 1986 there were 318 towns that had formed *kebele* associations.[3] *Kebele* are the lowest administrative unit in urban areas in Ethiopia and were established to provide for the social, economic and political needs of their inhabitants. For example, the preamble to Proclamation 104, 1976 states that "urban dwellers (are) to get organized in *kebele* associations and run their own affairs, solve their own problems, and directly participate in political, economic and social activities". *Kebele* had wide-ranging powers and intruded into the lives of their members in a great variety of ways. In summary, *kebele* had responsibility for welfare and social programmes including the maintenance and construction of dwelling units, mother–child clinics, *kebele* roads and paths, the maintenance of waste disposal facilities, and to conduct hygiene, vaccination and literacy programmes. Moreover, whenever possible *kebele* were to promote and encourage income-generating activities of a small-scale nature. *Kebele* were also responsible for keeping records of births, deaths and marriages.

Perhaps the most important component of the *kebele*, at least from the viewpoint of its members, was the *kebele* shop system whereby each *kebele* had its own shop where basic food and other items could be purchased at a subsidised price. As most commodities were in short supply, a rationing system was in operation but, nevertheless, this did allow residents the possibility of obtaining essential goods at reasonable prices. For the poor, who constitute the majority of urban dwellers in Ethiopia, *kebele* shops were essential to ensure survival. However, to gain access to *kebele* subsidised food and other commodities one had to be a *kebele* member, and in possession of a ration card (see Baker, 1991, for a discussion of the *kebele* system in Addis Ababa).

The consequences of these rural and urban land reforms and the associated reorganisation of economic, political and social life in Ethiopia has been dramatic. In the context of this present discussion, the most fundamental change has been the reduction in the rural–urban migration rate. As a result of insufficient data at the national level it is not possible to provide anything more than some general comments regarding the decline in-migration from the countryside to the towns. Data for Addis Ababa clearly show a dramatic decline in the growth rate of the city from 6.5 per cent in 1967 to 3.0 per cent in the mid-1980s, the latter figure is only marginally above the national population growth rate of 2.9 per cent (Solomon Mulugeta, 1985).

The reasons for the decline in rural–urban migration cannot be attributed to any single factor. First, there is no doubt that the rural land reforms had a major impact in that they provided would-be migrants with the means to survive in the countryside, instead of moving to the towns for work. The problem of landlessness which had been a major factor in pushing people from the land under the imperial regime, was overcome by land redistribution. Moreover, according to Clapham (1988:130), in the years immediately following the land reform, probably "quite a large number of recent rural emigrants" returned to the countryside to take advantage of the newly-acquired access to land.

Second, the establishment of two distinct institutions—the urban *kebele* and the rural peasant association—accentuated the distinctions between rural and urban dwellers. Henceforth, a person could be a member of a *kebele* or a peasant association, but not both. In practice, membership of these institutions introduced a degree of administrative rigidity and inflexibility which did not encourage rural–urban or urban–rural migration. For example, if a rural dweller wanted to leave the countryside to migrate to town, written permission from the peasant association was required. Even when permission was granted, the newcomer to town would require the consent of the *kebele* association. The official consent of the *kebele* was essential bearing in mind the need to acquire a ration card in order to obtain supplies of subsidised food. Although urban residence was possible without *kebele* consent "a poor immigrant not registered with the kebelle, and therefore not receiving rations, would find it hard to survive" (Clapham, 1988:147). A final hurdle to urban residence was to find somewhere to live. In view of the extreme shortage of available accommodation and the long waiting lists for housing, a newly-arrived migrant would need to rely on the goodwill of urban-domiciled kin and friends to provide a place to stay. This goodwill may certainly have been short-lived given the severe overcrowding of dwellings. In Addis Ababa, for example, seventy-five per cent of all houses have a surface area of less than 50 square metres, but are occupied by between 5 to 9 persons (Wendt *et al.*, 1990:234).

A final set of considerations which have had implications for reducing the level of rural–urban migration are the high levels of urban unemployment, coupled with declining real incomes and poverty. Poverty occurs right across the urban spectrum from Addis Ababa down to the smallest towns. In 1987 an estimated 65 per cent of households in the capital city lived below the absolute urban poverty threshold of 238 Birr per month[*] (World Bank, 1989:6). Data from 1988 for nine secondary towns show that the lowest levels of poverty among households were in the towns of Ambo (population, 19,900) and Arsi-Negele (population, 16,400) both with 69 per cent, and the highest level of urban poverty was found in Mizan Teferi (population, 7,600) with 86 per cent of all households living below the poverty threshold of 238 Birr per month (World Bank, 1989:162).

Obviously, such extreme levels of urban poverty are bound to have a disincentive effect on potential migrants. Moreover, poor urban households would certainly not appreciate poor country relatives adding to an already severely overstretched household economy unless, of course, they could contribute to it with regular supplies of rural produce.

High levels of unemployment are reported to be a major problem in urban areas in Ethiopia, although the data are inconclusive and conflicting. According to World Bank figures for 1978, the average estimated urban unemployment rate for males was 12 per cent and for women just under 31 per cent. These figures are considered to be even higher now (World Bank, 1989:6). While it is true that unemployment effects young people and females disproportionately, it is unlikely that the World Bank figures accurately reflect the actual situation given the widespread poverty among urban households and the necessity to obtain some income, however meagre.

Probably a more realistic picture would be widespread underemployment, whereby a great many people suffer from insufficient employment and very low remuneration. Data collected in two *kebele* in Addis Ababa revealed unemployment rates of 8.9 per cent and 11.6 per cent of the economically active populations. (Jonathan Baker and Pernille Baardson, unpublished data, 1985). Data on unemployment levels in small towns provided by the Central

---

[*]   At that time, the Ethiopian Birr had a fixed exchange rate of $1 : 2.07 Birr.

Statistical Office also conflict with the World Bank view of very high levels of unemployment in urban centres (Table 1).

Table 1. *Unemployment rates for selected small towns in Ethiopia, 1984*

Town	Population	Unemployment rate
Bedele	7,326	2.6
Gore	6,963	2.4
Metu	13,094	2.8
Mendi	3,962	5.0
Nejo	6,461	6.0
Shambu	8,654	3.6
Leku	4,783	3.1
Yabelo	6,249	10.5
Yirga Chefe	8,657	4.3

Source: Solomon Gebre, 1990. Data collected from Central Statistical Office, various issues of the analytical reports of the 1984 Census.

STATE INTERVENTION AND LARGE-SCALE MIGRATION

As mentioned earlier, north-south population migrations particularly since the end of the last century have been a common feature in transforming the settlement pattern in the southern regions of Ethiopia. The imperial conquests of Menelik and the consolidation of these conquests by Haile Selassie accelerated the process whereby northerners settled in the southern regions. Most of these movements were spontaneous. In the post-1974 period, the state played a much more central, perhaps even coercive, role in directing the flow of migration. There were two kinds of government sponsored and directed movements of population, namely villagisation and large-scale resettlement. A detailed discussion of villagisation is beyond the scope and intention of this chapter but some brief comments are appropriate. The basic philosophy which motivated villagisation was that to provide the scattered rural population of Ethiopia with essential basic services it was necessary to collect farm households into newly established villages. Parallels can be drawn with Tanzania's *ujamaa* programme. Specifically, it was hoped that villagisation would promote agricultural productivity through more effective extension services, bring about more rational land use patterns and conserve natural resources, provide access to welfare services such as schools, clinics, water supplies and strengthen security and self-defence. It has also been suggested that villagisation would make agrarian socialism and political control and education of the peasantry easier to achieve (Cohen and Isaksson, 1987; Lulseged, 1988:145–152). The effects of this programme were dramatic; by June 1987, 10 million people, accounting for 23 per cent of the rural population, had been villagised (Jansson, *et al.*, 1990:208).

Reasons for resettlement: ecological deterioration and inappropriate government policies

The establishment of a resettlement programme was initially undertaken following the famine in early 1974 which was partly responsible for the downfall of the *ancien regime*. Since then, the Relief and Rehabilitation Commission (RRC) has had overall responsibility for implementing population transfers from resource-depleted to supposedly resource-endowed regions of the country (Kirsch, 1989:1–2). In principle the programme is sound, and this view is endorsed by the former commissioner of the RRC, Dawit Wolde Giorgis (1989:281–308). Large areas of Tigray and Welo and portions of Shewa, Gojam and Gonder have suffered, and are suffering, from such severe environmental degradation that agriculture is increasingly becoming non-viable and peasant survival is at great risk.

According to data from the Food and Agricultural Organisation (FAO), fifty per cent of the Ethiopian highlands, which account for half of the total area of the country and contain 88 per cent of the total population, are affected by significant erosion. In 1974, the World Bank reported that "if major resettlement and land use improvement programmes were not implemented within the next decade, increasingly severe famines and further deterioration of living standards would follow" (World Bank, 1974). More recent recommendations by FAO indicate that if present demographic trends continue (the national population growth rate is 2.9 per cent a year) more than 150,000 people a year would require resettlement in order to prevent further serious land degradation (FAO, 1986).

Campbell sums up the situation as follows:

> Current agricultural and settlement practices are *not* responsible *per se* for the present extent of land degradation, rather the cause needs to be sought in the cumulative effect of agriculture over the previous centuries during which time a very long, slow process of erosion has gradually out-stripped the ability of soil formation by a factor of approximately 6:1, i.e. at 5–10 tons/ha. With the erosion of the 'A' soil horizon, and the subsequent loss of humus, the effect has been not only to drastically reduce the ability of crops to root and the ability of remaining soil to retain moisture (even with inorganic fertilizers) but also to increase soil erosion (Campbell, 1991:6).

While the above describes the *effects* of land degradation in the northern areas of Ethiopia, the *causes* are much more complex. Much of what follows is drawn from the excellent synthesis by Campbell (1991:5–21). After 1974, the government attempted to tackle the problem of land degradation and soil erosion by initiating a good deal of conservation work and, for example, between 1976 and 1985, 600,000 kms of bunds and 470,000 kms of hillside terraces were constructed and 80,000 hectares of steep slopes were closed. Most of this conservation effort was carried out by members of peasant associations in return for food-for-work provided by the World Food Programme. A top-down approach was applied whereby the Ministry of Agriculture and its regional and district officials planned, monitored and co-ordinated all activities.

This highly centralised system meant that peasants and peasant associations had no say in the decision-making process and on issues which directly affected their lives. The result of much conservation work has been to alienate peasants and to produce a number of inherent contradictions.

In a situation of increasing land scarcity[4] bunding removes agricultural land from production, while even controlled access to community forests, which are government owned, is often illegal. Consequently, the maintenance of community forests is not perceived as a local responsibility and any potential benefits of such schemes do not accrue to local households. Furthermore, there is evidence that peasant farmers deliberately destroyed bunds and terraces in order to gain access to scarce land. Implicit in the above is that for conservation efforts to make a real contribution to preventing and reversing land degradation it is essential to involve local people in all aspects of the work—from planning to implementation—and to allow them to reap the benefits.

The other area of concern, which tends to reinforce the problem of land degradation, was government policies towards the peasantry. The WPE government was committed to the socialist transformation of the country and a policy of industrialisation and collectivisation of agriculture was pursued.[5] In an attempt to realise these goals the government required resources, which under the circumstances, could only be derived by extracting larger amounts of the peasant surplus. From the mid-1970s onwards peasants were obliged to surrender increasing amounts of their surplus to meet obligatory fixed-priced quotas and to make a number of other contributions. Moreover, peasants were faced with the situation whereby their terms of trade deteriorated, and prices for fertilisers, improved seed and other inputs necessary (if available) to increase production shot up. All these measures had a disincentive effect on rural household production. And in a situation where fertilisers are too expensive or unavailable, and peasants burn plant and animal residue for fuel, intensification or even the maintenance of productivity is impossible.

Government restrictions on off-farm income earning possibilities such as trade or grain marketing removed an important cash source in times of need or for farm improvements. Government preference for and assistance to collective agriculture, for ideological reasons, meant the general neglect of the peasant sector.

While the rural land reforms brought about a greatly improved distribution of land, population growth leading to increases in the number of farm households has created an intractable problem. Peasant associations had responsibility for reallocating farm land between old and new households with the result that farmers, particularly in the land-scarce northern regions, would lose some of their land with each new round of allocations. Consequently, this exacerbated land degradation since peasant farmers had "little incentive to invest in the land they 'would' not be farming in years to come" (Campbell, 1991:14).

McCann (1987) demonstrates, for the period 1900 to 1935, how the problem of land scarcity was overcome among the historically northern-based Amhara with their traditions of ambilineal descent involving equal distribution of land among siblings. Under the pressure of scarce land resources, eldest sons inherited their fathers' land, while other children migrated downslope to the south to acquire land or to towns for work (quoted in Campbell, 1991:16).

Implementation and consequences of resettlement programmes

From 1974 resettlement was carried out in three phases. In phase I (1974–84) about 180,000 people were resettled by the RRC. The resettlement schemes organized during this decade have been criticized for their slow pace, high cost and their low productivity in terms of agricultural output. One of the major lessons learnt was the inadvisability of settling male heads of households on their own, as pioneer settlers, with their families to follow when the land had been cleared. Apart from the emotional problems of being estranged from their families, the added burdens of fetching water, gathering firewood and cooking led to high desertion rates (Pankhurst, 1989:320, 324).

In phase II (1984–86), which represented an emergency phase in response to the onset of drought and famine, the WPE took responsibility for the planning and implementation of resettling nearly 600,000 people over an eighteen-month period (Pankhurst, 1989:320). This phase is discussed in detail below.

Following a consolidation period from 1986–87, a small-scale resumption of resettlement was undertaken during 1987–88, and this involved the resettling of fewer than 10,000 persons (Kloos and Aynalem, 1989:116). There were no further reports of resettlement after 1988, and with the collapse of the WPE regime in May 1991, resettlement was officially abandoned (Tekleab, 1991).

The emergency phase of resettlement from 1984–86 raised a good deal of international criticism including, *inter alia* the way the transfers of population were conducted including lack of adequate planning, inhuman recruitment techniques, hastily devised and implemented resettlement schemes and inadequate transport facilities and arrangements. According to the former commissioner of the RRC, Dawit Wolde Giorgis, resettlement programmes devised by the WPE government were designed for political and security reasons, rather than for development purposes (Dawit, 1989:285). However, Dawit's allegations that resettlement was carried out for military reasons is refuted by Kurt Jansson, who was head of the UN Emergency Office in Addis Ababa (Jansson *et al.*, 1990:65).

Map 1 shows the source and destination of settlers during the period November 1984 to November 1985, while Table 2 provides actual figures by administrative regions.

Table 2. *Origins and destinations, by administrative regions, of settlers during the 1984–85 resettlement programme*

Origin of settlers		Destination of settlers	
Welo	353,151	Wellega	267,245
Shewa	108,241	Ilubabor	129,111
Tigray	89,716	Gojam	67,055
Gojam	16,425	Keffa	54,688
Gonder	6,387	Gonder	6,387
		Shewa	6,149

Source: Kloos and Aynalem, 1989:117.

Government criteria for selecting settlers were as follows: the willingness of heads of households to be resettled; to bring along their dependants; to be engaged in agriculture; and their physical fitness (Jansson *et al.*, 1990:173). At the regional level, local administrators added other criteria for resettlement. These included farm households whose *meher* (main harvest season—November–December) crop had completely failed; were in debt and unable to pay; were cultivating slopes steeper than 30 degrees; and families who had migrated to a feeding centre (Jansson *et al.*, 1990:173). The programme was

Map 1. *Settler origins and destinations, administrative regions, 1984–85*

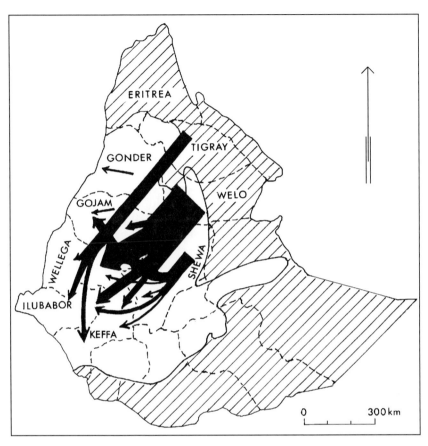

Areas where rainfed agriculture is unreliable or impossible because of moisture constraints. These areas cover about 55 per cent of Ethiopia

Source: Kloos and Aynalem, 1989:117 (on resettlement flows), Daniel, 1985:88 (for data on rainfed agriculture inadequacies)

to be entirely voluntary, but in some cases coercion and force were used by local authorities in an effort to meet quotas set by the government, to resettle families (Jansson *et al.,* 1990:66).

Serious criticism has been raised against inadequate preliminary studies of resettlement sites. And as Jansson *et al.* indicate "there is a growing realisation that investment in site selection and planning can be less costly than the failures that follow hasty decisions by a high-level team flying hurriedly around the western parts of the country" (1990:172). In some areas, there was an absence of drinking water, while in other areas, flooding and waterlogging presented serious problems. Black, clayish soils with limited agricultural potential covered many areas selected for resettlement (Jansson, *et al.,* 1990:174–175).

Resettlement programmes were of two types: conventional settlements (*medebajna*) were constructed in sparsely populated western lowlands, and this required much land clearance and disease and pest control. Much of these newly-settled areas are formerly under-utilised pastoral and geographically peripheral lowlands, although it is stated that one of the main reasons why resettlement areas were sparsely populated was because of high incidence of disease infestation (Getachew, 1989:363).

A total of 224,000 northerners were resettled in conventional settlements and by 1987, 123 new villages had been established in four *awraja* (sub-regional unit) of Wellega and the *awraja* of Gambella in Ilubabor (Legesse, 1988:127, 131). Because of the absence of infrastructure and the need to combat vector-borne diseases, the government played a major supporting role in the creation and administration of conventional schemes. Great efforts were made in organising settlers into mechanised collective farms, and extension agents from the Ministry of Agriculture, health workers from the Ministry of Health, and political cadres from the WPE all played major roles in promoting the productive, health and ideological well-being of the newcomers (Pankhurst, 1989:339).

The second type of resettlement schemes were known as integrated settlements (*sigisega)* and the idea was to create settlements in already inhabited, but under-populated, areas, which had some infrastructure and social services. Settler households were commonly integrated into already existing peasant associations. A total of 252,000 people were resettled in 15 of the 17 *awrajas* of the administrative regions of Wellega, Ilubabor and Keffa (Legesse, 1988:127).

There are a number of obvious distinctions between these two types of settlement programmes. Conventional schemes had strong *vertical* links with the state, while integrated schemes had *horizontal* links with local peasant associations. While conventional settlements have depended to a great extent on mechanised agriculture (with all the problems that this entails in terms of breakdowns, lack of spare parts, shortage of fuel and so on), settlers in integrated settlements have been provided with basic agricultural implements and oxen. In terms of scale, conventional schemes are much larger than integrated schemes, with the former comprising ideally 500 households and the latter 50 households (Pankhurst, 1989:340). Moreover, conventional settlements are often arranged into complexes of between 10,000 to 20,000 households within a radius of 100 kms and this concentration was justified because of the high investment costs involved (Pankhurst, 1989:340) and presumably the need to gain economies of scale.

According to statements made by government officials, resettlement was to have both short-term and long-term beneficial impacts. The short-term effects were to remove famine-stricken peasants from an environment which had become life-threatening and non-viable, while the longer-term effects were perceived as promoting the country's overall development strategy by opening up sparsely populated areas for productive purposes (Legesse, 1988:128).

The issues concerning the short-term effects have been addressed by a number of writers and these have focused on high mortality rates among the settlers (Savini, 1986:231–235; Getachew, 1989;364–366), the problem of the separation and splitting-up of families during the transportation of settlers to their new homes (Jansson *et al.*, 1990:174),[6] and the defection of settlers from resettlement areas (Dawit, 1989:297; Pankhurst, 1989:348). According to the latter writer, however, many men who left resettlement sites did so to take up seasonal work on the coffee plantations in the western parts of the country while women migrated to towns to work as domestic servants or in bars. This may have represented a short-term survival strategy, given the need for cash during the settling-in period, as a number of those who left settlement schemes, subsequently returned.

The longer-term negative impacts associated with resettlement in the western areas of Ethiopia appear difficult to resolve. Three major areas of concern centre on the prevalence of a range of diseases which are absent in the settlers areas of origin, the increasing pressure on natural resources given the increase in population through resettlement, and the potential for ethnic conflict.

While the government was aware of the problem of disease prevalence, it is apparent that the severity of the problem was underestimated or ignored, although government planners did admit to the fact that disease control was "an unfinished task and one of the main challenges in some places" (Legesse, 1988:128). A comprehensive review of the health hazards in the resettlement schemes is provided by Kloos (1989:61–94) who identified the following diseases as great health hazards: malaria, trypanosomiasis, onchoceriasis, yellow fever, podoconiosis (non-filarial elephantiasis) and sand-flea infestation, causing visceral leishmaniasis. Most of the settlers in the 1984–85 resettlement programme came from the malaria-free highlands of Welo, Shewa and Tigray and consequently many were at high risk of mortality. Also of great concern has been the appearance of chloroquine drug resistance in the administrative region of Wellega. Onchoceriasis (in Ethiopia, this causes low-level vision loss unlike blindness in Sudan, and central and West Africa) and trypanosomiasis are other major health hazards which settlers have had to face. The destruction of the habitats of the vectors of the diseases (the black fly and the tsetse fly respectively), through brush and woodland clearance, has had some control impact, although benefits have to be weighed against the negative environmental spin-offs such as the loss of valuable woodland.

Kloos points to the fact that the record of health programmes in settlement schemes elsewhere in the developing countries has been poor, and that the Ethiopian experience is no exception. He recommends that curative health schemes need to be supplemented by comprehensive, preventive health programmes (Kloos, 1989:76).

The relocation of thousands of northern rural households to the sparsely populated regions of the western lowlands had, in some cases, a dramatic effect on population. Overall, settlers represented six per cent of the population in the *awrajas* where resettlement took place. This figure, however, masks substantial variations. In Metekel *Awraja*, which covers exactly one-half of the Gojam administrative region, settlers constituted 25.5 per cent of the total *awraja* population, while in Gambella *Awraja*, which covers just over fifty per cent of the administrative region of Ilubabor, settlers made up 42.5 per cent of the *awraja* population (settlement figures from Pankhurst, 1989:348; area data from Central Statistical Office, 1982:20–21).

This increase in population in certain *awraja* put pressure on often fragile environments. Extensive tree felling and bush clearance to make way for ox-plough and mechanised agriculture led to soil erosion in a number of places. Because of the desire on the part of settlers and government agents to increase production, only lip-service has been paid to soil conservation endeavours (Jansson *et al.*, 1990:175). Moreover, tree felling for the construction of 30,000 settler dwellings in Metekel *Awraja* resulted in the utilisation of 15 million bamboos and 390,000 acacia and gum trees. In addition, the main sources of fuel for both settlers and the indigenous population were trees. Perhaps what is most disconcerting is the fact that 90 per cent of Ethiopia's savannah woodlands and forests are found in the areas designated for resettlement (Getachew, 1989:369), and these, it appears, are now under threat.[7] Attempts by the WPE government to solve the problems of land degradation and famine in the northern regions of Ethiopia through large-scale resettlement schemes may result, in the longer-term, in the replication of similar problems in the western regions of the country.

The western *awrajas* of the western administrative regions can be described as representing the political and economic periphery (although coffee is an important crop) of Ethiopia. These areas have traditionally been inhabited by ethnic minorities and even after the 1974 revolution were never brought into the mainstream of Ethiopian life and were rarely the focus of government attention. With resettlement, this peripheralization was reversed and the government obviously felt that the ethnic minorities should undergo "a process of socialization and cultural intermixture" (Legesse, 1988:128).

The Gambella *Awraja* in Ilubabor is inhabited by the Anuak and Nuer, the Asosa *Awraja* in Wellega by the Berta, and the Metekel *Awraja* by the Gumuz—more commonly referred to by outsiders as the Beja (Bender, *et al.*, 1976). These groups practise a range of production forms, including hunting and gathering, pastoralism, shifting cultivation and fishing, which is in sharp contrast to the grain/ox-plough production mode that the settlers brought with them from the northern regions.

Government pre-settlement programme aerial surveys of potential sites gave the impression of plentiful supplies of unused land suitable for plough agriculture. However, given the extensive production methods of the indigenous peoples and the unsuitability of much land for plough cultivation, it is apparent that there was little unused land.

Dessalegn (1988:14–34) provides useful documentation of the effects of resettlement on the indigenous Gumuz in the Metekel *Awraja* in Gojam. He describes how the clan system of land distribution operates and analyses the dominant production mode—shifting cultivation. He states that shifting cultivation is "adapted to and determined by a seasonally-arid savannah environment" as in Metekel, and that the finely-textured soil found in most Gumuz areas would quickly be damaged if exposed to plough or mechanised cultivation (Dessalegn, 1988:22). Moreover, inherent in the shifting cultivation technology of the Gumuz (and other groups) is the requirement for extensive fallowing (up to 15 years) to allow soils to recuperate. This effectively means that the land requirement per Gumuz household is three to four times greater that the land actually being cultivated at any given time (Dessalegn, 1988:25)—thus dispelling the government notion of large unused tracts of land. Dessalegn concludes on a sombre note: "the relation between the settler population and the Begga (Gumuz) will increasingly deteriorate as more and more resources claimed by the latter to be theirs by long tradition fall to the resettlement programme" (Dessalegn, 1988:32).

It would, however, be misleading to present a totally pessimistic picture of the resettlement programme and Pankhurst (1989), for example, presents a more positive view of resettlement based on fieldwork in western Wellega. He stresses the fact that although there were cases of misunderstandings and conflict, there were also many examples where settlers and the local population developed bonds of friendship and, in some cases, intermarriage occurred.

Another important consideration was that the local population felt that the central government was paying attention to the needs of these formerly forgotten people and that services such as schools and clinics were available to them. Pankhurst sums up the mood of the indigenous population by quoting a remark made to him: "Now the Government has no longer forgotten us" (352). On the other hand, the view could be taken that the WPE government by promoting and implementing large resettlement programmes in peripheral areas was merely extending central control and politicizing and incorporating all peoples into the Ethiopian state.

THE COLLAPSE OF THE MENGISTU REGIME AND EXODUS FROM RESETTLEMENT AREAS

The collapse of the WPE regime in May 1991 and the power take-over by the Ethiopian People's Revolutionary Democratic Front (EPRDF)—which established the Transitional Government of Ethiopia—is having far-reaching implications for Ethiopia. While the Transitional Government has stated that the villagisation and resettlement programmes have been discontinued, there is ambiguity regarding the present status of resettlement. On the one hand, it is stated that:

> In the past resettlement programmes were known to have faced fundamental political and economic problems and must be *discontinued*. Although voluntary resettlements which do not create conflicts between settlers and the local population would have to be carried out in the context of an agricultural development programme to relieve shortages of land and population density, they would have to be discontinued during the period of transition until conditions are ripe for such programmes.—emphasis added (Transitional Government, 1991:23).

And yet, on the other hand:

> ...efforts will be made to promote good relations between settlers who decided to stay on and the local population so as to enhance a climate of harmony and self-reliance. *Assistance will be extended to settlers to make them self-reliant and there will be a gradual reduction of public expenditure on resettlement*—emphasis added (Transitional Government, 1991:24).

The same source goes on to say that those settlers who wish to leave resettlement areas are free to do so (Transitional Government, 1991:24). From the fragmentary evidence that is available from the Ethiopian media, it appears that the majority decided to take the Transitional Government's advice and leave.

The experience of resettlement: an actor-oriented perspective

The following seven case histories were collected in July 1994 during a period of fieldwork in Welo Region—the worst effected by the 1984/85 famine. They briefly illustrate the range of experience which individuals, who returned to Welo from resettlement areas, underwent before, during and after resettlement. Cases 1 and 2 reveal the experiences of two individuals who resettled during phase I (1974–84) of resettlement, cases 3, 4, and 5 of those who resettled during phase II (1984–86), while cases 6 and 7 are of two women who refused to be resettled.

Some of these histories reveal harrowing and traumatic experiences—both prior to and during resettlement. Perhaps the most striking feature which can be discerned is the resilience of the individuals concerned. For some, resettlement meant the difference between life and death, for others, it meant fundamental psychological and emotional disruptions.

The case histories also provide some interesting insights into the fate of these individuals since their return to Welo. All have settled in small towns (with populations ranging from 2,310 to 4,511) which have provided them with some economic possibilities for survival. All, but one, have received small parcels of farmland (from the district governments) which help supplement income. For some, kinship networks have been important and have eased their re-integration into their areas of origin. Perhaps, above all, these stories provide some glimpses into the lives and experiences of individuals who so often are subsumed as aggregated data.

Case 1

Ato[*] Solomon Abebe was 68 years of age in 1979 when he volunteered to be resettled to the Ginir settlement area in the southern province of Bale. He was born in Welo Province and had grown up in a farming household. The reason he gave for wanting to be resettled was that he had insufficient agricultural land. His wife accompanied him to Bale, while his grown up children were independent and had already established their own households. They remained behind in Welo.

He found life hard at the resettlement site and agricultural production was organized on a collective basis. Settlers were paid (in kind) according to the amount of work done. However, he claims that he was able to receive sufficient food to provide for his wife and himself. With the collapse of the Mengistu government in May, 1991, and the decline in central control and protection, conditions in the resettlement area worsened as local people demanded the return of their lands for cattle grazing, and conflicts arose.

In 1992, Ato Solomon went to the town of Masha, near his birthplace, and asked the *Woreda* (district) council for some farmland. He was provided with 150 square metres—an amount too small to provide even for subsistence. As he has no money to purchase oxen (for ploughing), he allows his land to be farmed on a sharecropping basis by a farmer with oxen. The production from this land is shared equally between the two. At the age of 83, Ato Solomon works as a daily labourer in the town, where he makes three Birr[‡] a day. His wife's sister allows Ato Solomon and his wife to live, without charge, in one room in her house. His brother and sister who live in the surrounding countryside bring firewood and some grains when they visit about once a month.

Case 2

In 1979 when Mulatu Hailu was nine years old, his father volunteered to be resettled to the Ginir resettlement area in Bale Province (the same location as with Case 1). He moved

---

[*] Ato is the Amharic term for Mr.

[‡] In September 1994, the official exchange rate was $1 : 5.48 Birr.

alone. Two years later, Mulatu, his mother, three sisters and one brother joined him in Bale. According to Ato Mulatu the resettlement programme "was very good" as it enabled him to find work in a grain mill established in the settlement. However, with the collapse of the Mengistu regime, ethnic conflicts arose between the settlers and the local host population and in 1992 his family returned to their home area in Welo.

Ato Mulatu is now 24 years of age and was married on his return to Welo. He works in a grain mill in the town of Masha and earns 100 Birr a month. He was also provided with one quarter of a hectare of farmland by the local council, but as the quality of the land is poor he grows only 100 kgs of sorghum a year. He obviously considered the resettlement experience a positive one, and would like to return to Bale if the ethnic problem can be resolved.

Case 3

Ato Endris Ali was born in the countryside around the town of Wein Amba in Welo Province. In 1985, at the age of 31, he volunteered to be resettled in the Gesha settlement area in Keffa Province. He moved with his step-mother; his father had died as a result of the famine. He found the resettlement experience extremely difficult, not least because of malaria and other diseases, not found in the highlands of Welo. He said that many people died, including his step-mother. Following her death he married another settler because, as he stated, it was easier to survive having a wife who could help share the burdens of everyday life.

In 1991, following the collapse of the Mengistu government, Ato Endris returned to Welo and settled in the town of Wein Amba. He was given one hectare of farmland by the *Woreda* authorities—a relatively large piece compared to the average for the district of just under half a hectare (Baker and Tsion, 1994:21). His land is cultivated on a sharecropping basis as he is unable to afford oxen and other inputs. in 1993 he received 100 kgs of wheat as his share of the harvest.

Ato Endris is a poor man. He gathers and sells firewood and makes 20 Birr a month. His wife is a water seller (a very low status occupation) and earns roughly the same amount, while their eldest daughter of 18 works as a domestic servant and earns a meagre 6 Birr a month. He is unable to send his eight-year old son to school because of poverty.

Case 4

In 1985 Ato Indiro Yimer volunteered to be resettled in Gambella, in the province of Ilubabor. As his wife and daughter refused to leave, he left without them taking their eight-year old son. He left the resettlement area with his son in 1992 and returned to Welo and the town of Wein Amba where he was born. He was given 1,000 square metres of farmland by the *Woreda* council.

Subsequently, he married a divorcee who had also been given 1,000 square metres of farmland by the *Woreda* council. Both plots of land are cultivated on a sharecropping basis, as they lack oxen and other inputs. In 1993, they received 120 kgs of beans and 60 kgs of wheat as their share of the harvest. He works as a daily labourer and earns three Birr daily. He indicates that one of the advantages of living in the town is that casual work is always available and that he usually earns about 60 Birr a month. His son who accompanied him to Gambella is now 17 and is an eighth grade student attending Wein Amba junior secondary school. His wife's daughter from her previous marriage is 14, divorced, and illiterate. Ato Indiro states that he cannot afford to send her to school and consequently she helps in the house.

Case 5

Wizero[*] Zeritu Demissie is 55 years of age and divorced. She lives in the town of Bistima, where she was born, with her three daughters aged 20,18 and 14. The eldest and youngest daughters are divorced and look after the house, while the 18-year old daughter is a sixth grade student.

In 1985 she and her husband with their three daughters applied to be resettled and were sent to the Qeto resettlement area in Wellega Province. Wizero Zeritu described the

---

[*] Wizero is the Amharic term for Mrs.

horrifying famine conditions which prevailed in Welo prior to their departure. She stated that the decision to leave was difficult, but that there was no alternative.

However, her experiences in the resettlement area were bad. Her husband divorced her almost immediately on arrival and subsequently married and divorced four other women in the resettlement area. He died just prior to Wizero Zeritu's return to Welo in 1992. She married another settler but the marriage did not last.

She found conditions in Qeto difficult, particularly the first three years when land was cultivated on a collective basis. Distributed food was barely sufficient for subsistence. However, food intake improved considerably following the central decision to allow settlers to cultivate land on an individual basis. Wizero Zeritu stated that she was very ill in Qeto due to malaria. In contrast to some of the other cases reported here, she did not find conflict with the local host population a problem. On the contrary, she felt that the local population welcomed the settlers as they could purchase food from them.

She decided to leave Qeto when she heard that farmland in the district surrounding Bistima town was being distributed by the *Woreda* authorities. She was allocated 0.4 hectare which is cultivated on a sharecropping basis. Her share of the harvest in January 1993 was 50 kgs of beans and 50 kgs of lentils. Wizero Zeritu's main income source is from selling red peppers in Bistima town market. She estimated her monthly income at around 100 Birr. Her father, who also lives in Bistima, gave her a plot of land within the compound of his house where she built a one-room dwelling with a separate kitchen.

Case 6

Wizero Maritu Berhanu was born in the countryside around the town of Bistima 60 years ago. In 1985, her husband left for a resettlement area but she does not know where, and she has not seen or heard from him since. However, she refused to leave. She recounted the appalling conditions and starvation which prevailed in Welo in 1984 and 1985. She survived by eating soil mixed with sugar and dissolved in water. When the official zeal of the resettlement drive had subsided, she moved to Bistima town and got a job as a housemaid for a teacher.

She now works as a petty spice trader and makes three Birr, three times a week (approximately 36 Birr a month) in the Bistima market. She has a non-related female of 72 who lodges with her, and she also looks after her niece. She has two married daughters who live elsewhere in the rural areas of Welo, and occasionally the niece's mother visits and brings some food. Wizero Maritu is undoubtedly poor and stated that "there are no benefits of living in this town, but I live here because I have nowhere else to go".

Case 7

Wizero Fatuma Hussein is a Muslim of 29 who was born in the countryside in Welo Province. She was married to a farmer. However, on divorcing him in 1983 she moved to Bistima town where she found work in a bar. To earn extra income she also engaged in prostitution. With the onset of famine in Welo in 1984, many prostitutes, as part of government policy, were obliged to go to resettlement areas.

To avoid being forcibly sent, Wizero Fatuma married one of her clients, a much older man, wealthy and a Christian. To her the marriage was one of convenience, and she stated that she did not love him because he was old and a Christian. A daughter was born but she died at the age of three. Finally, she divorced her husband and started prostitution again. She married once more and had another daughter. This marriage too failed, and in 1992 she started prostitution which she was continuing at the time of the interview (July, 1994).

She is, however, very concerned by the threat of AIDS and is thinking of stopping. She would like to make and sell *tela* (a local beer), but the economic returns would be much less than from prostitution. Wizero Fatuma earns, on average, 150 Birr per month from prostitution. Her daughter, whom she visits weekly, lives with Wizero Fatuma's parents three kilometres from the town. She also has 1,600 square metres of farmland which was obtained from the *Woreda* council during her last marriage. In 1993, she received 300 kgs of sorghum from this land through a sharecropping agreement. She likes living in the town because "living is easier than living and working in the countryside".

Conclusion

This chapter has attempted to provide a review of Ethiopian state policies regarding migration since 1974. The emphasis has been on processes, the overall context, and on some of the actors involved. The effects of institution building on slowing down the rate of rural–urban migration were discussed. The reasons behind the WPE government decision to encourage and expedite the movement of nearly 600,000 people over an eighteen-month period, and the consequences of this in resettlement areas, were outlined.

With the collapse of the Mengistu regime in May 1991, and the accession to power of the Transitional Government, resettlement programmes have been discontinued. The right of free movement of people within the country is guaranteed (EPRDF, 1991:7). However, this decision raises a central issue. The Transitional Government has created a federal system based on ethnic regions which provides fairly wide powers of autonomy to these regions. The migration of people from different ethnic groups into other ethnic regions may certainly exacerbate conflict and tension. There were reports of a number of incidents following the take-over of power by the Transitional Government as Amhara settlers in the south were attacked by non-Amhara local populations.

Whatever transpires, however, the Transitional Government will be obliged to confront the continuing problems surrounding the degradation of the northern highland zones, and as a corollary the need to cope with the permanent out-migration of an estimated 150,000 people annually until at least the end of the first decade of the next century (FAO, 1986). One scenario which seems inescapable will be that spontaneous population migrations will have to re-occur, as during the imperial regime, as poor rural households search for survival options in towns and in rural areas of the south.

Notes

1　While the Transitional Government has promulgated a wide range of fundamental legisla-tion which has led to the re-designing of the political and administrative map of Ethiopia, especially the creation of a federal state based on ethnic regions, many of the institutions established during the Mengistu era remain intact. For example, the *kebele* and peasant association still exist and function, although in a modified form. The sub-regional adminis-trative unit (*awraja*) has been abolished, while the district level administrative unit (*woreda*) has been retained and its powers enhanced. The provinces of Ethiopia, created during Haile Selassie's regime and maintained by Mengistu, have been abolished and replaced by, in some cases, much larger ethnically-based regions. For the purposes of this discussion reference is made to the names of these earlier provinces.

2　The amount of land actually available per farm household is much smaller than 10 hec-tares. Data for 1979–80 show that in Gonder region the average farm size was 2.048 hec-tares, the largest of any administrative region, while in Gamo Gofa, the region with the smallest farms, households had access to only 0.728 hectares (Griffin and Hay, 1985:42). Very recent data from Welo Region (the main source area of settlers during the 1984–85 resettlement programme) show very small mean sizes of farm holdings for three locations of 0.169, 0.368 and 0.483 hectares per household (Baker and Tsion, 1994: 21).

3　Some larger towns and cities have more than one *kebele* and Addis Ababa, the capital city, with a 1984 population of 1.4 million, has 284 *kebele*. Dire Dawa (98,104) and Harer (62,160), both in Harerge region, have 23 and 19 *kebele* respectively. Debark (8,484) and Dabat (7,488) both located in Gonder region, and typical of roadside towns in Ethiopia, have two *kebele* each. The average size of a *kebele* ranges from about 3,000 to 5,000 peo-

ple (data on number of *kebele* from the Ethiopian Mapping Authority, 1988:51 and population figures from the 1984 census—see Office of the Population...1984).

4 An example from the highland area of Harerge administrative region, where 200 new rural
   households were waiting for land to be allocated to them, illustrates this problem of land
   scarcity (Campbell, 1991:13).

5 While the WPE government gave great support to collective farms (producer co-operatives)
   the vast majority of land (94.7 per cent) was still cultivated by individual peasant households; only 3.5 per cent was under state farms and 1.8 per cent under collective farming
   (Cohen and Isaksson, 1987).

6 Among some peasant households who were resettled, some family members, mostly older
   people and young children, were left behind on the farm. This provided members of the
   resettled household with the option to return home if conditions improved, by maintaining
   a claim to the land, and it also allowed the remaining members to do some cultivation if
   conditions permitted (Kloos and Aynalem, 1989:124; see also Dessalegn, 1991: 369–370).

7 In 1955, forests covered 15 per cent of Ethiopia's land area. By 1986, these had dwindled to
   an estimated 2.5–4 per cent. Savanna woodlands have decreased over the same period from
   72 million hectares to 20 million hectares (Getachew, 1989: 369–370).

References

Baker, Jonathan, 1990, "The Growth and Functions of Small Urban Centres in Ethiopia" in
   Jonathan Baker (ed.) *Small Town Africa: Studies in Rural–Urban Interaction.* Seminar Proceedings, 23. Uppsala: Scandinavian Institute of African Studies.

Baker, Jonathan, 1991, "Managing the Third World City: The Experience of Addis Ababa".
   Paper prepared for the *XI International Conference of Ethiopian Studies,* Addis Ababa,
   March 1991.

Baker, Jonathan and Tsion Dessie, 1994, *Rural Towns Study in Ethiopia.* Report prepared for
   SIDA, October.

Bender,M.L., J.D.Bowen, R.L.Cooper and C.A.Ferguson, 1976, *Language in Ethiopia.*
   London: Oxford University Press.

Campbell, John, 1991, "Land or Peasants?: The Dilemma Confronting Ethiopian Resource
   Conservation", *African Affairs,* 90.

Clapham, Christopher, 1988, *Transformation and Continuity in Revolutionary Ethiopia.* Cambridge: Cambridge University Press.

Cohen, John M. and Nils-Ivar Isaksson, 1987, "Villagisation in Ethiopia's Arsi Region", *The
   Journal of Modern African Studies,* 25, 3.

Cohen, John M. and Dov Weintraub, 1975, *Land and Peasants in Imperial Ethiopia: The
   Social Background to a Revolution.* Assen: Van Gorcum and Co.

Central Statistical Office, 1982, *Statistical Abstract, 1982.* Addis Ababa.

Daniel Gamachu, 1985, "Peripheral Ethiopia: A Look at the Marginal Zones of the Country",
   in Peter Treuner, Tadesse K. Mariam and Teshome Mulat (eds.), *Regional Planning and
   Development in Ethiopia,* vol. 1. Addis Ababa: Institute of Development Research and
   Stuttgart: Institut fur Raumordnung und Entwicklungsplanung.

Dawit Wolde Giorgis, 1989, *Red Tears: War, Famine and Revolution in Ethiopia.* Trenton,
   New Jersey: The Red Sea Press.

Dessalegn Rahmato, 1988, "Settlement and Resettlement in Mettekel, Western Ethiopia",
   Africa (Rome), 43, 1.

Dessalegn Rahmato, 1991, *Famine and Survival Strategies: A Case Study from Northeast
   Ethiopia.* Uppsala: Scandinavian Institute of African Studies.

Donham, Donald and Wendy James (eds.) 1986, *The Southern Marches of Imperial Ethiopia:
   Essays in History and Social Anthropology.* Cambridge: Cambridge University Press.

EPRDF, 1991, *Documents from the First National Congress of the Ethiopian Peoples Revolutionary Democratic Front,* January 1991.

Ethiopian Mapping Authority, 1988, *National Atlas of Ethiopia.* Addis Ababa: Ethiopian
   Mapping Authority.

FAO, 1986, *Highlands Reclamation Study, Ethiopia,* vol. 1. Rome.

Getachew Woldemeskel, 1989, "The Consequences of Resettlement in Ethiopia", *African
   Affairs,* 88, 352.

Griffin, Keith and Roger Hay, 1985, "Problems of Agricultural Development in Socialist Ethiopia: An Overview and a Suggested Strategy", *The Journal of Peasant Studies,* 13, 1.

Halliday, Fred and Maxine Molyneux, 1981, *The Ethiopian Revolution.* London: Verso.

Jansson, Kurt, Michael Harris and Angela Penrose, 1990, *The Ethiopian Famine.* London and New Jersey: Zed Books.

Kirsch, Ottfried C., 1989, *Resettlement and Relief in Ethiopia.* Discussion Paper. Heidelberg: Forschungsstelle fur Internationale Agrarentwicklung.

Kloos, Helmut, 1989, "Health and Resettlement in Ethiopia, with an Emphasis on the 1984/85 Resettlement Programme: A Review", *Ethiopian Journal of Development Research,* 11,1.

Kloos, Helmut and Aynalem Adugna, 1989, "Settler Migration during the 1984/85 Resettlement Programme in Ethiopia", *Geojournal,* 19, 2.

Legesse Gebeyehu, 1988, "Resettlement as a Tool of Regional Development with Special Reference to Western Ethiopia", in Peter Treuner, Tadesse Kidane Mariam and Teshome Mulat (eds.), *Regional Planning and Development in Ethiopia,* vol. 2. Addis Ababa: Institute of Development Research and Stuttgart: Institut für Raumordnung und Entwicklungsplanung.

Lulseged Decassa, 1988, "Villagization as a Tool for Regional Development with Reference to Eastern Ethiopia", in Peter Treuner, Tadesse Kidane Mariam and Tesome Mulat (eds.), *Regional Planning and Development in Ethiopia,* vol.2. Addis Ababa: Institute of Development Research and Stuttgart: Institut für Raumordnung und Entwicklungsplanung.

McCann, James, 1986, "Household Economy, Demography, and the 'Push' Factor in Northern Ethiopian History, 1916–35", *Review,* IX, 3, Winter.

McCann, James, 1987, *From Poverty to Famine in Northeast Ethiopia: A Rural History 1900–1935.* Philadelphia: University of Philadelphia Press.

McClellan, Charles W.,1978, "The Ethiopian Occupation of Northern Sidamo—Recruitment and Motivation", *Proceedings of the Fifth International Conference on Ethiopian Studies,* Session B, April 1978. Chicago.

McClellan,Charles W., 1980, "Land, Labor, and Coffee: The South's Role in Ethiopian Self-Reliance, 1889–1935", *African Economic History,* 9.

McClellan,Charles W.,1984, "State Transformation and Social Reconstitution in Ethiopia: The Allure of the South", *International Journal of African Historical Studies,* 17,4.

Negarit Gazeta, 1975, Proclamation 31, *A Proclamation to Provide for the Public Ownership of Rural Lands,* April 1975. Addis Ababa.

Negarit Gazeta, 1975, Proclamation 47, *A Proclamation to Provide for Government Ownership of Urban Lands and Extra Urban Houses,* July 1975. Addis Ababa.

Negarit Gazeta, 1975, Proclamation 71, *A Proclamation to Provide for the Organization and Consolidation of Peasant Associations,* December 1975. Addis Ababa.

Negarit Gazeta, 1976, Proclamation 104.,*Urban Dwellers' Associations Consolidation and Municipalities Proclamation,* October 1976. Addis Ababa.

Office of the Population and Housing Census Commission, 1984. *Ethiopia 1984 Population and Housing Census Preliminary Report,* September 1984, Addis Ababa.

Pankhurst, Alula, 1989, "The Administration of Resettlement in Ethiopia since the Revolution", in Abebe Zegeye and Shubi Ishemo (eds.), *Forced Labour and Migration: Patterns of Movement within Africa.* London: Hans Zell.

Pausewang, Siegfried, 1983, *Peasants, Land and Society: A Social History of Land Reform in Ethiopia.* Munich: Weltforum Verlag.

Savini, Giordano, 1986, "Famine and the Resettlement Program in Ethiopia", *Africa* (Rome), 41, 2.

Solomon Gebre, 1990, "The Interaction between Small Towns and their Hinterlands: Implications for Rural Development in Ethiopia". Paper presented to the joint SIAS/CDR Conference on *Small Towns and Rural Development in Africa under Conditions of Stress-Adaptive Strategies and Survival Mechanisms,* Gilleleje, Denmark.

Solomon Mulugeta, 1985, *Meeting the Housing Shortage in Addis Ababa: The Case of Housing Cooperatives.* Unpublished MA thesis, Department of Geography, Addis Ababa University.

Tekleab Kabede, 1991, "The Current Political Changes in Ethiopia". Paper presented at a conference on *The Current Situation in the Horn of Africa,* August 1991. Uppsala.

Transitional Government of Ethiopia, 1991, *Ethiopia's Economic Policy during the Transitional Period.* Addis Ababa.

Wendt, Sabine *et al.*, 1990, "Ethiopia", in Kosta Mathéy (ed.), *Housing Policies in the Socialist Third World*. London: Mansell Publishing Ltd.

World Bank, 1974, *Resettlement Strategy Proposals,* Agricultural Division, 444, June. Washington DC.

World Bank, 1989, *Ethiopia: Market Towns Development Project,* Infrastructure Operations Division, Eastern Africa Department. Washington DC.

Part IV

Gender Issues

Gender and Migration in Africa South of the Sahara[*]

Josef Gugler and Gudrun Ludwar-Ene

Migration research, like much of social research, is only beginning to redress a severe imbalance that is the legacy of the male domination of the profession. First of all, most migration research deals only with the migration of men.[1] Most books and articles purporting to deal with the migration of people in fact focus on the migration of men. There is a second problem that arises from the fact that such migration research as does include women in its purview usually treats women as dependents of migrating men. One of the authors of this paper pleads guilty to both charges. And while he recognized the first problem quite a while ago (Gugler, [1972] 1981), he assumed until recently that, in Africa at least, women come to town by and large as dependents (Gugler, 1989).

In the case of rural–urban migration in Africa, the assumption that women migrate as dependents was bolstered by the often repeated assertion that men predominate in the urban population. The set of census data on urban sex ratios in Africa presented in Table 1 shows such assertions to be ill-founded. Women predominate in the urban population of a number of countries.[2]

In considering these census data we note that substantial deviations from parity, say sex ratios above 1,050 or below 950 (males per 1,000 females), cannot be explained by sex differences at birth or in mortality, but indicate sex selectivity in migration. Such unbalanced urban sex ratios indicate which sex predominates among migrants but underestimate the degree of sex selectivity in migration in so far as they are affected by the more balanced sex composition of the urban-born. We should further emphasize that we are presenting sex ratios for entire urban populations, i.e. including children as well as adults,[3] and that, as a rule, sex selectivity in rural–urban migration is more significant among adults than among children. The sex ratios for the entire

---

[*] An earlier version of this chapter, entitled "Many Roads Lead Women to Town in Sub-Saharan Africa," was presented at the World Congress of Sociology, Madrid, July 1990. "Africa South of the Sahara," while cumbersome, is preferable to the racist "Black Africa" and the eurocentric "Sub-Saharan Africa." Throughout this chapter, "Africa" and "African" will stand as shorthand for Africa South of the Sahara.

Table 1. *Urban Sex Ratios in Africa South of the Sahara, 1951–91*

Country	Year	Sex Ratio: Males per 1,000 Females		
		National	Urban	Adjusted Urban[a]
Benin	1961	961[b]	960[b]	999[b]
	1975	961	967	1,006
	1979	921	928	1,008
Botswana	1971	840	942	1,122
	1981	890	1,065	1,197
Burkina Faso	1985	928	1,045	1,126
Burundi	1965	975	1,085	1,113
	1979	935	1,266	1,354
Cameroon	1976	960	1,077	1,122
Central African Republic	1959	915[b]	961[b]	1,051[b]
Chad	1964	904[b]	964[b]	1,067[b]
	1978	1,062	1,062	1,000
Congo	1960	853	988	1,158
Côte d'Ivoire	1975	1,074	1,177	1,096
	1988	1,045	1,070	1,023
Equatorial Guinea	1983	926	966	1,042
Ethiopia	1968	1,025	903	881
	1984	994	867	872
Gabon	1960	891	1,114	1,251
Gambia	1973	1,030	1,091	1,060
Ghana	1960	1,022	1,062	1,039
	1970	985	996	1,011
	1984	973	949	976
Guinea	1955	909	970	1,067
Kenya	1969	1,004	1,386	1,380
	1979	985	1,216	1,234
Lesotho	1972	992	843	850
Liberia	1971	977	1,153	1,180
	1974	1,020	1,135	1,113
Malawi	1977	930	1,168	1,255
	1987	946	1,103	1,166
Mali	1960	989	904	914
	1976	955	966	1,012
	1987	956	982	1,027
Mauritania	1973	1,006	1,041	1,035
	1977	968	1,178	1,217
Mozambique	1980	945	1,097	1,161
Namibia	1951	1,366	1,245	911
	1960	1,018	1,268	1,246
Nigeria	1963	1,020	1,149	1,127
Rwanda	1970	923	1,033	1,119
	1978	944	1,216	1,288
Senegal	1971	976	967	991
	1976	979	973	993
Somalia	1986–7	1,109	1,008	909
South Africa	1951	1,031	1,192	1,156
	1960	1,010	1,150	1,138
	1970	973	1,119	1,151
	1980	1,035	1,068	1,032
	1985	975[c]	1,007[c]	1,032[c]
	1991	998[c]	1,032[c]	1,034[c]
Sudan	1973	1,023	1,131	1,105
	1983	1,031	1,133	1,098
Swaziland	1986	895	1,065	1,190
Tanzania	1967	955[d]	1,180[d]	1,236[d]
	1973	969	1,078	1,112
	1978	962	1,075	1,117
Togo	1959	919	913	993
Uganda	1969	1,019	1,191	1,169
Zaïre	1984	988	992	1,004
Zambia	1980	958	1,027	1,072
Zimbabwe	1969	1,012	1,412	1,395
	1982	960	1,140	1,188

[a] The adjusted urban sex ratio is the urban over the national figure, multiplied by 1,000; slight divergences are due to rounding.　[b] African population only.　[c] Excluding Boputhatswana, Ciskei, Transkei and Venda.　[d] Tanganyika.

Sources: Ratios calculated from national censuses and estimates for the 1950s, 1960s, and 1970s compiled by the United Nations and provided to Josef Gugler on tape; and from census data in the *Demographic Yearbook* (United Nations), various years.

urban populations presented here thus doubly understate the sex ratios of adult migrants.

High urban sex ratios, a substantial preponderance of males, are reported from a number of African countries. The extreme examples are Zimbabwe, 1,412 males for 1,000 females in 1969, Kenya, 1,386 males for 1,000 females in the same year, and Namibia, 1,268 males for 1,000 females in 1960—not surprisingly in view of their history as settler colonies. The time series available for countries with high urban sex ratios indicate a strong trend towards a more balanced composition of the urban population in Kenya, South Africa, Tanzania, and Zimbabwe. We will address possible explanations for these trends at a later stage of the argument. The reverse trend, the urban sex ratio becoming more preponderantly male, is particularly strong in Burundi, Mauritania and Rwanda. Both trends are due to differentials in internal rather than international migration: the trends persist when changes in the national sex ratio are taken into account in the adjusted urban sex ratio.

Before we proceed further, we need to consider the sex ratios of national populations. Three censuses report males outnumbering females by a substantial margin in the country's total population. The large excess of males over females in the population of Namibia in 1951 seems utterly implausible —and has vanished by the next census nine years later. The dramatic change in the national sex ratio in Chad similarly raises questions about the reliability of the data. In the case of the Côte d'Ivoire, on the other hand, the excess of males over females can be explained by the influx of male labour from neighbouring countries, an influx that has become less significant in recent years.

Quite a number of countries report that women predominate in their total population. In the most dramatic case, Botswana where only 840 men per 1,000 women were reported in 1971, predominantly male emigration to South Africa explains the low sex ratio. Indeed, when the urban sex ratio of Botswana is adjusted for the national sex ratio, it appears that men are much better represented, relative to women, in the urban areas than in the country at large. The low sex ratios of the total population in a number of other countries are presumably also due to emigration. Such an interpretation is plausible given that all these countries have rather small populations, and in fact most of them are well known as major exporters of—primarily male— labour: Benin, Burkina Faso, Burundi, Central African Republic, Congo, Equatorial Guinea, Gabon, Guinea, Malawi, Mozambique, Rwanda, Swaziland, Togo. Most of these countries combine the emigration of men with substantial rural–urban migration of men as indicated by high urban sex ratios.

Contrary to the generalization commonly made about Africa, women predominate in the urban population of a number of countries.[4] An extremely low urban sex ratio, 843 men for 1,000 women, is reported for Lesotho in 1972. And Ethiopia shows a consistent pattern of very low urban sex ratios over two decades. These data force us to question current assumptions as to what changes in rural–urban migration explain the trend towards more balanced urban sex ratios in countries such as Kenya, South Africa, Tanzania, and Zimbabwe.

Women could be said to be "the second sex in town" (Gugler, [1972] 1981) in colonial Africa in that men predominated in the new towns spawned by the political economy of colonialism. An explanation has to consider both, employment and family separation. The major employers—colonial government, missions, commercial firms, mines—recruited men. It is not clear to what extent this was a matter of preference on the part of employers rather than the response of peasant households to the demand for labour. The reasons that they should supply labour at all, the role of coercion, whether directly in the form of forced labour or indirectly through the imposition of tax, and the integration of peasant households into the cash economy, are not at issue here. Rather we would like to know more about village opposition to the out-migration of single women. Whatever the role of employers and households, respectively, in determining the gender composition of urban labour, the result was quite remarkable to anybody assuming a fit between female socialization—in terms of technical skills as well as deferential attitudes—and the sex stereotyping of jobs: in many African colonies domestic servants, secretaries, and nurses were, as a rule, male.[5]

The preponderance of men over women in most African towns reflected a second fact: the tendency of men to move on their own while their wives and children remained in their rural area of origin. If the Industrial Revolution engendered the distinction of workplace and home, the separation of worker and dependents was drastically magnified for many African families. Extended family support typically facilitates such dual involvement in the urban and the rural economy. For the wife managing the farm, the extended family presents a mixed blessing. It can provide support, but the absent husband can call on male agnates to exert close control over his wife.[6]

The migration of individuals, whether single or separated from their family, has distinct economic advantages: it optimizes labour allocation, and, at least in rural–urban migration, it minimizes the cost of subsistence. Employers save on wages and retirement benefits, and public authorities face less demand for housing and infrastructure. But there were also gains to migrants that motivated them to accept family separation. Living costs in the city were high. Typically wife and children remained on a family farm growing their own food, and perhaps raising cash crops. Virtually everywhere land was communally controlled and could not be alienated. Thus, there was no compensation for those who gave up farming it. A wife who came to town had to abandon an assured source of income to join a husband on low wages. Of course, there have always been women who contributed incomes to urban households as well as their services as wives and mothers. Indeed, their numbers were substantial in some regions. Generalizations, however, are frequently misleading, e.g. the stereotype about women traders omnipresent in West African cities holds only for part of the region.

Colonial policies affected the labour market and rural–urban migration. In settler colonies in particular, policies were pursued to discourage the permanent establishment of Africans in town: labour was recruited on temporary contracts, only bachelor accommodations were provided. Such policies were pursued in South Africa until recently. Thus the gold mines were prohibited by law from providing family accommodation for more than three per cent of their African work force until 1986. And many men were recruited on short-term contracts, not only in the mines, but in various other sectors of the economy. More generally, colonial regimes pursued a cheap-labour policy. The colonial administration and other employers kept wages so low that labour shortages were common, complaints about high labour turnover and absenteeism near universal. Explanations that traced these ills to a lack in "labour commitment" among Africans were proven to be but ideological underpinnings for the cheap-labour policy when increased wages, in many countries around the time of independence, brought forth an abundant supply of labour, and urban unemployment became the concern of the new age. This new age also had its share of obscurantists explaining the new state of affairs in terms of the attractions of the cities' bright lights rather than the profound inequality that characterizes the urban/rural divide in Africa and throughout the Third World.[7]

Circular migration constituted an adaptation to family separation. After a period of employment lasting six months, perhaps, or a couple of years, the migrant returned for an extended stay with his family. In the ideal case, the return coincided with peak labour requirements on the farm. In some areas, such migrants went as contract labour, i.e. they were recruited for a fixed period of time at, or close by, their home place, and provided with return transportation. This strategy failed with the appearance of large-scale urban unemployment. When the search for a job takes months, circular migration is no longer a viable proposition. The migrant who wants to be assured of urban employment has to cling to his job. Instead of extended stays with the family there are short visits, as employment conditions and distance permit. What had been an economic cost to employers—a labour force characterised by high turnover and absenteeism—became an increase in social costs for workers: more severe strains in their relationships with wife, children, extended family, and village community.[8]

We can thus distinguish two phases in the urbanization of Africa. First, the pattern of circulatory migration of men during a period characterized by low wages and labour shortages; second, the pattern of men who have become long-term urban workers, but whose families continue to live in the rural area of origin. In the second phase substantial numbers of women come to town to visit their husbands for shorter or longer periods. Weisner (1972) describes such a pattern for Kenya, Potts and Mutambirwa (1990) for Zimbabwe. The extent of such visiting will vary seasonally with the agricultural cycle, and so will its reporting in censuses depending on when they are taken.

A third pattern of rural–urban migration, the long-term migration of families who maintain strong ties with rural areas they intend to return to, became more common with the increase in urban incomes and benefits that were the rule around the time of independence and the neglect of rural areas that has characterized much of the post-independence era. Such long-term, but non-permanent family migration can be quite enduring. A 1961–62 study found this third pattern dominant in south-eastern Nigeria, a replication survey in 1987 found it just as dominant a generation later (Gugler, 1991).

The independent rural–urban migration of women has been grossly neglected in African studies to date. Still, the census data attest to the significance of such migration, and a number of studies allow us to delineate three categories of women who move on their own. In many countries, substantial numbers of young, unmarried women with little formal education come to town. They are not attracted by factory jobs such as have become available to young women in some rapidly industrializing countries.[9] Rather, they typically work at first as domestic help. Guigou and Lericollais (1992) report from the Serer region of Senegal that unmarried girls between the ages of 10 and 20 began to migrate to work as domestics in Dakar in the 1950s. They describe a seasonal pattern of migration for an average six months. Once the women have reached the age of marriage, they are usually repatriated to the village by their parents. Hamer (1981), in her study of Diola migrant women from the same region, describes a similar pattern of seasonal migration for girls and young unmarried women who leave their village during the dry season to work as maids in town, preferably Dakar. The majority are between the ages of 10 and 19 when leaving. While in town, they usually stay with a male relation. After about seven years of seasonal migration they return permanently, usually for reasons of marriage.[10] Grosz-Ngaté (1991) reports from Bamana communities in central Mali that unmarried girls between the ages of about 15 and 18, or at most 20, go to Bamako to work as domestic servants. They return to the village for the cultivation season, but do not necessarily stay until the harvest is completed. The first teenage girls left to work in regional towns or in Bamako in the mid-1970s; by the end of the decade most were away during the dry season. In Ghana and Nigeria, many female domestics in urban households are poor relations from the countryside attracted by the educational and training opportunities in the city (Anker and Hein, 1986). Such a pattern can be seen in the context of the traditional institution of child fostering which is still current in many parts of Africa (Atto, 1994; Goody, 1986; Nelson, 1987; Page, 1989).

With the expansion of secondary education outside the major cities, increasing numbers of educated young women move to the cities in search of employment (Hollos, 1991; Sudarkasa, 1977; Wurster, 1995). Many postpone marriage or prefer to remain unmarried, while improving their standard of living with the contributions of male friends. Dinan (1983) and Seibert (1995) provide case studies of such a pattern in Accra and Lomé respectively. Behrman and Wolfe (1984) suggest that the rural–urban migration of women is affected not only by the labour market. They propose a model which—like the Harris and Todaro (1970) job search model—includes both the probability of finding a companion and the earnings of such a companion.[11]

Widowed, divorced or separated women constitute a third category of women who move from the countryside to the city on their own. From Ethiopia Baker (1994) reports that women have equal land rights, but that cultivation is almost entirely the domain of men. Cultural, physical, and capital constraints bar women from ox ploughing, the dominant mode of production in many areas. Divorce rates are high and, given very limited rural employment opportunities, urban areas offer much better options.[12] This situation presents a sharp contrast with most of Africa where hoe cultivation is the norm, and women play a major role in agriculture. The extremely low urban sex ratio in Lesotho apparently reflects the large number of women who receive insufficient support from husbands working in South Africa and seek urban earning opportunities to support themselves and their children (Sembajwe and Makatsjane, 1992). In Bamako, eleven per cent of female migrants in a large-scale survey were widows or divorcees (van Westen and Klute, 1986). In Kampala, Obbo (1980:76–77) found that an unsatisfactory marriage was the reason most commonly given by women for coming to town alone. Others were widows or divorced. In Northern Nigeria, Hausa girls and women sometimes flee from home due to the imminence, or the existence, of an unwanted marriage and eventually become karuwai ("courtesans") or independent women in the city. According to Pittin (1983), the harshness of rural life and the social network built up during the years of residence in the city with its greater opportunities for trade and economic independence may act as barriers to returning.

Polygamy encourages separation. And losing a husband through death is a common experience where women are considerably younger than their husbands. Residence is patrilocal in most African societies, and a woman's village of origin can typically offer not much more than refuge. The village of her in-laws, on the other hand, has little to keep a woman who has lost her husband, and whose sons may have moved to the city.[13] Witchcraft accusations are common in many rural areas, culminating at times in the emergence of organized witch persecutions aimed at eradicating "evil" and restoring order.[14] Women, especially older women without the protection by a husband or an adult son, are likely to be blamed for misfortunes that befall the family or the wider community and to be treated accordingly (Ludwar-Ene, 1986). Other women come to the city to stay with a married son. Peil *et al.* (1988) report such a pattern from Southern Nigeria. These women may resume child rearing, this time of their grandchildren. In any case, staying with a son or other relative promises care in old age, and urban residence in general gives access to better health facilities than can be found in rural areas.[15]

So far we have distinguished three patterns of temporary migration. A fourth pattern of rural–urban migration, permanent settlement in the city, continues to be the exception in most of Africa. The reasons are not far to seek. Most Africans rely on the security the village continues to provide. Few are entitled to pensions, covered by social security, or assured a living from urban property. Even for that minority political upheavals can destroy such urban security overnight. In contrast, most Africans can return to their village of origin at any time, find an abode, claim land to farm. The contrast is striking with Latin America where permanent migrants have established powerful trade unions and obtained social security protection to various degrees. Latin America is different also in that squatter movements have provided many permanent migrants with housing, as well as rental income, especially in old age (Gilbert and Gugler, [1982] 1992:192–200). Such organized large-scale invasion and appropriation of urban land is unknown in Africa.

The exceptions to the rule that Africans find their ultimate security in the village, are of three types. First, some Africans have lived in cities for generations and are without a rural connection. Second, some rural areas can no longer provide land to farm for returnees. Third, and this is the issue of particular interest for the topic at hand, the security the village offers is more problematic for women than for men. If the patrilocal village tends to release abandoned, separated, divorced, and widowed women, it has little to attract such women from the city. And their relationship with their village of origin is tenuous as well. Such women, as well as never married women, are more likely than men to settle in the city permanently.[16] To put it in a nutshell: women are more urban than men.

There is some evidence to support this view. Peil with Sada (1984:145) summarize surveys in Sierra Leone, Ghana, Nigeria, and Zaïre in which more women than men indicate that they intend to stay in the cities permanently. Surveys in Calabar, Nigeria, in 1989 and 1990 show a difference between female and male migrants in their preference for an urban place to retire to. While among the women 36 per cent intend to settle in a town on retirement—either in Calabar or in a smaller town nearer to their own or their husband's village of origin—only 20 per cent of the men indicate such an intention. Particularly striking is the difference among blue-collar workers. Whereas 29 per cent of the women in this group would like to live in a town on retirement, only 3 per cent of the men express a similar wish. This wide gap may be accounted for by the fact that the women in this group are unskilled workers—cleaners and garden-hands—who would stand little chance of eking out a living in the countryside. On the other hand, the men's expertise as skilled workers—carpenters, masons, plumbers—is in demand in rural areas where they can set up small workshops of their own. The surveys also show a difference between female and male migrants in their involvement in urban associations. Whereas for men associations oriented towards the development of the rural home area are of major importance, for women Christian church congregations and associations are most important (Ludwar-Ene, 1993). This difference in associational behaviour is indicative of the women's weaker attachment to the rural area. And their involvement in urban-centred congregations and associations proclaiming a universalist commitment further promotes their dissociation from the village (Ludwar-Ene, 1991:137f.). According to estimates of age-specific migration rates, urban areas in Ghana in the 1960s and in Kenya in the 1970s saw net emigration of men over age 45, but net in-migration of women over age 45 (Singlemann, 1993). And census data presented by the Office of Women in Development (U.S. Department of Commerce, 1984:41) show a lower urban sex ratio among the elderly than among the working age population in 16 out of 21 African countries.[17]

These observations prompt us to take another look at those countries where high urban sex ratios have dropped rapidly, i.e. Kenya, South Africa, Tanzania, and Zimbabwe. The sex ratios have become more balanced at such a fast pace that a declining share of migrants in the urban population cannot suffice as an explanation. Rather, the preponderance of men in rural–urban migration must have disappeared quite abruptly. The assumption is easily made that this reflects a shift to the third pattern we have outlined: women increasingly join their husbands in town. However, Sabot (1979:90) reports that women began to outnumber men among rural–urban migrants in Tanzania in 1970. And Vorlaufer (1985) found that women predominated in net migration to Nairobi and Mombasa, Kenya, in 1978–79. Conceivably this could be a transitory phase as men who previously stayed alone in the city are now joined by their wives. However, recent research in Nairobi indicates that it is still quite common for men to leave their wife and children in the countryside (Tostensen, 1990; Curtis, 1993).

It appears then that there is a large and growing number of women who come to African cities on their own. This development is part of a broader transformation, the emancipation of the young from their elders. In much of

Africa this transformation has been gathering strength for several generations. Earning opportunities beyond the village confines gave the young a
chance of economic independence denied earlier generations. This independence was complemented by individualistic norms that found expression in
colonial law and Western-type education. The emancipation of the young is
most obvious in the control the young have wrested from their elders over
marriage decisions.

Both single women migrants and women who have lost their husbands in
town tend to settle permanently. The living conditions and strategies of survival employed by such women in Nairobi have been described and analysed
by Nelson ([1979] 1988). The policy implications are obvious. Efforts to alle-
viate urban poverty have to recognize and address the poverty of independent
women raising children and of old women in terms of earning opportunities,
income transfers—whether private or public—and housing.

Notes

1 The recent shift towards a focus on the gender dimension of migration is reflected in the
   review essays by Pedraza (1991) and Tienda and Booth (1991) and the bibliography by
   Findley and Williams (1991).
2 Urban sex ratios provide an attractive proxy for sex selectivity in rural–urban migration
   because they are available for most countries, usually at several points in time. Singelmann
   (1993) presents estimates of the proportion of females among rural–urban migrants, using
   the census survival ratio method, for six African countries. They show a predominance of
   males in Botswana, Kenya, Tanzania, and Zimbabwe in the 1970s, in Togo in the 1960s;
   and virtually equal proportions of male and female migrants in Botswana and Ghana in the
   1960s. They are thus by and large in line with the implications of the urban sex ratios presented in Table 1.
3 Using data including all ages rather than age-specific data avoids the problems arising from
   the widespread—and gender-specific—misreporting of age.
4 Distinct patterns of sex selectivity in rural–urban migration characterize some Third World
   regions. Women outnumber men among rural–urban migrants in Latin America, men predominate in South Asia (Gilbert and Gugler, [1982] 1992:74–79).
5 The gender dimension of the demand for and supply of labour in Africa has received very
   little attention to date. Most Africanists seem to take it for granted that wage employment
   is a male domain, that women find little scope for earnings outside trade, prostitution, and
   illegal brewing. A notable exception is Hansen (1989) who painstakingly seeks to explain
   why men continue to dominate in domestic service in Zambia to this day. She adduces economic as well as cultural and ideological factors. See Schmidt (1992:155–79) for an
   account of the positions various protagonists took in the controversy over female domestic
   labour in colonial days in what has since become Zimbabwe.
6 Sharp and Spiegel (1990) emphasize the domination absent husbands exert through male
   kin over their wives. Contrasting Matatiele and Qwaqwa in South Africa, they show the
   importance of local resources in the form of agricultural land and cattle in allowing women
   some degree of autonomy and dignity. Nelson (1992) concludes from a review of the literature on Kenya that the autonomy of *de facto* female heads of rural households is primarily
   a function of the strength of the patrilineal, extended family or local lineage. Webster
   (1991) emphasizes the solidarity of women in Kosi Bay, another rural periphery in South
   Africa, who, in resisting the domination of their absent spouses, affirm a separate ethnic
   identity.
7 See, however, Jamal and Weeks (1993) who argue that the income gap between urban
   wage-earners and the rural population narrowed in most African countries, even disappeared in some, due to the dramatic fall in the real wages of urban workers since the 1970s.
8 For a more detailed discussion of rural–urban migration, see Gilbert and Gugler ([1982]
   1992:62–86).
9 Not only is the manufacturing sector in Africa minute, but it employs a very small proportion of women. Women hold 2% of the manufacturing jobs in Chad, 22% in The Gambia,
   12% in Kenya, 5% in Niger, 10% in Tanzania, and 5% in Zimbabwe; only in Botswana

and Swaziland, countries where men prefer to find work across the border in South Africa, do women hold about a third of the manufacturing jobs (International Labour Office, 1992, 1993).

10 Sudarkasa (1977) reports that young girls working as domestics for relatives in a small Yoruba town in Nigeria in the early 1960s, used to return to the village when they reached marriageable age. Since then, however, it has become increasingly common for young women who have been brought to town as girls to remain there up to and after marriage.

11 Obbo (1980:74) reports that young women who had been persuaded by urban-dwelling boyfriends to come to Kampala stayed around when the relationship broke up because they had decided that urban husbands had more to offer than rural husbands.

12 Pankhurst (1992:114–123) provides an account of high marital instability in an Amhara village. She suggests that the high divorce rates reflect both women's power to exit from a relationship in search of a better one, and their dissatisfaction resulting from stress, poverty, and oppression. The divorcees with few resources were most likely to migrate to urban areas.

13 For an account of the precarious access of unmarried, separated, and divorced women to land in two regions in Kenya, see Davison (1988).

14 On such organized persecution of witches in south-eastern Nigeria, see Offiong (1982).

15 Our discussion does not address the record numbers of refugees in Africa. The great majority are women and their children, and much of their movement is rural to urban.

16 Trager, in this volume, emphasizes the home ties of women from the Ijesa region in Nigeria and their return migration.

17 The exact implications of these data for migratory patterns are difficult to assess. On the one hand, differential mortality explains at least part of these differences. On the other, men were more likely to predominate among earlier cohorts of rural–urban migrants than among the more recent.

References

Anker, Richard, and Catherine Hein, 1986, "Introduction and Overview" in *Sex Inequalities in Urban Employment in the Third World*, edited by Richard Anker and Catherine Hein, 1–56. New York: St. Martin's Press.

Atto, Ulla, 1994, "'... et tout le reste pour les filles.' Zur Hausarbeit von Kindern in Abidjan." Doctoral dissertation, Bayreuth University.

Baker, Jonathan, 1994, "Small Urban Centres and their Role in Rural Restructuring ". In *Ethiopia In Change: Peasantry, Nationalism and Democracy* edited by Abebe Zegeye and Siegfried Pausewang, 152–71. London and New York: British Academic Press.

Behrman, Jere R., and Barbara L. Wolfe, 1984, "Micro Determinants of Female Migration in a Developing Country: Labor Market, Demographic Marriage Market and Economic Marriage Market Incentives." *Research in Population Economics* 5: 137–166.

Curtis, John William, 1993, "Rural Ties Among Men Working in Nairobi: Social Networks and Differentiation in the Political Economy of Kenya." Ph.D. dissertation, Johns Hopkins University.

Davison, Jean, 1988, "Who Owns What? Land Registration and Tensions in Gender Relations of Production in Kenya." In *Agriculture, Women, and Land: The African Experience* (Westview Special Studies on Africa), edited by Jean Davison, 157–76. Boulder/London: Westview Press.

Dinan, Carmel, 1983, "Sugar Daddies and Gold-Diggers: The White-Collar Single Women in Accra." In *Female and Male in West Africa*, edited by Christine Oppong, 344–66. London: George Allen & Unwin.

Findley, Sally E., and Lindy Williams, 1991, "Women Who Go and Women Who Stay: Reflections of Family Migration Processes in a Changing World." Population and Labour Policies Programme, Working Paper 176. Geneva: International Labour Organization.

Gilbert, Alan, and Josef Gugler, (1982) 1992, *Cities, Poverty, and Development: Urbanization in the Third World*. Second edition. Oxford/New York: Oxford University Press.

Goody, Esther, 1986, "Parental Strategies: Calculation or Sentiment? Fostering Practices among West Africans." In *Interest and Emotion. Essays on the Study of Family and Kinship*, edited by Hans Medick and David Warren Sabean, 266–277. Cambridge: Cambridge University Press.

Grosz-Ngaté, Maria, 1991, "Gender, Generation and Power: Labor Migration as a Terrain of Contest in Rural Mali", paper presented at the Institute for African Development, Cornell University.

Gugler, Josef, (1972) 1981, "The Second Sex in Town." *Canadian Journal of African Studies* 6:289–301. Reprinted in *The Black Woman Cross-Culturally*, edited by Filomina Chioma Steady, 169–184. Cambridge, Mass.: Schenkman.

Gugler, Josef, 1989, "Women Stay on the Farm No More: Changing Patterns of Rural–Urban Migration in Sub-Saharan Africa." *Journal of Modern African Studies* 27:347–52.

Gugler, Josef, 1991, "Life in a Dual System Revisited: Urban–Rural Ties in Enugu, Nigeria, 1961–87." *World Development* 19:399–409.

Guigou, Brigitte, and André Lericollais, 1992, "Crise de l'agriculture et marginalisation économique des femmes sereer siin (Sénégal)." *Sociétés—Espaces —Temps* 1:45–64.

Hamer, Alice, 1981, "Diola Women and Migration: A Case Study." In *The Uprooted of the Western Sahel*, edited by L.G. Colvin *et al.*, 163–203. New York: Praeger.

Hansen, Karen Tranberg, 1989, *Distant Companions: Servants and Employers in Zambia, 1900–1985* (Anthropology of Contemporary Issues). Ithaca/London: Cornell University Press.

Harris, John R., and Michael P. Todaro, 1970, "Migration, Unemployment and Development: A Two-Sector Analysis." *American Economic Review* 60: 126–42.

Hollos, Marida, 1991, Migration, Education, and the Status of Women in Southern Nigeria. *American Anthropologist* 93:852–70.

International Labour Office, 1992, *1992 Yearbook of Labour Statistics*. Geneva: International Labour Office.

International Labour Office, 1993, *1993 Yearbook of Labour Statistics*. Geneva: International Labour Office.

Jamal, Vali, and John Weeks, 1993, *Africa Misunderstood or Whatever Happened to the Rural–Urban Gap?* (ILO Studies). Geneva: International Labour Office.

Ludwar-Ene, Gudrun, 1986, "Explanatory and Remedial Modalities for Personal Misfortune in a West African Society." *Anthropos* 81:555–65.

Ludwar-Ene, Gudrun, 1991, "Sind Frauen urbaner als Männer? Eine These zum Urbanisierungsprozeß im subsaharischen Afrika." In *Ethnologische Stadtforschung*, edited by Waltraud Kokot and Bettina C. Bommer, 123–44. Berlin: Dietrich Reimer.

Ludwar-Ene, Gudrun, 1993, "The Social Relationships of Female and Male Migrants in Calabar, Nigeria: Rural Versus Urban Connections." In *Gros-plan sur les femmes en Afrique/ Afrikanische Frauen im Blick/Focus on Women in Africa* (Bayreuth African Studies Series 26), edited by Gudrun Ludwar-Ene and Mechthild Reh, 31–47. Altendorf: D. Gräbner.

Nelson, Nici, (1979) 1988, "How Women and Men Get by: The Sexual Division of Labour in the Informal Sector of a Nairobi Squatter Settlement." In *Casual Work and Poverty in Third World Cities*, edited by Ray Bromley and Chris Gerry, 283–302. Chichester/New York/Brisbane/Toronto: John Wiley. Reprinted revised in *The Urbanization of the Third World*, edited by Josef Gugler, 183–203. Oxford/New York: Oxford University Press.

Nelson, Nici, 1987, "Rural–Urban Child Fostering in Kenya: Migration, Kinship Ideology, and Class." In *Migrants, Workers, and the Social Order* (ASA Monograph 26), edited by Jeremy Eades, 181–98. London/New York: Tavistock Publications.

Nelson, Nici, 1992, "The Women Who Have Left and Those Who Have Stayed Behind: Rural–Urban Migration in Central and Western Kenya." In *Gender and Migration in Developing Countries*, edited by Sylvia Chant, 109–38. London/New York: Belhaven Press.

Obbo, Christine, 1980, *African Women: Their Struggle for Economic Independence*. London: Zed Press.

Offiong, Daniel A, 1982, "The 1978–1979 Akpan Ekwong Antiwitchcraft Crusade in Nigeria." *Anthropologica* 24:27–42.

Page, Hilary J, 1989, "Childrearing Versus Childbearing: Coresidence of Mother and Child in Sub-Saharan Africa." In *Reproduction and Social Organization in Sub-Saharan Africa*, edited by Ron J. Lesthaeghe, 401–41. Berkeley, Cal.: University of California Press.

Pankhurst, Helen, 1992, *Gender, Development and Identity: An Ethiopian Study*. London, New Jersey: Zed Books.

Pedraza, Silvia, 1991, "Women and Migration: The Social Consequences of Gender." *Annual Review of Sociology* 17:303–25.

Peil, Margaret, Stephen K. Ekpenyong, and Olotunji Y. Oyeneye, 1988, "Going Home: Migration Careers of Southern Nigerians." *International Migration Review* 22:563–85.

Peil, Margaret, with Pius O. Sada, 1984, *African Urban Society*. Chichester/New York/Brisbane/Toronto/Singapore: John Wiley & Sons.

Pittin, Renée, 1983, "Houses of Women: A Focus on Alternative Life-Styles in Katsina City." In *Female and Male in West Africa*, edited by Christine Oppong, 291–302. London: George Allen & Unwin.

Potts, Deborah, and Chris Mutambirwa, 1990, "Rural–Urban Linkages in Contemporary Harare: Why Migrants Need Their Land." *Journal of Southern African Studies* 16:677–98.

Sabot, Richard H., 1979, *Economic Development and Urban Migration: Tanzania 1900–1971*. Oxford: Clarendon Press.

Schmidt, Elizabeth, 1992, *Peasants, Traders, and Wives: Shona Women in the History of Zimbabwe, 1870–1939*. Portsmouth, NH: Heinemann; Harare: Baobab; London: James Currey.

Seibert, Jutta, 1995, "Lebensstrategien unabhängiger junger Frauen in Lomé, Togo." Doctoral dissertation, Bayreuth University.

Sembajwe, Israel, and T. Makatsjane, 1992, "Migration and Rural Crisis in a Labour Reserve Economy: Lesotho." In *Migrations, Development and Urbanization Policies in Sub-Saharan Africa*, edited by Moriba Toure and T.O. Fadayomi, 237–76. Dakar: CODESRIA.

Sharp, John, and Andrew Spiegel, 1990, "Women and Wages: Gender and the Control of Income in Farm and Bantustan Households." *Journal of Southern African Studies* 16: 527–49.

Singelmann, Joachim, 1993, "Levels and Trends of Female Internal Migration in Developing Countries, 1960–1980." In *Internal Migration of Women in Developing Countries: Proceedings of the United Nations Expert Meeting on the Feminization of Internal Migration, Aguascalientes, Mexico, 22–25 October 1991*, 77–93. New York: United Nations.

Sudarkasa, Niara, 1977, "Women and Migration in Contemporary West Africa." *Signs* 3:178–89.

Tienda, Marta, and Karen Booth, 1991, "Gender, Migration and Social Change." *International Sociology* 6:51–72.

Tostensen, Arne, 1990, "Industrialization in Kenya: Quasi-Proletarianization and Labour Migration." In *Industrialization in the Third World: The Need for Alternative Strategies*, edited by Meine Pieter van Dijk and Henrik Secher Marcussen, 105–22. London: Frank Cass.

United Nations, 1994, *1992 Demographic Yearbook*. New York: United Nations.

U.S. Department of Commerce, 1984, *Women of the World*. Volume 1. Washington, D.C.: U.S. Department of Commerce.

Van Westen, A.C.M., and M.C. Klute, 1986, "From Bamako, with Love: A Case Study of Migrants and Their Remittances." *Tijdschrift voor Economische en Sociale Geografie* 77:42–49.

Vorlaufer, Karl, 1985, "Frauen-Migrationen und sozialer Wandel in Afrika. Das Beispiel Kenya." *Erdkunde* 39:128–43.

Webster, David, 1991, "*Abafazi Bathonga Bafihlakala*: Ethnicity and Gender in a Kwa Zulu Border Community." In *Tradition and Transition in Southern Africa: Festschrift for Philip and Iona Meyer*, edited by Andrew D. Spiegel and Patrick A. McAllister, 243–71. Johannesburg: Witwatersrand University Press.

Weisner, Thomas Steven, 1972, "One Family, Two Households: Rural–Urban Ties in Kenya." Ph.D. dissertation, Harvard University.

Wurster, Gabriele, 1995, "Beruf und Karriere im Leben gebildeter Frauen in Nairobi, Kenia." Doctoral dissertation, Bayreuth University.

Women Migrants and Rural–Urban Linkages in South-Western Nigeria[*]

Lillian Trager

> We are just sojourners here, whereas our place of abode is at home; attachment to home is always there. (Statement by Lagos-based woman who is a chief in her hometown, June 18 1992).

In Africa, as elsewhere in the third world, migration involves not only the movement of individuals from one place to another, but also the maintenance of ties between those who move and those who do not. The extent, frequency, and importance of such ties vary considerably, depending on gender, socio-economic status, occupation, and the nature of social networks. In many societies of West Africa, migrants not only maintain ties with family at home, but also with the home community itself, by participating in hometown-based organizations and contributing to local development. Return migrants often take on prominent leadership roles in their local communities.

Research on these issues has primarily emphasized the role of men in these processes, with the implication that women participate little in such linkages. This chapter will argue to the contrary, that the majority of women migrants, of all statuses and occupational groups, maintain some connection with family and kin in their home communities, at least while close kin are resident there. These ties involve visiting, contributions of money and goods both from migrants to those at home and from those at home to migrants, and participation in organizations based on place of origin.

The chapter examines the interrelationship between women's status, their economic roles, and participation in local-level community development among women migrants and return migrants in south-western Nigeria. It is based on in-depth interview and survey data collected among migrants and return migrants in five communities in the Ijeṣa region of Yorubaland (the urban centre of Ileṣa, two medium-sized towns, and two villages), as well as among migrants from those communities now resident in the large cities of Lagos and Ibadan.

---

[*] A somewhat different version, entitled "Women Migrants and Hometown Linkages in Nigeria: Status, Economic Roles, and Contributions to Community Development" was presented at the International Union for the Scientific Study of Population Seminar on Women and Demographic Change in Sub–Saharan Africa in Dakar, Senegal in March, 1993, and is being published in *Women and Demographic Change in Sub-Saharan Africa* by An-Magritt Jensen and Paulina Makinwa-Adebusoye, (eds.), published by Ordina Editions for IUSSP, Liege 1995.

The first part of the chapter briefly reviews literature on three interrelated issues: women in the migration process; rural–urban linkages; and the economic roles and activities of Nigerian women. The chapter then examines data from the study area, showing that a majority of women have participated in migration, and that many of those maintain linkages with their home communities, including returning to those communities to live.

However, active participation in hometown organizations and local community development activities is less widespread. Female migrants of high status and in professional occupations, like men of similar background, participate in hometown organizations and make substantial contributions to community development efforts. These activities in turn enhance the status of the migrants, who are seen as non-resident community leaders. On the other hand, women migrants with fewer economic resources, who participate in informal sector occupations, are less likely to be involved in activities in their own hometowns. They have neither the financial resources necessary, nor the requisite status, for being seen as community leaders or potential leaders. Return migrants from this group are not likely to be well known locally or to play leading roles in community organizations and development.

This chapter has implications for our understanding of the role of women migrants in the migration process and in local development activities, and demonstrates the ways in which social status and economic role affect such participation. Female migrants, like male migrants, are seen as part of extensive social and economic networks linking rural and urban areas, with status and role in one place having implications for status and role in the other.

MIGRATION, WOMEN AND RURAL–URBAN LINKAGES

In considering the involvement of migrant women in their home communities, this chapter assumes a complexity to the migration process, in which rural and urban places are part of a single social field, and in which migrants move between a number of different places and may have social networks and resources in several. The questions addressed here are not simply those of "who migrates?" and "do women migrate?" Rather, this chapter addresses the issue of what happens during the migration process and after, both to those immediately involved (the migrants) and to others with whom they have ties. It incorporates an understanding that women involved in migration, like men, may differ in their characteristics, and that some may participate in a wide range of activities in their home communities and others may not. In addressing these issues, the chapter focuses on three interrelated themes: women and migration; rural–urban linkages; and the economic roles and activities of women. Earlier research on these themes provides the background and context for the present study.

Women and migration in Nigeria

Until recently, most research on migration in Nigeria, as elsewhere in Africa, focused on men. Perhaps this was due to the assumption, stated in a recent article, that "Migration by women until recently [in Nigeria] was primarily to join husbands" (Hollos 1991:854). For example, Makinwa's comprehensive study of migration in Bendel State (1981), mentions that female migrants, like their male counterparts, tend to be young, and includes an analysis of the fertility of female migrants in comparison with women of urban origins, but it provides little data or analysis of other characteristics of those females who migrate.

Those studies which do focus on women in the migration process have been largely concerned with the relationship between migration and women's status, as reflected in education and employment characteristics. In his study of female migrants in south-western Nigeria, Adepoju found that urban migrants tended to be younger and better educated, and hence to be employed in "diversified economic activities," as compared with rural migrants (1984:74). Lacey, likewise, investigated the relationship between migration and economic opportunities. She argues that, unlike men, women do not improve their occupational status as a result of migration. She found that few women moved from what she terms "traditional sector activities" (such as trading) into professional, clerical, or skilled occupations, and further, that some women "even experienced downward shifts from the modern economic sector to informal sector activities such as trading" (1986:16). This assumes, of course, that trade represents downward occupational mobility, whereas in fact, both men and women in some regions of Nigeria choose self-employment in business and trade after a period of time working in the formal sector and see such self–employment as a preferred occupation.

A more complex analysis of the relationship of migration to women's status is that of Hollos (1991), who is concerned not simply with occupational status but also with the status of women in the household, as reflected in decision-making and autonomy. She argues that it is not urban migration as such that leads to a change in women's status, but rather educational and employment characteristics which determine whether she is part of a nuclear family urban household, or whether she is part of an urban household similar in structure to rural households. According to her, it is the less-educated woman, usually working in an informal sector occupation, who has greater domestic status and power, in contrast to the better educated woman whose public status may be higher but whose domestic autonomy is reduced.

Other studies which focus on specific forms of migration also demonstrate the complex ways in which migration may be related to status. Watts (1983) shows that marriage migration to the city of Ilorin may improve the opportunities for women to engage in trade and other informal sector occupations, while in a contrasting case, Pittin shows that some young Hausa women who engage in autonomous migration are able to "parlay their earnings into considerable wealth through shrewd investment, careful planning, and a great deal of hard work" (1984:1308).

Like the study of migration in general, the research on women in the migration process in Nigeria is based largely on survey data and focuses on the individual migrant in her new, urban setting. Yet there is ample evidence to indicate that migration is not a simple one-way process. Nor is it a process in which individuals engage on their own. The complexity of migration, involving social networks and connections in a number of different places, as well as moves of individuals and groups between several places over time, needs to be considered for a more complete understanding of the role of women in migration.

Rural–urban linkages

As the understanding of the complexity of migration has increased, more attention has been paid to issues such as circular migration and the role of migrants in their communities of origin. In other regions of the third world, studies have focused on the connections migrants maintain to families in the place of origin and to the ways in which migration is a part of family strategies of survival and mobility (Chapman and Prothero 1983; Hugo 1982; Trager 1988). Some have argued that the migration of women is best understood in the context of such strategies (Trager 1984). Maintenance of ties with rural areas, including the rural community itself, has been recognized as being particularly important in Africa, and a number of studies have shown the ways in which connections with the hometown are maintained and utilized by migrants (e.g. Weisner 1976; Moock 1978–79; Gugler 1971, 1991; Aronson 1971). Recent research on hometown associations also reflects the importance of the participation of migrants in local-level community development activities in their home areas (Barkan, McNulty and Ayeni 1991; Trager 1992).

However, little of the research on rural–urban linkages in Africa considers the participation of women in these networks. As with migration research in general, there seems to be an assumption that women play a less important role in maintaining the connections with family and community in the place of origin. Gugler and Ludwar-Ene argue that evidence from a number of countries indicates that women show "weaker attachment to the rural area" (1990:10). Similarly, in a recent article Ludwar–Ene and Reh argue that evidence from south-eastern Nigeria indicates that women are less involved in their hometowns than are men, and that "[women's] ties with the rural area seem to rest more on the existence of personal relationships there, whereas men's rural ties are stronger, based not only on personal relationships but also on a more general concern for the welfare of their rural home place" (1993:45).

On the other hand, a study of return migrants in southern Nigeria shows that both men and women tend to return to their hometowns before retirement (Peil, Ekpenyong and Oyeneye 1988). The type and extent of contact maintained seems to vary considerably, depending both on the specific context and the socio-economic circumstances of the migrants. In Zimbabwe, for example, Schlyter (1990) found that low-income urban women drew on contacts in the rural areas in times of crisis, whereas in Bamako, Mali, both men and women send money back to their families in the village, and those who have lived longer in the city also tend to send gifts to the village (Vaa, Findley and Diallo 1989).

Further consideration of this issue necessitates examining the specific socio-economic circumstances of those involved, and recognizing that different types of migrants may participate in such networks in varying ways.

Economic roles of Yoruba women

The Yoruba of south-western Nigeria are well known for their entrepreneurial and trade activities. Women's role in trade has been examined both in terms of its importance within the local and regional economy (Trager 1976–77, 1981) and in terms of its relationship to household and family organization (Afonja 1981; Sudarkasa 1973). While Yoruba women in rural communities also participate in farming, they tend to have an independent source of income through trade in both rural and urban areas. Economic change in recent years has affected women's participation in trade and other informal sector activities; in some cases opportunities have expanded, with access to new sources of income-generating activities (Trager 1985). However, the economic crisis and the Structural Adjustment Program of the past few years has increased the burden on both rural and urban women (as well as on men) (Dennis 1991a, 1991b). Women, in particular, have fewer opportunities in the informal sector, while greater demands are placed on their income-generating capacities since there is a decrease in formal-sector and wage labour jobs for men (Dennis 1991b:100).

One question that arises in the current circumstances is the extent to which both rural and urban residents rely on support from kin located elsewhere, or conversely the extent to which people cut off ties with those elsewhere in order to reduce the demands on their limited incomes. The data to be considered in the following discussion will begin to address that question. By considering women migrants and return migrants in one specific set of communities and by examining their different socio-economic and class statuses, it will allow us to begin to consider the complexity not only of migration itself, but also of the continuing links maintained by those resident in different locales.

WOMEN AND MIGRATION IN IJEŞALAND

In this section of the chapter, I consider results from research carried out in the Ijeşa area of Yorubaland between October 1991 and July 1992. The Ijeşa are one of the Yoruba subgroups, located in the eastern part of Yorubaland, and include people with allegiance to the city of Ileşa, which is the traditional capital of the Ijeşa kingdom, and a number of smaller towns, villages, and hamlets in the surrounding hinterland. As Peel has pointed out, the Ijeşa "only came to consider themselves 'Yoruba' in the course of the twentieth century" (1983:15). The research took place in five Ijeşa communities—the city of Ileşa, two medium-sized towns, Oşu and Ijebu-jeşa, and two villages, Iwoye and Iloko.[1]

For the Ijeşa, as for the Yoruba in general, a crucial concept that informs behaviour and motivates action is the concept of *ilu*, translated in English as "hometown". The hometown is the place where one has kinship connections, basically the place where one's father's lineage is from. It is, however, more than the place of origin; it provides a source of social identity and a web of social connections, which influence actions regardless of where a person is residing. In general, the Ijeşa feel that people with origins there who live elsewhere "should associate themselves with the town, build houses and spend money there, and above all give it effective leadership in the competition of communities for the resources of the state" (Peel 1983:260). In the following discussion, I will consider some of the current importance and dynamics of connections with the hometown.

The Ijeṣa, like many other Yoruba, have tended to be highly mobile, at least in the twentieth century. Evidence from other Yoruba areas shows that people move in and out of their hometowns, residing there for some period of time, moving to other places, including larger cities, and moving back to the hometown. For example, Berry found that in one village over a period of seven years, the total population remained stable but 60 per cent of the people counted the first time had left and been replaced by others seven years later (1985:70; see also Aronson 1978). For the Ijeṣa in particular, mobility has been influenced by the fact that many people have worked as traders, known as *osomaalo*. Particularly in the first part of the twentieth century, the major reason for men to migrate out of Ijeṣaland was to work as *osomaalo*, meaning that they traded in cloth in small towns around Nigeria (Peel 1983:148–159). Although few people today claim to be *osomaalo*, many of those interviewed in the current research had relatives who were in the past. Although the term most frequently applies to men who worked as traders, many women are also involved in trade and they, too, have been mobile in connection with their trading activities.[2]

The following discussion is based both on survey data collected in a sample survey in the five communities under study, carried out in May–June 1992, and on extended interviews carried out throughout the research period.[3] While the survey focused on people who are currently residing in the communities under study, and therefore includes migrants, return migrants, and non-migrants, the interviews provide case study material on people who are from the Ijeṣa region but who are not currently residing there. Furthermore, the survey was designed to provide information on a wide variety of characteristics of current residents in the communities, whereas the case study and interview material focused on people who were identified as being actively involved in their hometowns.

Women migrants and return migrants in Ijeṣa communities

As noted above, survey data was collected in five Ijeṣa communities in May–June 1992.[4] The following analysis is based on a portion of the survey data—that from the two medium-sized towns of Oṣu and Ijebu-jeṣa. There were 119 respondents in those communities, of whom 66 are women. The sixty-six respondents range in reported age from 18 to 105; the mean age is 47. Forty-seven per cent have had no formal education; 28.8 per cent have had some primary school, and the rest include people with at least some middle or secondary school. There is one university graduate in the sample. Seventy-one per cent are married, while twenty-two per cent are widowed. In terms of occupation, these respondents reflect the occupations typical of women in small and medium-sized Yoruba towns: 59 per cent are traders, and 21 per cent are in other informal sector occupations such as seamstressing and hairdressing. The remainder include farmers (7.6 per cent) and women with no occupation, including a student, someone looking for work, one who terms herself a "housewife" and several others who either are retired or report no occupation.

Most significant for the present discussion is that of these 66 respondents, only nine (13.6 per cent) report having lived in only one place during the course of their lives. The other 57 (86.4 per cent) have lived in more than one place. They are either women who have previously been migrants who have now returned to live in their hometowns, or they are currently migrants who have moved to Oṣu and Ijebu-jeṣa from somewhere else.[5]

The rest of the discussion focuses on these 57 respondents, thirty of whom are return migrants and twenty-seven of whom are current migrants. In the first part of this discussion, I consider both return migrants and current migrants as one group. I then consider whether there are differences between migrants and return migrants in terms of involvement in hometown affairs.

The 57 respondents who are either currently migrants or are return migrants are similar in most respects to the sample of women as a whole. They are somewhat younger and somewhat better educated. Whereas 66 per cent of the whole sample is under 60 years old and 33 per cent is over 60, 72 per cent of the migrants/return migrants are under 60 and 28 per cent are over 60. This is largely due to the fact that it is the oldest women in the over-all sample who have never moved; six of the nine women who are non-migrants are over 60 years old. Forty per cent of the migrants/return migrants have no education, 31.5 per cent have had some primary school, and 28 per cent have middle school or above, including six with secondary school certification and one university graduate. Seventy-five per cent are married and 17.5 per cent widowed. In terms of occupation, 57.8 per cent are traders and 24.5 per cent are in other informal sector occupations; 7 per cent are farmers and 10.5 per cent have no occupation.

In how many places have women migrants lived, and what kind of places are they? The majority have lived in either three or four different places, or in other words, have moved two or three times; 42 per cent have lived in three places and 28 per cent in four places. Twelve per cent have lived in two places and 18 per cent report having lived in five or more different places. The places in which respondents have lived are spread throughout Nigeria and even beyond, but for most, their moves have been to centres which are quite close to their current residence. Of the 51 who reported the location of their first move, seven (13 per cent) moved to other towns in Ijeṣaland, and 23 (45 per cent) moved to places in what was formerly Oyo State (now divided between Oyo and Oṣun States); the latter include ten who moved to the city of Ibadan. Interestingly, only five respondents reported moving to Lagos, the capital of Nigeria, for their first move, but another five report it as the place of their second move. Other moves included several locations in Eastern and Northern Nigeria, as well as Ghana.

The most common type of reason that respondents gave for moving was family: 25 per cent reported that their first move was to join or accompany their spouse, and 10 per cent gave that as the reason for their second move as well. Other family reasons were to go with their parents or to stay with other relatives, and for those who are older, to stay with their children; in all, 62 per cent of first moves and 66 per cent of second moves were due to such reasons. Eighteen per cent of first moves and 22 per cent of second moves were for work or trade, and 16 per cent of first moves and 11 per cent of second moves were to study or learn a trade. Similar responses were given by those who are currently migrants to Oṣu and Ijebu-jeṣa, for the reasons why they left their hometowns and the reasons for their move to their current residence.

On the other hand, for those who are now living in their hometowns (return migrants), the reasons given for their return home are more varied. While nine per cent stated that they came with their spouse, another ten per cent simply stated that it was time to return or settle at home. Still others reported financial problems or illness, and several reported that they returned because of specific problems where they were living, including being expelled from Ghana (two respondents) and the religious situation in Northern Nigeria (two respondents).

In sum, in the two medium-sized towns of Oṣu and Ijebu-jeṣa, a large majority of the women surveyed have been involved in the migration process; most have lived in several different places for varying lengths of time. Although their reasons for moving are largely based on family considerations, all have been involved in some type of occupation (including those who are currently not working) and, like Yoruba women in general, earn income and participate in economic activities separately from the activities of their spouses.

The discussion to this point has included both women who are migrants to Oṣu and Ijebu-jeṣa from other places and women who have returned to their hometowns after being migrants elsewhere. While all have been or are migrants, their current residential situation differs in significant ways, especially for the consideration of linkages with family and community. One might expect that those who have been migrants but are now resident at home would be more involved in hometown activities than those who are living outside their hometowns. On the other hand, one might expect those living away from home to be more involved in visiting and sending things to relations elsewhere. The following section examines these issues by considering current migrants and return migrants separately.

Migration, linkages, and hometown involvement

Among the 57 women who have participated or are currently participating in the migration process, 30 are women whose hometown is either Oṣu or Ijebu-jeṣa and who are now residing in one of those towns, after having moved elsewhere. The other 27 are women whose hometown is elsewhere and who have moved to Oṣu and Ijebu-jeṣa from somewhere else.[6] The hometowns of those who are not from Oṣu or Ijebu-jeṣa are primarily located in the Ijeṣa region or nearby; eight (29 per cent) are from other Ijeṣa towns, and 17 (63 per cent) are from Oṣun State or a neighbouring state in south-western Nigeria. Only two come from places that are farther away, one from Kwara State and one from eastern Nigeria; in other words, there are few major ethnic or cultural differences within this group.

Table 1 examines data on the extent to which migrants and return migrants are involved in maintaining ties with family members residing elsewhere. For those who are return migrants, the issue considered here is whether they visit family members who do not reside in the hometown; whether those family members visit them; and whether they send things to family elsewhere in addition to, or instead of, visiting them. For those who are current migrants, the question is whether they visit family who reside in the hometown; receive visits from them; or send things to them. As is clear from Table 1, visiting is much more common than sending. Seventy-six per cent of return migrants and 100 per cent of current migrants report that they visit family, while 100 per cent of return migrants and 92.5 per cent of current migrants report that they get visits from family elsewhere. Fifty-nine per cent of current migrants also report sending things to relatives at home, but only 23 per cent of return migrants send things to relatives who live elsewhere. The majority also bring things with them—usually money or goods—when they visit.[7]

Table 1. *Contact with family elsewhere among women migrants*

Visiting/sending	Return migrants[a] (N = 30)		Current migrants[b] (N = 27)	
	no.	%	no.	%
visit family elsewhere	23	76		
visit hometown			27	100
family visit respondent	30	100	25	92.5
send to family elsewhere	7	23		
send to family in hometown			16	59

[a] Return migrants are women who have lived outside the hometown and have now returned there to live.
[b] Current migrants are women whose hometown is outside the survey community and who have moved to the survey site from somewhere else.
Source: Field survey data collected by Lillian Trager in Ọṣu and Ijebu-jeṣa, Nigeria, May-June 1992.

It is clear from Table 1 that both current migrants and return migrants maintain relationships with relatives elsewhere with whom they exchange visits and goods. Women migrants, like men reported on in earlier studies, are clearly involved in visiting their hometowns and maintaining contact with family not only in the hometown but elsewhere as well.

Table 2 examines participation in hometown activities and ownership of property in the hometown. Among return migrants, currently living in their hometowns, 50 per cent are members of hometown organizations, compared to 40 per cent of current migrants not resident in their hometowns. While 20 per cent of return migrants have a house, only 3.7 per cent of current migrants have built a house in their hometown. There are somewhat higher numbers who own farms, and some have property elsewhere (including land). Finally, 23 per cent of return migrants and 14 per cent of current migrants report having contributed to an activity in their hometown, primarily by donating money for a project such as the building of a school, town hall, or palace.

To judge by the data presented here, it appears that women participate to a limited degree in hometown activities. Relatively few have built their own houses or contributed to local projects; on the other hand, 50 per cent of return migrants do belong to at least one hometown organization (and some belong to several). However, this data must be viewed in light of who the

Table 2. *Participation in hometown activities by women migrants*

Type of participation	Return migrants[a] (N = 30)		Current migrants[b] (N = 27)	
	no.	%	no.	%
belongs to hometown organization(s)	15	50	11	40.7
has house in hometown	6	20	1	3.7
has farm in hometown	8	26.6	5	18.5
has other property in hometown	13	43.3	4	14.8
has property elsewhere	3	10	5	18.5
contributes to hometown activities	7	23.3	4	14.8

[a] Return migrants are women who have lived outside the hometown and have now returned there to live.
[b] Current migrants are women whose hometown is outside the survey community and who have moved to the survey site from somewhere else.

Source: Field survey data collected by Lillian Trager in Oṣu and Ijebu-jeṣa, Nigeria, May-June 1992.

women in the sample are: they have relatively low levels of education and they work in occupations, primarily trade, which, while they can be lucrative, most often are not. For the most part, then, these are not women who are likely to have money available for acquiring property or for contributing extensively to hometown activities.

Lagos-based Ijeṣa migrants

The discussion to this point would seem to lead to the conclusion that while women are involved in migration in the Ijeṣa area and that many maintain ties with family and relatives living elsewhere, fewer are involved in community-based activities in their hometowns, whether or not they are living in those communities. However, broadening the set of people studied, to include those who are based outside of the hometown and readily identified as being active in it, provides a different view of the situation.

I turn now to consider data from case studies of women who have migrated from the Ijeṣa area to Lagos; all have been living outside Ijeṣaland for long periods of time but retain connections with their home communities. Unlike the people considered in the preceding section, those discussed here were selected through network sampling. During the course of interviews in the communities under study, I asked for names of individuals from Ijeṣaland and of Ijeṣa organizations in Lagos and other large cities.[8] Initially, I was primarily referred to men and men's organizations. However, after some time, I was given names of a number of key women as well as introductions to several women's organizations. I followed two procedures in obtaining data on these women: I carried out extended interviews with those identified as leaders and I circulated written questionnaires through the organizations to reach a wider number of respondents. I also attended meetings of several organizations in Lagos, and met some of these same individuals at events in Ijeṣaland. The following discussion is based on the information obtained from eight women.

All of those considered here were already identified as being involved in some way in Ijeṣa activities. The characteristics of these women are considered below. It is clear that they differ in significant ways from most of those in the samples taken in the hometowns. These differences derive not simply from the fact that they are currently living in Lagos, but involve a variety of socio-economic characteristics. Overall, they comprise a set of women, who, like many men of similar status and background, are involved in Ijeṣa affairs in multiple ways, and for whom the connection to their hometown remains important despite the fact that they have long lived elsewhere and may never actually return to live in Ijeṣaland.

Of the eight women considered here, six consider the city of Ileṣa to be their hometown, while one is from Oṣu. One other is not herself from the Ijeṣa area at all. Rather, it is her husband who is from Ileṣa, while she is from Lagos; however, she is very active in Ijeṣa activities, viewing her husband's hometown as her "home", along with the city of Lagos. Only four were actually born in Ileṣa, and two others spent part of their childhood there, returning when their parents decided to do so. One has never lived in Ileṣa, having been born in Lagos and lived there essentially all her life, except for a period when she studied overseas. The oldest of these women, who is now in her late seventies, first came to Lagos in 1926, although she later spent some time back in Ileṣa working, before returning again to Lagos. The woman whose husband is from there also lived and worked there briefly, before her marriage.

Six of the women under consideration are between the ages of forty-five and sixty, and the other two are over seventy. They have all lived in Lagos for very long periods of time. One woman, now forty-six, has lived there for 22 years, while those who are in their fifties and sixties have all lived there more than thirty years. Like the two in their seventies, one of whom came to Lagos in 1926 and the other of whom has always lived in Lagos, these women have essentially spent their entire adult lives in Lagos. Further, they left Ileṣa even earlier, having travelled out of their hometowns both for education and for work before their marriages. All except the oldest have lived elsewhere in Nigeria, and three, including one of those in her seventies, have also studied in England.

The educational and occupational backgrounds of these women are remarkably similar. Of those who are now between forty-five and sixty, all but one have had specialized post-secondary education in teacher training; the other finished secondary school but did not receive additional education. However, she, like the others, worked for some time in a formal sector occupation; the woman with only secondary school worked as a secretary while the others worked as teachers. Likewise, the woman in her late seventies received specialized training in nursing and worked for a short time at a hospital in Ileṣa when she was young. The other woman in her seventies is more highly educated, having received medical training and having then worked for many years in government as a doctor. While all have previously worked in formal sector occupations, only one, a teacher, continues to do so. The doctor is retired but involved in numerous organizations, including ones which draw on her medical experience. The others are all in business, with several who state their current occupation as "trading" and others in catering and book selling. One, a widow, took over her husband's business when he died about twenty-five years ago. Although their current occupations may be termed informal sector occupations, they are different in crucial ways from the informal sector occupations of those women who are traders in the medium-sized towns of Oṣu and Ijebu-jeṣa, involving greater capital investment and leading to considerably better incomes (see Trager 1987).

It should be clear from the description above that the set of women considered here are people who are established in Lagos and who have been, in broad terms, successful there. Given their long residence in Lagos, and their educational and occupational backgrounds, one might well expect that they would have little reason or motivation to remain in contact with their hometowns. However, the reverse is the case.[9] All of these women visit Ijeṣaland regularly. With the exception of the doctor, who goes only occasionally, and mainly for special events, the others report that they go to Ileṣa at least several times a year, with three stating that they go monthly and one stating that she goes every two weeks. All, including the ones who do not go frequently, had actually been in Ileṣa at some time in the previous three months, and most had visited during the month when they provided the data (June or July 1992). Despite the fact that their own immediate families (i.e., children) are largely resident in Lagos and that their parents are dead, all report visiting home to see relatives and to attend a variety of events, including weddings and funerals. One woman pointed out that she had made a policy of visiting her father every two weeks for the five years before he died, because she "didn't want to wait until he died and then just go home to bury him".

But their involvement in Ijeṣaland is not limited to visiting relatives there and attending social events. Four of the women have houses in Ileṣa, and a fifth is building one. This includes the woman in her late seventies who has lived in Lagos since 1926, as well as the woman whose husband died a number of years ago. None report having their own farm there, but two refer to their father's farmland; further, four report having land there, including the woman who has lived her entire life in Lagos who stated that she had bought land in Ileṣa and was thinking about establishing a farm on it.

Even more significant is these women's involvement in hometown organizations and activities. All are members of at least one Ijeṣa organization, and several are members of more than one. For example, one woman is active in a woman's organization, which she helped to form in the early 1970s; she is a member of a recently formed organization that includes both men and women, based both in Ijeṣaland itself and outside; and she is a representative to the Council of Ijeṣa Societies in Lagos. In addition, she has recently been installed as a chief, having taken a traditional chieftaincy title. While she is no doubt one of the most active, the others tend to have multiple involvement in organizations, including social and service organizations, church organizations, and chieftaincy organizations. Three of these women have been given traditional chieftaincy titles and are therefore members of the Ijeṣa Council of Chiefs in Lagos, which includes all Ileṣa chiefs—both men and women—who are based in Lagos. The oldest woman in this set is the head of an organization of Ileṣa women in Lagos, a member of several church organizations, including ones both in Lagos and in Ileṣa, and a chief.

With their organizational commitments, these women are frequently called on to contribute to activities in Ileṣa and Ijeṣaland. All have made monetary contributions in the recent past. For example, two report contributing to a

Development Fund, and others say they have contributed at various fund-raising and launching ceremonies. Still others have made even more substantial financial contributions, including one who is helping to pay the salary of teachers in an adult education program organized by one of the churches in Ileṣa.

Their efforts tend to go beyond monetary contributions to involvement, both formally through their organizations and informally through their personal social networks, in a variety of other issues in the Ijeṣa area. During the period of the research, there were many meetings and discussions in Ijeṣaland concerning disputes among various chiefs; women's organizations, like men's organizations, sent delegations as part of efforts to settle these disputes.

Women are also involved in efforts at community development in Ileṣa and the Ijeṣa area more generally. Two of the women's organizations have purchased land in Ileṣa with the intention of establishing something for children and students. As individuals, several have been involved in discussions with other people from Ijeṣaland to try to find ways to promote economic development there. In general, the women interviewed focus on the importance of assisting women in their hometown; one emphasized the importance of education, another stated that she would like to see more "industrial development involving women".

Like many men of similar status and backgrounds, the women discussed here are involved in hometown affairs in multiple ways and at many levels. They share a personal commitment to the place, which is in part an emotional tie; as the oldest stated, "No matter where you are you have to continue to maintain contact with home." For the most part, they continue to have relatives in Ijeṣaland, even though their immediate families are not there, and they feel an obligation to maintain ties with those relatives. Even though they have long lived outside, most have built houses at home or invested in other ways, such as through the purchase of land. They belong to hometown organizations and contribute both financially and in other ways to hometown activities. The participation of women, like that of men, has important implications for both the migration process and for local development.

DISCUSSION

Some years ago, Abu-Lughod noted the passing of simplistic notions in the study of migration, in which "human beings, like iron filings, were impelled by forces beyond their conscious control" (1975:201). In recognizing the complexity of migration, scholars have increasingly sought conceptual and methodological tools for helping to understand that complexity. One crucial aspect of this development has been to consider individual migrants within broader contexts of family and community, and to examine the ways in which migrants continue to be tied to, and maintain connections with, people and institutions in a variety of locales.

Emerging out of much of the research in recent years is a sense that, in many situations, individual migrants form a part of a nexus of relationships that span rural and urban areas. It is that nexus that must be understood to grasp the actions and motivations of many of the people involved in the migration process, and to consider the implications of those actions for other societal processes. Too often, for example, we consider the "rural" and the "urban" to be entirely separate, with developments in one type of locale bearing little relation to those in the other. How, then, to understand what is immediately apparent to anyone travelling the roads of south-western Nigeria on a Friday afternoon or Saturday morning—the long lines of cars leaving Lagos travelling to smaller cities and towns of the region? And, even more significant, how do we understand the contribution of large sums of money at a fund-raising ceremony ("launching") in a small rural community, made by visitors from Lagos who have spent four hours travelling there on a weekend when there is a fuel shortage and some are not sure they have sufficient fuel to return to Lagos after the ceremony?

The data considered in this chapter contribute to our understanding of the migration process and to considering some of the broader implications of that process in one particular setting and among one set of people. In this discussion, I want to briefly examine the following issues: 1) the role of women in the migration process; 2) the importance and extent of maintenance of hometown ties; 3) the implications of this data for understanding rural–urban linkages and local development.

Women and migration

It is clear from the data considered here that there is high mobility among the women studied in the Ijesa area. Of those surveyed in the two medium-sized towns of Osu and Ijebu-jesa, 86 per cent have moved at some point in their lives, and the majority have moved more than once. These include women who have returned to their hometowns after having lived elsewhere, as well as women who have migrated to the towns from other places. While it is not surprising perhaps that women have returned to their hometowns to live, it is noteworthy that this occurs at a number of different points in the life cycle; some have returned when they are elderly, but many are still quite young, and it is quite possible that at least some of them will move again at some stage in their lives. It is also interesting that there are considerable numbers of in-migrants to the towns studied, making clear that migration among the Yoruba does not simply involve movement to big cities but also includes smaller cities and medium-sized towns.

The data also indicate that women involved in the migration process in south-western Nigeria come from a variety of socio-economic backgrounds. Most of those in the sample in the two towns have little or no education, and nearly all work in informal sector occupations, with trade as the dominant occupation. On the other hand, elite women are also involved in migration, as is clear from the network sample of Ijesa women based in Lagos, who are highly educated and who have worked at some point in formal sector occupations, although most are now engaged in small business.

While most of the women included in the survey data moved for family reasons, education and work are also important motivations for migration, especially among those who are better off. However, given the economic independence of Yoruba women, it would be misleading to assume that they move simply because they must follow their spouses; in fact, older women frequently live apart from their spouses and some of those interviewed are return migrants who have come back to their hometown while the spouse has remained elsewhere.

Overall, it is evident that migration is a common process for Yoruba women in general, as it is for Yoruba men. It is perhaps the rare woman who has not lived for some period of her life in a place other than her home; in fact, in the sample, it is only among the oldest women that one finds a considerable number who have never lived anywhere else.

Women and attachment to home

The simple fact of migration, however, tells us little about the extent to which women migrants maintain ties with people elsewhere. Is there a "weaker attachment" to home among women than among men, as Gugler and Ludwar-Ene (1990) have suggested?

The data considered here suggest that, in general, "attachment" is quite strong. Among those in the survey who are migrants currently living outside their hometowns, all report that they visit their hometowns, as do all of the Lagos-based women in the network sample. Likewise, most of those who have returned home to live report that they visit family elsewhere, and all state that family members currently residing elsewhere come to visit them.

However, there are many different types and degrees of attachment. The women in the sample survey are less involved in a variety of hometown activities than might be expected. As we have seen above, among both those who have returned home to live and those who are still living outside their hometowns, there are rather low rates of participation and involvement. While it is true that 50 per cent of return migrants are members of hometown organizations, only 23 per cent report contributing to hometown activities. Likewise, 40 per cent of current migrants belong to hometown organizations, and 14 per cent have contributed to an activity at home.

In contrast, those in the network sample participate in a wide variety of activities in their hometowns. They own houses and land, belong to organizations, make financial contributions, and are engaged in efforts to improve the home community. Three have taken chieftaincy titles.

How to explain the difference between the participation and "attachment" to home among those in the network sample and those in the survey sample? For the Lagos-based women in the network sample, their own view of attachment to home is expressed in the statement quoted at the beginning of this chapter: "We are just sojourners here, whereas our place of abode is at home; attachment to home is always there." This may seem to be an emotional expression of an attachment to a place which they left long ago. And certainly that is one element of the connection.

But the degree to which people travel back and forth and contribute in substantive ways suggests that it is not simply an emotional and symbolic link. Rather, for these women, as for men of similar status, their involvement in hometown affairs is an important aspect of their overall status. I would argue that while some degree of attachment and involvement is important for just about everyone, the extent of that attachment varies with socio-economic status; it is much more crucial for those of higher status to be visibly involved at home. To be a person of importance means that one's status is recognized at home, and part of the process of achieving that recognition is carried out by engaging in activities that are seen as having significance to the home community. This includes participation in a range of activities: membership in organizations; giving contributions for special events; assistance in settling disputes.

It is significant that three of the women in the network sample have been given chieftaincy titles, and are clearly proud of those titles, especially of the fact that these are "traditional" titles, not just honorary ones. As one explained to me, these positions are still very important "at the grassroots," and therefore she has decided that it is worthwhile to become involved in the chieftaincy institution. Not everyone shares this view; there are many elite men and women who avoid being given chieftaincy titles and who state that they would not accept them if they are offered. However, as this woman indicates, it is an institution that is still viewed with considerable importance by many, and one that has considerable status.

For these women, then, their success and status achieved through migration have enhanced their status and recognition in their hometown, and have led to participation in a variety of hometown activities. In this, they are like many men of similar backgrounds, although it is probably the case that more men than women are engaged in such activities, and that the participation of men is seen as being, in general, more important than that of women. For example, one elite woman who has returned to live in Ileṣa with her husband explained to me that she stays in the background so that her husband can play an active role in hometown affairs and so that they are seen as speaking with one voice; she views her role as a supportive one played behind the scenes.

On the other hand, women with fewer financial resources are less likely to participate in hometown activities while they are still migrants, and when they return home, they participate in more limited ways than do those who are elite. They have neither the financial resources nor the requisite status for being seen as community leaders, although in some cases they do take on leadership roles in the organizations to which they belong, and in some cases, they take traditional chieftaincy titles, as in the case of one woman in the survey.

Rural–urban linkages and local development

The notion of "attachment to home" makes clear that there are a variety of connections that span location. For the Yoruba women considered here, the locales in which people are involved include not just "rural" and "urban" (i.e., large city), but a range of places in between—smaller cities such as Ileṣa, as well as medium-sized towns like Oṣu and Ijebu-jeṣa. People participate in social activities and organizations in more than one place, and move regularly between these places. In this discussion, I have emphasized the ties with hometown, but those currently resident in urban areas such as Lagos are also incorporated into activities and institutions there as well. For example, women in the network sample described Lagos-based church organizations in which they participate. The point here is simply that we cannot fully understand the social organization and behaviour of migrants by focusing on what they do only in the place to which they have moved. Nor can we understand the impact of migration by focusing only on the social structure of the city.

In other words, we need to examine this population in terms of its *multilocality*, that is the attachment to and participation in social and economic activities in a number of places.[10] In a society such as Nigeria, and elsewhere in Africa as well, where the commitment to the hometown remains strong, the linkages to place, and among people in different places, form the crucial web of connections that influence individuals' actions and behaviour. Hence, all those cars leaving Lagos on Fridays and Saturdays: they carry people going to visit relatives at home, people attending ceremonies at home, and people going to the ceremonies of friends in the friends' hometown. There are strongly felt obligations to participate in such activities; one can hear discussions among Lagos residents about how they met a variety of—often conflicting—obligations on a given weekend, in some cases by travelling to a number of different places.

These obligations probably affect members of the elite most, in that they are the ones who are expected to appear and participate in a range of social events, and for whom it is most important to do so. But they affect everyone to some degree, as is clear by the fact that all of the current migrants in the survey in Oṣu and Ijebu-jeṣa report visiting their hometowns.

One question that must be raised is whether the current socio-economic crisis in the country is affecting people's willingness and ability to continue to fulfil these obligations, and hence the continued maintenance of linkages. For the elite, for example, there seem to be an increasing number of demands on their resources; do they—or have they—reached a point where they must cut back on the ties maintained, declining to visit their own or others' hometowns or declining to attend ceremonial events, in order to conserve their resources? For the vast majority of others, who are not well off and whose lives have become increasingly difficult in the past few years, the situation is much more serious; are such individuals making fewer visits home, sending less to kin elsewhere, and in general cutting back on their involvement in social networks? Or, conversely, are they contributing more because of the greater need?

The data considered in this chapter do not provide specific answers to these questions. Elsewhere, I have discussed some of the effects of the economic situation and the Structural Adjustment Program on the perceptions and activities of migrants (Trager 1993). In brief, it appears that all of these possibilities may be taking place. That is, some people may be cutting back on their ties, while others are finding it even more important to maintain them.

One thing is clear, however. The participation of elite in hometown social networks is not just a matter of attending a variety of ceremonial events. Rather, both men and women in this set of people are contributing in substantial ways to local development activities in their hometowns. They do this primarily by contributing money to development funds and at launchings, as described by the women in the network sample. Some go further than this, and contribute to a specific project that they have organized, usually as part of the activities of an organization to which they belong. One result of this is that what might be considered "local development" is in fact heavily dependent on the contributions of those who reside outside the local area. In other words, what is crucial for local development activities is the ability to mobilize externally-generated resources through a variety of both local and external social connections.

Most research on migration, and on rural–urban linkages in the migration process, focuses on those who are low-income urban migrants, who make up the great majority of migrants throughout the third world. In my research on migrants in the Philippines, for example, I stressed the way in which rural–urban linkages are crucial in the survival and maintenance of low-income families, and demonstrated the key role played by young women in those linkages (Trager 1988). However, that is just part of the picture. By including migrants who are elite and relatively well-off, the present research indicates the importance of rural–urban linkages for communities as well as for individuals and families. The nexus of connections that span place plays a role not only in family support and maintenance, but also in the support of local community development activities.

Migration is a complex process, involving people and institutions in different locales interacting in a variety of ways over time. Rather than focusing on those in a single place, this chapter has focused on the connections between people and places, specifically, the connections with the hometown. For women as well as men, such connections are crucial, and continue to influence behaviour and actions long after the specific act of moving takes place. The maintenance of connections across place has implications not simply for what individuals do, but also for the larger community of which they are a part. Our understanding both of what happens in the places to which migrants move, and in the hometowns from which they come, necessitates further research from such a perspective.

Notes

1 In the 1963 census, Ijeṣa had a population of about 160,000; Oṣu and Ijebu-jeṣa were in the range of 5,000–10,000. These are not terribly useful figures for knowing present population of these communities; once details of the 1991 census are released we will presumably have a better idea.
2 Peel's discussion of *osomaalo* trade focuses only on male heads of households (Peel 1983).
3 The research continued in May–June 1993, with further interviews of these individuals. However, the discussion here is based on data collected in the 1991–92 research period.
4 In each of the five communities, sections of the town or city were delineated, to include all types of housing and residences. In the city of Ijeṣa and the two medium-sized towns of Ijebu-jeṣa and Oṣun samples were selected in several of the delineated sections; in the two small towns, the sample was taken from the entire town. Preliminary mapping identified residences and compounds; a ten per cent sample of residences and compounds was then taken in each delineated area. Interviewers were instructed to interview one adult male or female in each of the residences or compounds selected. The survey included data not only on the individual interviewed but also on other household members and on non-resident members of the family. However, the following analysis focuses on the individual data. A total of 281 people were interviewed in the five towns studied.
5 The return migrants were not necessarily born in their hometowns, although most in fact were. Birthplace is not the same as hometown; hometown rather than birthplace defines "home".
6 There is one woman in the sample who reports that she moves back and forth between her residence in her hometown and a residence elsewhere.
7 The data includes considerable detail on the frequency of visits, the types of remittances, and so on, which will be considered in detail in later analyses.

8 There are numerous hometown organizations of Ijeṣa people in Lagos. Some are single sex organizations, others include both men and women. Some are social clubs, others are service organizations, while some also take on lobbying and community development activities.
9 Certainly there may be comparable individuals who do not retain strong connections with their hometown; they of course are much more difficult to identify in a city like Lagos.
10 In his comments at the IUSSP seminar, John Clarke used this term, which seems to me particularly appropriate for the situation I am describing. Locoh has recently suggested a similar term, "multipolarity" (1991).

References

Abu–Lughod, Janet, 1975, "Comments. The end of the age of innocence in migration theory", in B.M. DuToit and H.I. Safa (eds.), *Migration and Urbanization*. The Hague: Mouton.

Adepoju, Aderanti, 1984, "Migration and female employment in South-western Nigeria", *African Urban Studies*, 18, 59–75.

Afonja, S.A., 1981, "Changing modes of production and the sexual division of labour among the Yoruba", *Signs*, 7, 299–313.

Aronson, Dan R., 1971, "Ijebu Yoruba urban–rural relationships and class formation", *Canadian Journal of African Studies*, 5, 263–279.

Aronson, Dan R., 1978, *The City is Our Farm: Seven Migrant Ijebu Yoruba Families*. Cambridge: Schenkman.

Barkan, Joel D., Michael L. McNulty and M.A.O. Ayeni, 1991, "'Hometown' voluntary associations, local development, and the emergence of civil society in Western Nigeria", *The Journal of Modern African Studies*, 29, 457–480.

Berry, Sara S., 1985, *Fathers Work for Their Sons: Accumulation, Mobility and Class Formation in an Extended Yoruba Community*. Berkeley: University of California Press.

Chapman, Murray and R. Mansell Prothero, 1983, "Themes on Circulation in the Third World", *International Migration Review*, 17, 597–632.

Dennis, Carolyne, 1991a, "The limits to women's independent careers: gender in the formal and informal sectors in Nigeria", in D. Elson, (ed.), *Male Bias in the Development Process*. Manchester: Manchester University Press.

Dennis, Carolyne, 1991b, "Constructing a 'career' under conditions of economic crisis and structural adjustment: the survival strategies of Nigerian women", in H. Afshar (ed.), *Women, Development and Survival in the Third World*. London: Longman.

Gugler, Josef, 1971, "Life in a dual system: Eastern Nigerians in Town, 1961", *Cahiers d'Etudes Africaines*, 11, 400–421.

Gugler, Josef, 1991, "Life in a dual system revisited: urban–rural ties in Enugu, Nigeria 1967–87", *World Development*, 19, 399–409.

Gugler, Josef and Gudrun Ludwar-Ene, 1990, "Many roads lead women to town in Sub-Saharan Africa", paper presented at the World Congress of Sociology, July 1990, Madrid.

Hollos, Marida, 1991, "Migration, education, and the status of women in Southern Nigeria", *American Anthropologist*, 93, 852–870.

Hugo, Graeme, 1982, "Circular migration in Indonesia", *Population and Development Review*, 8, 59–83.

Lacey, Linda, 1986, "Women in the development process: occupational mobility of female migrants in cities in Nigeria", *Journal of Comparative Family Studies*, 17, 1–18.

Locoh, Therese, 1991, "Structure familiales d'accueil des migrants et developpement des structures familiales multipolaires en Afrique", in P. Vimard et A. Quesnel, (eds.), *Migration, Changements Sociaux et Developpement*, Colloques et Seminaires de l'ORSTOM, Paris.

Ludwar–Ene, Gudrun and Mechthild Reh, 1993, "The Social Relationships of Female and Male Migrants in Calabar, Nigeria: Rural versus Urban Connections," *Focus on Women in Africa*, Bayreuth African Studies Series 26.

Makinwa, P.K., 1981, *Internal Migration and Rural Development in Nigeria: Lessons from Bendel State*. Ibadan: Heinemann Educational Books.

Moock, Joyce L., 1978–79, "The content and maintenance of social ties between urban migrants and their home–based support groups: the Maragoli case", *African Urban Studies*, 3, 15–31.

Peel, J.D.Y., 1983, *Ijeshas and Nigerians: The Incorporation of a Yoruba Kingdom, 1890s–1970s*. Cambridge: Cambridge University Press.

Peil, Margaret, S.K. Ekpenyong, and O.Y. Oyeneye, 1988, "Going home: migration careers of Southern Nigerians", *International Migration Review*, 22, 563–585.

Pittin, Renee, 1984, "Migration of women in Nigeria: the Hausa case", *International Migration Review*, 18, 1293–1314.

Schlyter, Ann, 1990, "Women in Harare: gender aspects of urban–rural interaction", in J. Baker, (ed.), *Small Town Africa: Studies in Rural–Urban Interaction*. Uppsala: The Scandinavian Institute of African Studies.

Sudarkasa, N., 1973, *Where Women Work: A Study of Yoruba Women in the Market Place and in the Home*. Ann Arbor: Museum of Anthropology, University of Michigan.

Trager, Lillian, 1976–77, "Market women in the urban economy: the role of Yoruba intermediaries in a medium–sized city", *African Urban Notes*, 2, part 2, 1–9.

Trager, Lillian, 1981 "Customers and creditors: variations in economic personalism in a Nigerian marketing system", *Ethnology*, 20, 133–146.

Trager, Lillian, 1984, "Family strategies and the migration of women: migrants to Dagupan City, Philippines", *International Migration Review*, 18, 1264–1277.

Trager, Lillian, 1985, "From yams to beer in a Nigerian city: expansion and change in informal sector trade activity", in S. Plattner (ed.), *Markets and Marketing* (Monographs in Economic Anthropology No. 4). Lanham: University Press of America.

Trager, Lillian, 1987, "A re–examination of the urban informal sector in West Africa", *Canadian Journal of African Studies*, 2, 238–255.

Trager, Lillian, 1988, *The City Connection: Migration and Family Interdependence in the Philippines*. Ann Arbor: University of Michigan Press.

Trager, Lillian, 1992, "The hometown and local development efforts: implications for civil society in Africa", paper presented at the Conference on Civil Society in Africa, January 1992, Jerusalem.

Trager, Lillian, 1993, "Structural Adjustment and Local Development in Nigeria", paper presented at the Society for Economic Anthropology meetings, April 1993, Durham New Hampshire.

Vaa, Mariken, Sally E. Findley, and Assitan Diallo, 1989, "The gift economy: a study of women migrants' survival strategies in a low–income Bamako neighbourhood", *Labour, Capital and Society*, 22, 234–260.

Watts, Susan J., 1983, "Marriage migration, a neglected form of long–term mobility: a case study from Ilorin, Nigeria", *International Migration Review*, 27, 682–698.

Weisner, T., 1976, "The structure of sociability: urban migration and urban–rural ties in Kenya", *Urban Anthropology*, 5, 199–223.

Women in Rural–Urban Migration in the Town of Iwo in Nigeria

Lai Olurode

Though academic work on migration in Nigeria is indeed extensive, there is still none that is devoted exclusively to women. This should probably be expected. The tremendous social change throughout society has not been accompanied by a commensurate shift with respect to the perception of gender roles. This, in spite of the changes in Nigeria's economic base from being dependent on cash crops to oil revenues.

The question then is whether or not the set of changes and social values which were triggered off by the introduction of cash crops (cocoa, cotton, palm oil, rubber, etc.) were similar to the ones unfolding with the injection of vast and unprecedented oil revenues into the Nigerian economy? Whatever the change, my interest is on the effect of this change on perception of gender roles and on women's migration.

Much that has been written on migration simply excluded women as migrants on their own, or merely categorised them as dependent migrants and thus numerically insignificant for social analysis. For example, I often come across cases where women as wives join their husbands in the city.

This lacuna is ideological as well as historical. It derives from a body of ideas that has evolved in society from generation to generation. The world is a male-dominated one and more often scholars present only this one-sided view of the world because it is the one with which they are familiar. Most of the biases that are often observed in practice are based on culture.

Thus the typical reason for refusals by female respondents was the absence of the male head of household. For example, a demographer in Nigeria once recorded this experience:

> An illiterate woman aged 35 said that her husband was not in town and for this reason would not answer the questions. Although another four families answered the questions in the actual house, she said that her husband had told her never to answer any question without permission (Olusanya, 1985:81).

Even in popular fables, discussions and academic novels, women are expected not to be heard. They are only to be obedient to their husbands, keep good homes and look after their children (Obbo, 1980:ix–x and Ezeigbo, 1990:119–120).

It should now be understood why women as migrants have attracted little serious work of scholarship. This chapter should be regarded as an attempt to help fill this gap. Apart from this introductory section, there are four others. The second section discusses aspects of bias in migration studies. Some recent attempts to overcome this bias are briefly mentioned in section three. In section four, a profile of women migrants that were studied is presented as well as the research methodology. The last section contains the conclusions and there I spell out the main obstacles to independent migration by women in Nigeria. By independent migration, I mean the ability of women to exercise the right to decide when and where to migrate. Women's migrations often tend to be in association with that of their husbands.

ASPECTS OF BIAS IN MIGRATION STUDIES

There is an unpardonable bias in the presentation of migration studies. Some writers make no reference to women as migrants at all, whereas others refer to them as associational migrants. The pioneering work on rural–urban migration in Nigeria was essentially male-oriented (see, for example, Lloyd, 1967, Olusanya, 1969, and Adepoju, 1976). Writing about a typical migrant in the city, Lloyd said the following.

> In leaving his village society, the African becomes detribalised...The migrant, taking employment as a labourer in a large company or government department... But on arriving in the town, he will most probably have lodged with distant relatives or other people from his home community, and his behaviour towards these will follow that of the village (Lloyd, 1967:116–117).

There is no doubt that the author has in mind only a male as a migrant. Also writing about the migrant's relationship to the home areas, the following was written:

> He makes sure that he visits there at least once a year for the annual family reunion. In some cases, his children are sent there to live with relatives when they reach school age. He considers himself a failure in life unless he can erect a building of his own, superior in architectural design to the dwelling units in the lineage compound, or refashion the family house (Olusanya, 1969:343–344).

Thus, whenever migration is discussed in the academic literature on Nigeria, the reference is most often to males.

In most of the theoretical formulations on migration which have been advanced by scholars, a greater weight is patently given to economic considerations (see Todaro, 1968, Olusanya, 1969 and Caldwell, 1969). This economic theory of migration presents a number of hypotheses. The usual argument is that the disparity in economic conditions between two areas determines the direction of flow of migration.

Though Caldwell (1969) recognized that "no single feature of a rural area determines the volume of migrants travelling to the towns", he nevertheless asserted that "socially and economically advanced areas can produce a high proportion of young people who would prefer to work in the town" (p.55). Caldwell, however, cautioned that "no one factor can fully determine an individual's propensity to migrate... the application of any form of multifactorial analysis is fraught with difficulty, largely because it is impossible to define neatly the original condition of migrants" (p. 56).

The central element of the economic factor in migration was also empha-sized in the work of Olusanya (1969). Olusanya, however, pointed out that there are many factors that influence the decision to migrate. Some of these factors may be purely personal and others may be factors operating within the larger society. Some scholars prefer to stress the psychological factors (see Imoagene, 1967).

Bjerén (1971:29–30) has presented a restatement of this theory, when in reference to the historical development of Africa, she says that:

> Large-scale labour migration, and later rural–urban migration, started first in areas where European techniques of production and new cash crops were first introduced. Once the new crops and techniques had been established, these first-favoured areas developed at a rate much faster than the rest of the regions and... the economic differential between the earn-ings of subsistence farmers and wage labourers is considered to be the main factor behind African rural–urban migration.

Thus the division between town and country is said to be a major factor in migration. It is important to stress that a number of factors influencing the decision to migrate are endogamous, while there are others which may be regarded as exogamous. Among the factors in the former are scarcity of land, the desire to escape from the authority of elders, and rivalry between family members. The exogamous factors include colonialism, the degree of capitalist penetration and the exploitation of mineral resources. It needs to be said that these factors do not exert the same effect on the two sexes. A number of scholars have reminded us that there are also non-economic factors in opera-tion with regards to the decision to migrate (Norman, 1969).

Some of the non-economic factors that have received attention include socio-cultural factors such as the desire to escape from the traditional author-ity of the elders, and the lure of modern amenities, such as electricity, good roads, cinemas, telephones and so on.

Whatever the form of analysis that recent migration experiences in Africa take, such a discussion would be incomplete without reference to the impact of colonialism. Though there were large population settlements in Nigeria that preceded colonialism, migration into cities became pronounced with the establishment of administrative towns (political capitals) and commercial towns (Mabogunje, 1968 and Krapf-Askari, 1969).

In its development policy, the colonial regime favoured areas of intense cash crop production and mining centres, and these centres had the greatest concentration of social amenities. Railway lines and roads merely connected these centres to Lagos. The situation that emerged was one where an adminis-trative centre may be poorly connected to surrounding rural settlements but, nevertheless, well connected to major towns such as Lagos, Enugu or Kaduna.

When after independence the educated élites succeeded the colonial admin-istrators, they found it difficult to reverse an already entrenched practice which was to the benefit of those at the centre of power. For various reasons, the immediate beneficiaries of this process of lop-sided transformation were predominantly male. A few females managed to be incorporated into this process, either by engaging in independent political activities or by being mar-ried to men that had captured state power (Mba, 1982 and Olojede, 1990).

Given the fact that colonial policy favoured male as opposed to female migration, few women migrated to the cities. In most cases, there was not even marginal reference to them. More recently, however, a number of researchers have started to correct this imbalance in the presentation of reality which hitherto has excluded females. Not surprisingly, a majority of these pioneering works are by females themselves.

OVERCOMING THE GENDER BIAS

In a culture that has in-built prejudices against females, it is not surprising that women brought up under a male-dominated culture take up academic positions that further justify their unequal treatment. It was not expected that overcoming the bias that had developed over the years would be easy.

Initially, women were thought not to be fit for education as this may affect their reproductive capabilities (George, 1990). This was because:

> To be a woman is to be a mother. Whatever else she may do in the way of routine activities, and however else she may participate in society's life, her primary function is to reproduce (Murdock, 1937:37).

The result of this in-built bias is that:

> What women do is perceived as household work and what they talk about is called gossip, while men's work is viewed as the economic base of society and their information is seen as important social communication (Reiter, 1975:12).

One of the few earlier academic works to challenge the male preoccupation with themselves as the only ones who migrate was that of Christine Obbo (1980). The women to whom she spoke in her work also cherished power. They could achieve their aims through various strategies. Migration was one option and this enabled them to be mobile and also to "escape from obstacles to individual progress in favour of creating or taking up more options" (Obbo, 1980:5).

Generally, colonial policy was opposed to women as independent migrants. Obbo presented the general attitude toward migration as follows:

> Females migrating alone have always been seen as a problem by both urban authorities and migrant men.... urban migration is bad for women because it corrupts their virtue, leads to marital instability and erodes traditional norms. This leads to the weakening of the family structure, an increase in juvenile delinquency and violent crimes. But the worst perceived influence of the town is the idea that prostitution is encouraged among women. This seems to be the rationale for the preoccupation of the public and the law and policy makers with the problem of female migration. Branding female rural–urban migrants as prostitutes has been a strong weapon repeatedly used to discourage female migration (1980:26–28).

Through her research, however, Obbo was able to show that not all women who migrated to the towns of Uganda were "loose" women. A number of them accompanied their husbands, while a few migrated on their own. As for the reasons why the latter category of women migrated, such expressions as "to seek my fortune", "to improve my opportunities", and "to try my luck" were common. Yet, others migrated for reasons connected with sorcery, barrenness, divorce, for the desire to be able to read and write and for reasons of frustration with village life. There were others that migrated in order to "fish" out their husbands who had failed to return after a period of migration.

The edited work by Christine Oppong (1983) also contains chapters which specifically look at women as migrants to the cities of West Africa. In the same volume, Margaret Peil (1983) compared the social contacts which were established by men and women in six towns in Nigeria and The Gambia and concluded that when it comes to problem solving, men had more resources than women. But she concluded that the social networks which women and men engage in were similar.

The study by Gunilla Bjerén (1985) on Ethiopia also made reference to the place of gender in migration to Ethiopian towns. A number of the women studied were divorcees. The author noted as well that "women were an integral part of Ethiopian towns from their inception" (p. 159). The author also discussed a few factors that made it possible for women to use men in the town of Shashemene.

A most recent intervention at overcoming the evident bias against women in migration studies is that of Ann Schlyter (1990). Her focus was on Harare where she looked at the strategies being employed by poor women to improve, in particular, their living and housing conditions. She was critical of the situation where, while women had been *de facto* heads of households for half a century for reasons of male migration, "women were never recognized as such. A woman was under perpetuous supervision of a man—a father, husband, brother or son" (p. 183).

Schlyter presents three case studies which are indicative of the complex social circumstances which may dictate the decision to migrate. It could be because the migrant wishes to escape from being forced to marry someone, for reasons connected with childlessness, or because the woman became widowed. Some of the women lived up to the challenges of urban life. They engaged in purely urban networks by participating in political activities, being church members as well as belonging to neighbourhood or work-place associations. There were also cases where some women exploited, to their advantage, the rural–urban network.

Today, the realities of poor economic conditions in Africa are such that it is no longer possible for scholars to ignore the fact of women as independent migrants to the towns of Africa. The rural sector has suffered a serious decline which has made living there intolerable, not only for men but for women as well.

Theoretically, I am of the view that the shift of the revenue base of the town of Iwo, the study area, from cocoa to petroleum could probably have triggered off certain conditions that make people in this town more tolerant of women migrants than they would have been in the era of cocoa. Historically, oral tradition points out that apart from a few migrants from the middle-belt, there were not even many male migrants during the cocoa period (1920s–1950s). As cocoa is obviously different from oil, both will have generated different sets of social values.

PROFILE OF WOMEN MIGRANTS

Iwo: The research setting

Iwo, a predominantly Muslim society, is located in western Nigeria, north-east of Ibadan. It had a population of over 53,000 in 1962 and its present population is estimated at over 700,000 (see Oyo State *Abstract of Statistics, 1988,* for the most recent estimate). The first primary school in Iwo was established by the Baptist Mission in 1919. In 1927, a bridge was built across the main river, Odo Oba, and the town became linked with Ibadan, and thus with the outside world.

Mention needs to be made of two major international events that have shaped the development of the town. The town was first drawn into the global capitalist system of production and exchange during the British period when it became a centre for cocoa production for the world market.

Apart from cocoa, oil revenues have also influenced the transformation processes unfolding in Iwo. Nigeria's oil industry, though located hundreds of kilometres away from Iwo has definitely left its mark, and will continue to do so for a long time. Iwo has been the headquarters of a local government since 1976, and since then it has remained heavily dependent on financial subventions from the central government. Nigeria's oil revenues are recycled into the Iwo local economy. Iwo has shifted the basis of its dependence from cocoa to oil revenues (see Olurode, 1984 for details).

In 1970, more than 6,000 soldiers were garrisoned in Iwo, and again in 1972 an additional 5,500 soldiers were transferred there. For the first time in its history, a large number of migrants came to live in the town. During the duration of their stay of more than five years, there were widespread social dislocations and vast conflicts in social values, all of which have left their mark on social attitudes in Iwo.

At this point, it needs to be stressed that the Nigerian state is the main influence as to who migrates and in what direction, as the military posting mentioned above indicates. So also are specific acts of the state such as the local government reforms of 1976 and the creation of more states. Thus, unlike the period of cash crop production during which there was a good deal of voluntary migration into the regions of cash crop production, today state intervention in the realm of migration is more crucial than ever before. Government decisions to locate a project in one town and not another may have significant implications not only for migration but also for differences in the tempo of development between areas or towns of the country. Hence, the frantic fight among politicians and military men to ensure that a new government project is located in their part of the country.

Today, Iwo has 25 primary schools, 12 secondary schools, a post-secondary institution, two hospitals and several private clinics. It has facilities such as electricity and water supplies and roads which link it to the towns of Ibadan, Lagos, Osogbo, Oyo, Ile-Ife and Ejigbo.

But Iwo also has well over 200 Islamic institutions where pupils are taught the Islamic way of life. A few of those that attended such schools had no western education at all. Some women are also kept in purdah. There are some opportunities for self-employment outside teaching and the government service sector. There are small-scale industries such as brick-making, cassava processing and saw-milling.

Today, Iwo ranks third after Osogbo, and Ilesa in the new Osun State into which Oyo State was divided in August 1991. This latest political move will no doubt accelerate movement of people into Iwo.

It should be mentioned that in spite of its large population size, over 80 per cent of its male population practise peasant farming as a full-time or part-time occupation. Women are generally traders in farm crops, processed goods and imported items which are often sold in smaller units for a livelihood. Hence, the reference to Iwo as "urban" is misleading, as its urbanness is not defined according to occupational structure or population heterogeneity.

Research methodology

Because of my prior knowledge of Iwo, I suspected and found that there were not many women who would have been independent migrants. Since the universe of such women is small, a purposive sampling technique was employed. Women were selected whom I knew personally or through my informants to be independent migrants. A number of these women denied this description which, given the stigma attached to being alone, is understandable. A total of 55 such women were interviewed.

Research findings

The research findings have been summarised in table form. What follows is only a brief account of those findings.

Most of the women were aged 40–49 (41.8%), although a few (7.3%) were aged 20–29. The majority, about 70 per cent, were however above 40 years of age (Table 1).

They were mostly married (72.7%), although 3.6 per cent were divorced and the same number had re-married. Those who were single constituted 7.3 per cent (Table 2). There were more Christians than Muslims (Table 3). Trading was a major occupation of these migrant women (65.5%) and 14.5 per cent were teachers (Table 4).

More than a third had lived in Iwo for a period of 15–24 years, while 7.3 per cent had lived there for 25 years or more. About a third had been there for between 6–12 years (Table 5). More than two-thirds of the migrants came from other parts of the western region, while 1.8 per cent came from the north and 3.6 per cent from the east. The rest were immigrants from neighbouring African countries (Table 6). Those who said they came with their husbands were 38.2 per cent which we learnt to be untrue, 10.9 per cent said they came with relatives and 50.9 per cent did not reply to this question (Table 7). The latter category may be women who came with husbands but subsequently became divorced.

About three-quarters had visited home in the twelve months preceding the interview, while about a quarter had visited home more than a year previously. More than a third of them pay rent for their accommodation, while 21.8 per cent said that their husbands pay; 30.9 per cent obtained their accommodation through friends and with the help of relatives and 3.6 per cent live in their own houses (Table 8).

About 90 per cent earn more than 500 Naira monthly. This is well above Nigeria's average income of less than 300 Naira (Table 9). Most of the women live with their children and grandchildren. But not all those who claimed to have come with their husbands were actually living with them. Those who live alone constituted 14.5 per cent. Although those who replied positively (29.1%) to having plans to return home were more than those who responded in the negative (14.5%), a majority of them were yet undecided as to their future plans (Table 10).

Most had primary education though a few had more, and some were illiterates. About half had between 4–6 children while 9.1 per cent had seven children or more, 34.5 per cent had 1–3 children and 7.3 per cent had no children (Table 11).

DISCUSSION

As would be expected, most of these women had been married before. This explains the preponderance of those aged forty and over. Yoruba society, from where most of these women came, frowns on single women who migrate unaccompanied. So also does the dominant Islamic culture of the people in Iwo. It appears however that the town is more tolerant of women with children than those without. This may explain why the economic value to be derived from rents probably outweighs the prejudice that the town's landlords have for single mothers.

Only a few of these women had lived in Iwo for more than 25 years. Most were recent migrants. This finding supports our earlier stated theoretical position that oil wealth has opened up Iwo more than was possible during the cocoa era. A number of people had come to Iwo because of certain specific state interventions, and some because Iwo now offers a wide range of opportunities on a scale that had never been known before.

It is a sign of a significant change in social values that Iwo as a community tolerates these women who live on their own and also lets houses to them. This could have been because of greater religious tolerance than that which prevails in the north. It could be the result of economic pressure on landlords, some of whom were reported to be indebted to the banks. A third reason that has probably facilitated this process is the availability of houses on the outskirts of the town, and the availability of living quarters which were built by the local government authority. Finally, there is the often discussed concern on the part of the people from the town on the need to allow strangers to settle as a means of transforming the town economically; those who refuse to let out their apartments on flimsy grounds are nowadays regarded as retarding the town's development, so also are those who refuse to give up their land for development purposes. It is a common belief that migrants help to accelerate the tempo of development in any community as they create demands for goods and services. Generally, however, Yoruba women tend to gain in status as they grow older and have enhanced economic capacity. They could at that stage decide to live in their own built houses, separate from their husbands. We came across two instances in which husbands lived with their wives in the houses built by the latter. Though Yoruba women have a certain degree of

Table 1. *Age distribution*

Age	Frequency	Per cent
20–29	4	7.3
30–39	13	23.6
40–49	23	41.8
50+	15	27.3
Total	55	100.0

Table 2. *Marital status*

Status	Frequency	Per cent
Single	4	7.3
Married	40	72.7
Widowed	7	12.7
Re-married	2	3.6
Divorced	2	3.6
Total	55	100.0

Table 3. *Religion*

Religion	Frequency	Per cent
Christianity	28	50.9
Muslim	26	47.3
Others	1	1.8
Total	55	100.0

Table 4. *Occupational characteristics*

Occupation	Frequency	Per cent
Trading	36	65.5
Teaching	8	14.5
Others	11	20.0
Total	55	100.0

Table 5. *Length of stay in Iwo*

Length of stay	Frequency	Per cent
> 5 years	11	20.0
6–14 years	18	32.7
15–24 years	22	40.0
25 years and over	4	7.3
Total	55	100.0

Table 6. *Place of origin*

Origin	Frequency	Per cent
West	37	67.3
North	1	1.8
East	2	3.6
Others	15	27.3
Total	55	100.0

Table 7. *Person with whom the migrant came*

With whom	Frequency	Per cent
Husband	21	38.2
Relatives	6	10.9
No response	28	50.9
Total	55	100.0

Table 8. *Provision of accommodation*

By whom	Frequency	Per cent
Husband	12	21.8
By self	20	36.4
Friends/relations	17	30.9
Others	4	7.3
Own house	2	3.6
Total	55	100.0

Table 9. *Income per month*

Amount in Naira	Frequency	Per cent
201–499	6	10.9
500–799	24	43.6
800 and above	25	45.5
Total	55	100.0

Table 10. *Plan to return home*

Response	Frequency	Per cent
No	8	14.5
Yes	16	29.1
Undecided	31	56.4
Total	55	100.0

Table 11. *Number of children*

No of children	Frequency	Per cent
0	4	7.3
1–3	19	34.5
4–6	27	49.1
7 and above	5	9.1
Total	55	100.0

autonomy, the Iwo women studied have some constraints which are imposed by religion. Not a few of the town's women are kept in seclusion.

From my personal knowledge of the migrants and from their neighbours' accounts of them, these women migrated to the community alone. That they were unwilling to admit this, could be for fear that the government wants to deal strictly with unmarried mothers and this theme is often the subject of ridiculous debates on the radio and in the popular press. Children brought up by single mothers are often argued to be among the major causes of child delinquency and crime.

It is surprising that most of these women even visit home at all. However, as they earn a reasonable income, they may think that they have something to show for their "deviant" behaviour back in their hometown. It is even suspected that their estimated incomes may be on the low side. It is common for these women to combine a main occupation with others, such as being a schoolteacher and a hairdresser. The schoolteacher would employ someone to take care of the hairdressing business while she was away at school. If this schoolteacher were to come by a windfall, she would most likely invest this in expanding her hairdressing business. Peil (1981:159–163) found that nearly half of the Nigerian women in her sample agreed that they would use a windfall to expand their businesses. This was unlike their Gambian counterparts who would rather spend a windfall on food and clothing. This was less surprising as "Nigerian housewives were six times as likely as Gambian ones to aspire to trading if they could get capital to start" (Peil, 1981:159).

These women tend not to belong to the hometown associations which are often formed by men, and later joined by their wives who form the women's wing. As most of them did not belong to these associations, they are thus excluded from significant social contacts and resources that these associations do provide during periods of personal crises in the urban centres. It has been found that a large number of women in southern Nigeria participate more than their male counterparts in the new religious movements that are found mostly in the cities (Ludwar-Ene, 1991). These religious associations may be seen as an alternative to the hometown associations that are often dominated by men.

Even though some of these women do visit home, they are undecided as to whether and when they would return home permanently. This finding is unlike most of the findings on male migration in Nigeria in which men readily express a desire to retire to the hometown. As for women who are single mothers, they cannot be said to have a hometown as such. At marriage, a woman is often expected to move to her husband's residence. As over 70 per cent of these women have stayed in Iwo for more than fifteen years, it is not surprising that over 50 per cent are undecided whether to return home. The longer a migrant stays in a town the more likely he or she is to consider such a place as a permanent home. Also, over a third of the migrants have between four and six children who were probably born in Iwo and who may be attending schools there. This may constitute a factor in the decision to stay longer in a place. The status of the majority of these women as single mothers is another factor in the decision to stay longer and this creates a dilemma which may not make for a happy return to their birthplaces.

This dilemma for women migrants may mean either a longer period of stay in Iwo until it is possible to acquire sufficient money to build one's house in the hometown, or until one's children are able to do so, and are thus able to be shielded from insults.

The above discussion shows the kinds of constraints that women as independent migrants confront. Obbo (1980) also found that there was a general negative attitude toward female migration. Before we set out these constraints more fully, a case study will illustrate what it takes for a woman to be alone in Yoruba (Iwo) society.

Mama Wale, as she is called by neighbours, is 31 years of age and teaches in one of the primary schools as a grade two teacher. She finished school in 1983 and was transferred to Iwo in 1985. Here is the rest of her story:

> I had my first child in 1986 for a soldierman whom I met in Iwo in 1985. He has always lived in Port Harcourt, some three hundred or so kilometres away. He told me that his prospects for promotion will be narrow if it is known to his bosses that he is married. So I had to stay at Iwo. Also for reasons of his frequent transfer we both agreed that it was better for me to remain at Iwo because of future children.
>
> When I became pregnant for him I had to register myself in the hospital. I also had to pay the hospital fees. These were uncommon for a woman of my education. It is for the husband to do all these. He came on a visit when the pregnancy was three months old. By then my ears had become full of all sorts of stories from the so-called friends and neighbours. Some said it to my face that I had no husband and that I was expecting a child without a father. After all, a co-tenant in a similar position had regular visits from her husband who works in Ibadan.
>
> My mother was not happy about this development at all. She had hoped that I would be happier in marriage. How could I alone be carrying those financial burdens? It was enough for her that my husband's relations used to bring food from the village.
>
> It was after I had paid him a visit in Port Harcourt and there I met a woman who lived with him permanently that I then decided to divorce him at the customary court. This second baby of mine is for another person. He lives with his family in this town but at least I see him more often, unlike my former husband whom I see twice or thrice a year.
>
> But I must say that it is a bitter experience for a woman to stay alone—it brings insults and all sorts of male characters come to solicit for your friendship. Men just regard you as a free woman.

CONCLUSIONS: CONSTRAINTS ON FEMALE MIGRATION

It is possible to identify five major constraints which are socio-cultural, political, religious, legal and academic as well.

The socio-cultural elements have to do with the stigma that Yoruba society attaches to single parenthood, especially mothers and single girls. The young ones are taught from birth that a proper family life requires a man as the family head and the wife is only to play a supportive role. The head is the provider in the family. Migration is perceived as the pursuit of wealth and this falls within the domain of the head of the household.

Thus in spite of the shift from cocoa to oil, perceptions of gender roles have changed very little. Attitudes favourable to women as independent migrants are just beginning to develop. This slowly changing view of the world is reinforced by such other institutions as the religious institutions which are critical of single parenthood as it is a sign of social malady which may lead to the ruin of a nation. In contemporary Nigeria, there is a proliferation of new religious movements which, it is alleged, enjoy foreign financial support.

The school curriculum, especially the teaching of social studies still emphasizes that men are the heads of the households who provide for the members. A component of this social constraint is formal education itself in which women's participation is low and most of the job opportunities in the urban centres require formal education.

A related factor to the socio-cultural constraint is physical. Generally, until recently, men preferred to re-build their parents' houses which are often located in the older part of the town. Female migrants would hardly be tolerated in the older part of the town. And when physical development started on the outskirts of the town, the preference was for male migrants. Even in Lagos, this experience of a woman is not uncommon: "Do you know I had to tell my landlord that I was engaged before he agreed to rent out my flat" (*The Guardian*, Nigeria, 10 February, 1985).

In its attempt to control crime, the police may even arrest landlords that let accommodation to single women. One may not even be able to enjoy the society's sympathy for being so harassed by the police. Single women have lower status in society. Thus many women, in spite of being divorced from their husbands, still prefer to use their married names. This is partly to shield them from insults.

The second constraint is political. Men without women under their control and care are as well looked down upon and such men command little or no respect. If such men attempt to mediate in a conflict, such a remark as "even you who cannot control a woman" is common. This means that a man without at least one woman under his care cannot be an opinion leader. His views would hardly be respected by society and he may even be ridiculed by women as well.

A Ugandan female academic who divorced her first husband for a businessman once spoke to me about her experience with this new husband. Though they live apart as husband and wife, the new husband often complains about his wife's frequent trips abroad to attend conferences, which creates the impression that he has no control over her. Paradoxically, the businessman boasts to some people that his wife's trips abroad cost him so much. The husband was quoted as saying that he never knew he was getting married to a globetrotter as a wife. The husband, however, enjoys the prestige which the wife's frequent trips abroad confer since those who are widely travelled are respected for they are believed to have seen the world and are thus assumed to have better experience.

Also, since the migration of young male school leavers is more common, women remain the only resource that men as politicians can draw on. Men as politicians find it easier to coerce women to go and queue in all weather in order that they might vote for the predominantly male politicians. For men therefore to maintain their hegemony over Iwo, and indeed that of the larger society, they create obstacles for women as migrants both at the place of origin and at the point of destination.

There is also the religious constraint. Both Islam and Christianity stress that it is part of a woman's duty to minister unto her husband's needs. Iwo is a predominantly Islamic society and enrolment of girls in school is still low. It is unimaginable that girls without western education would migrate on their own or would be able to mobilize the technical and financial resources that migration entails. Some of the Muslims even keep their girls in purdah (in seclusion) before attaining the age of maturity. A woman's place is still believed by some to be in the home.

Migration on the part of the woman who is alone to the city would render more difficult this primary role of a woman. The belief is strong that men own their wives. This reminds me of a story that is often told as to why the railway line did not pass through Iwo town instead of about five kilometres south of Iwo. The chiefs of the town were said to have opposed this move because they feared that the train would take away their women.

A fourth constraint is legal. Nigerian statute books are full of laws which do not make for the wide participation of women in the process of social change. For example, laws on who is legally competent to sue as the head of the family or the one that can bail out an accused from police custody, discriminate against women. Moreover, men to the exclusion of women are landowners. It is for all these reasons that an expert on the subject commented recently as follows "... the Nigerian woman has been subjected to discriminatory and disadvantageous treatment in matters ranging from marriage, succession and other social rights" (Ibidapo-Obe, 1990:141).

Of course, there are patently academic constraints as we have shown in the section on gender bias in migration studies. The production of social knowledge that focuses only on a part in order to explain the whole even though it often claims to be explaining the complex whole is falsification of such knowledge. Academics must seek to present the complex social realities and not merely reproduce the usual and familiar stereotypes and prejudices which, though they may conform to the dominant populist expectations, may not be true.

References

Adepoju, A., 1976, "Some Aspects of Migration and Family Relationships in South-West Nigeria", *Seminar on Rural and Urban Family Life in West Africa*. Legon: University of Ghana.

Bjerén, G., 1971, *Some Theoretical and Methodological Aspects of the Study of African Urbanization*, Research Report No. 9. Uppsala: Scandinavian Institute of African Studies.

Bjerén, G., 1985, *Migration to Shashemene: Ethnicity, Gender and Occupation in Urban Ethiopia*. Uppsala: Scandinavian Institute of African Studies.

Caldwell, J.C., 1969, *African Rural–Urban Migration: The Movement to Ghana's Towns*. Canberra: Australian National University Press.

Ezeigbo, T., 1990, "Women and Social Change in Nigeria: A Literary Perspective", in Lai Olurode (ed)., *Women and Social Change in Nigeria*. Lagos: Unity Publishing and Research Co. Ltd.

George, U., 1990, "Theoretical Positions on Gender Roles in Society", in Lai Olurode (ed.), *Women and Social Change in Nigeria*. Lagos: Unity Publishing and Research Co. Ltd.

Ibidapo-Obe, A., 1990, "Aspects of Law and the Changing Status of Women in Nigeria", in Lai Olurode (ed.), *Women and Social Change in Nigeria*. Lagos: Unity Publishing and Research Co. Ltd.

Imoagene, O., 1967, "Psycho-Social Factors in Rural–Urban Migration", *The Journal of Economic and Social Studies*, 9, 3.

Krapf-Askari, E., 1969, *Yoruba Towns and Cities: An Enquiry into the Nature of Urban Social Phenomena*. London: Clarendon Press.

Lloyd, P.C., 1967, *Africa in Social Change*. Harmondsworth: Penguin Books.

Ludwar-Ene, G., 1991, "Spiritual Church Participation as a Survival Strategy among Urban
    Migrant Women in Southern Nigeria", in G. Ludwar-Ene (ed.), *New Religious Movements
    and Society in Nigeria*. Bayreuth: Bayreuth African Studies, Series 17.
Mabogunje, A.L., 1968, *Urbanization in Nigeria*. London: London University Press.
Mba, N.E., 1982, *Nigerian Women Mobilized: Women's Political Activity in Southern Nigeria,
    1900–1965*. Berkeley: University of California.
Murdock, G.P., 1937, "Comparative Data on the Division of Labour by Sex", *Social Forces,*
    17.
Norman, D.W., 1969, "Economic and Non-Economic Variables in Village Surveys", *Rural
    Africana*, no. 8, Spring.
Obbo, C., 1980, *African Women: Their Struggle for Economic Independence*. London: Zed
    Press.
Olojede, I., 1990, "Women, Power and Political Systems", in Lai Olurode (ed.), *Women and
    Social Change in Nigeria*. Lagos: Unity Publishing and Research Co. Ltd.
Olurode, Lai, 1984, *Social Structure and Spatial Form: A Case Study of a Nigerian Town*
    Working Paper no. 8, Urban and Regional Studies. Brighton: University of Sussex.
Olusanya, P.O., 1969, *Socio-Economic Aspects of Rural–Urban Migration in Western Nigeria*.
    Ibadan: Nigerian Institute of Social and Economic Research.
Olusanya, P.O., 1985, *A Handbook of Demographic Research Methods for African Students*.
    Lagos: Olu-Nla Publications.
Oppong, C., (ed.), 1983, *Female and Male in West Africa*. London: Allen and Unwin.
Peil, M., 1981, *Cities and Suburbs: Urban Life in West Africa*. New York: Africana Publishing
    Company.
Peil, M., 1983, "Urban Contacts: A Comparison of Women and Men", in C. Oppong (ed.),
    Female and Male in West Africa. London: Allen and Unwin.
Reiter, R.R., (ed.), 1975, *Towards an Anthropology of Women*. London: Monthly Review
    Press.
Schlyter, A., 1990, "Women in Harare: Gender Aspects of Urban–Rural Interaction", in
    Jonathan Baker (ed.), *Small Town Africa: Studies in Rural–Urban Interaction*. Uppsala:
    Scandinavian Institute of African Studies.
Todaro, M.P., 1968, "A Model of Labour Migration and Urban Unemployment in Less Devel-
    oped Countries", *American Economic Review*, 59, 1.

The Girls of Nyovuuru[*]

Dagara Female Labour Migrations to Bobo-Dioulasso

Jean-Bernard Ouedraogo

Migration studies have characterized Burkina Faso as a country subject to strong migrations, but the considerable volume of literature on the subject has almost always neglected the role of women. With respect to their volume, migrations are men's business: the latest population census, from 1985, reports a ratio of 130 males per 100 females among internal migrants, and 349.1 males per 100 females among international migrants. "The majority of persons migrate in search of work, and these migrations are essentially composed of men" (Institut National, 1990). It is also stressed that female migrations are closely linked to male movements: women merely accompany their husbands and appear to have no real dynamic or strategic autonomy. The figures seem to confirm this passivity of Burkinabè women. But has the reality of migration ever been examined in another way?

One credible hypothesis states that migratory movements are subject to history, the history of African social formations, and that the unfolding of this historic process determines the interaction of the various components of those societies. Women are also subject to this rule, despite being left out in limbo for a long time, women are now more clearly proclaiming their own identity.

In this sense, studying the degree of autonomy of women provides the opportunity to understand the mechanisms of geographic mobility and also the modalities of an undeniable social change. But what relationships can be established between migration and the Dagara country?

We may also ask under what conditions are this society's traditional collective migrations being perpetuated today? It seems that the central issue here, is to grasp the meaning of the shifts in female population, primarily from the Dagara Dissin area towards Bobo-Dioulasso—shifts which are singular both in form and content. What makes Dagara women migrate more than other women, given that female labour migration is rare in Burkina Faso? Dagara girls, together with perhaps Dogon girls, who migrate to Ouagadougou, emerge as pioneers. Is the flow of female migration taking on an identity of its

---

[*] a Dagara word which can mean both 'economy' and 'well-being'.

own? Is this due to the particular nature of the aspirations which feed it, or to the form of professional integration at the place of destination? In which ways are female strategies deployed? In response to which social constraints? And, finally, can we, on the basis of these migrations, attempt to understand the process of increasing autonomisation of women as being a response to specific contradictions within a Dagara social structure which is undergoing change?

This chapter does not survey the entire Dagara country. The girls interviewed come from the villages of Ouéssa, Nakar, Tangsebla, Benvar, and from Dissin town itself (Map 1). This Dagara area has a predominantly young population, with the exception of Dissin town, which has an ageing population. Population density is high, (nearly 80 inhabitants per km²) but that is true of a wider area and is not specific to the Dagara country. In the 1985 census, the 2350 migrants in Bougouriba Province were all heading for town. In the absence of statistics it is impossible to furnish a quantitative estimate of female migrations and many factors concerning destinations, length of stay, and employment remain unknown. This chapter is based on information drawn from about twenty interviews carried out between April and September 1992.[1]

Map 1.   *The study region, south-western Burkina Faso*

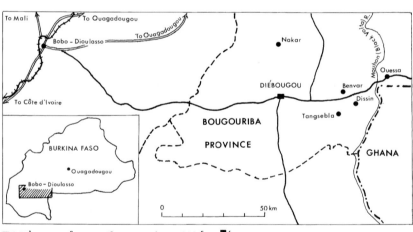

THE CUL-DE-SAC FOR WOMEN ON THE DAGARA 'OLD PATH'

The Dagara are an ethnic group whose territory stretches over both banks of the Black Volta river, called Mouhoun in Burkina, which constitutes a natural frontier between Ghana and Burkina-Faso. It has been established that the Dagara on the left bank of the Mouhoun migrated by crossing the river in the course of the 19th century. Some writers, (Hébert, 1976), however, suggest that this mobility of the Dagara people may go back to the 13th century and that they may then have originated on the Atlantic coast. The reasons behind this first migration have not been clearly established, but researchers have indicated that the new Dagara domestic units, in their search for independence, and fearing excessive authority, moved away from the 'mother house'. In their own language, 'Da-gara' can be taken to mean 'rebellious man'.

Traditionally, the Dagara are farmers, herders, and hunters. Like the other peoples of the 'Lobi branch', the Dagara have never formed an organized political state. Dagara community life never evolved a real centralised political hierarchy, on an ethnic, regional, or even village level (see Savonnet, 1976:23–40).

Dagara socio-political structure is segmentary. Kinship is the chief regulator of social life. Kinship is dual in nature and the agnatic axis is combined with the uterine axis, resulting in a form of filiation which requires the Dagara to subscribe to dual membership. He is simultaneously attached to his mother's clan—the matriclan—by the uterine link, and also to his father's—the patriclan—by the agnatic link.

The dual nature of the social membership has multiple consequences for the individual. First, on the level of his identity, for, in addition to the personal name, *yuor*, and the religious name, *sighaa*, there are two other frames of nominal reference: the *doglu* name, which is common to all members of the patriclan, and the *bellu* name, common to all descendants of the same matriclan. The *bellu* is exclusively transmitted by the women. In line with this same social logic, the system of transfer of wealth also bears the hallmark of this system of double descent.

Dagara social organisation states that long-life immovable goods such as land and its produce, houses, as well as certain social positions such as religious or divinatory roles are the property of the patriclan. The matriclan, for its part, can only transmit short-lived goods such as cattle and money, for it possesses neither land, nor houses. Interference of the mother and her clan might lead to the conclusion that they were pre-eminent in the Dagara social system. This point gives rise to numerous discussions seeking to establish whether the type of kinship which predominates in Dagara country is matrilineal or patrilineal. One of the forms of matrilineal intervention is the special relationship which links the uncle to his sister's son—his uterine nephew. The maternal uncle believes he can be certain that his nephew is really of his own blood—something which he cannot confirm concerning his own direct descendants.

The woman, as the means of reproduction of the groups, is the most precious object in the social exchange system. The definition of the terms of exchange of this particular form of wealth is a political act regulating potential conflict relationships between patrilineages. As Mauss has already observed, "both morality and economics intervene in these transactions" (1968:148).

As the object of a clan transaction, and exchanged for material compensation, the Dagara woman is made community property. The virilocal form of Dagara marriages makes her a stranger in her husband's clan. Since she is never integrated into the husband's clan, she will, until death, remain linked to her original clan, which she may rejoin at any time, yet this original clan is also structured by male domination. "She is 'present' in the clan", Balandier stresses, "but in terms of a communal female with limited capabilities, termed 'stranger-wife', she is confined to a domestic universe. Conditionally linked to the place in which she does not reside (her group of origin), she is virtually isolated there where she resides (her allegiance group)" (1974:41). This ambivalent situation has social and economic consequences in daily life for the Dagara woman. Being a possession herself, she does not inherit, except small things from her mother or sister. By virtue of her foreign status, she owns no fields of her own, and in most cases, her economic activities are under her husband's control. On the other hand, domestic work is her exclusive domain, and, in conformity with a sexual division of labour, the man does the clearing and ploughing in the fields, while the women sow, plant, and harvest. In the non-agricultural domain, certain handicrafts are allotted to her. Traditionally, unmarried girls would 'steal' a little of the harvest on the way home from the fields, which they then used in their money-earning activities. From such activities they were able to derive an income which, though insufficient, still guaranteed them a small degree of financial independence. But today, the arrival of imported goods, new lifestyles, and male competition are considerably reducing their economic scope. It must, however, be stated that the structurally marginal place of women within the traditional social system of production and distribution of material goods and positions of prestige does allow them a relatively free sentimental life within the institution known as *sesenu*. According to this custom, the Dagara woman has the right to freely choose boyfriends, who give her shea butter (*sumbala)*, millet for preparing millet-beer (*dolo)*, and invite her out to 'cabarets'. Generally, this sentimental freedom never goes as far as extra-marital sexual relationships, which are prohibited and severely punished. From it, the woman will derive an emotional well-being, a significant compensation for the constraints of clan-made marriage. But she will not be alone in benefiting from this customary arrangement, for, the husband's clan can heighten the value of this special form of property, the married woman, by accumulating external resources, and by partly divesting itself of certain specific requirements of the wife's.

This 'sentimental friendship' can also become a sexual freedom granted to the 'two friends'. This is a case of *sesen sebla* or 'black sentimental friendship'. The 'black friend' is the man who, because he has been so helpful and has given so many presents to his girlfriend, gets her husband's permission to share her bed. On close examination, we see that this curious custom seems to imply that, beyond a certain limit, an essentially free gift shifts in nature so as to require a counter-gift. The woman derives her status from a transaction, and therefore is deemed to have a material and moral value. The significant 'down payments' of the 'black friend' are also evaluated and this necessarily leads to a socially-inscribed value of these 'gifts', the absence of which would risk devaluing the value-system on which the 'proprietary rights' to the acquired goods, the woman, are founded.

Is it really a question of 'gift' and 'counter-gift', a social exchange, if we examine the *sesenu* mechanism of compensation? The deed of transfer is not free of charge despite the investments which brought it about, and the value of the compensation is established with regard to the social status of both the legal husband and the 'lover-candidate'. Thereafter, the woman may receive her 'lover' freely, but the children of their union belong to the legal husband as a right. It is clearly visible in this rule of exchange that the woman is a means to regulate the relationships between groups, and this makes it possible to go beyond individual cases in the application of the economic, legal and moral rules which guarantee social harmony. Female Dagara are subject to very strong male political domination, though this is masked by undeniably egalitarian social relationships which, however, are sexually stratified to the advantage of men. There is, for example, a Dagara saying which states: "one man is not held higher than another man; one woman is not held higher than another woman".

This original social structure in which a woman was allotted a status of dominee while enjoying, within this domination, a relative degree of freedom and a certain social value in one respect, is experiencing serious turbulences due to the combined action of colonisation, evangelisation, and present-day transformations of the Burkinabè rural environment. The colonial system, by imposing an external political framework, by employing outsiders *(mande-dyula)* to administer indigenous populations, as well as by an enforced regroupment policy, attempted to establish an efficient colonial framework for the Dagara populations. The colonial power sought to replace the genealogically-based clan units by territorially-based village units. This colonial intervention at all levels was, by reorganizing the territory, simultaneously changing Dagara social organisation and beginning to undermine the clan's traditional social control structures. The impact of evangelisation by the White Fathers and the widespread conversion to Catholicism were decisive factors of social change in Dagara country. Madeleine Père (1988:105) draws attention to the opportunist nature of the Catholic missions which took advantage of the social fragility resulting from various conflicts the country experienced with its neighbours. The first missionaries arrived in the Dissin region in 1933.

These foreigners came and imposed profitable agriculture, a money-based social life, and new norms for the conduct of communal affairs. The Church instated the monogamous family model, a new morality in male-female relationships taught in home-care centres, and required its faithful to avoid initiation ceremonies. Here again, we have an instance of the exercise of symbolic violence towards local populations recently subjected to military violence. "The European Missionary", Linton remarks, "is always at pains to put forward his beliefs and his own rites in their original form and is always upheld by the prestige connected with everything European—when the latter is not being imposed by more direct agents, in such a way that, if the natives adopt the new faith, they have to take it on in the exact form presented to them, (1968:386)." The consequence of all these changes is the gradual and irreversible destruction of the old social relationships, especially of the rules which govern the life of the lineages. The changes all aim to help Dagara country to 'evolve' towards western-type structures or attitudes. There is 'progress' from clan to household. The joint clan, spanning several generations, is tending to be replaced by the western-style household. The *yir*, the basic family community[2], is splitting up to produce smaller domestic units that are, above all, jealous of their recently acquired economic independence. One can easily understand how this process of separation exacerbates the pressure which the new head of the household brings to bear on those directly under his authority, i.e., chiefly upon the young and women. The spirit of calculation brought in by the spread of monetary exchanges undermines the spirit of brotherhood and fosters individualism, which leads to many break-ups. But as yet, the new configurations under construction have not laid down either a stable framework or, more importantly, a mode of social regulation. Not everything is disappearing, but everything is undergoing transformation.

In the new social units, some traditional rules of social constraint are being maintained as instruments of accumulation for the benefit of the new domestic authorities, which themselves are under increasing pressure due to the impoverishment of the countryside. The already unenviable situation of women is being extended into a second, perhaps even stronger degree of marginalisation. Their position as structural dominees is reproduced in the new society, leaving them with very few opportunities for accumulating personal wealth, because they feel perhaps more strongly than ever the pull of modern life. A recent study claims that "a woman works twice as hard as a man and earns twice as little," (Dabire, 1984:106). How does one improve one's lot, if the social environment sets firm limits on economic emancipation? Excluded from the ownership of the means of production, and kept away from indispensable rural modernisation (agricultural techniques, credit/loan systems, the commercialisation of cotton and groundnuts), women are obliged to find other strategies for self-advancement. Emigration has become a sort of new female 'industry'. But what do they have to offer in that universe where exchange is the rule? The policies aiming at female emancipation constantly face traditional resistance to the new vocation of the Dagara 'old path'. Trapped within this double marginalisation, the politically and economically dominated women, particularly the younger ones, find their status as 'outsiders' more and more unbearable and, by emigrating, reject it. Will they succeed in altering the course of the 'old path', of tradition, towards new routes to emancipation?

Perhaps emigration will enable young women to gain a new social identity?

FEMALE ESCAPE: NOTIONS, OPPORTUNITIES AND MEANS

The routes used by women to escape from their downgraded economic and social situation are multiple. Because it is rooted in social contradictions, when geographic mobility takes on a migratory form it traces out a variety of patterns, thus allowing us to measure the extent and depth of the migratory process, viewed as an expression of the transformations taking place in the Dagara social system.

The primary lever of the migratory movement is the establishment of a special relationship with the 'outside'. This connection contributes to building up a social representation of mobility and of its characteristics—some of which is real, and most of which is dreamt up. An understanding of this process will enable us to examine the mechanisms which do not necessarily generate excursions out of the homeland, but which encourage their emulation.

TOWARDS ANOTHER WORLD, IN THE WAKE OF THE PASSERS-BY

> Yes, I know some people who have already come to Bobo: my brothers who were on the way from Côte d'Ivoire and the girls from Ghana who were passing through our village (Jeanne, 23, maid).*

> ...some of our family-people were coming back from Côte d'Ivoire, they were bringing me shoes, so I realised there is another world, better than my village. And also, there were the stories of the older girls who had already gone to the town (Marie, 20, waitress).

> I was fascinated by the way of dressing and the style of my friends who were returning from the town, especially the boys coming back from Côte d'Ivoire, so I said to myself, there is a world that's different from my village" (Caroline, 20, waitress).

> I used to see these girls coming back from Bobo and talking about this town. I saw they had succeeded in their life, 'cos they had nice clothes, they were shining (Perpetua, 24, waitress).

> Me, I was born in Ouaga; my father was a civil servant; due to the revolution he was laid off, so he takes us back to the village, but I couldn't live there no longer (Laure, 18, waitress).

> Since my early age, I was in Bobo, at a cousin's, as housemaid; now, he is in Ouaga with all his family. After, he took me back to the village, I spent a bit of time there and I came back here (Eugenie, 21, salesgirl).

The desire to migrate springs from the evolution of the social structure as well as from the constraints which face young Dagara girls. But, in order for this desire to be translated into an actual change of place, through migration, there needs to be some focus on a locality, some particular perspective from which the new space can be compared with the old in such a way that its characteristics are measured up against the goal of resolving the contradictions in present experience.

Female migrations reproduce a traditional migratory process, which at first pertained to men, but is nowadays undergoing change induced by an independent dynamism and leading to its reproduction in a broader context.

As is often the case, through the dissemination of an urban ideal, the first migrants draw other young people into migrating. The accounts of the young girls' journeys demonstrate, however, that there are typically female routes. Civil servants exploit family networks to obtain the services of a 'sister' as housemaid, or again, the long-standing flow of girls coming from Ghana who provide a model, if not a guarantee, of potential female dynamism.

The special attraction of Bobo-Dioulasso, which remains the preferred destination of the young Dagara, might be explained in terms of the conjunction of three factors. The first is historical: it is an old, cosmopolitan merchant town with a degree of social tolerance not found in the austere Mossi capital of Ouagadougou; second, it is a compulsory stop en route to Côte d'Ivoire— a rail link was established in 1954; and, third, one can conjecture that the market for small jobs there is less subject to monopoly forces than in the capital, since this type of activity only figures to a very minor extent in secondary towns. One may also hypothesise that a special concentration of former Dagara migrants in the bar sector may make it easier for the migrant women to gravitate towards those jobs. Our research has not yet studied in depth these structural effects upon the birth and development of female labour migrations. Whatever the circumstances, the town appears to be the most accessible path to 'well-being', to the resolution of the contradictions of vil-

---

* The names given here are fictitious, but the ages and occupations are real.

lage life, and, if we observe those who are thinking of leaving for Bobo, it is the obvious solution. As we have seen, the young Dagara girls confronted by the social obstacles to their advancement are left vulnerable and are tempted to follow the example of those men who left much earlier in search of 'well-being'.

THE OCCASIONS FOR LEAVING: BRINGING ABOUT A SOLITARY ESCAPE

I prepared *dolo* to get my transportation costs (Claire, 22, waitress).

I made *dolo* and doughnuts for quite a while to be able to pay my fare (Sidonie, 17, waitress).

In the village, making *dolo* and doughnuts is the way for women to earn money. But often, they sell at a loss, which means they can't afford to buy what they want, unless it's near a feast like Easter or Christmas. They have very little scope, so they get married very early and the problems start. I didn't want to suffer the same fate, so I decided to go to town, because my friends coming back from there were fine and brought back all sorts of stuff with them (Eveline, 22, waitress).

One of the village schoolteachers took advantage of me. He'd even promised to marry me and some time later I was left with a child which he won't recognise; (...) Three years later, my mother suggested I go to town to find a way of taking care of my child because, having no father, life was very hard for us (Rose, 22, waitress).

My parents arranged to marry me to a man who was much older than me but I didn't want, so I decided to run away from all the bad spells, 'cos I could be poisoned or killed. I tried a first time: my father threatened to kill me. So this time, I decided to go very far away, to the town, to get the money to repay the dowry and get free from that engagement (Ziem, 21, waitress).

I was on the way to Abidjan with my husband: once in Bobo we had an argument about another man and he told me he couldn't go on with me and to go back to the village. So I decided to take the child back to the village and to come back alone so as to get some clothes. It's mainly for the pagnes (loincloths) that I came here (Tina, 21, waitress).

... because of the tale-telling in Dissin, I didn't want to stay there. People are too nosey about other people's business. Dissin people criticise too much. If you do something today, tomorrow people are talking about it (Charlotte, 22, waitress).

Also, there were problems I didn't know about: my mother was pregnant before her marriage: when her friend came to pay the dowry, his parents refused because they wanted to claim the child. One of my mother's brothers offered to give his name for the birth certificate. That child was me. So I lived with the family of my mother who later married the same young man. I had a child by a young Dagara boy. The child got sick and they advised us to go to the local medicine-man. But unfortunately, the child died. A friend brings the corpse to his home; his parents chase us away, the child doesn't belong to them; at my place, they tell me I don't belong there. I cried, and afterwards, my uncles buried the body.(...) My mother advised me to leave my boyfriend, but here in Bobo we still go together, but he doesn't want me to work in the bar; but he, he hasn't got a job, how are we going to live without any money? (Marie, 21, waitress).

Barbara Hagaman (1977) has no doubt exaggerated the part that *dolo* plays in establishing a female power-group in Lobi country, an ethnic group with a social system similar to that of the Dagara. As we have seen, the mode of regulation of political power leaves little leeway. One must not, however, lose sight of the contribution, however minimal, which these activities make to the lives of these women as the Dagara economic structure leaves them with few opportunities. In the case of *dolo*-making, for instance, the proliferation of brew-houses, which reflects women's growing need for money, is reducing the profit-margins; today, a single production will barely bring in between 500 CFA and 1000 CFA. In this formerly exclusively female domain, men are appearing with proposals to create modernised 'cabarets' and to subcontract to the female beer makers. The same can be seen in the harvesting of karite and shea* beans, where men are intervening more and more to take control of this produce, which has a high export-value. There is a gradual intensification of the domination and exploitation of women, and this nullifies opportunities which used to be in their favour.

The obstacles take various forms. Faced with an impasse, women have a number of strategies at their disposal, and migration will be an ultimate recourse in this desire to escape. One thing, however, must be underlined: experience, under these conditions, is not always personal and direct; it is diffuse, collective, and each one deals with it according to her own capacities. In this confusing context, the mothers and the elders act as privileged consultants who attempt to link the old structures with the new. Early marriage is the first choice, but such matrimonial strategies do not always have a happy ending. For instance, a young village-girl may naively invest in a match with a school-teacher, or the family may plan a marriage with a migrant without taking into account the possible discrepancies between the collective ideal and individual plans, especially if, as is often the case, urban life has been experienced before the contract is made. "Discord" must be kept concealed. This discrepancy is revealed by the incompatibility between sexual freedom and the strict system of customary regulation. Adultery[3] is severely punished in Dagara country, and disregard of the rules leads to an immediate, but maybe momentary, severing of marital bonds. The gap between the widespread practice of sexual freedom and the constraints of collective censorship via gossiping, is reason enough to run away. The necessity of putting geographic distance between oneself and one's home-community may become evident under more dramatic circumstances. The contradictions inherent in the kinship system can lead to instances of total exclusion. Such a tragedy becomes an even more intense experience when a bereavement and a difficult love-affair are piled on top of it. The last case-history, Marie's, is a good illustration of the way in which the old laws are being modified, in the old social exchange system, owning a wife was an asset for the clan, but nowadays, it has a reduced value.

"Man means wealth" goes a Dagara proverb, and in that context, ethnic endogamy is still in fashion. For example, a child born of a Turka father does not belong to that community, it will go to enrich another; it does not enter into the logic of the clan. The impossible love affair with the taximan makes her return to the village premature, and so staying in town becomes compulsory.

These departures from the norms demonstrate how women are gradually deviating from the 'old path', but we do not yet know their new destination(s). We have the feeling that, despite their evident desires to break away, and perhaps because of them, these ruptures will never be more than partial; their identities are still largely centred on the old society. 'Final' liberation from the past must follow ancestral paths. "Buying" one's own freedom, which is allowed for under Dagara jurisdiction, is the true means to enfranchisement, and migration serves this purpose.

---

*   African locust tree beans (parkia biglobosa)

DEPARTURES: THE INDIVIDUAL FACETS OF A COLLECTIVE ENTERPRISE

Yes, I left without telling my parents, but my girlfriends knew I wanted to go to Bobo. They weren't happy about it (Eugenie, 27, waitress).

My parents said OK, but the only thing they told me was: find what I've gone to find, so I don't destroy myself; roughly speaking what they meant to say was, that I should not go to 'pull the curtain' (Caroline, 18, waitress).

They thought, like me, that with my School Certificate I was going to find work (...) my mother gave me some charms to protect me (Elene, 20, maid).

Every time, my mother didn't stop reminding me I have to go to the town to find work to help them. For my transportation, she made me prepare *dolo* three times (Caroline, 20).

Because I was running away, my mother couldn't give me nothing to protect me, and if my father finds out she was in the know, she'd be driven away from the family (Ziem, 21, waitress).

I told my parents before I came. My father is dead and my mother had no objections; she advised me to come back to get married. When I was coming, my mother took me along to my uncle's and he gave me his blessing (Catherine, 21, waitress).

I told them I was coming to continue my studies (Agnes, 17, waitress).

My grandmother told my sister to not get married, to not suffer, and to go to the town to get work (Perpetua, 20, waitress).

My father didn't want, he thought I was too young, so I told him I was coming to my uncle's and not to worry (Marie, 17, waitress).

The discussions concerning the last remaining links with the village show that mobility is both a break-off point and a new strategy for survival—the plan to migrate is a social plan. The clandestine organisation of the departure is itself a proof of the extent of female solidarity, the men are often opposed to migration. The accomplices are female: the circle of girlfriends who do not betray, together with the mother, who is an accomplice in her heart, at least.

The migration undertaken by the migrant is a collective enterprise, for it associates the domestic unit which is seeking to arm itself against the ups and down of modern life. The urgency with which the plan to migrate is invoked makes its success a shared dream. Migration paves the way for the future, and expresses the expectation of a positive reconstitution based on an idealized model: to get married, to get stable, paid employment. This future is equally impregnated with old values, for within it we recognise the traditional role-distributions.

We have not sufficiently stressed the importance of the female ties of solidarity. Where the grandmother, the 'sister' according to the classification by generation, is absent, that link is broken. One has to go along with a different life-stream. Female mobilisation brings out the influence of the elders on their juniors; the mothers and grandmothers have deeper dreams, and promote a joint ambition for social success. Such an ambition corresponds to their social functions, since they have the duty to promote the lives of the children, especially the girls, and to prepare their futures, hopefully better than their own.

This complicity in migration, however, remains perfectly moral in nature. The town is a means to attain the predefined goal of well-being; it must not destroy that which the village has built up for the good of all. The town must not alienate morality: one must not 'draw the curtain' (this expression means to become a prostitute) on the fundamental values of the 'old path'. Herein arises an opposition between what was laid down in the past, and the demands of the new rules of life.

A NEW SOLIDARITY OF THE EXCLUDED

Migration is an uprooting, but at the same time, it is the occasion to adopt a new social and spatial identity, temporarily at least. Just as the separation can be painful, so too, settling in town, in Bobo-Dioulasso, is fraught with difficulties. Coming from Dissin, how does one cope with urban life?

THE KEYS TO THE TOWN

...my luck: a young man I knew took me to some girlfriends who had rented a house together, friends from the village who left before I did. I had a little money, but my girlfriends gave me food until I found work (Eugenie, 27, waitress).

I was put up at my direct uncle's, my father's brother (...). I did not suffer hardship because I was at my uncle's. I didn't pay for house or food or water (Eveline, 18, waitress).

I was staying at a first cousin's, quite all right, in spite of the small problems I had with his wife who wanted me to work for her. She couldn't admit that I could sleep there for free without doing nothing and going to work somewhere else (Aghate, 20, maid).

First, I was at my cousin's; she works at the cash-desk. A little while later, she found me a job with a French couple (Rose, 20, waitress).

I did not know where my friend lived. The driver proposed to shelter me until I find her (...). I then realized that he wanted to use me; he wasn't married. He promised to find me a job. Meanwhile, I had to put up with his whims. I was sleeping with him for a month (Ziem, 21, waitress).

When I arrived I looked for a friend to stay with her. Later on I left her for my own house, because I had a boyfriend who paid the rent (Solange, 22, waitress).

I use to live at my uncle's, one day we came close to fighting with his wife, so I preferred to rejoin my elder sister who is married here (Andréa, 22, salesgirl).

"Good luck", when reaching the town, is to be able to avail oneself of an established network of old acquaintances. Kinship is highly valuable in the first period of settling down in town. In the old context, it would seem that distance does not diminish the strength of kinship bonds. Present-day migratory experience reveals other aspects of kinship availability. The extended family is narrowing down, often becoming limited to the family of procreation. In the management of daily life, the newly-arrived girl appeals to this new-style family. Yet its availability is not unlimited, for the emergence of the nuclear family is a powerful counterpoint in opposition to the old solidarity bonds. The "new paths" are narrower, whereas the old paths, though broader, stop short. The standards of hospitality and of clan solidarity are undergoing change in response to availability in urban life, which is sometimes individualistic, and often money-based.

Exposed to risks and exploitation by their forerunners, the lonely young girls form new groups, and forge new bonds of solidarity with their workmates.

FINDING WORK: A STAGE OF FREEDOM OR OF EXPLOITATION?

I'm a waitress. I got this job through my girlfriends (Rose, 27, waitress).

I'm a waitress at the 'Trinity Bar', I found this job by myself (Caroline, 18, waitress).

I'm a maid, it's not the job I wanted, but I have no choice (Marie, 20, maid).

Thanks to my aunt, I found a job: I work in a kiosk. I sell sheep's heads every evening from 4 pm on (Eugenie, 21, salesgirl).

I'm a waitress at the 'La Liberté' bar. I found this job through a friend of my boyfriend's (Phelicité, 21, waitress).

I was working in a family as a maid, then my girlfriend found me a job in the bar. The wages are higher: in the family I was earning 4,000 CFA, in the bar I get 15,000 CFA per month (Madeleine, 22, waitress).

I'm a salesgirl in a shop which sells ready-made clothes and various articles. It's my cousin who found this job for me (Marie, 22, salesgirl).

The urban solidarity networks come into play at this crucial stage of 'job-hunting'. But what is interesting in this search for work is not so much the structure of the support, but rather, the types of activity carried out. We observe that the girls find their niches in the informal sector, within which the jobs primarily assigned to women are in leisure activities, domestic service, and, less frequently, employment in small businesses.

The structure of the labour market leaves the female workforce with almost no choices. They can only offer their physical qualities and the attributes socially considered to be inherent to womanhood. Thus, the female workforce, in response to the hurdles in the labour sector, takes up positions in the socially-assigned niches. In so doing, it experiences the third stage of marginalisation. The Dagara girls, whom the urban crisis thrusts into the least sought-after spaces, those that are financially unrewarding and socially despised, share this status with foreign girls, though with the added disadvantage that, against their wishes, they are under the thumb of a community to which they supposedly belong. Under such conditions, the financial and social management of their working life is all the more difficult.

WORKING, TAKING RISKS, BEING FREE

Yes, I've changed: I am more free, I am more responsible (Rose, 27, salesgirl).

Of course I've changed: I've put on weight, I've become a mature girl. Except that sometimes, I think about how my mother suffers (Ziem, 21, waitress).

I've changed because now I've had my hair straightened (laughter), I've got clothing. Nowadays I have things to wear, I eat well and I sleep well (Eveline, 21, waitress).

I send gifts to my mother. I've helped to pay the school fees for one of my brothers. Him— he's through school, Thank God, he works well. He's taking the entrance test for the Tax Office. With the help of the bar manager, I've opened a savings account. I will have money when I go back to the village (Eugenie, 22, waitress).

In the bar, you work, your salary is 15,000 CFA; but maybe you earn 4,000 CFA. Sometimes the managers are crooks. I never imagined I would find myself in this situation, but I can't go back without any goods. It's very shameful, so I've got to work under miserable conditions to reach my goal (Sidonie, 17, waitress).

I've forgotten my earlier sufferings. I take care as best I can of my mother and brothers and sisters, and especially of my child, because I want him to be a good boy, proud of his Mummy (Caroline, 22, salesgirl).

The girls repeatedly say that they came to town in search of plates, dishes, and clothes. For them, the aim of paid employment is that they gain access to modern consumer goods. This accumulation remains linked to the community plan which was the starting-point of the migration. Though at one point, the strategy of accumulation is directed towards the search for greater individual and collective security, over a period of time it is very often devoted to satisfying immediate needs. Clothing seems to be central to these needs. Père[4] observes this overvaluation of clothing among the Lobi neighbours. This rapid change in dress-behaviour among the Dagara is in step with people's openness towards the outside world. The reports of the first European visitors have much to say about this cultural metamorphosis.[5] The social value attributed to an object is never a matter of mere chance.

The highly integrated personality of the Dagara, which permeates their material[6] and spiritual life, became more and more frail under the impact of cultural isolation, evangelisation, and colonisation. This latter shock-wave brutally brought on a process of individualism, the emergence of differentiation, and the weakening of collective pride, which has laid the way open to the new cult of appearance as a new form of power, defining a nascent 'personality'.

This desire to have a 'look' is itself the zero degree of Dagara community personality. Once freed from the levelling-down and egalitarian rules of community life, the individual's "new territory" maintains the same "value" as that great bastion, lineage (both material and spiritual), once so proudly defended. This is the confirmation of one of the consequences of the tremendous cultural shock caused by contact with the western forces of domination. This re-construction of the Dagara personality also expresses allegiance to colonial logic, implying a kind of symbolic adoption of some of the justifiable attributes of what is perceived as a power-symbol. Thus, a neat appearance is not a mere cultural illusion, since it is a spur to action—to migrate. Neither is it pure ostentation, since its basically political function is perfectly obvious. Might we, however, be overestimating the leading part that appearance plays in female migrations? This frantic scramble for modern glamour-goods might appear to be heralding the establishment of new social norms.

We must now turn to the mode of consumption of these 'superfluous elements', as Veblen would call them, and to their social value. We shall relate the original starting point of the migrations to the utilization of the resources which the latter provides. Indeed, studies of the Mossi have demonstrated that the major part of the money earned during the migration was not destined for the resolution of local problems, but for purchasing goods for personal enhancement, such as transistors and town clothes, in particular. Without necessarily sharing the conclusions of Remy *et al.* (1977) concerning the alleged ineffectiveness of the power of transformation of the migratory enterprise, their observations lead us to make a fundamental conclusion; both in Mossi and in Dagara societies, the upsurge of migrations particularly affects the subordinate categories such as the young and women, i.e. those victims of the legal and economic constraints which deny them access to the means of livelihood. Under these circumstances, one can formulate the hypothesis that the rationalisation of migration cannot be disconnected from this original reaction to conditions which, on the migrants' return, have not really altered. Such forms of behaviour will always originate from a more or less clear vision of a particular shape of individual and collective future.

The decision to invest, though limited by the amount accumulated, is determined by interests linked to social position. Economic applications follow a social logic, and one cannot comprehend the "meaning" of the ways in which objects circulate, before having identified the social necessities which they fulfil. The economic logic is the product of "particular situations", yet these are determined by history. Also, the failure to integrate into these new behavioural norms gives rise to a new kind of "shame", not the same as under the old rules, but just as real. The old Dagara used to predict that "a time will come when there will be no more 'shame'." But did they not know that every age has its own 'shame'?

OLD AND NEW ALLIANCES

> I know all kinds of people, but I mostly see my workmates, because in spite of jealousies, we give each other moral and material support (Caroline, 22, waitress).

> No, I don't have friends among the Dagara women who live here, because they say bad things about us. They don't want to understand us (Rose, 27, waitress).

> Here, I see a few relatives, but mainly people in my own category (Marie, 27, waitress).

> I see a lot of my girlfriends who come from other countries, especially the Togolese girls, I trust them more than those gossiping Dagara girls (Perpetua, 18, waitress).

> I'm in touch with my uncles, since they are my relatives, I can't avoid seeing them (Eugenie, 21, waitress).

> I don't see any Dagara women except the girls from home who work in the bars. At first, I used to go to see them but my brother-in-law forbade me to see them, because I might be tempted to imitate them (Marie, 22, salesgirl).

The circle of relationships takes on a particular configuration based on social-identity criteria; one only sees 'people in one's own category', having the same social status. In town, the migrant Dagara women experience a double marginalisation: confined to highly despised occupations, they are also cut off from the Dagara community established in Bobo, which views them as the expression of collective disgrace. A Dagara notable in Bobo told us of his indignation: "Before, the Dagara woman was gold, but that is not the case now, since married women started coming here. For the price of a beer, you can have a Dagara girl for the night. Because you've spoken to her, or given her 100 CFA for her lunch, that's enough for her to follow you. We claim to be mature, serious people, but things are so bad that, when you hear that, it makes you mad. Take Koko, that working-class district; you find them left and right, and they have no other name than 'dagari'—and they answer to it! What does that tell you? I know that we Dagara, we've had it forever, we are no longer respected in town." Some people are really seriously considering sending these girls back to the village. The Dagara community would like to present a different image of the homeland and its children from that given by these girls and their unworthy, immoral conduct.

Here again, we come across the struggles for identity of African urban contexts. Indeed, the construction of a "Dagara identity", which is not necessarily an exact reflection of the "original" one, allows the urban elite to play a part on the national political scene and to claim some rewarding power of representation. This reconstituted identity is founded upon human qualities dangerously disturbed by these girls who flout a conflicting social reality, and which is an unbearable threat to the new urban Dagara systems of representation.

This conflict situation lies at the origin of a campaign for exclusion which consists in marginalising this 'unworthy' element, by means of depriving them of any opportunity to utilize the community identity. The migrants have fully grasped this situation, and, in turn, develop an 'avoidance strategy' along the lines of "I have nothing to do with the Dagara". But, in town, the girls have had experience of another kind of life, and, in response to the community's barriers, establish new social networks and form new alliances. These regroupings are based on a double shared-experience system, work-associations, and cohabitation. These girls, lost in town, often from different cultures and nationalities[7], feel a need for solidarity. These new forms of cooperation compensate for the effects of the ruptures caused by migration. Is the strength of these new bonds only valid for the duration of their urban residence?

LIVING TOWN LIFE

The town is good and bad at the same time. Good: everyone does what he wants, whereas in the village you always have to deal with 'what people say'. Bad: if you've got a problem, you're on your own, except in the case of a death: there, the Dagara stick together (Perpetua, 18, waitress).

For me, town and village both suit me because in both places I can get enough to eat, but the problem is clothing, that's what's missing in the village. If I have to choose, I'll choose the village because that's home and no-one can drive me away, whereas in town, you don't know when you're going to be told to leave (Eugenie, 21, salesgirl).

In town, after work, you can rest, but in the village, after the field work you have to go home late at night to start cooking, that's a big chore (Eveline, 21, waitress).

In town, there's the problem of fatal diseases, I'm scared. But I find the town more bearable because in the village you sell *dolo* and the money doesn't allow you to buy much; you sell at a loss, credits here and there, which means it's hard to make progress back there (Caroline, 22, waitress).

Here, when you have nothing to do, your life is ruined, you can't live well. It's this situation that makes others turn to prostitution. The town can just as easily suit people as harm them. If you have a wage, then you're OK (Marie, 22, salesgirl).

The ways in which the migrant girls perceive the town are as diverse as their individual trajectories. Country life seems to be the seat of rare qualities even though these are disappearing. It is both the starting-point and the root-cause of migration, and migrants judge it severely. But the nostalgia for the secure feeling of belonging to the homeland, still persists.

It can be observed that the only value ascribed to the town is the paid work it can offer, and that remuneration itself is valued for the goods it can procure, and lastly, those goods only acquire real value from the standpoint of the village, whatever each girl imagines that to be. These "migrant goods" are brought back into the village context and, for a while, confer the illusion of having achieved betterment.

How long can this disconnection from urban centrality hold out? The evolution of the extension of urban values may influence the direction of the migrants' life-strategies in the future.

RETURNING TO THE VILLAGE

I haven't gone back to the village because I'm not ready (Eugenie, 20, maid).

Criticism is inherent in Dagara nature. I don't last long in the village. The village has changed. All my girlfriends are married, the village isn't the same like before; people are a bit lazy and look at you with contempt (Sidonie, 17, maid).

What I've noticed, children seem to be more free, and education isn't as strict as it was in our time. Anybody can come to town as they like, which means that the number of migrants has grown a lot (Eugenie, 27, waitress).

Some of the migrant girls have made the journey home, although this particular journey requires a great deal of preparation. How many of them return for good? We do not yet know. The girls say they have noticed a general change in the village. But perhaps it would be truer to say that the change has taken place among the migrants themselves. For one must state that the ordeal of returning can be interpreted as a stage of re-deployment of the migratory phases; we have already stressed that the return is an opportunity to 'enact', to 'stage the migratory expectations' symbolically meant to ensure the reproduction of the phenomenon. It is also a sort of a 'bounce-down' for the migrant, to the extent that this return is often necessarily followed by a "return" to migration; the temporary becomes long-term and reinforces, or redefines, the migratory strategies. Diarra (1974) has provided a good description of the position of Zarma ex-migrants who, as a result of their migratory experience, are condemned to remain in the big town. Whether mythical or real, the return to the village is a kind of rebirth of migration.

FROM NEED SATISFACTION TO ACCUMULATION STRATEGIES

> As a woman, I appeal to all the young girls not to stand with their arms crossed, waiting for happiness to fall from the sky. We must fight (Rose, 27 waitress).

> As some men think, the work in the bars is not as bad as all that. It's only gossips that give the wrong idea about the work. A waitress in a bar is not necessarily a tart. Some of them get husbands and run their household properly (Ziem, 21, waitress).

> For the future, I hope to have a secure job and get married (Marie, 22, salesgirl).

> My only wish: to earn my dishes, clothes and go back to the village to get married some day. I want to continue to sell my *dolo* and my doughnuts (Sidonie, 17, waitress).

> ...'tis because of the word 'money' that you see Dagara girls working in bars. This thing used to be unknown. Money has come to spoil everything. Today without money you are nothing (Rose, 21, waitress).

> For my future life, I intend to keep working as a maid and in the evenings with a little money I'll try to sell something at the roadside on my own account (Eugenie, 21, salesgirl).

> In the future, I would like to learn a job, if I get some support in addition to my savings, I shall pursue some studies in a centre, even if it is learning to sew, to weave clothes and also to create a family (Caroline, 18, waitress).

> It is because Dagara women have no initiative that the girls who come to work as maids or in the bars are only looking for material goods, without thinking of building a solid future. A Togolese girl was telling us that she had come to Burkina to fetch the running funds to do some trading. I want to succeed like my Ghanaian or Togolese sisters (Noëllie, 20, waitress).

> As a woman, one must think of the future and I say that if one finds the minimum, one must invest in another domain to make some progress. There is no promotion to be sought in a bar. It is essential to save to invest elsewhere (Perpetue, 19, waitress).

One of the first consequences of labour migration is precisely this need for one's work to be respected, perhaps in response to the social pressure which downgrades women, or leads to their exclusion from the only places in which they are accepted and which constitute their sole means of livelihood. What is at stake is giving a moral value to gaining greater occupational and social autonomy, because the experience of migration has proven to these women that plans can only be realized through struggle.

This struggle begins with the decision to migrate, but then gradually changes its nature; from the satisfaction of immediate needs, it develops into more or less elaborate strategies of accumulation. Because the "happiness", as originally perceived, not only refuses to retreat, but persistently calls for greater and greater means for implementation. The "well-being" which gives life its value is insatiable. It is not always a matter of 'great plans', but rather of 'great ambitions', at the individual level. Above all, the girls want to set up home, have a husband, and bring up children.

In all cases the rule remains either, to work hard for a wage, or else, be more autonomous and set up your own business. The ambitions follow three main streams 1) return to the village, disappointed, and conform to the 'traditional' woman's role; 2) stay 'where you are' and seek less precarious employment; 3) express a determination to break with village egalitarianism and demand continuous social mobility for oneself. The labour migration trajectories demonstrate quite clearly that women are clamouring for an ever greater degree of autonomy, and the journeys described here are all "moments" in the Dagara women's struggle against the consequences of a lifestyle that others want to define on their behalf.

"Happiness" is the fact of eluding the unpleasant constraints of existence, and, drawn by *Nyovuuru*, that well-being which makes life worth living, the Dagara girls leave for Bobo-Dioulasso where they work hard.

Notes

1 I would like to thank Bernadette Dabire for her invaluable assistance during the interviews.
2 The Dagara language does not seem to have a word for the 'nuclear family' in the Western sense. 'Yir' is the name of the more or less extensive family group, and of the building itself.
3 M. Père writes: "On every occasion that a woman's sexual organ has been touched, even accidentally, it's considered to be a case of adultery." (1977:722).
4 M. Père writes:"All the interviews of men and women on the reasons for emigrating bring out the need for money, to buy clothes first of all. Being dressed has become a real need for the younger generations." (1977:371).
5 On this point, refer to M. Paternot who, from his paternalist and European-centred viewpoint, notes the changes in dress which even then he connected with the consequences of migrations. He wrote "the men wear a few torn rags, or a skin thrown over the shoulders; the children simply have a string; whereas the women make do with a slight belt of thongs which maintains the leaves with which they adorn themselves (...) Since more and more young people are going to trade centres on the Gold Coast in search of paid employment, we see them returning in shorts, straw hats, dark glasses, braces, parasols, etc... The women are happy to receive brightly-coloured cloths which their gallant fiances bring them back from their trips to the land of "Paradise." (1954:34–35).
6 On the relationship between architecture and social organisation, see Savonnet, (1976); Pradeau (1970).
7 They are often Togolese or Ghanaian, and the latter community may also be composed of Dagara from the north of Ghana. Such cultural proximity could favour the integration of Dagara girls from Burkina into the bar-waitress' milieu.

References

Balandier, G., 1974, *Anthropologiques*. Paris: Presses Universitaires de France.
Dabiré, A., 1984, *La femme rurale dans la societe Dagara en mutation: quelle formation pour développement. Le cas de centre formation féminine rural de Dissin*. Haute Volta: DUFPS, Université de Tours.

Diarra, F.A., 1974, "Les relations entre les hommes et les femmes et les migrations des Zarma", in Samir Amin (ed.), *Modern Migrations in Western Africa.* London: Oxford University Press for the International African Institute.

Hagaman, B.L., 1977, *Beer and Matriliny: The Power of Women in a West African Society.* Ph.D dissertation, Northwestern University.

Hébert, J., *et al.*, 1976, *Esquisse d'une Monographie Historique de pays Dagara.* Diocèse de Diébougou. Burkina Faso, Ronéo.

Institut National de la Statistique et de la Demographie, 1990, *Direction de la Démographie Recensement général de la Population, 1985.* Ouagadougou.

Linton, R., 1968, *De l'homme.* Paris: de Minuit.

Mauss, M., 1968, *Sociologie et Anthropologie.* Paris: Presses Universitaires de France.

Paternot, M., 1954, *Lumière sur la Volta, chez les Dagari.* Paris: Association des missionnaires d'Afrique.

Père, M., 1988, *Les Lobis: tradition et changement.* Laval: Siloë.

Pradeau, C., 1970, "Kokolibou (Haute Volta), ou le pays dagari à travers l'étude d'un terroir", *Etudes Rurales,* 37,38,39, Janvier-Septembre.

Remy, G., J. Capron and J.M. Kohler, 1977, "Mobilité géographique et immobilisme social: un exemple voltaïque", *Revue Tiers-Monde,* XVIII, 71, pp. 617–653.

Savonnet, G., 1976, "Inégalités de développement et organisation sociale (exemples empruntés au Sud-Ouest de la Haute-Volta)", *Les Cahiers de l'ORSTOM,* XIII,1.

Non-Metropolitan Migration in Botswana with an Emphasis on Gender

Elvyn Jones-Dube

Circulating migration, the movement between rural and urban abodes, in the context of non-metropolitan migration, and its occurrence in Botswana is the subject of this chapter. The movement of ethnic groups and individuals has been a constant feature of life in southern Africa for several thousand years. It continues today, and lies at the heart of human existence and survival in both rural and urban settings. While migration in southern Africa has most often been associated with young, single men who migrate to the mines in search of work (Chaney, 1980), this chapter suggests that, at least in Botswana's case, migration has been a constant feature of life dating back to the last century, but which has taken on a much different character since Botswana's independence in 1966 and particularly since the economic boom years of the 1980s. Unlike earlier periods, migration has now become commonplace amongst women as well as men, with a numerically significant population of females also migrating for survival and advancement. In fact, according to recent census figures, it is likely that female migration will outstrip male migration by the first decade of the next century (CSO, 1991).

The chapter is divided into three parts. The first section presents an overview of past external and internal migration trends and explains how these are rooted in the geographic, cultural and economic context of the region. The second section focuses on census data from the National Migration Study, and the 1982 and 1991 censuses, the latter of which identifies current migration trends and Botswana's new growth points. It is suggested that the continued undirected shift in population away from rural areas towards urban and peri-urban areas defeats current government efforts to revitalise and support the growth of non-metropolitan centre (agro-town) development. It is further suggested that without concerted governmental and private sector effort, the agro-towns are unlikely to foster new non-metropolitan growth which would help develop Botswana's rural areas. The final section of the chapter discusses circular migration from a gender perspective. It discusses how migration has historically affected women in Botswana and of late, contributed towards a "feminization of poverty" in a patriarchal society. This section argues that although women are not alone in their need for improved living standards and employment opportunities, the continuing deterioration of traditional social and economic support systems for women and their families and the large numbers of rural and urban women in search of secure income generating opportunities is negatively affected by the paucity of employment options presently available. Lack of viable employment particularly affects women, many of whom are single parents. Therefore, potential female wage earners find it extremely difficult to remain in the rural areas on a permanent basis. Income and life style differences between rural and urban areas coupled with the difficulties of rural life continue to encourage rural flight. The chapter concludes that Botswana's interests would best be served by policy and programme strategies which aggressively seek to create and employ enlightened rural development strategies to provide the conditions necessary to support and sustain non-metropolitan development.

MIGRATION RESEARCH

Research interest in the effects of migrant labour on peasant economies and their resultant underdevelopment were part of the development debate of the 1970s which sought to generate economic strategies to assist the entry of pre-industrial societies into the industrialised era. In Botswana's case, its large migrant labour population, an outcome of the peripheral economies characteristic of the Southern African economic context had not fostered its internal development. While the debate raged in Northern capitals, research efforts were launched in Botswana to investigate the extent of migration and its effects. Brown (1983) has noted, in her research on the impact of male migration on women in Botswana, that early researchers including W.A. Lewis, Todaro and Harris focused on the "who" and the "why" of the migration cycle from a purely economic perspective, the latter having concluded that individuals migrate in order to maximise the returns from perceived opportunity sets. This early research argued that migration was economic in nature and a rational response to a limited range of resources and choices, and that, as such, the family unit, already suffering from the effects of out-migration, benefited from the migratory movements of family members. Writers such as Gunder Frank and Samir Amin criticised the economists' approach arguing that migration was a consequence of the historical development of capitalism and that the geographic concentration of the factors of production in particular regions should be taken into account. A further group, those consisting of specialists on southern Africa, including Giovanni Arrighi, Colin Bundy, Harold Wolpe and Martin Legassick drew attention to the workings of extant pre-capitalist society within the modern sector and the process and impact of migration on the peasant family. It was not until almost a decade later that writers such as Izzard (1982), Kerven (1982), Bozolli (1983) and Brown (1983), upon whose writings this chapter is largely based, began to focus on how migration had an impact on women and the Tswana family. These female writers represented a new contingent of researchers who, following the 1970 publication of Esther Boserup's *Women's Role in Economic Development*, began to question existing beliefs about women's contribution towards Third World development. Previously, scant attention had been paid to the effects of migration on women or on women as migrants in southern

Africa. The chief source of such ethnographic research, dating back to the 1940s, had been Isaac Schapera (1947), who had painted a different picture of the effects of migration on Batswana from that advanced by the economists mentioned earlier. As early as 1947 Schapera's research had shown that male labour migration had had a negative impact on the social and economic fabric of Tswana society resulting in fundamental changes in the economics and structure of the family.

Subsequent research such as that cited above, has indicated that women in particular, have been hard hit by the aftershocks of migration to the extent that both their economic and social position have been significantly affected resulting in what Brown (1983:387) has characterised as the "feminization of poverty". However, as this essay will show, male and female migration is also a direct result of a weak rural sector in which arable agriculture is risky and unproductive; to the point where, as the economists had earlier noted, security-minded families must engage in varied survival strategies in order to maintain the family. In the light of economic insecurity, it is not uncommon to find members of some extended families abandoning their rural family units to their own resources. Therefore, in a country with few prosperous non-metropolitan centres capable of supporting and sustaining rural or peri-rural life, out-migration or circular migration has become an irresistible alternative to rural poverty and stagnation.

CULTURE OF MIGRATION

Pre-colonial

Botswana has been described as having a "culture of migration" which pre-dates labour migration to South Africa and Zimbabwe (Kerven, 1982). Given Botswana's geographical position at the centre of the Southern African plateau, the peoples of the region have traversed this area for centuries. The earliest known settlers were Southern Africa's aboriginal inhabitants, the San and the Khoi (Campbell, 1982), followed by iron-working Bantu from central Africa who migrated south and then north again in small bands. Modern Sotho-Tswana groups are known to have moved into Botswana around 1500 A.D., as a result of the expansion and break-up of kingdoms to the south which distributed Sotho-Tswana peoples, and their language and culture over much of the southern African plateau (Ngcongco, 1982). Other tribal groups which migrated and settled in Botswana include the BaTawana, BaKalanga, SiYei, SiMbukushu, and BaHerero (Campbell, 1982). Group migrations were a function of populations accommodating themselves to an array of pressures including warfare, famine, pestilence, political upheavals, repression and the desire for a better life.

Individual migration, on the other hand, started in the nineteenth century in response to natural and man-made pressures. These included the large scale movement of Africans to escape the *difaqane* or "Time of Great Troubles" associated with the Zulu chief Shaka and his successors (Nangati, 1979); the "Great Trek" involving the mass movement of the Boers away from British rule in the Cape Province, the introduction of corvée labour usage by Tswana chiefs to acquire cash to buy guns and powder for defence against invaders; the need for cheap labour for the newly opened gold and diamond mines in South Africa; and the decimation of African cattle herds as a consequence of a rinderpest epidemic in 1896 (Alverson, 1978).

Institutionalised wage migration

It is commonly accepted that the rinderpest epidemic of 1896-7 was the greatest catastrophe to strike Batswana and which prompted the cycle of migratory labour common today. The loss of the herds, a traditional source of wealth and status, coupled with drought, brought on considerable famine during this period (Chirenje, 1977). Thereafter, many thousands of men were driven to seek wage employment in order to obtain cash, food and to rebuild lost herds. Following the introduction of the "head and hut" tax in 1899, the need for cash and the wage paying jobs to provide it were actively sought after and consequently became a permanent aspect of economic life for Africans.

By 1940, figures for Batswana working in the mines of South Africa totalled 18,400 (Kerven, 1982), and up until 1981, approximately 25 per cent of men aged between 20-40 and 4 per cent of women were migrants outside Botswana's borders (CSO/SIDA, 1991). Tlou and Campbell (1984:198) have summarised the effects of the migrant system on Botswana (Table 1).

Table 1. *Advantages and disadvantages of migrant labour system in Botswana*

Disadvantages	Advantages
1. Workers paid low wages because they could not sell their labour wherever they liked.	1. Dikogsi (chiefs) got part of the tax money so they tended to encourage mine labour.
2. Agricultural production declined as men left Bechuanaland and agricultural work left to old and women.	2. The Protectorate Administration received revenue through taxation and recruiting licence fees.
3. Batswana developed South Africa instead of developing their own country.	3. Social unrest due to unemployment was avoided.
4. Families often collapsed due to long-term spouse absences.	4. The mines got cheap labour and huge profits.
5. Miners returned with new diseases which badly affected those left behind.	5. Migrants obtained cash for domestic consumption and were able to pay taxes

Source: Tlou and Campbell (1984).

In the last ten years, Botswana has experienced a welcome change regarding the out-migration of her people to work in the more industrialised neighbouring countries. Recently, more jobs have become available within Botswana in relation to four growth areas. These include (a) the economic expansion of the peri-urban areas near Gaborone; (b) the new towns created to support Botswana's mining industry; (c) government expansion of local authorities and amenities in the Districts; and, (d) new growth centres in previously undeveloped or underdeveloped portions of the country. In addition to increased public and private sector activity, the expansion of the Botswana Defence Force (BDF), whose 1991–92 budget reached P136 million, has fostered non-metropolitan growth in selected areas in the countryside (Botswana, 1991:123). However, while these developments have fostered some new population centres as well as created formal and, indirectly, informal sector employment, they have not been sufficient to stem the tide of undirected rural out-migration, unemployment or rural poverty, especially among the young. Therefore, whereas young men, and to a lesser extent women, used to migrate to the mines, factories, farms and kitchens of South Africa and Zimbabwe, they now migrate to urban and peri-urban areas or set up in squatter camps on the peripheries of new population centres.

FACTORS INFLUENCING MIGRATION

Continued out-migration is related to conditions in the rural areas which make life there increasingly difficult. These conditions include recurrent drought which makes arable agriculture risky, a stark difference in rural and urban incomes and life styles which require rural (and urban) dwellers to employ a range of coping strategies which are almost universally employed to diversify income sources. The overall situation is complicated by the low level of rural investment with which to support and sustain rural industry in a country largely without indigenous artisans or entrepreneurs (Jones-Dube, 1984). Taken together, there is little incentive to remain in the rural areas or to develop non-metropolitan centres in the light of existing rural stagnation and better conditions in urban and peri-urban areas.

Some expansion of these ideas is necessary. First, unlike other sub-Saharan countries where agriculture contributes substantially to household income and GDP, this is not the case in Botswana where drought is frequent, soil productivity is low and many households lack draught power. In Botswana, drought occurs on average 7 out of every 10 years. In three of these years, drought is particularly severe so that rural households are either having to cope with rain failure or trying to recover from it. Over time, this has led to erosion of the rural economy, declining rural incomes and a widening gap between the asset rich and the asset poor, of whom women constitute the majority. An analysis of GDP (Table 2) covering the years 1966–1988/89 shows that agriculture's contribution to GDP has fallen from 39.6 per cent in 1966 to just 3 per cent in 1988/89 whereas mining, trade and government contributed 51 per cent, 16.4 per cent and 12.8 per cent respectively or a total of 80.2 per cent of GDP (Botswana, 1991:13). Economists believe that the population growth rate of 3.4 per cent, many female-headed households, a high dependency ratio and questionable land grazing policies also contribute to a low and declining rate of rural agricultural productivity (Valentine, 1990). Added to this scenario is Botswana's young population, of which 29.5 per cent is below 15 years of age and the fact that over 80 per cent of the young have access to at least free Universal Primary Education (Botswana 1991, 11; 319). On the one hand, this has created a better educated, young population, while on the other hand, it has produced one or two generations of young people who are disinclined to remain in undeveloped rural areas, in contrast to their parents and grandparents.

A second factor which influences out-migration is the difference between rural and urban incomes. Table 3 gives figures for distribution of cash income for the period 1985–86 and shows (a) that in virtually every category, urban

Table 2. *Gross domestic product, 1966–1988/89 (selected years)* (Constant 1988/89 Prices)

	1966		1977/78		1982/83		1988/89[a]	
	Pm	Share %	Pm	Share %	Pm	Share %	Pm	Share %
Agriculture	124	39.6	309	19.9	153	5.8	149	3.0
Mining	–	–	241	15.5	815	31.2	2 542	51.0
Manufacturing	25	7.9	106	6.8	165	6.3	209	4.2
Water & Electricity	3	0.8	44	2.8	65	2.5	93	1.9
Construction	18	5.7	73	4.7	142	5.4	166	3.3
Trade, hotels	58	18.6	311	20.0	556	21.3	818	16.4
Transport	13	4.1	65	4.2	66	2.5	82	1.6
Finance	21	6.6	129	8.3	174	6.6	263	5.3
Government	52	16.7	253	16.3	451	17.2	638	12.8
Social Services[b]	–	–	65	4.2	87	3.3	118	2.4
Dummy Sector[c]	–	–	-42	-2.7	-58	-2.2	-91	-1.8
Total	313	100.0	1 554	100.0	2 613	100.0	4 988	100.0
GDP/capita, in Pula	578		1 982		2 677		4 115	

[a] 988/89 figures may be subject to revision.
[b] Included under Government in 1966.
[c] The dummy sector is a correction for imputed bank service charges.
Source: Republic of Botswana, 1991, *National Development Plan 7, 1991–97.*

households earned more than rural households; (b) with few exceptions, both rural females and males earned similar amounts illustrating the extent of Botswana's cash-poor rural population; (c) while the table also indicates the significant differences between cash earning of female and male urban dwellers, it also shows that except for the lowest level of income, males earn more than females. Given these differences in cash income potential, it is difficult to argue a case for rural dwellers to remain on the land.

Table 3. *Distribution of cash income by households, 1985/86*

	Urban Areas			Rural Areas		
	Head of Household			Head of Household		
Pula per Month	Male	Female	All	Male	Female	All
	%	%	%	%	%	%
–100	10.5	32.4	19.6	62.3	69.4	65.8
100–125	4.5	9.4	6.6	6.5	6.2	6.4
125–150	3.6	5.9	4.6	4.6	5.8	5.2
150–200	10.2	11.1	10.6	6.3	5.0	5.7
200–250	7.5	8.5	7.9	3.7	2.9	3.3
250–300	9.5	7.1	8.5	1.9	1.9	1.9
300–400	9.5	5.0	7.6	2.9	2.9	2.9
400–500	9.7	6.4	8.3	2.7	1.1	1.9
500–750	9.6	9.9	9.7	5.2	3.6	4.5
750–1,000	4.2	1.4	2.9	2.0	0.5	1.2
1,000–2,000	14.2	2.4	9.2	1.5	0.9	1.2
2,000–	7.2	0.6	4.4	0.4	0.0	0.3
ALL	100.0	100.0	100.0	100.0	100.0	100.0

Source: CSO, 1988, *Household Income and Expenditure Survey (HIES) 1985/86.*

Table 4 indicates the extent of earning power differentials by sex and educational attainment levels for the same period. Males have significantly higher levels of earning power compared to females in similar circumstances. Hence, in the face of higher returns for wage employment and better informal sector opportunities in urban and peri-urban areas, there is little incentive for males or females to resist the pull of rural out-migration to the cities. Further, given that a higher proportion of women reside in the rural areas as heads of households (about 50 per cent), the pull of non-rural areas where the possibility of work exists, is doubly strong. Given these facts and trends, it would seem that, given its monetary advantages over the poverty inherent in rural life, growth in urban areas is clearly the way of the future for Batswana. The question then becomes one of whether the present trend of movement can be re-directed so that non-metropolitan centres become viable and attractive alternatives to movement into major population centres.

Table 4. *Earning power differentials for 1985/86* (Pula per month)

Location	Sex	No Education	Primary	Secondary
Urban	Male	226.77	416.82	1149.64
	Female	95.25	208.49	464.28
	Male/Female	2.38	2.00	2.48
Rural	Male	105.59	190.32	595.74
	Female	58.52	109.01	412.89
	Male/Female	1.80	1.75	1.45
Urban/Rural	Male	2.21	2.19	1.93
	Female	1.63	1.91	1.12

Source: CSO, 1987, *National Manpower Development Planning Report.*

MIGRATION TRENDS

The national migration study

While the international studies mentioned earlier had helped to establish the extent and causes of international migration, similar information about the movements of the population *within Botswana* were unknown. This gap in knowledge was further intensified by extended periods of drought which made rural people fearful to continue to engage in subsistence agriculture and drove many to leave the land altogether. Hence, in 1985 it could still be said that more was known about the migratory habits of the Bushmen minority than was known about the majority of the population (Taylor and Tumkaya, 1985:128).

In 1975 the National Migration Study (NMS) was commissioned (and implemented in 1977 and published in 1982) to provide government with information and policy analyses on the magnitude, causes and effects of national and international migration streams (Kerven, 1982:16). Research was conducted over several years covering 8 out of 10 districts in Botswana, and 3 per cent of all households. Despite reported shortcomings (Taylor,

1985; Taylor and Tumkaya, 1985), the report helped to identify patterns of migration and to isolate its effects on Tswana life. Case (1982) established the existence of four networks of primary migration, which were the North-West, North, Central and Southern parts of the country. Within each of these networks there exist primary centres, central places, peripheral areas and sub-peripheral areas from which migration takes place. Map 1 shows primary migration streams in Botswana, while Map 2 shows population distribution.

Map 1. *Primary migration streams*

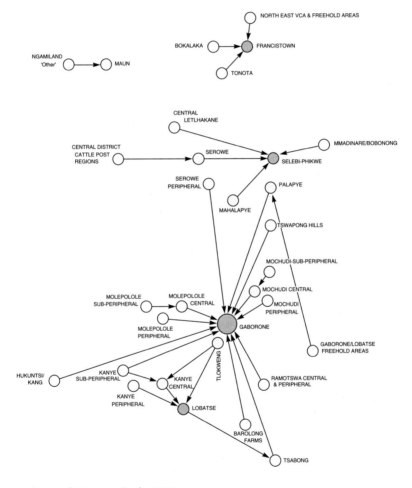

Source: National Migration Study, 1982

Map 2. *Population distribution 1981 census*

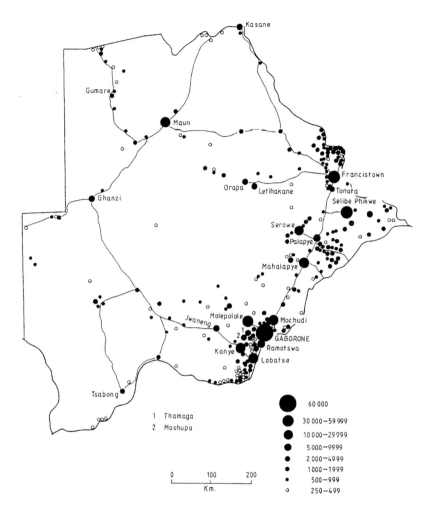

By the conclusion of the NMS an array of information on internal migration flows had been amassed, the information from which can be summarised as follows: (a) in all instances, central areas exhibited a net gain in rural migrants illustrating the continuing pull of urban employment opportunities; (b) rural/rural migrants tended to migrate within their own localities (central, peripheral, sub-peripheral); (c) migrants tended to move within their own districts indicating that districts were more than mere administrative units but rather, served as bases of ethnic solidarity; (d) in the South-East, North-East and Kgalagadi Districts, inter-district migration was larger than intra-district migration (Case, 1982:112–114).

Case's analysis also showed that there were distinct differences between districts. In the southern districts, the major migration from the South-East District is to the Southern District (11 per cent) and to the Central District (17 per cent). There is considerable inter-district movement in both directions which is not surprising given their proximity. Movement to the Central District, however, is explained as the movement of farm labourers from Lobatse Freehold Farms to Tuli Block Freehold Farms—a distance of several hundred kilometres. In the case of the North-East, migration to the Central District became the norm owing to (i) the lack of grazing and farm land; (ii) the paucity of employment options in the region capable of absorbing the wage-seeking population; (iii) a historical linkage between the BaNgwato and BaKalanga which predisposed the latter to migrate to the Central District. Therefore, based on the NMS data, an image of a large-scale rural exodus to urban areas was created and the non-metropolitan shifts documented by Silitshena (1978 and 1982) were viewed with disbelief.

The 1981 census

The 1981 census provided additional data to substantiate Silitshena's claim that significant rural/rural migration as well as rural/urban migration was taking place. This was made possible due to the inclusion, for the first time, of a question regarding internal migration. From these data, the census was able to calculate that of the de facto population for 1980–81, 16.6 per cent of the population had moved at least once during the year preceding the census. Of this number 49.5 per cent had moved within the same District, while 50.5 per cent had moved between Districts. Based on the same data, it was possible to conclude that "the vast majority of migrants in Botswana move from one rural area to another and an almost equal proportion migrate from the towns as to them" (Taylor, 1985:91). As for the importance of towns and other non-metropolitan centres, Taylor concluded that "away from the influence of towns, long distance migration appears to be reduced with the most important flows occurring between contiguous rural Districts [where]... the District capitals would no doubt be revealed as the pivot of intra-District migration flows". This supposition has largely been proven by shifts in population within the rural areas where the large central villages *cum* agro-towns such as Serowe, Kanye, Molepolole and Mochudi, received many migrants drawn from the peripheral and sub-peripheral areas surrounding the large villages. Taylor's research would seem to support the belief, therefore, that non-metropolitan development is viable and that it is occurring with or without government intervention. And, as data in the next section will show, in recent years some of these former central villages *cum* agro-towns have grown sufficiently to have been upgraded to rural towns due to increases in population from rural areas.

The 1991 census

Results from the most recent census, conducted during 1991, indicate that a number of significant changes in Botswana's population distribution have taken place. First, figures show that the total population has more than doubled over the last twenty years from 597,000 in 1971 to 1,334,000 in 1991. There has been a steady increase of population in urban and peri-urban areas while rural areas have suffered a net loss. Whereas in 1981 50 per cent of the population resided within 200 kilometres of the capital, latest census figures show that 50 per cent of the population now resides within 100 kilometres of

Gaborone, much of it concentrated in peri-urban areas and in the former central villages close to the capital. As a result, the number of urban areas (defined as places with populations of 5,000 or more, with 75 per cent of population engaged in non-agricultural pursuits) have increased considerably (Table 5), while total urban population has increased from nearly 18 per cent in 1981 to 33 per cent in 1991 (CSO, 1991:2). These figures present adequate evidence to conclude that Botswana's rural population (65 per cent) is moving away from rural areas and into semi-rural (villages of 12,000–20,000 people retain much of their rural character despite their size), peri-urban and urban settlements at a rapid rate. It would therefore appear that if these population movements were directed and more organised, those individuals and family groups, which have already become transient or are contemplating movement away from rural environments could, under the correct circumstances, be encouraged to populate re-vamped older villages, or altogether newly established non-metropolitan centres. However, without adequate town planning and the availability of industrial and service jobs, these non-metropolitan centres cannot realistically be expected to progress beyond the status of rural or semi-rural out-posts or peri-urban "bedroom communities" for more dynamic nearby larger urban centres.

Table 5. *Actual and estimated urban population, 1981–2001*

Settlement	1981	1986	1991	1996	2001
1. Gaborone	59 657	94 211	136 396	184 594	239 367
2. Francistown	31 065	43 399	58 234	74 787	93 280
3. Selebi-Phikwe	29 469	40 960	54 556	69 587	86 345
4. Lobatse	19 034	23 591	28 439	33 130	37 779
5. Jwaneng	5 567	10 205	16 361	23 973	33 054
6. Palapye	9 593	13 676	19 027	25 493	33 028
7. Tlokweng	6 653	9 800	13 326	18 055	23 721
8. Orapa	5 229	7 361	9 834	12 687	15 900
9. Ghanzi	–	4 528	6 102	7 926	10 064
10. Kasane	–	2 563	3 056	3 607	4 234
11. Sowa	–	–	2 158	3 783	4 359
12. Mogoditshane[a]	–	–	6 127	8 316	11 108
13. Mahalapye[a]	–	–	28 809	33 790	39 211
14. Maun[a]	–	–	19 842	22 375	25 142
15. Serowe[a]	–	–	30 083	33 576	37 134
16. Letlhakane[a]	–	–	8 958	11 277	13 809
17. Kanye[b]	–	–	–	36 566	43 109
18. Mochudi[b]	–	–	–	35 267	40 824
19. Ramotswa[b]	–	–	–	24 747	29 939
20. Molepolole[c]	–	–	–	–	50 689
Urban Total	166 267	250 302	441 308	663 536	872 096
National Total	941 027	1 125 008	1 338 386	1 566 615	1 822 398
Urban share	17.7%	22.2%	33.1%	42.4%	47.9%

[a] Mogoditshane, Mahalapye, Maun, Serowe and Letlhakane were expected to have attained urban status by 1991.
[b] Ramotswa, Mochudi and Kanye may attain urban status during the NDP 7 period (1991–1997).
[c] Molepolole may attain urban status by 2001.
   A dash indicates that the locality was not urban at that date, apart from Sowa, which was only constructed in 1990.
Source: Republic of Botswana, 1991, *National Development Plan, 7 1991–97*:406.

Several non-metropolitan areas have been affected by population shifts since the 1991 census. Enumeration areas which have lost population include Central Bobonong, North East and Central Mahalapye. In these areas, low growth rates or stagnation has occurred due to prolonged drought, lack of grazing or farm land, inferior infrastructure and lack of jobs. Many people, particularly the young and educated, have left for more urbanised centres and only return to the rural areas on short visits and at holidays. Conversely, other non-metropolitan areas such as Chobe, Kweneng and South East Districts have grown during the past ten years. In each instance, growth can be attributed to factors such as commercial farming, increased tourism, construction of military installations and family housing, border posts, airports, and to the creation of suburbs contiguous to the capital and other larger towns, such as Francistown and Jwaneng, where the cost of living and land are less expensive.

Smaller villages continue to suffer population losses in favour of the larger villages and urban areas (Botswana, 1985:80) which has implications for Botswana's development planning objectives, two of which are rural development and employment creation. On the other hand, it would appear that the National Settlement Policy, a concept introduced during the 1979–85 Plan Period aimed at counteracting the prevailing bias of investment to, and the migratory attractiveness of the urban areas, especially Gaborone, could have the desired effect of transforming the larger agro-towns into modern centres if conditions such as those at Chobe, Kweneng and South East Districts were suitably adapted and replicated in the requisite areas. This would require extensive changes in the administrative arrangements in such areas as well as substantial physical modifications to help redefine them as towns and cities rather than as traditional villages. Central to these changes and renovations would be the provision of more serviced land, replacement or modernising of tribal administrations, provision for new or more modern physical infrastructure and improving financial assistance and training for empowerment, particularly of women (Morapedi and Jones-Dube, 1988).

RURAL WOMEN AS MIGRANTS

For many years, much of the recorded data about Third World migration caused researchers to conclude that only males had been participants in migration. This was particularly true for southern Africa, with its history of migrant labour to farms and to the mines. According to this view, women were presumed to have played a limited and passive role in the migration process by either having merely followed their husbands, or male family heads such as fathers, uncles or brothers, to new locales or having been "left behind" in the rural areas (Brown 1983). Recent research has shown that many southern African women engaged in some form of migration and that they have suffered both from the effects of migration vis à vis its long-term debilitating effects on family structure, economic security, and child-rearing, as well as freeing them from a staunchly patriarchal society (Lucas, 1981, 1982; Bozzoli, 1983; Brown, 1983; Cooper, 1982; Izzard, 1982, 1985).

In Botswana's case, the fact that women have migrated on both a seasonal and a permanent basis, with and without men, has been a common phenomenon. Traditionally, they have migrated on a seasonal basis between their village homes and lands areas to produce food, they have migrated for marriage, and have moved between the freehold farms in Botswana, South Africa and Zimbabwe as labourers. They have worked in the same countries as domestics, factory workers, nurses and teachers. Thus, as in other non-Muslim, Sub-Saharan countries which have experienced extensive European influence, women in Botswana have migrated for a variety of reasons as Obbo (1980), in her study of women in Uganda, states:

> Women...migrated for personal, matrimonial, social and economic reasons. They regarded the towns as areas of expanded opportunities and resources. Some had lived in the area before the city boundary enclosed it, others came with or followed their husbands, while still others came alone. In some cases migration was intermittent as in the case of Luo women who shuttled between town and country. The reasons for migrating were often reflected in the styles of migration. An immediate reason such as witchcraft accusation, pregnancy or quarrels caused women to migrate directly from the country to the town. Long-term planning resulted in either direct migration or stage-by-stage migration through urban centres of varying size culminating in the city itself. Stage-by-stage migrants tended to be women who migrated alone and were highly motivated (Obbo, 1980: 85).

While men have also been exposed to the positive and negative effects of migration, women in southern Africa in general and in Botswana in particular, can be seen in the context of a "worst case" scenario of having been exposed to permanent rural underdevelopment and dire poverty which has caused many to migrate even when they would have preferred not to do so. As the figures in Table 6 indicate, median monthly household income for rural females and males is several times lower than that which can be obtained in urban areas. Why this is so has much to do with the economic limitations of rural life where:

> The opportunities for women to earn cash ... are extremely limited, with beer-brewing (or cash brewing as it is so aptly called) the most common activity. The alternative means of earning cash in the villages are mostly informal pursuits, including various handicrafts (such as knitting or crocheting), hawking fruit, vegetables or prepared food, as well as a small range of activities for which payment tends to be in kind, for example, providing agricultural labour (usually at harvest time) or various odd jobs done on a "once only" basis such as washing or mending clothes, or baby-sitting (Izzard, 1985:268).

Table 6. *Median monthly household income, 1985/86* (Pula per month at 1985/86 prices)

Household Type	Rural Households	Urban Households	All Households
Male headed HHs			
Cash income	59	342	110
Non-cash income	93	41	86
All income	152	383	196
Female headed HHs			
Cash income	47	161	66
Non-cash income	69	32	62
All income	116	193	128
All Households			
Cash income	53	254	83
Non-cash income	79	28	78
All income	132	282	161

Source: CSO, 1988, *Household Income and Expenditure Survey (HIES) 1985/86.*

In the rural areas where they predominate, women are faced with a three-fold regime of work and responsibility. First, they are responsible for the domestic work within the household, second, they are expected to organise and carry out subsistence agriculture to feed the family and, third, where possible, they are expected to create and engage in some type of income generation to obtain cash income. However, in the main, their economic activity is not reflected in the Gross Domestic Product and, as a result, women remain as unacknowledged producers in the national economy. Therefore, females constitute a large labour reserve which is under-utilised given their greater reliance on informal sector non-wage employment. Although the situation is improving with higher numbers of educated women and improved work opportunities in certain sectors of the economy (banking, accountancy, secretarial, teaching), there are still few empirically-based examples of female economic activity associated with non-metropolitan migration, other than earlier research devoted to domestic servants, prostitution, seasonal movement for subsistence, or farm labour and 'piece jobs' such as bird scaring.

Women in rural areas usually lead a hard, monotonous life punctuated by field work, occasional day trips to shop or seek medical attention in town, weddings and funerals. Household maintenance tasks are mainly done by women in an environment where processed and semi-processed foods are largely absent and where there are limited alternatives to the traditional fuel source, firewood. The tasks of food preparation and collection of water and firewood occur often and are time-consuming leaving little time for income generating activities which provide opportunities for women to work in order to bring cash into the home. Similarly, in a country where the female headed household (55 per cent) is becoming the norm (CSO, 1988), high child dependency is common, and where difficult physical conditions are commonplace, these conditions necessarily restrict labour, time and mobility to engage in other productive activities (Jones-Dube, 1990). Given the present situation, an increase in available time to engage in income generation work can only be envisioned once constraints on women's daily household maintenance tasks are reduced. Until conditions in rural areas have improved however, rural women, like rural men, will naturally opt for circular or permanent migration which, depending on their marketable skills and prevailing economic conditions, often leads them to non-metropolitan or metropolitan centres where they may find a means to earn an income.

Lastly, many women are engaged in agriculture, particularly crop production. Owing to historical conditions related to male migrant labour, and the continuing trend for male household members to leave rural areas in search of work, many women work on the land without male labour input, draught power or material inputs sufficient to make agriculture an economically viable undertaking. Despite the absence of male labour input, however, women continue to practise agriculture, at times taking on the roles and responsibilities traditionally held by men, and to make fundamental economic decisions even though their positions as minors, in accordance with common and statutory law, render them unable to enter into or make binding agreements without their husbands (or male guardian's) consent or assistance (Molokomme, 1983). In light of these constraints on women's participation in rural development and their overall lack of integration into the national development process, government's recent acknowledgement of the need to see women as "equal partners in the nation's economic and social development" is welcome (Botswana, 1991:85). However, mere words alone have neither made the less favoured status of women more palatable, nor reduced the need for rural (and urban) women to migrate in search of work in an attempt to optimise personal and family welfare.

To date, the main sources of recorded female migration currently taking place in Botswana revolve around individuals moving between rural/rural and urban/rural locations in a circulation of labour associated with linkages between family members engaged in income maximization.

In her research on female migration, Izzard (1985:260) has characterised women as "non-participants, participants and former participants" in labour migration whose movements are dictated by social and economic factors related to their life cycle. The case study below of a rural woman was collected by the author (Jones-Dube, 1990), and is included here as a guide to an approach which avoids the usual temptation to view the migrant as the unit of analysis or in terms of absenteeism. Instead, it allows for examination of the migratory movement of a woman during her life cycle and draws attention to the kind of activities women have undertaken in order to ensure the survival of the household. Izzard's use of case studies is helpful in illuminating a cycle of migration amongst women not readily discernible through the use of statistics or in much of the migration literature. Izzard's use of case studies and the one presented below, reveal cycles of rural/rural and rural/urban movement common among female migrants in Botswana today. Through the use of a case study it is possible to discern the vulnerable economic status of women and the distribution of the family over space and time, in a variety of income earning situations of which agriculture plays a minimal role. The study is indicative of the limited range of economic opportunities available to women, commonly practised family survival strategies, circular migration destinations and the importance of linkages between urban and rural families. The case study also focuses attention on the continuing importance of the family in Botswana society. From the study it is clear that income from a variety of sources is used to benefit the family, not the individual; linkages between a family's rural and non-rural members are maintained through remittances, gifts, clothing and visits to the village of origin.

Case Study—Patience

Patience was born in 1950 in Mapoka village in the North East District within walking distance from the then Rhodesian border. She was the fourth child and eldest daughter in a family of six children. Her parents were well educated for the period. Her father worked as a shop-manager in Plumtree (Zimbabwe) throughout her childhood. He would cycle to and from Zimbabwe at weekends to see his family. Her mother had trained as a nurse's assistant but had become a housewife once the children began to arrive. Patience's mother worked in the community throughout her life, managed the cattle in her husband's absence, tended the family fields and, as the wife of the first born, was often consulted by her husband's siblings and their spouses who resided in the same village.

Patience attended primary school but, unlike her brothers, failed to complete it. Before leaving school, two of her siblings, one brother and one sister had died in infancy. At 16 she became pregnant and had her first child, a son. Her parents were awarded damages by the father of the child but he eventually left the village in search of work. She did not hear from him again. Patience continued to live at home with her parents for a time and later married a man from Zimbabwe and lived there with him for four years, having left her first born in the care of her mother. While she was married in Zimbabwe she had twins boys. The marriage eventually failed and she returned to her parents' home with her children where she stayed for a number of years, working in the fields to assist her mother. In 1973 she became pregnant again and had a daughter. The father was a married man and friend of the family. Faced with friction from the man's wife, she left Mapoka and migrated to Francistown in search of work. She lived with one of her uncles and obtained employment as a domestic servant where she worked until 1975. In that year she fell pregnant again and returned to Mapoka with a second daughter. Following the birth, she returned to the fields with her mother and looked after her children. She had no income during this period and was unable to find employment in the village.

Faced with the responsibility of feeding and clothing five children and with less than a primary education, Patience set out for Gaborone in 1978 where she lived with her older, married brother. She helped out in his home and was given an allowance. After some time she found a job as a domestic servant. She held this job for several years. During this time she visited home every other month and during long holiday weekends, sent money whenever she could, and took clothing for her children whenever she went home. Her brothers assisted her financially whenever they could, but with their own families to look after, they did not have much income to share with her. By this time her father had died and the mother was left alone with Patience's five children to look after as well as Patience's younger brother, now in his twenties, who was moderately retarded and only occasionally able to find work on construction sites. Her other brothers often argued with her about her inability to support and care for her children, and the hardship this situation brought upon their mother. However, according to Patience, the mother never complained and had been happy to raise her children during her absence. During this period Patience became used to town life and felt confident enough to move to the mining town, Jwaneng, where she had relatives who helped her find work as a cleaner in the mining offices. In 1983 she fell in love and became pregnant with her sixth and final child, a son. When the relationship failed she moved back to Gaborone where she first found day work as a domestic and later as an office cleaner.

By 1988 Patience had secured a plot in Tlokweng where she has been building a small house for herself and her remaining dependent children. She has no plans to return to Mapoka where she says, 'There is too much jealousy and too little to do". Her oldest son now lives and works in Gaborone. The first daughter, although bright, left secondary school before completing it and is unemployed and unmarried with two children of her own. The remainder reside in Mapoka with their elderly grandmother.

CONCLUSION

This chapter has attempted to show that as a result of factors in Botswana's history and geographical position, a culture of migration, largely founded on the need for cash income, developed. This movement of individuals and families has implications for non-metropolitan development as well as gender considerations. Until recently, it was thought that migration was mainly a male affair, but an increasing number of empirical studies now indicate that women are also full participants in this process. These studies indicate that women, like men, migrate in order to improve their lives and to maintain their families—and not merely as passive participants. This is further supported by census figures which estimate that by the year 2015, women will have overtaken men in their rate of movement in search of work and opportunity. Given the shift in development from older, established urban centres to a wider range of growth points it could be expected that a considerable portion of this movement is likely to be centred on new non-metropolitan centres.

Faced with the option of a lifetime of hard work for minimum returns in rural areas and limited control over their lives compared to the possibility of a fuller life and employment adequate to maintain their households, few women are likely to opt for the former. However, two major issues are still important. The first is the question of the fuller participation of men and particularly women in the development process and the recognition of their roles, needs, capabilities and problems as farmers, workers and members of families with mouths to feed and how these impact the efficiency and effectiveness of government projects. Fuller participation by women in the development process and their access to means of income generation and financial empowerment can only contribute towards improved levels of welfare for women and their offspring. At present, constraints retarding women's progress in taking their rightful place in the community at large rest on the overall socio-economic fabric of property relationships and tradition which relegate women to second class status.

Second, as regards non-metropolitan migration, women and men should both be seen as prime targets for government intervention to carry on with the strengthening and implementation of the National Settlement Policy of 1979 and to introduce further policies and projects aimed at increasing rural incomes and reducing urban/rural inequalities. By so doing, government will be taking direct action to reduce out-migration from rural to urban and peri-urban areas. Recent census data indicates that this is happening most frequently in the poorest districts where land scarcity is rife and few alternatives to subsistence agriculture exist. Steps could be taken to facilitate the expansion of existing non-metropolitan centres and provide the impetus for further development of new growth points thereby encouraging development throughout the country, a trend which has already been started by the people themselves in their search for wage income and alternative lifestyles. Having aided this development, government and the private sector will be facilitating the stabilization of rural (and urban) family life, providing concrete reasons for people to remain in rural and peri-rural areas, as well as providing a rationale for investment to encourage non-metropolitan growth.

References

Alverson, H., 1978, *Mind in the Heart of Darkness*. New Haven: Yale University Press.

Botswana, Republic of, 1985, *National Development Plan 6, 1985–91*. Gaborone: Ministry of Finance and Development Planning.

Botswana, Republic of, 1991, *National Development Plan 7, 1991–97*. Gaborone: Ministry of Finance and Development Planning.

Bozzoli, B., 1983, "Marxism, Feminism and South African Studies", *Journal of Southern African Studies*, 9, 2, 1983:139–171.

Brown, B., 1983, "The Impact of Male Labour Migration on Women in Botswana", *African Affairs*, 82, 382: 367–387.

Campbell, A.,1982, "Some Aspects of Settlement in North-Western Botswana", *Settlement in Botswana*. Gaborone: Botswana Society.

Case, J., 1982, "Migration Flows, Sizes, Directions and Composition", in *National Migration Study*, Vol. 2. Gaborone: Government Printer.

Central Statistics Office and Ministry of Finance and Development Planning, 1982, *Migration in Botswana: Patterns, Causes and Consequences*, Vols. 1–3. Gaborone: Government Printer.

Central Statistics Office, 1984, *1981 Population and Housing Census*. Gaborone: Government Printer.

Central Statistics Office, 1985, *Employment Survey, 1984*. Gaborone: Government Printer.

Central Statistics Office, 1986, *Labour Force Survey, 1984–85*. Gaborone: Government Printer.

Central Statistics Office, 1987, *National Manpower Development Planning Report*. Gaborone: Government Printer.

Central Statistics Office and Ministry of Finance and Development Planning, 1988, *Population Report, 1986–87*. Gaborone: Government Printer.

Central Statistics Office, 1988, *Household Income and Expenditure Survey, 1985–86*. Gaborone: Government Printer.

Central Statistics Office, 1991, *Population and Housing Census Enumeration: Preliminary Returns*. Gaborone: Government Printer.

Central Statistics Office and Swedish International Development Authority, 1991, *Women and Men in Botswana*. Gaborone.

Chaney, E., 1980, *Women in International Migration: Issues in Development Planning*. Washington, D.C.: USAID.

Chirenje, M., 1977, *A History of Northern Botswana, 1850–1910*. London: Associated University Press.

Cooper, D., 1982, "Socio-Economic and Regional Factors of Wage Migration and Employment", in *National Migration Study*, Vol. 2. Gaborone: Government Printer.

Izzard, W., 1982, "The Impact of Migration on the Roles of Women", in *National Migration Study*, Vol. 3. Gaborone: Government Printer.

Izzard, W., 1985, "Migrants and Mothers", *Journal of Southern African Studies,* Vol. 11, No. 2, April 1985, 258–280.

Jones-Dube, E., 1984, "Indigenous and Nonindigenous Entrepreneurs in Botswana: Historical, Cultural and Educational Factors in Their Emergence", unpublished Ed.D dissertation. Amherst: University of Massachusetts.

Jones-Dube, E., 1990, *Training and Educational Needs of Women in Botswana*, report prepared for African Association of Literacy and Adult Educators. Nairobi: Kenya.

Kerven, C., 1982, "Botswana—A Synopsis", *National Migration Study,* Vol. 1. Gaborone: Government Printer.

Lucas, R., 1981, *The Distribution and Efficiency of Crop Production in Tribal Areas of Botswana*, Working Paper, No. 44. Boston: African Studies Center, Boston University.

Lucas, R., 1982, "Outmigration, Remittances, and Investment in Rural Areas", in *National Migration Study*, Vol. 3. Gaborone: Government Printer.

Molokomme, A., 1983, "The Legal and Cultural Barriers which Prevent Women's Full Participation in National Development: Some Proposals for Change", paper presented at a National Conference on *Women in Botswana—Strategies for Change*. University of Botswana, 10–14 October, 1983.

Morapedi, N. and E. Jones-Dube, 1988, *Evaluation of the Financial Assistance Policy: Background Information on Small Scale Enterprises*. Gaborone: Ministry of Finance and Development Planning.

Nangati, F., 1979, *Constraints on a Pre-Colonial Economy: The BaKwena State and the Beginnings of Labour Migration c. 1820–1855*, NMS Workshop on Migration Research, (ed.) C. Kerven. Gaborone: Government Printer.

Ngcongco, L., 1982, "Precolonial migration in Southeastern Botswana" in *Settlement in Botswana*. Gaborone: Botswana Society.

Obbo, C., 1980, *African Women. Their Struggle for Economic Independence*. London: Zed Press.

Schapera, I., 1947, *Migrant Labour and Tribal Life: A Study of the Condition of the Bechuanaland Protectorate*. London: Oxford University Press.

Silitshena, R., 1978, "Notes on some characteristics of population that has migrated permanently to the lands in the Kweneng District". *Botswana Notes and Records*, 10:149–157.

Silitshena, R., 1982, "Population Movements and Settlement Patterns in Contemporary Botswana", in *Settlement in Botswana*. Gaborone: Botswana Society.

Taylor, J., 1985, "The migration element in the 1981 Botswana Census", *Botswana Notes and Records*, 17: 89–98.

Taylor, J. and N. Tumkaya, 1985, *Population Research in Botswana. Research for Development in Botswana*. Gaborone: Botswana Society.

Tlou, T. and A. Campbell, 1984, *A History of Botswana*. Gaborone: Macmillan.

Biographical Notes

Aderanti Adepujo, a Nigerian economist-demographer is currently United Nations Population Fund (UNFA) Training Coordinator at the African Institute for Economic Development and Planning (IDEP), Dakar, Senegal. Previously, he was Professor, Head, Department of Demography, University of Ife (now Obafemi Awolowo University) (1980–1984); Research Professor, (1984–1990) and Dean (1988), Faculty of Business Administration, University of Lagos; United Nations' Expert/Professor, University of Swaziland (1985/1986); and Regional Adviser, Population and Labour Policy, International Labour Office, Addis Ababa (1977–1978).

He has written extensively, including articles and books on migration (internal and international), on the rural–urban interface, population policies and population-development interrelations in Africa.

Tade Akin Aina is a sociologist who was educated at the University of Lagos, the London School of Economics and the University of Sussex. He has taught sociology and researched at the University of Lagos for 17 years. He is currently the Deputy Executive Secretary (Publications) at CODESRIA, Dakar, Senegal. He has written extensively on development planning and policy issues, and on problems relating to the environment, health and human settlements. He is an Editor of *Environment and Urbanization*, the journal of the International Institute for Environment and Development.

Samir Amin was born in Cairo, Egypt in 1931 and received his Ph.D degree in Economics from the University of Paris in 1957. During his career he has been a scholar, researcher and administrator. He has worked at the Ministry of Development in Cairo (1957–60) and was advisor to the Malian Government (1960–63). Between 1963 and 1980, he was Professor at various universities, including Dakar and Paris. From 1970 until 1980 he was Director of the UN African Institute for Economic Development and Planning (IDEP) in Dakar. Since 1980 he has been Director of the Third World Forum, an international non-governmental association for research and debate. Professor Amin has published more than 20 books, many of which have been translated into several languages including French, English, Arabic, and Spanish. Some of his latest books are *Maldevelopment*, 1987, *Eurocentrism*, 1988 and *The Empire of Chaos*, 1992.

Jonathan Baker was born in London and obtained his Ph.D. degree from the London School of Economics. He is currently a senior research fellow and leader of the *Urban Development in Rural Context in Africa* programme at the Scandinavian Institute of African Studies. While he has conducted research on energy and aid issues in both Africa and the former centrally-planned economies, his primary research interests relate to urbanisation and urban processes in Africa, particularly Tanzania and Ethiopia. He is the author of *The rural–urban dichotomy in the developing world: A case study from northern Ethiopia* (Norwegian University Press, 1986), editor of *Small town Africa: Studies in rural–urban interaction* (1990), and co-editor of *The rural–urban interface in Africa: Expansion and adaptation* (1992)—the latter two books published by the Scandinavian Institute of African Studies.

Johnathan Bascom is assistant professor of geography at East Carolina University. This is his tenth publication related to refugees. His ongoing research in east Africa is supported by external grants from the National Science Foundation, the Fulbright-Hays Program, and the American Philosophical Society. During the last three years he has been invited to lecture on refugee issues at Oxford University, the University of London, the University of Glasgow, Cornell University, and the University of North Carolina. He has served as the chair of the African Specialty Group in the Association of American Geographers and coordinated a conference, "Africa's Refugees: Durable Solutions?", held in 1986 at the University of Iowa.

Hugh Evans runs a small consulting firm engaged in urban and regional planning in developing countries, and is also Adjunct Professor in the School of Urban and Regional Planning at the University of Southern California in Los Angeles.

Bill Gould is Professor in Geography and Director of the Graduate School of Population Studies in the University of Liverpool, U.K. He has published extensively on several aspects of population movements in East Africa in particular and in Africa in general, including invited contributions to the *Migration in the 1990s* conference of the Union for African Population Studies, Nairobi, 1991, and to the *Population dynamics of Sub-Saharan Africa* study of the Committee on Population of the American National Science Foundation, 1993. His most recent book is on *People and education in the Third World* (Longman, 1993).

Josef Gugler is Professor of Sociology at the University of Connecticut, USA. Previously he was Director of Sociological Research at the Makerere Institute of Social Research, Makerere University College, Kampala, Uganda. Research and teaching have taken him to India, Kenya, Nigeria, Senegal, Tanzania and Zaïre.

He is the co-author of *Urbanization and Social Change in West Africa* (Cambridge University Press, 1978) and *Cities, Poverty, and Development: Urbanization in the Third World* (Oxford University Press, 1982; second edition 1992), the editor of *The Urbanisation of the Third World* (Oxford University Press, 1988), and the co-editor of *Literary Theory and African Literature* (LIT Verlag and Westview Press, 1994). His edited collection, *Patterns of Third World Urbanization,* is to be published by Oxford University Press in 1995.

Elvyn Jones-Dube holds a Ed.D. in International and Comparative Education from the University of Massachusetts and a A.B. in Sociology from Lincoln University (Pa.). A former Peace Corps volunteer in Botswana, she has since lectured at the Agricultural College and been a member of staff at the Institute of Adult Education, University of Botswana. She has carried out research for the Department of Information, the Ministry of Finance and Development Planning and for AALAE, USAID, UNDP and UNICEF. Her interests lie in the areas of gender and feminist issues in the southern African context. She is currently undergoing training in psychoanalytic psychotherapy with the Arbours Association in London.

Christer Krokfors has an MA degree in geography from the University of Helsinki. He is a researcher and lecturer with the Unit for International Development Studies at the University of Uppsala. He has wide research experience of Africa, mainly in resource use, population geography, settlement structure and African arid lands. He has done fieldwork in Tanzania, Mozambique, Somalia and Morocco and his publications concern politics and ecology, land management, camel pastoralism and conceptual issues relating to the areas of interest mentioned above. He has worked as a lecturer at the Universities of Helsinki, Uppsala, Gothenburg and Örebro, and as a researcher at the Bureau of Research Assessment, University of Dar es Salaam, The Scandinavian Institute of African Studies, the Somali Camel Research Project, and the Environmental Policy and Society research programme at the University of Uppsala.

Vesa-Matti Loiske is a Human Geographer in the Environment and Development Studies Unit, School of Geography at Stockholm University. His research, which is part of a research programme entitled "*Man Land Inter-Relations in semi-arid Tanzania*", is oriented towards the socio-economic aspects of land management and land degradation processes at the local level.

Gudrun Ludwar-Ene, an anthropologist, is a Research Fellow involved with the Africa Research Programme at the University of Bayreuth, Germany. She has conducted research on sociocultural change among Tibetan exiles in Nepal and since 1982 on new religious movements, urban–rural linkages and gender issues in Nigeria, and has taught at the universities of Cologne, Calabar (Nigeria) and Bayreuth. She authored *Die Sozialisation tibetischer Kinder im soziokulturellen Wandel,* Franz Steiner Verlag 1975, edited and contributed to *New Religious Movements and Society in Nigeria* (Bayreuth African Studies Series 17, 1991) and is co-editor of and contributor to *Focus on Women in Africa* (Bayreuth African Studies Series 26, 1993) and *Gender and Identity in Africa*, LIT-Verlag 1994.

Anders Närman is a lecturer in Development Studies and Geography at the University of Gothenburg, Sweden. Most of his research has been concentrated on Eastern and Southern Africa and is related to issues concerning education and the labour market. Some of the research work has been on a consultancy basis for, *inter alia*, SIDA, DSE and IIEP/UNESCO.

Lai Olurode is a sociologist who was educated at the University of Lagos. He received his D. Phil. from the University of Sussex in 1984. At present, he is senior lecturer in the Department of Sociology, University of Lagos. His research interests include the political economy of inequality and social change.

Jean-Bernard Ouedraogo is currently mâitre-Assistant of sociology at the University of Ouagadougou, Burkina Faso. He obtained his Ph.D. at the University of Nantes, France. In 1989 he received the Harmattan Thesis Award. He is the author of *The formation of the working class in Black Africa*, and has published numerous articles and participated in collective works on labour, the city, migration, entrepreneurship, and the cinema.

Margaret Peil is Professor of the Sociology of West Africa at Birmingham University, U.K. She has an M.A. from Fordham University and a Ph.D. from the University of Chicago. She spent five years lecturing at the University of Ghana and has also lectured and/or carried out research in The Gambia, Nigeria, Sierra Leone and Zimbabwe. She is the author of eight books and numerous papers on African societies.

Gazala Pirzada has recently completed her doctorate at the University of Southern California, and is currently working as an Associate Planner at the Community Redevelopment Agency of the City of Los Angeles.

Christian M Rogerson is Professor of Human Geography and Head, Department of Geography and Environmental Studies, University of the Witwatersrand, Johannesburg. He has authored over 140 research publications concerning development issues in southern Africa. Recent co-edited books include *South Africa's Informal Economy* (Oxford University Press, Cape Town, 1991), *Geography in a Changing South Africa: Progress and Prospects* (Oxford University Press, Cape Town, 1992) and *Finance, Institutions and Industrial Change: Spatial Perspectives* (Walter de Gruyter, Berlin, 1993).

M.A. Mohamed Salih has a Ph.D. in Social Anthropology, University of Manchester. He is currently a Senior Lecturer at the Institute of Social Studies, The Hague, The Netherlands.

Previously he was Associate Professor in Social Anthropology, University of Khartoum (1983–1991) and Senior Research Fellow at the Scandinavian Institute of African Studies (1987–1993), where he was leader of the *Human Life in African Arid Lands* research programme .

He is a member of the editorial board of *Nomadic Peoples*, the Journal of the International Union of Anthropological and Ethnological Commission and several other journals. He has lectured in many African, Nordic and European Universities. He has published widely, including the Scandinavian Institute of African Studies, Macmillan Press, St. Martins, Westview Press, Pinters Publishers, and the *Review of African Political Economy, Ambio,* and *Geojournal.*

Lillian Trager is Professor of Anthropology and Director of the Center for International Studies at the University of Wisconsin-Parkside. Her research in Nigeria and the Philippines has focused on market women, the informal economy, and rural–urban linkages. From 1985–87 she was Program Officer and Assistant Representative in the Ford Foundation's West Africa office, and since that time she has been increasingly interested in local-level and indigenous approaches to development.

Index